Concepts in World Politics

SAGE was founded in 1965 by Sara Miller McCune to support the dissemination of usable knowledge by publishing innovative and high-quality research and teaching content. Today, we publish over 900 journals, including those of more than 400 learned societies, more than 800 new books per year, and a growing range of library products including archives, data, case studies, reports, and video. SAGE remains majority-owned by our founder, and after Sara's lifetime will become owned by a charitable trust that secures our continued independence.

Los Angeles | London | New Delhi | Singapore | Washington DC | Melbourne

Concepts in World Politics

edited by

Felix Berenskoetter

Los Angeles | London | New Delhi
Singapore | Washington DC | Melbourne

Los Angeles | London | New Delhi
Singapore | Washington DC | Melbourne

SAGE Publications Ltd
1 Oliver's Yard
55 City Road
London EC1Y 1SP

SAGE Publications Inc.
2455 Teller Road
Thousand Oaks, California 91320

SAGE Publications India Pvt Ltd
B 1/I 1 Mohan Cooperative Industrial Area
Mathura Road
New Delhi 110 044

SAGE Publications Asia-Pacific Pte Ltd
3 Church Street
#10-04 Samsung Hub
Singapore 049483

Editor: Natalie Aguilera
Editorial assistant: Delayna Spencer
Production editor: Katie Forsythe
Copyeditor: Sharon Cawood
Proofreader: Clare Weaver
Marketing manager: Sally Ransom
Cover design: Stephanie Guyaz
Typeset by: C&M Digitals (P) Ltd, Chennai, India
Printed and bound by CPI Group (UK) Ltd,
Croydon, CR0 4YY

First published 2016

Library of Congress Control Number: 2016934261

British Library Cataloguing in Publication data

A catalogue record for this book is available from the British Library

ISBN 978-1-4462-9428-4
ISBN 978-1-4462-9427-7 (pbk)

Table of Contents

Acknowledgements

This volume has its origin in a meeting I had with Natalie Aguilera, editor at SAGE, during the BISA conference in Manchester in April 2011. It was one of those conversations academics have with publishers about where they see the discipline heading. At one point I mentioned that much of my teaching at SOAS revolved around concepts and how, in my view, there was little material in IR dedicated to concepts aimed at students. When Natalie followed up a year later, I began to see the contours of a project. A successful application to the International Studies Association (ISA) for a Venture Workshop Grant on *Concept Analysis* enabled me to organize two workshops in Toronto and London in 2014, which eventually led to this volume.

The journey was enjoyable but also hard work, and I am grateful to a number of institutions and people for their support. The ISA grant was crucial for getting the project off the ground and Laura Gottschalk helped with the organization of the Toronto workshop. At SOAS, the Faculty of Law and Social Sciences and the Department of Politics and International Studies provided financial support for the London workshop, with Nadiya Ali providing valuable assistance. My contacts at SAGE, especially Natalie, Amy Jarrold, and Katie Forsythe were fantastic to work with, as they competently and cheerfully shepherded the project towards and through the production process. Alexej Ulbricht skillfully compiled the index.

And, of course, I thank the contributors for joining and believing in the project. This was a collective endeavor and I am grateful for their insights, efforts and patience during many rounds of revisions. Their chapters bring this book to life. My deepest gratitude goes to my partner Caroline, who supported me in various ways, not least by tolerating me working long hours on too many occasions. Our son Hugo was born when I started this project; now it is done and, well, he likes the cover. So I dedicate this book to him, with love.

F. B.
London, April 2016

About the Editor and Contributors

Tanja Aalberts is Senior Researcher at Transnational Legal Studies, VU Amsterdam and co-director of the Centre for the Politics of Transnational Law. Her fields of interest are International Relations theory, international legal theory and international political sociology, and her research focuses on the interplay between law and politics in practices of global governance. She is co-editor of *The Power of Legality: Practices of International Law and their Politics* (Cambridge University Press, 2016) and has published in *inter alia* the *European Journal of International Relations*, *Review of International Studies*, and *Millennium*. She is founder and series editor of the Routledge book series on the *Politics of Transnational Law*, and editor for the *Leiden Journal of International Law*.

Felix Berenskoetter is Senior Lecturer (Associate Professor) in International Relations at SOAS, University of London. He holds a PhD from the London School of Economics and Political Science (LSE) and specialises in international theory and concepts, in particular friendship, identity, power, security, peace, and time; as well as German foreign policy, European security and transatlantic relations. He has published articles in various journals, including *International Studies Quarterly*, *Security Studies* and *European Journal of International Relations* and co-edited *Power in World Politics* (Routledge, 2007). Felix is a former editor of *Millennium: Journal of International Studies*, founder and former chair of the ISA Theory Section, and currently an Associate Editor of the *Journal of Global Security Studies*.

Maria Birnbaum is Research Associate on the ERC-funded project "ReligioWest" at the European University Institute (EUI) in Florence and a post-doctoral fellow at the University of Oslo. She holds a PhD in International Relations from the European University Institute. Her work focuses on the international politics of religion and culture as well as different forms and critiques of recognition in international politics, especially in relation to the colonial history of British India and Palestine. Recent publications include 'Emerging International Subjects: The Royal "Peel" Commission, Palestine Partition and the Establishment of Religious Difference at the United Nations', in: Stensvold (ed.) *Religion, State and the United Nations*, (Routledge, 2016); 'Exclusive Pluralism', in: Stack et al. (eds.) *Religion as a Category of Governance and Sovereignty*, (Brill, 2015). Current projects include *Non-Representational Agency in International Relations and Traveling Knowledge: The Connected Histories of Pakistan and Israel.*

Antoine Bousquet is Senior Lecturer in International Relations at Birkbeck College, University of London. His main research interests are concerned with the entangled relationship of war and society, the history and philosophy of science and technology, and social and political theory in the digital age. He is the author of *The Scientific Way of Warfare: Order and Chaos on the Battlefields of Modernity* (Hurst Publishers, 2009) and has published various articles in a range of peer-reviewed journals. He is currently completing a second monograph on the logistics of military perception entitled *The Martial Gaze*.

David Chandler is Professor of International Relations, Department of Politics and International Relations, University of Westminster, London. He is the founding editor of the journal *Resilience: International Policies, Practices and Discourses*; his latest books are *Resilience: The Governance of Complexity* (Routledge, 2014) and *The Neoliberal Subject: Resilience, Adaptation and Vulnerability* (Rowman & Littlefield, 2016).

Alejandro Colás is Reader in International Relations at Birkbeck College, University of London where he directs the MSc in International Security and Global Governance. He is author of *Empire* (Polity Press, 2007) and co-editor with Bryan Mabee of *Mercenaries, Pirates, Bandits and Empires: Private Violence in Historical Context* (Hurst, 2011). Alex has published on issues such as jihadist terrorism in Spain, American imperialism, Islamism in North Africa and cosmopolitan solidarity in *International Affairs*, the *European Journal of International Relations*, *Development & Change* and the *Review of International Studies*.

Thomas Diez is Professor of Political Science and International Relations at the University of Tübingen and President of the European International Studies Association (EISA) 2015-7. From 1997 to 2000, he was Research Fellow at the Copenhagen Peace Research Institute and subsequently taught at the University of Birmingham. Among his publications are *The Securitisation of Climate Change* (Palgrave, 2016), *Key Concepts in International Relations* (co-author, Sage 2011), and *European Integration Theory* (Oxford University Press, 2009). In September 2009, he received the Anna Lindh Award for his contribution to the field of European Foreign and Security Policy Studies.

Annette Freyberg-Inan teaches International and European Politics and Political Economy as well as Social Science Methodology at the University of Amsterdam and is a member of the research program on Political Economy and Transnational Governance at the Amsterdam Institute for Social Science Research. Her recent books include *Human Beings in International Relations* (Cambridge University Press, 2015), with Daniel Jacobi; *Evaluating Progress in International Relations: How Do You Know?!* (Routledge, 2016), with Ewan Harrison and Patrick James; and *Growing Together, Growing Apart: Turkey and the European Union Today* (Nomos, 2016), with Olaf Leisse and Mehmet Bardakci. She chairs the Theory Section of the International Studies Associations and has since 2012 co-edited the *Journal of International Relations and Development*.

Stefano Guzzini is Senior Researcher at the Danish Institute for International Studies, Professor at Uppsala University and at PUC-Rio de Janeiro. His research focuses on international theory, security studies, approaches to foreign policy analysis, concepts and theories of power, as well as interpretivist methodologies. He has published nine books, including *The Return of Geopolitics in Europe? Social Mechanisms and Foreign Policy Identity Crises* (Cambridge University Press, 2012), and *Power, Realism and Constructivism* (Routledge, 2013), winner of the 2014 ISA Theory Section Best Book Award. He currently serves as President of the *Central and East European International Studies Association* (CEEISA).

Benjamin Herborth is Assistant Professor at the Department of International Relations and International Organization, History and Theory of International Relations, at the University of Groningen. His research interests include social and political theories in and of international relations, world society studies, critical theory and international politics, the politics of security, and reconstructive methodology. Recent and forthcoming publications include 'Theorizing Theorizing: Critical Realism and the Quest for Certainty', *Review of International Studies* 2012, 'The Elusive Nature of Human Nature', *International Studies Review* 2012, 'Recognition and the Constitution of Social Order' (with Oliver Kessler), *International Theory* 2013, 'The West: A Securitizing Community?' (with Gunther Hellmann, Gabi Schlag and Christian Weber), *Journal of International Relations and Development* 2014 and 'Imagining Man – Forgetting Society', in Jacobi/Freyberg-Inan, *Human Beings in International Relations,* Cambridge University Press 2015. An edited volume *Uses of the West* (with Gunther Hellmann) is forthcoming with Cambridge University Press.

Piki Ish-Shalom holds the A. Ephraim and Shirley Diamond Family Chair in International Relations at the Hebrew University of Jerusalem. He is the author of *Democratic Peace: A Political Biography* (University of Michigan Press, 2013), as well as articles in different scholarly journals and edited volumes.

Richard Ned Lebow is Professor of International Political Theory in the War Studies Department of King's College London, Bye-Fellow of Pembroke College, University of Cambridge and the James O. Freedman Presidential Professor (Emeritus) of Government at Dartmouth College. His most recent books are *Return of the Theorists: Dialogues with Dead Thinkers* (Palgrave, 2016), coedited with Peer Schouten and Hidemi Suganami, and *National Identifications and International Relations* (Cambridge University Press, 2016). His edited volume *Max Weber and International Relations* will be published by Cambridge in 2017. In December 2015, he completed fifty years of university teaching.

Alex Prichard is a Senior Lecturer in International Relations at the University of Exeter. His research brings together IR theory, political theory and anarchist political thought, in order to rethink the constitutional potential of anarchy for a post-sovereign politics. He gained his PhD from Loughborough University in 2008, and has since published widely on the thought of Pierre-Joseph Proudhon, anarchism and IR theory. He is co-editor of the monograph series 'Contemporary Anarchist Studies', published by Manchester University Press.

Rahul Rao is Senior Lecturer (Associate Professor) in Politics at SOAS, University of London. He holds a DPhil in International Relations from the University of Oxford. His research interests encompass critical international relations theory, comparative political thought, and gender and sexuality, with an area focus on South Asia and East Africa. He is the author of *Third World Protest: Between Home and the World* (Oxford University Press, 2010) and of articles in numerous journals. He sits on the editorial boards of *International Feminist Journal of Politics* and *South Asia Research*, is a member of the *Radical Philosophy* editorial collective, and blogs at *The Disorder of Things*.

Oliver Richmond is Research Professor of International Relations, Peace & Conflict Studies at the University of Manchester. His primary area of expertise is in peace and conflict theory and practices, and in particular its inter-linkages with IR theory, and he has published widely on this topic. He is currently working on a book on Progress, Peace and Intervention. His most recent work has been on peace formation and its relation to state formation, statebuilding, and peacebuilding (*Failed Statebuilding and Peace Formation*, Yale University Press, 2014, and *Peace Formation and Political Order*, Oxford University Press, 2016). This area of interest has grown out of his work on local forms of critical agency and resistance, and their role in constructing hybrid or post-liberal forms of peace and states (*A Post-Liberal Peace*, Routledge, 2011). He has also recently written *Peace: A Very Short Introduction* (Oxford University Press, 2014) and is co-editor of the journal *Peacebuilding*.

Stephan Stetter is Professor of World Politics and Conflict Studies at the University of the Bundeswehr in Munich. He holds a PhD from the London School of Economics and Political Science (LSE) and specializes in world society theory, Middle East politics and conflicts as well as EU foreign policy. He has published numerous articles in various journals and is the author of *World Society and the Middle East* (Palgrave, 2008). Stephan is an editor of the leading German-language IR journal the *Zeitschrift für Internationale Beziehungen* and chairperson of the IR-section of the German Political Science Association.

Holger Stritzel is Lecturer at King's College London, University of London. He holds a PhD from the London School of Economics and Political Science and specializes in security theory and German foreign policy and transatlantic relations. He has published articles in various journals including *European Journal of International Relations*, *Review of International Studies* and *Security Dialogue*. His most recent book *Security in Translation* (Palgrave, 2014) explores the spread and translation of security concepts in international affairs.

Benno Teschke is Reader in the IR Department at Sussex University and an Affiliated Visiting Professor in the Politics Department, Copenhagen University. His research interests comprise IR Theory, International Historical Sociology, Marxism and the Philosophy of the Social Sciences. He is the author of *The Myth of 1648: Class, Geopolitics and the Making of Modern International Relations* (Verso, 2003), which was awarded the 2004 Isaac Deutscher Memorial Prize, and has published widely in the field of IR and the Social Sciences, including in *International Organization* and the *New Left Review*.

Teschke is an editorial board member of *International Theory* and a Management Committee Member of the Sussex Centre for Advanced International Theory.

Juha A. Vuori is acting Professor of World Politics at the University of Helsinki, and an Adjunct Professor of International Politics at the University of Tampere. His main research focus has been on the critical development of securitization theory through illocutionary logic, semiotics, and the application of the approach to the People's Republic of China. He is the author of *Critical Security and Chinese Politics* (Routledge, 2014) and co-author of *A History of the People's Republic of China* (in Finnish, Gaudeamus Helsinki University Press, 2012).

Frido Wenten received his PhD in Development Studies from SOAS, University of London in 2016. His research is on labour relations, movements and development in the Global South, with a particular focus on transnational automotive production in China and Mexico. He has published on IR and IPE theory and the post-1978 socio-economic transformation, labour and migration in China.

1

Unpacking Concepts

Felix Berenskoetter

Like everyone else, scholars of international relations use concepts to make sense of what they look at and to have conversation about it. While it is common to portray academic inquiry into world politics as exploring a set of salient issues with the help of a range of theories, concepts are central to this undertaking as they enable us to intellectually frame issues and formulate theories in the first place. They are devices we use to order and make sense of a messy reality by reducing its complexity and naming and giving meaning to its features; they provide mental shortcuts through which we navigate and grasp the world by allowing us to cluster, classify and categorize everything we encounter into something manageable and meaningful. In doing so, concepts guide thought and provide a language that enables scholars to communicate their theoretical arguments and empirical findings. And by guiding thought, concepts also guide action.

Most of the time, we take the meaning of our concepts for granted. Of course, we know that our conceptual language is an invention and that the meaning of key terms is not carved in stone. We are aware that a particular concept may be interpreted differently and we have seen insightful explorations of concepts prominent in the discipline of International Relations (IR), many of them covered and cited in this volume. However, existing studies dedicated to opening up concepts and showing their complexity tend to be highly specialized and rarely explore a range of concepts side by side (for a recent exception, see Adler-Nissen 2013). Moreover, these studies are only reluctantly acknowledged, let alone integrated in mainstream conversations. Usually concepts tend to be reduced to static "variables", which are broken down into "indicators", without taking into account the rich history and multiple meanings of the concept underpinning the variable.[1] The reasons for this range from the modern belief

[1] As Giovanni Sartori (1970) observed over four decades ago, missing reflection on concepts is especially prevalent in quantitative research.

that we actually can arrive at the true meaning of a concept, which is singular and simple, to the more pragmatic view that opening up concepts sows unnecessary confusion and goes against their very purpose of reducing complexity. And so we usually resort to an authoritative definition that settles the matter by quoting a well-known scholar who presumably thought about the matter carefully and whose definition is popular and/or makes intuitive sense. Having fixed the meaning of our concept (or so we believe) we go on with our research.

But we cannot ignore the fact that behind each concept lurk multiple meanings that have evolved over time and space, are embedded in different theoretical frameworks and empirical expressions, and are displayed in political and public discourses and action (Connolly 1993). As students and scholars, we need to spend some time thinking about these various manifestations and how they affect our research. And so, whereas most IR textbooks focus on "issues" and "theories" without paying much attention to the multifaceted nature of concepts, this volume takes this task head on. Specifically, it has three aims. First, it seeks to display multiple meanings of a concept across historical, theoretical and cultural contexts to make students sensitive to the openness and contestedness of concepts and to processes of meaning creation. Second, it seeks to highlight the role concepts play in scholarly research and in political decision-making to remind students of the analytical and practical consequences of using a concept in one way rather than another. Third, by showcasing different ways of unpacking concepts and discussing their contingency and performativity, the volume hopes to make students familiar with different approaches to concept analysis and their potential for investigating world politics. In other words, the objective is to improve awareness of the historical evolution(s) and plural meaning(s) of key terms, to encourage critical and productive engagement with key concepts and to demonstrate how concept analysis contributes to an analysis of politics.

The study of concepts has long been prominent among historians and philosophers and has never been absent from IR, yet over the last two decades it has gained in prominence. Despite the stubborn resistance in some quarters, it has become increasingly difficult for IR scholars to ignore that our perception of and engagement with the world is structured by language(s) and that we need to pay more attention to how this affects political action and research. Specifically, two related developments make an engagement with concepts unavoidable. First, constructivist angles inspired by, above all, the linguistic turn have relentlessly pushed for a more critical attitude towards the categories and terminologies we use and the mentalities behind them. Disillusioned with grand theories as analytical devices, scholars now increasingly organize their research and, indeed, research communities around key concepts like security (Buzan and Hansen 2009; Bourbeau 2015), gender (Tickner 1992; Steans 2013) and, most recently, practice (Adler and Pouliot 2011; Ringmar 2014). Second, there is a sense that we are living through a period of social and geopolitical transformation, entering a world with late-modern features accompanied by challenges to structures of Western dominance that have shaped the IR discipline since its inception. While these changes are experienced differently depending on one's position, they often make established concepts feel out-dated, prompting modifications and even inventions of new concepts. This can be witnessed in the formation of new terms like globalization (Held et al. 1999) and the re-reading of old ones like war (Kaldor 2012), as well as the broader critique of Eurocentric speaking and thinking and the corresponding emergence of and search for "non-Western" voices (Tickner and Blaney 2012; Hobson 2012), and the recovery of long-neglected concepts like race (Vucetic 2015).

The main objective of this introductory chapter is to assist reflection on how we might "unpack" a concept. It thus is broadly methodological in character by laying out key parameters of concept analysis and providing an overview of three different approaches, called here "historical", "scientific" and "political(critical)". My hope is that offering these general frameworks will serve both as a useful background when reading individual chapters and as analytical guidance for those wishing to unpack concepts themselves. They also flow from my experience on how this book developed. When inviting the authors to join the project, I asked for contributions showing the plural/complex meanings of a given concept as well as its use/performance in world politics. At that stage, I did not provide much guidance as to how this might be done, assuming that my colleagues had an approach at hand. Yet, I soon realized that few of us, including myself, had thought carefully about the methodological aspects of "unpacking" a concept or possessed the vocabulary to spell out the analytical approach. So, while I had expected (and welcomed) differences in how authors would deal with their respective concepts, it turned out that the challenges this project faced were not only disagreements about what "concept analysis" actually entails, but also the need to systematically reflect on how and why we unpack our concepts in the first place. In fact, when the question "what is a concept?" was raised at one of our workshops, the room was split between those who thought it would be a good idea to come up with a clear answer and those who argued that doing so would be detrimental to the project. From an editor's perspective, this could be seen as an insurmountable hurdle for constructing a volume that "hangs together". To me, it only affirmed the importance of the project as, hopefully, a contribution to an informed conversation about how we use and study concepts – not only among established scholars but, more importantly, also among students who begin to learn about the subject.

One fundamental issue such a conversation inevitably touches on is the epistemological debate around whether language can provide an accurate description of reality, draw its meaning(s) from or merely invent this reality. Different ways of conceiving of the relationship between word (concept) and world (reality) underpin the tension between positivist and non-positivist perspectives in the social sciences (Smith et al. 1996; Jackson 2011). This division overlaps with two different approaches to knowledge production: the modern view that categorization is necessary for systematic analysis and action and that diligent scholarship can provide objective categories that reflect reality; and a stance combining postmodern and critical sensitivities holding that all concepts/categories are political products, which not only are contingent in meaning but also limit the scope of thought and action. While taking its motivation from the latter position, the spirit of this volume is to leave the matter open, not least because the authors assembled here have their own reading of, and way of navigating through, these debates and the purpose of scholarship.

Parameters of Concept Analysis: Core, Web, Context

Let us begin by looking at the parameters that inform the assumptions and strategies underpinning all scholarly engagement with concepts. While the sequence in which they are discussed here might suggest a movement outwards from the thing itself in concentric circles, it is more accurate to view these parameters as three intertwined dimensions of the same thing.

So, what is a concept? At first sight, there is something paradoxical about defining a concept for a project that seeks to highlight its plurality. But, as will become clear shortly, these two tasks do not necessarily stand in contradiction to each other. In general terms, a concept is an image formed in the human mind that helps us to generate knowledge about the world by organizing, naming and giving meaning to its features. As an abstract heuristic device, it is not considered an accurate representation of reality/the world – regardless of the fundamental question of whether such representation is possible – but, rather, an image which meaningfully organizes this reality/world, perceived through sensory experiences, in the mind. The appeal of a concept is largely pragmatic, namely to enable us to communicate and research this reality/world, although it also owes much to the belief that once we name something we can control it. A concept tends to be attached to a word, although – and this is important – not necessarily always to the same word and, as such, is more than a word. Whereas the meaning of a word points to one particular thing, a concept catches and bundles multiple elements, aspects and experiences and relates them to each other. It would be misleading, though, to simply think of a concept as an umbrella term. Its meaning is not arrived at by simply "adding up" the constituting elements, not least because it is the concept which enables us to organize and make the connections between those "elements". In the words of Reinhart Koselleck, a concept "is not simply indicative of the relations which it covers, it is also a factor within them" (Koselleck 2004 [1979]: 86).

Because concepts contain and bundle many elements and meanings, it is difficult to define them. Indeed, if we understand the purpose of a definition to be fixing meaning, concepts cannot be defined. As Nietzsche famously put it, "only that which has no history can be defined",[2] and as the chapters in this volume show, all concepts have a history. Having said that, only by defining concepts can we move beyond the word to express the concept's constitutive elements and their configuration. Of course, every definition is partial – think, for instance, about the different ways "the state" can be defined. And so we need to look carefully at every definition and ask how and why certain elements and relations are highlighted over others. But even then, defining a concept is only a starting point for its exploration. The mistake is to think that once we have a definition, we have fixed meaning. This is not the case. As Koselleck notes, concepts cannot be given definite meaning, they can only be interpreted (2011 [1972]: 20). Once we look closely, we can see that even a seemingly clear definition of a concept remains vague and ambiguous, allowing for an interpretative space that can contain multiple readings.

[2] Quoted by Koselleck in his introduction to *Geschichtliche Grundbegriffe* (see Koselleck 2011 [1972]).

From recognizing the ambiguity and openness of concepts, it does not follow that we can fill them with whatever meaning we want. The range of elements a concept contains and how they are related is not completely random. Rather, it seems sensible to assume that beneath a particular configuration, each concept has some sort of internal logic, structure, perhaps even properties, which form its core. This core allows us to identify and trace the concept through time and space, especially when attached to different words. That said, this view, often attributed to Socrates and Plato, is not unproblematic. Where does the structure, where do these properties, where does the logic come from? Unless we take the (difficult to defend) position that they are read off nature, they must be an invention of the human mind. But if the internal logic/structure only exists per human agreement, then how and why do we come to agree (if, indeed, we do)? Even if we have an answer to this question, a second problem arises: the assumption that concepts have intrinsic features comes close to claiming an essence, which seems detrimental to highlighting multiple and fluid meanings of a concept. How can this be reconciled? Does it make sense to speak of a contingent core? Again, it is important to avoid dogmatism. Rather than stylizing the issue of the internal logic/structure to a debate about foundations and locking modern and post-modern positions against each other, it is more fruitful to be pragmatic and contemplate that something holds a concept together from within and lends it internal coherence, without insisting on an essence.

One way to think about the parameters of the core is to ask about the internal logic/structure that gives a concept its "basic" quality. For Koselleck, a concept is basic if it plays a central role in our socio-political language, in this case our language of international relations/world politics. That is, we consider it a concept "we cannot do without". In his words, "basic concepts combine manifold experiences and expectations in such a way that they become indispensable to any formulation of the most urgent issues of a given time" (Koselleck 1996: 64).[3] This points to two interrelated features, which can be seen as forming the core of a concept. First, basic concepts grasp, or refer to, fundamental features of our **socio-political** system. They are leading terms [*Leitbegriffe*] of our vocabulary trying to grasp (links between) fundamental structures, processes and events; they are keywords [*Schlüsselwörter*] and slogans [*Schlagwörter*] used by major social, economic and political organizations and movements, and scholarly attempts to describe them; and they are core terms found in major theories and ideologies (Koselleck 2011 [1972]: 8). As such, basic concepts do not merely exist as specialized terms within academic circles but permeate public discourse. One could call them "fundamental codes of a culture" (Foucault, 1970 [1966]). Second, basic concepts have a **temporal** structure containing a stock of experiences and an aspirational outlook. Koselleck argues that the ability of a basic concept to grasp key features of social relations is tied to the "experiential content" (*Erfahrungehalt*) it has accumulated and to the "innovative expectations" it raises. This feature of concepts as both backward- and forward-looking conveys not only that concepts have a temporal dimension, but also that they may allude to movement and contain a promise of progress, thus

[3] See also Connolly's "terms of political discourse" and his discussion of whether it makes sense to distinguish "normative" from "descriptive" concepts (Connolly 1993, Ch. 1).

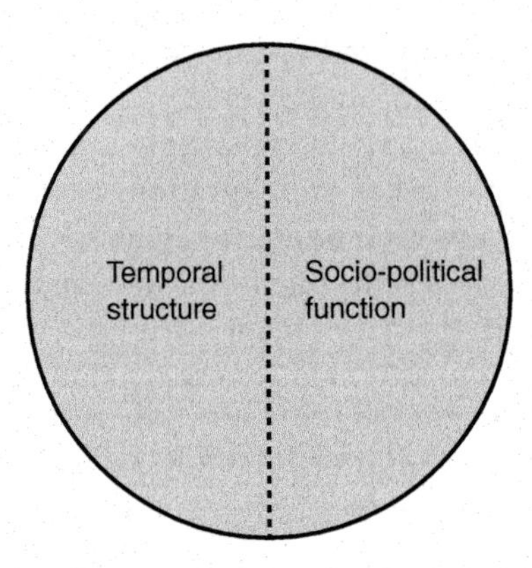

Figure 1.1 Concept core

pointing to their normative content. One might say that the quality of "basicness" is, above all, attributed by those who use a concept. However, this does not imply that within a particular community there is consensus on the concept's meaning – if anything, the opposite is the case. As Koselleck notes, basic concepts tend to be contested precisely because they are basic and open to interpretation, which prompts different actors to try and claim a monopoly on its meaning (Koselleck 1996: 65).

The attempt to delineate the core already shows that it makes little sense to see a concept as a stand-alone entity, as a free-floating unit of knowledge. Concepts come to life and gain meaning only within particular contexts. But there are different ways to think about "context" – the frame, environment or field within which a concept is embedded – and to study how a concept is situated within a particular context. So it is important to think carefully about which contexts we look at, and about the relationship between concept and context or, rather, different contextual layers.

Scholars of concepts (and political thought more generally) usually start by emphasizing the importance of language and, hence, the linguistic context. Influenced by structural linguistics going back to Saussure, they maintain that concepts gain their meaning from being situated in a "semantic field", loosely understood as a group of terms and symbols that relate to each other in a particular way. This involves looking at how a concept is linked to other concepts and, thus, embedded in a web of concepts that supports its meaning. Without delving into semantics, three kinds of relations are prevalent: with **supporting** concepts which are integral to the meaning of our concept (*sovereignty* for *the state*); with **cognate** concepts with similar meanings, or whose meanings correspond with each other and bear what Wittgenstein called a family resemblance (football and basketball are both *games*, to use his famous example); and with **contrasting** concepts that are opposite in meaning, sometimes even taking the form of counter-concepts (as in reactionary-revolutionary), which relate to and (in)form each other through a dialectic.

These relations forming a conceptual web do not need to be grounded in logic but can be habitual, sentimental or normative, and thus seemingly arbitrary in character. Their links become particularly interesting when they are said to present a causal relationship, as in the case of "democracy" and "peace" cherished among liberal IR theorists (Doyle 1983; Chan 1997; see also Ish-Shalom in Chapter 13, this volume). Analysts also need to be aware of how supporting concepts are embedded in semantic

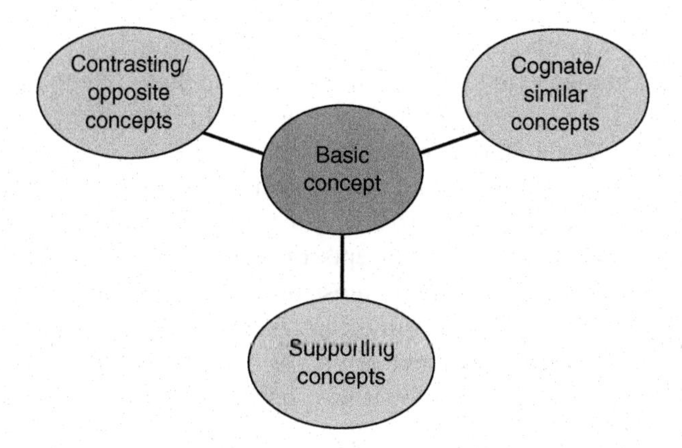

Figure 1.2 Concept web

fields of their own, the configuration of which affect the concept at hand. Finally, we need to pay attention to what happens to a concept, usually a noun, when an adjective is added to it. For instance, the concept of "liberty" takes on a particular meaning when "civil" or "economic" are added (Koselleck's example), or "positive" and "negative" (Berlin's famous distinction). The use of such qualifiers is quite common in International Relations, especially for long-standing basic concepts such as security (national, collective, human, cyber, etc.), power (hard, soft, civilian, structural, etc.) and war (civil, total, old, new, etc.), and it is important to ask how these qualifiers change the meaning of a concept and whether/at what point they create a new concept.

While analysing context in terms of semantic fields is important, it also risks reducing concepts to words and blending out their socio-political appropriation and function. After all, we want to know not only how concepts gain meaning within a linguistic structure but also how they are used and understood, that is, who speaks these words, to whom, how they are received by the audience and with what effect. We also need to take into account that the meaning of our concept is shaped through its association with extra-linguistic forces like ideas, images and practices, which often are captured in the broader notion of a "discursive field". Whatever we call it, I suggest it is useful to distinguish between four contextual layers: temporal, theoretical, material and socio-political.

Paying attention to the **temporal context** involves studying the historicity of a concept and how its meaning content is formed and evolves over time. It views concepts as embedded within a particular historical moment and/or particular structures stretching over time into the future. Conversely, analysts may ask how a concept shapes our understanding of time, namely how it directs our temporal orientation and privileges certain readings of past and future. The **theoretical context** directs attention to how the concepts and its web are situated in a broader ideational framework, or narrative, whether that is a political ideology or a theory (which, for critical scholars, is often the same). It requires exploring the role a concept plays in a particular theoretical ontology and argumentative logic and how it acquires meaning through this role, including how this meaning changes when the concept is placed in a different theory. Reversely, it asks us to understand what the concept does for/to a theory, including how and why theorists build their theories around, or through, particular concepts. One might also extend this to investigate the place of concepts in methodological frameworks of investigation more generally, including quantitative and qualitative methods. The **material context** asks us to look at the material space(s) and bodies in which the concept is used and manifests itself, including what happens to meaning when the concept travels from one material context to another. Equally, it asks us to be sensitive about how concepts organize and shape (our awareness of) material spaces and bodies. This angle most directly raises the question of how we should conceive the relation between meaning (thought/language) and material matter. Finally, the **socio-political context** points to the practice and performance of a concept in (international) society and within a political system. It asks us to trace how a concept is used and its meaning manifested by political actors, its diffusion throughout society/the system and the different understandings and usages seen in different parts of that society/system. It also directs attention to how a concept shapes society and how its meaning becomes a subject of political contestation.

These four contexts hang together and none can be ignored. Most obviously, the temporal and the socio-political reach directly into the internal structure of a basic concept. Yet those two only come to life within the ideational structures and material conditions that make the "stuff" of history and politics. And the socio-political dimension perhaps most clearly permeates the other three and is the reason why concept analysis is interesting for students of (world) politics in the first place. To use a metaphor, these four contexts can be seen as layers of a cake and any piece we cut out, that is, any particular meaning we give the concept, is informed by all four layers. Moreover, we should conceive of contexts not as static/stable environments, but as dynamic practices, processes and flows. At the same time, contexts do not expand indefinitely but end somewhere, and where and how we conceive of their boundaries is an important question. Finally, accounting for concepts in context not only involves asking about how the former is placed in the latter and how this imbues the concept with meaning. It should also have an eye on how the concept performs in a particular context and affects our understanding of it. Indeed, one might say that a basic concept functions like a keystone holding the context together, yet also is supported by it. However we conceive of the relationship, the bottom line is that we need to pay attention to how concept and context are interwoven and shape each other.

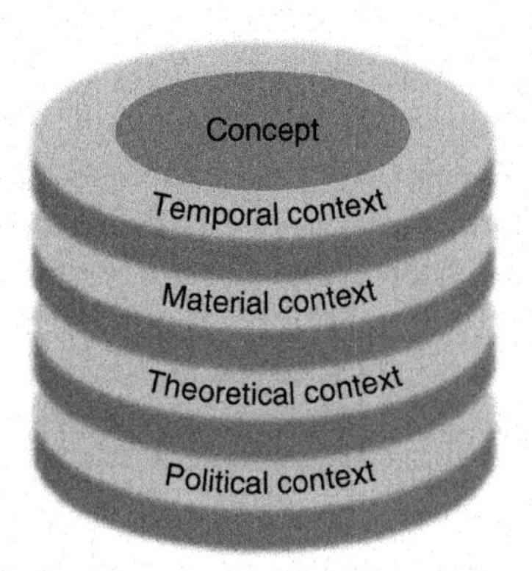

Figure 1.3 Context cake

Three Approaches to Concept Analysis

Unpacking a concept, its meanings, functions and performances by taking into account all the above is challenging and there is no simple recipe. Moreover, as the contributions to this volume testify, there is more than one way to unpack a concept. One reason for the multitude of possible approaches is that we choose and design our approach according to our motivation for doing concept analysis. In other words, our approach is significantly influenced by what we consider its purpose to be, what we want to achieve with it. Thus, the question of *what is* concept analysis is tied to *how to* and *why should we* do concept analysis. This is related to the question *whose* concept we study: is it "our" analytical category or is it a socio-political resource used by those we study? The answer is usually "both", and every approach must grapple with the interplay between these two levels and the tension it generates in its own way. As a consequence, tracing concepts within or through the above contexts always oscillates between deconstruction (or disaggregation) and reconstruction (or concept formation). The following pages show that this can occur in rather different ways. Here, it suffices to say that disaggregation is not simply about showing shattered pieces but about outlining the concepts' different associations in the above contexts. Equally important, reconstructive moves tend to advance a particular reading of the concept and, in doing so, establish a hierarchy between "better" and "worse" readings, which need to be justified. With this in mind, the remainder of this chapter will outline three approaches to concept analysis, which are labelled historical, scientific and political(critical). Each approach is discussed with reference to a particular scholar, namely Koselleck, Sartori and Foucault, respectively, serving as a representative and source of inspiration.

The historical approach

The historical approach foregrounds the temporal context and focuses on a concept's place in and its evolution throughout "history". The starting point is the recognition that using contemporary basic concepts to grasp historical events and periods is problematic because it shapes our understanding of the past and makes us see/write one kind of history rather than another. Can we use basic concepts that did not exist in the past to reconstruct that past? And even if a concept did exist back in the period we are examining, how do we know it did not mean something completely different then? Grappling with this basic problem of representation, the historical approach takes up the notion that concepts have a history and seeks to improve our awareness of their historical depth. However, the motivation is not simply historical curiosity to explore how concepts were used in the past, but also to provide a better understanding of how they evolved and how we arrived at the meanings we employ today. Thus, the aim is to make us aware of both continuity and contingency of meanings under, and in interaction with, specific historical conditions.

Historians of ideas, philosophers of history, and political and literary theorists, have presented rich studies in this regard that can be subsumed under the label of "history of concepts" or "concept history". Perhaps the most ambitious project emerged in postwar Germany under the stewardship of Reinhart Koselleck, which culminated in the eight volumes of *Geschichtliche Grundbegriffe* (Koselleck et al.

2004 [1972]).[4] Koselleck's approach of concept history [*Begriffsgeschichte*] is complex and evolved over many years (Richter 1987; Lehmann and Richter 1996; Steinmetz 2008), yet its intellectual baseline is an attempt at combining linguistic analysis and historical analysis to explore how a concept is understood and employed differently throughout history. This goes far beyond etymology – the tracing of a word's evolution from its alleged "roots" or "origins" to current usage – by investigating the evolution of language and thought in the context of historical experience. Assuming that concepts are "in motion", the approach is especially interested in tracing changes in a concept's meaning. Crudely put, one could say that the historical approach lends itself to explore four instances in the life of a concept: (1) concept **invention** (emergence): how a new concept establishes itself in a particular historical context; (2) concept **fixation** (reification): how a particular meaning becomes hegemonic and gains "common sense" status; (3) concept **transformation** (modification): how a term takes on a new meaning or meanings; and, finally, (4) concept **disappearance**: how a concept ceases to be used and drops from our vocabulary. Although a complete approach takes into account all four phenomena, concept history in Koselleck's tradition is primarily interested in tracking change and so fixation/reification is discussed here as a distinct concern of the third approach outlined below.

Tracing the life of a concept is not mere description. It also involves explanation of why concepts emerge, are modified or disappear. Koselleck's approach offers a largely structural account of change. It is especially interested in how conceptual change correlates with the discontinuity of political, social and economic structures, and in exploring how and why certain experiences and structural changes are grasped as, for instance, "revolutions". It explores convergences and divergences between "real" history and how that "history" has been understood by contemporaries, and sees divergences as tensions which prompt the emergence of new concepts or a change in meaning of existing ones.[5] In doing so, the historical approach tells us something not only about the life of a concept but also about the configuration of the societies and historical periods in which concepts emerge or are transformed. It not only illuminates conceptual change but also provides a window into understanding societal transformations and, hence, historical change. This dual character is expressed in Koselleck's note that concepts are not only *indicators of* but also *factors in* change (Koselleck 2004 [1972]: 86). The latter suggests that concepts do something. It asks analysts to trace their representational performance by asking how concepts guide the thinking and behaviour of actors and shape the organization of (international) society and, consequently, how they influence the course of history.

Analysing how concepts, concept webs and socio-political structures implicate each other and, thus, understanding a concept's historical evolution *and* its social organization and use, are ambitious and come with challenges. One such challenge

[4] The full title (translated) is *Basic Concepts in History: A Historical Dictionary of Political and Social Language in Germany*.

[5] Thus, despite emphasizing the primacy of language, Koselleck's approach does not take the radical position that there is nothing outside language. If that was so, it could not investigate the relationship between concepts and socio-political structures, including material context, in a way that lends the latter some sort of causal force.

is the question of agency. Concepts do not act (on their own) – looking at a "concept in action" requires looking at who is using it. So to understand their historical evolution, we must also ask what historical actors do with concepts, why and how they assign and manipulate meaning and, thus, influence the shape and life of a concept. Yet, tracing the use of concepts among a variety of agents in a given society is not an easy task and requires a fine-grained analysis difficult to reconcile with a macro-historical perspective (Steinmetz 2008). This points to perhaps the greatest challenge, namely the methodological demand to both trace patterns of political language surrounding a particular concept in a specific place and time (synchronic analysis) *and* follow the concept throughout history, that is, across space and time (diachronic analysis). Whereas for Koselleck the two modes of analysis are inseparable, historians of political thought such as J. G. A. Pocock (1996) are sceptical about the possibility of both tracing the evolution of a concept through time and adequately accounting for socio-political context. They argue, instead, that the latter should take priority. This preference for a synchronic perspective stems from the commitment to a mode of historical analysis also known as the "Cambridge School",[6] which holds that a concept's meaning is bound to particular discursive and, especially, ideational structures governing a society at a particular point in time. And these structures, including the concept web any given concept is embedded in, are seen as multi-layered living organisms of which those using a concept may not be consciously aware (Pocock 1989: 33).

The Cambridge School thus reminds us of the need to think carefully about how we conceive of and capture historical context and what we consider adequate sources for reconstructing a concept's meaning. However, we must also be careful not to throw the baby out with the bathwater by dissolving a concept in a socio-political language system. In the end, there is no fixed formula for how to balance and combine diachronic and synchronic analysis and for sorting through the relationship between concept and context(s). The chosen mode of analysis is not least informed by the kind of change one wants to look at: whether one seeks to trace "concepts in motion" from a macro-historical perspective, which analyses the evolution of a concept across multiple generations, or to reconstruct "concepts in action" in a micro-diachronic analysis, which delves into the complexity of how a concept performs and changes in a temporally and spatially confined setting. Both are perfectly valid versions of the historical approach.

The scientific approach

What is termed here the scientific approach sees concepts as methodological tools to grasp the contemporary world, to measure, explain and predict political dynamics across different geographical and cultural locations. Its main objective is tied to the modern ambition of demystifying the world and to developing better, in the sense of both more accurate and more useful, concepts for capturing that world. It is guided by the conviction that only "clear concepts" bring our knowledge "into close and self-correcting relations" with empirical reality (Blumer 1954: 5). Working towards this

[6] The other major representative of which, besides Pocock, is Quentin Skinner (1969).

aim, the scientist seeks to sharpen the conceptual toolkit by revising and refining or, if necessary, inventing and replacing basic concepts to build better theories and improve our measuring techniques. At first sight, this ambition to engage in what Herbert Blumer (1954: 6) calls "precision endeavors" to improve and refine concepts, runs counter to the objective to open them up and reveal their multifaceted nature. And yet, by directing attention to how concepts are used in comparative research, it highlights attempts at mastering the link between concepts and context and at dealing with the tension between universal and particular, which leads to a distinct approach to concept analysis.

One prominent representative of this approach is Giovanni Sartori, an Italian scholar trained in political philosophy who became a central figure in the emergence of the (sub)discipline of Comparative Politics in the United States. Aware that language mediates and guides knowledge production, Sartori's starting point is that concepts play a central role in data collection. That is, they function not only as elements of a theoretical system but also as "data containers" (Sartori 1970). This leads to a conundrum already encountered in the historical approach: because scientific research needs universal categories/concepts that can **travel** across space and enable analysts to compare, it must assume that concepts have core characteristics out of which indicators can be formed for collecting data in different places. At the same time, the meaning content of a concept is built up in the process of measuring "the world", which is to say that concepts only gain substance through empirical research in particular places. And so they are expected to function as "empirical universals" (Sartori). In navigating this tension between the universal and the particular, the temptation may be to put more weight on the former. However, Sartori (1970) warns, employing a concept across geographical and cultural spaces without understanding a concept's history and the discursive field it is made to work in will result in "conceptual confusion", namely a situation where the seemingly same concept ends up describing very different things.

To tackle such confusion, the scientific approach asks researchers to pay attention to the flexibility of a concept and its modification in the research process. Specifically, it looks at (i) the concept's "extension" – the process in which a concept widens and shifts its boundaries to include more and/or different elements, thus becoming broader and more complex in meaning, and (ii) the concept's "intension" – the process which zooms "inwards" and highlights its core elements, thus specifying its meaning. Scholars offering strategies to navigate this dynamic often do so in an overly technical discussion about logic, semantics and methods (Sartori 1984; Goertz 2006; Collier and Gerring 2009). Here it suffices to say that the approach requires the analyst to reflect on how a concept is **adjusted, translated** and, to a certain extent, **transformed** when it moves, or is moved, from one space to another. Importantly, this involves exploring what happens to a concept in the process of **application**, or **operationalization**, namely when research moves from theoretical reasoning to empirical investigation. That is, the approach seeks to understand how a concept is altered when it moves from the abstract level, where it carries a general meaning, to the concrete empirical level, where it functions as a "data container". To use a well-known metaphor from Sartori, it traces how a concept is modified when it (or, rather, the researcher) climbs down "the ladder of abstraction" (Sartori 1970: 1040-41). This also shifts attention to how the concept interacts with the chosen method, whether that is quantitative or qualitative in character.

However, the scientific approach is not content with tracing these travels and recording changes. After all, for the scientist the task is not simply "to understand our conceptual confusions" but "to clear them up" (Gaus 2000: 16). Driven by the aim to create ever more accurate concepts, the approach seeks to minimize "distortions" in the process of translation and operationalization by devising rules that keep flexibility in check and allow concepts to travel across contexts without disappearing. Ultimately, Sartori's solution is unsurprising: he calls for "minimal definitions" that define the concept's "basic structure" independent of context (Sartori 1984). In other words, he seeks to stabilize meaning by specifying the core attributes of a concept and anchoring them on a universal plane.

There are two problems with this strategy. First, seeing vagueness and ambiguity as "defects" (Sartori 1984) and a "basic deficiency" (Blumer 1954: 5) sits uneasily with Koselleck's insight, discussed earlier, that concepts are inherently and necessarily vague. Indeed, it ignores the idea that vagueness or ambiguity is often what makes a concept useful and gives it a long shelf-life, whether in scholarly debate or in political practice. Second, it ignores intractable disputes about the meaning of basic concepts, which W. B. Gallie (1956) famously captured in the notion that many concepts remain "essentially contested". As Gallie notes, often "endless disputes" about the proper use of concepts such as "democracy" or "justice" are "perfectly genuine: although not resolvable by argument of any kind, [they] are nevertheless sustained by perfectly respectable arguments and evidence" (Gallie 1956: 169). For the scientist, this state of affairs is puzzling and frustrating, especially as the dispute requires agreement between the two sides that, at some level, they are talking about the *same* concept. Gallie argues that this is the case when both derive their reading from the same "exemplar" (1956: 176), which functions as the source from which their respective reading of the concept flows. Because the "exemplar" – like all basic concepts – is internally complex and open/ambiguous, parties are able to focus on different elements and configurations and develop different adaptations. As such, both parties can claim "ownership" of the exemplar, yet neither is able to persuade the other that its claim is ill-founded or invalid.

Despite these limitations to the scientific ambition, not all is lost for the agenda to clear up confusion, as it invites an investigation into different readings of an "exemplar" and the establishing of a sensible **typology** of these readings without favouring one over another. The crucial question is whether (a) the different types are deemed compatible and can be integrated into a single research process, that is whether they can be combined, or are claimed to be combinable, into one master concept (one might call this the "Sartori position"), or whether (b) the types are deemed essentially contested and, thus, incompatible and cannot be combined and integrated into a single, coherent research process (the "Gallie position"). The answer has significant implications for how we use typologies in scholarly communication and collaboration. It either holds that a concept can serve as a bridge for scholars working in different theoretical frameworks, enabling fruitful exchange between and integration of paradigms, or it allows scholars to more clearly see and appreciate different readings, guarding against the belief that they are talking about the same thing when, in fact, they are talking past each other.

The political/critical approach

The political/critical approach starts from the famous dictum that knowledge is power. It accepts that concepts are central parts of knowledge production in modernity and that their purpose is to frame, categorize and organize reality, thereby bringing order and cognitive stability to our understanding of the world. Other than the scientist, however, it treats this stabilizing function with suspicion. Influenced by a post-modern stance, it considers the order created by concepts artificial, blocking out the complexity of the world and upholding certain power structures that benefit some and disadvantage others. The approach, discussed here through the work of Michel Foucault, has a dual aim: first, to explore how concepts form and their meaning becomes reified through their use across society, and to highlight that the formation and performances of concepts are implicated in structures of power. In doing so, it overlaps with concept history and it makes the scientific approach part of its object of analysis.[7] Second, the political/critical approach seeks to disrupt and challenge these reified meanings and underlying power structures to open the door for alternative conceptions and, ultimately, societal change. As such, of the three approaches outlined here, it is the one that most explicitly takes a critical stance and understands concept analysis as an engagement with politics, indeed it is political in motivation.

To understand **reification** processes, the political/critical approach investigates how particular kinds of knowledge are produced, that is, how concepts are used and **perform** in society and to what effect. It highlights that, by giving meaning to "things", concepts don't just make these things intelligible, they actually *make* things, that is, in the words of Foucault, they "systematically form the objects of which they speak" (1974: 49). As such, this approach focuses on the productive power of basic concepts in not merely guiding but constituting thought, action and identities or subjectivities, on both elite and subaltern levels, as well as altering material realities. One important aspect of this analysis is to explore how basic concepts and the *epistemes*, that is, the concept webs and broader discourses surrounding them, become institutionalized. Investigating the process of **institutionalization** involves tracing how the ideational content of the concept is formed and becomes entwined with material reality. In other words, it studies a concept's material manifestation, including the aesthetic expression of a concept in architectural designs or "hard" forms of infrastructure. Yet it also can take more intangible forms if "institution" is understood to not only encompass formal structures with a concrete physical presence, but also informal practices which are not centrally controlled, or monitored, and may not be localizable in one place, or space, but are diffused throughout society in a seemingly uncoordinated manner. Thus, the analysis of how concepts exercise power largely depends on how we think productive power works and, by extension, how it can be observed. Are concepts embedded in a dominant ideology imposed from the top, as in Gramscian hegemony, or do they emerge out of and are reproduced through everyday practices, as in Foucauldian governmentality? The answer may well be "a bit of both", but this cannot distract from the conundrum that any attempt to analyse the political performance of a particular concept – the production and effect of its meaning on society – relies on an understanding of another basic concept, namely power.

[7] Tellingly, Foucault (2003) at one point called his work "antiscientific" in orientation.

As noted, the political approach does not stop with exploring the reification and reproduction of basic concepts by unmasking power configurations. It also seeks to weaken these configurations and act as a critical voice against the temptation to find a singular meaning and accept a "common sense". It does so by highlighting techniques of resistance, subversion and **contestation** of meaning and, thus, showing that meaning is (or should be) a matter of politics. Indeed, as the name suggests, the political approach actively participates in and seeks to advance contestation and regards concept analysis as a mode of resistance. One approach exemplifying this is Foucault's **genealogy**, a method that overlaps with concept history in exploring the evolution of a concept within socio-political structures. Due to its focus on reification, genealogy differs from concept history in that it does not seek to trace change, whether in a macro- or micro-historical perspective, but how a concept is **assembled** into something taken for granted while, simultaneously, showing that any notion of unified or coherent meaning is an illusion.

The latter aspect most clearly sets this approach apart from those discussed so far. It brings to the fore the historical contingency of stabilized knowledge through the dual move of critiquing (deconstructing) the notion of a coherent historical narrative about a concept and bringing to the foreground (reconstructing) its disparity, the marginalized and forgotten aspects. Foucault adopts this approach from Nietzsche, specifically from Nietzsche's critique of the notion of "origin", which exemplifies the idea that there is an essence or singular truth that can be excavated. Instead, Foucault holds, if the genealogist "listens to history he finds ... the secret that they have no essence or that their essence was fabricated in a piecemeal fashion from alien forms. What is found at the historical beginning of things is not the inviolable identity of their origin ... it is disparity" (Foucault 1977, part 1). And so rather than trying to identify an origin (or "exemplar") and to trace an unbroken continuity in the historical life of a concept, the genealogical approach asks the analyst to "identify the accidents, the minute deviations ... the errors, the false appraisals, and the faulty calculations" that underpin the life of a concept (Foucault 1977, part 3). The study of discontinuity and **contingency** aims at revealing aspects of a concept's life which have been glossed over by conventional accounts and thus become invisible, to show that the concept has no unifying shape but only fragments of meaning. In other words, it seeks to carve out what Foucault calls "subjugated knowledges" (Foucault 2003: 7), namely meanings/uses that are ignored because they do not fit established discourses, which are considered irrelevant or invalid and, hence, are marginalized, squeezed out of sight.

Where and how one finds a concept's disparate, **subjugated fragments** depends, once again, on our reading of the power structure. Often, the search for these forgotten or silenced meanings takes place "on the local level", although, as Foucault reminds us, it is important not to mistake subjugated for "common-sense" knowledge, as the latter tends to be an expression of the dominant, taken-for-granted account and is exactly what genealogy works against. Also, finding this meaning does not necessarily require focusing on subalterns (a tricky concept in itself), but may also be found in the contradictions and tensions of dominant discourses, or in elite voices that have become forgotten. In any case, the genealogical approach requires attention to detail. As Foucault famously put it, "genealogy is gray, meticulous, and patiently documentary. It operates on a field of entangled and confused parchments, on documents that have been scratched over and recopied many times". Moreover, the researcher must explore how meaning is tied to "the most uncompromising places, in what we feel is without history – in sentiments, love, conscience, instincts" (Foucault 1977: 1). This not only poses significant methodological challenges but also opens up a very different understanding of what concept analysis entails: it not only asks analysts to explore the grey zones and lived experiences outside established frameworks, but may also require a different style of analysis that replaces conventional logics and rigid systematicism in favour of a playful, improvised and disruptive mode of research and writing.

Conclusion

The three approaches outlined here are ideal types, and while they can be seen as distinct they are not mutually exclusive. It is possible, for instance, to read the historical approach as a baseline for the other two, with the scientific approach and the political approach taking up certain aspects of the historical approach and developing them in different directions. Moreover, none of the three approaches offers a polished roadmap. Rather, they are dynamic intellectual projects which have created distinct spaces for conversation containing different, at times diverging, views about how to engage concepts. So, while the differences between these three approaches should be taken seriously, in practice one may well end up with a combination. Thus, it is not surprising that the chapters in this book do not fit neatly into one or the other approach but can be seen as highlighting and combining certain themes and angles, as well as adding others. As such, even if those three approaches delineate the playing field of concept analysis, one might well come to the conclusion that the book does not present three but 17 approaches.

On that note, a word should be said about how the concepts covered in this book were selected and clustered. All of them are basic concepts in the field of IR; certainly each author seems convinced that their respective concept fits this category. Variation in emphasis makes it possible to devise four categories along which concepts were classified for the purpose of this book: (1) fundamental human *claims* (traits or goals) attributed to political actors (power, security, rationality, identity); (2) pertinent *conditions* of human existence characterizing international relations (war, peace, anarchy, society, capitalism); (3) prominent *systems of governance* underpinning world politics (sovereignty, hegemony, democracy, religion); and (4) central *modes of transformation* marking the current period (revolution, intervention, integration, globalization).

Of course, this classification is far from perfect. Apart from the fact that many of the concepts have a place in each other's conceptual web, the four categories overlap. Thus, as will be clear to the reader, the concepts discussed in this book fit in more than one category. One could reasonably ask, for instance, why security and peace are in different sections, why capitalism is not categorized as a system of governance, or why hegemony or globalization are not listed under conditions. Going a step further, one could also come up with alternative clusters. Taking the sociology of the discipline as an organizing framework, one could label power, security, war, sovereignty, anarchy and rationality "dominant" concepts, with society, hegemony and democracy as "secondary" concepts. A third cluster containing identity, capitalism, religion and revolution, which had been pushed to the margins of the IR discourse, might be termed "forgotten" concepts; and a fourth group consisting of integration and globalization could be called "novel" concepts. And, of course, one could have chosen an entirely different set of concepts! Given the complexity and ever-growing diversity of angles on "world politics", the options are endless and the selection here is, to some extent, arbitrary. But then, as Koselleck concedes, this is still the case with the 122 concepts covered in the *Geschichtliche Grundbegriffe* (Koselleck 2011 [1972]: 8, 32). So, as long as the reader feels provoked to think about criteria for choosing and classifying concepts, the attempt will have been worthwhile. In the end, my hope is that the following pages will stimulate readers to think (more) carefully and critically about *their* favourite concepts, what we do with them and what they do with us.

Bibliography

Aalberts, T. E. (2012) *Constructing Sovereignty between Politics and Law*, London: Routledge.

Adler, E. and V. Pouliot (2011) 'International Practices', *International Theory* 3(1): 1–36.

Adler-Nissen, R. (ed.) (2013) *Bourdieu in International Relations: Rethinking Key Concepts in IR*, London: Routledge.

Blumer, H. (1954) 'What is Wrong with Social Theory?', *American Sociological Review* 19(1): 3–10.

Bourbeau, P. (2015) *Security: Dialogue across Disciplines*, Cambridge: Cambridge University Press.

Burger, T. (1987) *Max Weber's Theory of Concept Formation*, expanded edition, Durham, NC: Duke University Press.

Buzan, B. (1984) 'Peace, Power, and Security: Contending Concepts in the Study of International Relations', *Journal of Peace Research* 21(2): 109–125.

Buzan, B. and L. Hansen (2009) *The Evolution of Security Studies*, Cambridge: Cambridge University Press

Chan, S. (1997) 'In Search of Democratic Peace: Problems and Promise', *Mershon International Studies Review* 41(1): 59–91.

Collier, D. and J. Gerring (eds) (2009) *Concepts and Methods in Social Science: The Tradition of Giovanni Sartori*, London: Routledge.

Connolly, W. E. (1993) *The Terms of Political Discourse*, Princeton, NJ: Princeton University Press.

Doyle, M. (1983) 'Kant, Liberal Legacies, and Foreign Affairs', *Philosophy and Public Affairs* 12(3/4): 323–353; 1151–1169.

Foucault, M. (1970 [1966]) *The Order of Things: An Archaeology of the Human Sciences*, New York: Vintage Books.

Foucault, M. (1974 [1969]) *The Archeology of Knowledge*, London: Tavistock Publications.

Foucault, M. (1977) 'Nietzsche, Genealogy, History', in *Language, Counter-Memory, Practice: Selected Essays and Interviews*, D. F. Bouchard (ed.), Ithaca, NY: Cornell University Press, pp. 139–163.

Foucault, M. (1988 [1964]) *Madness and Civilization: A History of Insanity in the Age of Reason*, New York: Vintage Books.

Foucault, M. (1991 [1975]) *Discipline and Punish: The Birth of the Prison*, London: Penguin Books.

Foucault, M. (2003) *Society Must be Defended: Lectures at the Collège de France, 1975–1976*, New York: Picador.

Freeden, M. (1996) *Ideologies and Political Theory: A Conceptual Approach*, Oxford: Clarendon Press.

Gallie, W. B. (1956) 'Essentially Contested Concepts', *Proceedings of the Aristotelian Society* 56: 167–198.

Gaus, G. (2000) *Political Concepts and Political Theories*, Boulder, CO: Westview Press.

Goertz, G. (2006) *Social Science Concepts: A User's Guide*, Princeton, NJ: Princeton University Press.

Goodwin, C. and A. Duranti (eds) (1992) *Rethinking Context: Language as an Interactive Phenomenon*, Cambridge: Cambridge University Press.

Gumbrecht, H. U. (2006) *Dimensionen und Grenzen der Begriffsgschichte*, Muenchen: Wilhelm Fink Verlag.

Guzzini, S. (2013) 'The Ends of International Relations Theory: Stages of reflexivity and modes of theorizing', *European Journal of International Relations* 19(3): 521–541.

Held, D., A. McGrew, D. Goldblatt and J. Perraton (1999) *Global Transformations*, Stanford, CA: Stanford University Press.

Hobson, J. M. (2012) *The Eurocentric Conception of World Politics*, Cambridge: Cambridge University Press.

Jackson, P. T. (2011) *The Conduct of Inquiry in International Relations*, London: Routledge.

Jordheim, H. and I. B. Neumann (2011) 'Empire, Imperialism and Conceptual History', *Journal of International Relations and Development* 14(2): 153–185.

Kaldor, M. (2012) *New and Old Wars*, Third Edition, Cambridge: Polity Press.

Koselleck, R. (1996) 'A Response to Comments on *Geschichtliche Grundbegriffe*', in *The Meaning of Historical Terms and Concepts*, Lehmann, H. and Richter, M. (eds), Occasional Paper 15, Washington, DC: German Historical Institute, pp. 59–70.

Koselleck, R. (2002) *The Practice of Conceptual History: Timing History, Spacing Concepts*, Stanford, CA: Stanford University Press.

Koselleck, R. (2004 [1979]) *Futures Past: On the Semantics of Historical Time*, New York: Columbia University Press.

Koselleck R. (2011 [1972]) 'Introduction and Prefaces to *Geschichtliche Grundbegriffe*', trans. M. Richter, *Contributions to the History of Concepts* 6(1): 7–37.

Lehmann, H. and M. Richter (eds) (1996) *The Meaning of Historical Terms and Concepts: New Studies on Begriffsgeschichte*, Occasional Paper 15, Washington, DC: German Historical Institute.

Pocock, J. G. A. (1989) *Politics, Language, and Time*, Chicago: University of Chicago Press.

Pocock, J. G. A. (1996) 'Concepts and Discourses: A Difference in Culture?', in *The Meaning of Historical Terms and Concepts*, Lehmann, H. and Richter, M. (eds), Occasional Paper 15, Washington, DC: German Historical Institute, pp. 47–58.

Pocock, J. G. A. (2009) *Political Thought and Political History: Essays on Theory and Method*, Cambridge: Cambridge University Press.

Richter, M. (1987) 'Begiffsgeschichte and the History of Ideas', *Journal of the History of Ideas* 48(2): 247–263.

Richter, M. (1995) *The History of Political and Social Concepts: A Critical Introduction*, Oxford: Oxford University Press.

Ringmar, E. (2014) 'The Search for Dialogue as a Hindrance to Understanding: Practices as Interparadigmatic Research Program', *International Theory* 6(1): 1-27.

Sartori, G. (1970) 'Concept Misformation in Comparative Politics', *The American Political Science Review* 64(4): 1033–1053.

Sartori, G. (1973) 'What is "Politics"?', *Political Theory* 1(1): 5–26.

Sartori, G. (ed.) (1984) *Social Science Concepts: A Systematic Analysis*, London: Sage.

Skinner, Q. (1969) 'Meaning and Understanding in the History of Ideas', *History and Theory* 8(1): 3–53.

Smith, S., K. Booth and M. Zalewski (eds) (1996) *International Theory: Positivism and Beyond*, Cambridge: Cambridge University Press.

Steans, J. (2013) *Gender and International Relations*, Cambridge: Polity Press.

Steinmetz, W. (2008) 'Vierzig Jahre Begriffsgeschichte: The State of the Art', in *Sprache – Kognition: Kultur. Sprache zwischen mentaler Struktur und kultureller Prägung*, Kämper, H. and Eichinger, L. M. (eds), Berlin/New York: Walter de Gruyter, pp. 174–197.

Tickner, A. B. and D. L. Blaney (eds) (2012) *Thinking International Relations Differently*, London: Routledge.

Tickner, J. A. (1992) *Gender in International Relations*, New York: Columbia University Press.

Vucetic, S. (2015) 'Against Race Taboos', in *Race and Racism in International Relations*, Anievas, A. et al. (eds), London: Routledge, pp. 98–114.

Claims

2

Power

Stefano Guzzini

This chapter picks up the concept of power, perhaps the most important concept for analysts of world politics, to advance three ways in which we can analyze concepts. Rather than offering a survey of different conceptualizations of power, which have been well discussed elsewhere (Baldwin, 1989, 2002; Barnett and Duvall, 2005; Berenskoetter, 2007; Guzzini, 1993, 2000; for a succinct overview, see Guzzini, 2011), the chapter shows the crucial importance of conceptual analysis both for the critique and development of theory and as an empirical analysis of the performative effects of power analysis. In doing so, the discussion points to the analytical benefits and limits of taking a concept's theoretical and political contexts seriously.

The chapter proceeds in three parts. The first section will tackle how to understand or define a concept. Far from being a purely semantic exercise or a simple instrumental step in the operationalization of variables, I look at concepts from their context-specific usage, including our theoretical languages. Applied to the concept of power, I look at how the two overarching domains of power analysis, political theory and explanatory theory, can help us map the different concepts of the power family. The main purpose of this section is to justify my non-instrumental assumptions in conceptual analysis: analyzing the concept of power is more than defining it; and some definitions may seriously hinder analyzing it.

The second section looks at the role the concept of power plays in our theoretical languages and shows how conceptual analysis can be used for the analysis and critique of theories. It illustrates how the "scientific approach" to concept analysis laid out by Berenskoetter in the introduction to this volume can be adapted for critical purposes. It does so by addressing a paradox. On the one hand, concepts derive their specific meaning from the theoretical and meta-theoretical contexts in which they are embedded. On the other hand, meanings travel across the multitude of theoretical contexts. This can produce situations in which a concept considered central is, however, not best served by keeping it within the theoretical context in which it is predominantly applied. Also, importing conceptualizations from other theoretical contexts may not work because it produces contradictions within receiving theoretical contexts. Applied to the concept of power, I will use the mapping of power concepts of the first section for a theoretical critique of realism, a theory that is often identified with the analysis of power.

The third and final section focuses on the role of power in political discourse(s) and shows how the concept of power becomes itself the object of empirical analysis. This is a central issue for conceptual history in its different forms, but also for performative analyses of discursive practices, and hence the "political (critical) approach" (see Chapter 1). Power is performative in that it mobilizes ideas of agency and responsibility. It politicizes issues, since action and change are now deemed possible. Moreover, given that we have no objective measure of power, but practitioners need to assume one to attribute status and recognition, a part of international politics can be understood as the ongoing negotiation about who has the right to define and what is part of the definition of power. This struggle over the "right" definition of power, as used by practitioners, is part and parcel of power politics.

The Meanings of Power and the Theoretical Domains of Power Analysis

Concepts and theories are intrinsically connected. Not only do concepts appear as the terms of our theoretical propositions, but concepts, such as power, play a role in the constitutive function of theories in that they "conceive" the very things we theorize: "*Concepts are about ontology*. To develop a concept is more than providing a definition: it is deciding what is important about an entity" (Goertz, 2006: 27, original emphasis). In support of this stance and developing further the theory dependence of concepts, I will argue against conceptual analyses that are either "descriptive" and theory-neutral, or instrumentalist, where any conceptualization will do as long as it serves the explanatory purpose. In contrast, I will look at the meaning(s) of power by analyzing their role within the contexts of political and of explanatory theory.

Conceptual analysis as neither neutral nor instrumental

The attempt to find a neutral term is typical for more positivist understandings of conceptual analysis. They are perfectly justifiable for some specific purposes and contexts. It is easy to see how having several meanings of power impairs research communication and accumulation. The ideal is to imitate the technical cleanness of an almost mathematical language in which concepts are precisely defined and distinguished. As is typical for positivism, this technical language is not meant to literally reflect the world, but should provide a tool with which we can more efficiently study and deal with that world. In its most common version, such an approach to conceptual analysis aims at reconstructing a "descriptive" (Nagel, 1975), i.e. theoretically neutral, meaning of a concept(s), where concepts are defined "independently of any theories with the purpose of clarifying whatever isolated generalizations have been made or may be asserted" (Oppenheim, 1981: 189). Conceptual analysis is but a crucial first step for variable construction and for the transferability of analytical results.

This approach is useful, but only as far as it goes. Putting neutrality and operationalization first can easily end up in a dilemma: faced with the difficulties of pinning down a concept, scholars decide to go for its more neutral and easily operationalizable aspects, but they thereby incur the risk of emptying the concept of the very significance for which it had been chosen as a focus in the first place. For instance, analysts of power in international relations who start from a more empirical grounding, have often tried to express power either in mainly military indicators (Mearsheimer, 2001) or in some composite index usually including GDP (Merrit and Zinnes, 1989). But this then neglects other resources and the structural aspects of power so important to understanding domination in international politics. In addition, the descriptive approach faces a second problem. Here, the search for neutrality leads researchers to climb up the "ladder of abstraction" to such daring heights that these "overstretched" concepts can no longer function as data-containers viable for empirical analysis in the first place (Sartori, 1970, 1984; see also Collier and Mahon, 1993).

Most importantly, such neutrality may not be possible in the first place. It assumes that all concepts can function independently of the theoretical and/or meta-theoretical contexts in which they are commonly used. And this, precisely, does not work, since it rests on a basic paradox. Faced with the absence of a general social theory to build on, Oppenheim chose a strategy of "neutral concepts" as building blocks for such a theory, more inductive and more bottom-up. Yet for the very same reason that underlying meta-theoretical and theoretical differences thwart a general theory, they also thwart any theoretically significant concept to stay neutral to start with. And this produces a paradox for Oppenheim's strategy: neutrality is sought for, because it is a step towards an all-encompassing social theory, yet starting with neutrality is only possible if we already have one. Hence, concept formation and theory formation stand in a mutually constitutive relationship, and the philosophical and meta-theoretical assumptions which divide our social and political theories are inevitably reflected in the meaning and theoretical use of concepts. As a result, the meaning of these concepts is to be approached from the theoretical contexts in which they are used. This does not exclude translatability in general, but looking for translations is a different enterprise to looking for a neutral meta-language.

In addition to opposing a neutral conceptualization of concepts, the following analysis is also informed by a stance against instrumentalism in conceptual analysis. This refers to the idea that any definition of a concept will do as long as it is consistent with some usage and can be fruitfully fitted into an analysis. Such an instrumental view, if qualified, has been proposed in a recent re-discovery of Sartori (Collier and Gerring, 2009; see also the earlier writings of Gerring, 2001). But this neglects the fact that (our core) concepts are a repository of our accumulated knowledge. In a section entitled "the loss of historical anchorage", Sartori writes that "our understandings of meanings are not arbitrary stipulations but *reminders of historical experience and experimentation*" and that those who ignore how our political concepts were discussed in the past and how their meaning evolved "have freed themselves not only from the constraints of etymology, but equally from *the learning process of history*" (Sartori, 2009 [1975]: 62, original italics). So, while any conceptualization is a construction of the observer, we cannot just instrumentally define our terms as we feel best for coding, with no concern for their historical legacies and wider purpose: we would end up with a clean definition which remains blind to and does not reflect the historical and political legacy that gave that particular concept its significance to start with. Our concepts are living memory, and we must understand their meaning as embedded in theoretical contexts and political history (Guzzini, 1993, 2005).

The domains of power in International Relations

Power has been ubiquitous in the discipline of International Relations since its early days, when realism used it threefold to define the very nature of international politics ("power politics"), the main factor for explaining behaviour (in terms of the "national interest"), and the outcomes of interactions. The notion of power politics provided a demarcation criterion for the study of politics as opposed to law, and for the study of international as opposed to domestic politics. It did so by characterizing a qualitatively different nature of politics at the international level which is due to the absence of a world government, a state called "anarchy" (see Chapter 8, this volume). Not only did anarchy become a core concept for political realism; it was seen as the basis for understanding the special nature (and hence expertise) of international relations in general. By moving international, the nature of politics is profoundly affected. Whereas in domestic politics, power can be used synonymously with government, at least partly defined with regard to a common good, no such commonality exists at the international level, where "powers" meet unfettered. Power is still about political order, but merely about the "art of the possible" in support of the autonomy of a specific international "reason of state". And even scholars who may not agree with political realism implicitly pay tribute to this view, as long as they are wary about the "domestic analogy" of transferring the understanding and functioning of politics from the domestic to the international realm.

In addition to defining the nature of international politics, realists use power as the central variable for explaining interests and outcomes. As in Morgenthau's famous statement, "whatever the ultimate aims of international politics, power is always the immediate aim" (1948: 13). The accumulation of power is necessary to protect a country from aggression and, if that happens, from defeat. Moreover, under the assumption that countries will try to avoid any configuration that could be detrimental to their survival, an international "balance of power" ensues "of necessity" (1948: 125). For realists, then, power refers to two great theoretical domains: the political theory about the nature of order and government and the explanatory theory of behaviour and outcomes.

To come to grips with this dual heritage, I follow Morriss' move to study concepts from their usage in different contexts (Morriss, 2002 [1987]: Ch. 6). Such contexts may ask for different conceptualizations. For instance, in a practical context one wants to know what others can do to oneself, whether intended or not; in a moral context that assesses responsibility, such non-intentional power may be less relevant. The pertinence of certain conceptualizations is to be established through the purposes within such contexts.[1] Hence, by approaching power from the perspective of its context-specific

[1] Morriss excludes a scientific context for power, since power statements "*summarise* observations; they do not explain them" (Morriss, 2002 [1987]: 44, original emphasis). I approach that context differently, however, by not subsuming it under causal explanatory theorizing, as Morriss does.

usage, it is possible to establish its different conceptualizations in the two distinct yet intrinsically connected fields of political theory and explanatory theory.[2]

The purpose of power analysis in the field of political theory, as I understand it here, is to think about the nature of the "polity" in which questions of the organization of (organized) violence and of the common good, as well as questions of freedom, are paramount. Power here stands for "government" or "governance" and political order, as well as personal "autonomy". The logic in the field of explanatory theories is to conceive of power in terms of a (micro) theory of action or a (macro) theory of domination. Here, power is searched for the explanation of behaviour and the outcomes of social action. It is here that power is thought of in terms of "agency", "influence" or prevalence, if not "cause", but also, if used at the collective level, in terms of social rule and hegemony. Crossing the two theoretical domains with a focus on individual or structural aspects of power analysis gives the following table.[3]

Table 2.1 The domains and concepts of power (N.B. Dark shading refers to primary power concepts; light shading to centrally related terms).

<table>
<tr><th></th><th></th><th>Political theory (domain of constitutive knowledge)</th><th>Explanatory theory (domain of applied knowledge)</th><th></th></tr>
<tr><td></td><td></td><td colspan="2">Polity/Socio-political order</td><td></td></tr>
<tr><td>Macro level</td><td>Common good</td><td colspan="2">Government/Governance
Rule/Domination/Hegemony</td><td>Hierarchy
Stratification</td></tr>
<tr><td>Micro level</td><td>Freedom
Responsibility</td><td>Autonomy
Independence</td><td>Ability/Capacity
Influence</td><td>Disposition
Cause</td></tr>
<tr><td></td><td></td><td>Subjectivity</td><td>Agency</td><td></td></tr>
</table>

Source: Guzzini (2013: 10).

The matrix can do entirely without naming power, but for all of the terms used, "power" could be substituted. Moreover, this wide semantic field and the connected terms give a sense of the variety of concerns we raise when we embark on power analysis. Even if we explicitly relate only to one power term, it always reverberates with debates using the other ones – whether scholars are aware of it or not. For instance, when Dahl (1961) analyzed influence in specific policy domains, he wished to understand "who governs" in social science terms and yet through this also the nature of democratic government, while explicitly mobilizing a certain vision of causality for understanding power (Dahl, 1968).

[2] For a first exposition of this approach, see Guzzini (2007), later developed in Guzzini (2013, Introduction); see also Haugaard (2010).

[3] For graphic reasons, the table does not include "authority" and the related issue of legitimacy. I would place authority in the exact middle of the matrix, where domains and levels overlap.

Conceptual Analysis as Theoretical Critique: A Power Analysis of Power Politics

One might distinguish between three types of theoretical critiques for which conceptual analysis can be mobilized. A historical take would consist in unpacking the political battles that concepts carry with them and seeing whether they fit or contradict the theories in which they are used. Here, I will develop two analytical ways of using conceptual analysis as an avenue for critiquing the internal logic and consistency of theories.[4] The first way investigates whether the assumptions underlying a conceptualization within its theoretical context can actually be met empirically. If concepts cannot just be instrumentally defined, then their underlying assumptions, including ontological/empirical ones, are up for a check – and with the assumptions also the actual theorization. And the second way checks whether a given conceptualization is coherent within the meta-theoretical framework of the theory and/or across the two theoretical domains that encompass power concepts (see above). This section will illustrate the first by discussing realist assumptions of power in the analysis, and the second by looking at recent attempts to import or combine power concepts from other theoretical contexts.

A conceptual critique applied to assumptions: realism and the measure of power

The Melian Dialogue, *The Prince*, and *Leviathan* are star witnesses testifying to the immutability of human nature, the wisdom of the *raison d'état*, or the brutish consequences of a state of nature. It was self-evident to classical realists à la Morgenthau, or for the English School for that matter, that realism drew its wisdom from political theory. It is "an attitude regarding the human condition", as Gilpin (1986 [1984]: 304) put it. The concern with power was fundamentally linked to a materialist theory of politics, accompanied by a cyclical view of history that teaches prudence and offers no redemption (Bobbio, 1981). When realism turned into a social science, it could not let power go. It constitutes its philosophical core. The transfer seemed easy enough through the specific anarchical context of world politics. With no world government, the international system seemed to lack not only an ordering authority, but a polity altogether. This made it possible to think of world politics simply as the attempt to aggregate and balance capacities to affect outcomes.

In the explanatory domain, power thus became a central variable in a double causal link. Understood as resources or "capabilities", power was an indicator of the strength

[4] The historical and analytical takes might not converge. A historical approach does not necessarily view concepts from any external position, let alone a telos; they are mere outcomes of historical epistemic struggles. Yet embedding concepts in different theoretical and meta-theoretical contexts provides the observer with an external viewpoint of the concept. Ideally, the two must be made to meet by, for instance, embedding concepts in language games or historically contingent purposes, which include scientific ones.

of actors, and consequently of the capacity to affect or control events. Likewise, a general capacity to control outcomes has been used as an indicator for the ruling of the international system. Rather than seeing the two domains as separate, the anarchical nature of world politics could combine them in an explanatory sequence: by knowing and aggregating *who can be expected to win conflicts*, we would also know *who or what governs international politics*. Within Table 2.1, we can see how the analysis of government (top left) is done through the analysis of influence (bottom right) and its aggregation – and is also reduced to it.

But both links have become heavily disputed. The causal link from resources to outcomes was duly criticized by David Baldwin in the context of the Vietnam War. For Baldwin, the assumed link produced either unfalsifiable ad hoc patches or the "paradox of unrealized power" (Baldwin, 1979: 163). Either the US was more powerful than its adversary but lost the war, which would however mean that the causal link from power to influence was gone and with it the very relevance for looking at power as resources; or the causal link was there, but that meant the US was (militarily) weaker than Vietnam, which was surely not what appeared on the balance-of-power sheets, although the latter were busily redrawn to accommodate the unexpected outcome.

That such patches were logically possible in the first place has to do with the conceptual "flexibility" provided by the fact that power is not objectively measurable and is hence adjustable to fit assumptions and analysis. One of the reasons is the interrelatedness of resources: to be potentially efficient, they need to be combined in specific packages. Relatedly, and more generally: how do we aggregate resources – military, financial, cultural, moral and others – into one single unit? This assumes a common measuring rod into which the different units can be converted. Unfortunately, no such thing exists, at least not in an objective sense (for a constructivist reading of this conversion, see below). In other words, by assuming a single measure of power, balance of power theories applied what Robert Dahl (1976: 26) has pointedly called the "lump of power" fallacy.

The underlying reason for this lack of convertibility is that power cannot be conceptualized in close analogy to money, at least not for the purpose of building an explanatory (and causal) theory of action. As Raymond Aron (1962), a classical realist, argued a long time ago, whereas economists can reduce the variety of preferences (guns or butter) into a unified utility function through the concept of money, and whereas people can apply this in *real existing* monetarized economies in their everyday economic behaviour, there is no equivalent in politics. In real-world politics, we have no existing measure to tell us how much a billion inhabitants weigh in power as compared to a nuclear weapon, or hundreds of them. And this qualitative difference undermines the attempt to model power in analogy to money. Put into power jargon: power is not just less "fungible" (convertible across domains) than money, although it is this, too. More importantly, power cannot fulfill the same functions in political exchanges as money does in economic ones: it does not provide a standardized measure of economic value (Baldwin, 1993: 21). As a result, the analysis of power would have to be multidimensional, avoiding statements that assume either a single power index (where resources are fungible) and/or a single world issue area (in which one resource would necessarily trump the others).

To complicate things even more, a third problem in established power analysis has to do with the *relational* character of power that problematizes what counts as a capability in the first place. For Dahl, "A has power over B to the extent that he can get B to do something that B would not otherwise do". The main characteristic of a relational approach is that it locates power as a counterfactual in a human relationship, thus distinguishing it from the sheer production of effects (power in nature). Such relational concepts of power take issue with a vision of power in terms of its resources or instruments: power exists in and through a relationship; it is not the possession of any agent (Dahl, 1957: 202–3).

Bachrach and Baratz (1970: 20–1) illustrate the relational view in a famous thought experiment. A sentry levels his gun at an unarmed intruder, whom he orders to halt or else he will shoot. If the intruder stops, it seems the threat has worked: the sentry has exercised power. Not necessarily, they say. If the intruder was himself a soldier, he may obey because that is what a soldier does when receiving an order from a sentry. The alleged power resource is ineffectual here, since it was the intruder's value system that made him obey, not the gun. Inversely, if the intruder does not obey and gets himself killed, we may again not be seeing a power relationship. Since the intruder apparently valued entering the base more than his own life, the killing only shows the ultimate powerlessness of force (violence) in the face of a suicide attack. But the example can be pushed to its extreme: the intruder may have wanted to commit suicide but gets the sentry to do it for him. In this case, the intruder, by "forcing" the sentry to shoot him, exercises power over the sentry.

Put in general terms, no empirical analysis of power can be made without knowing the relative importance of conflicting values and preferences in the mind of the power recipient, if not also of the supposed power-holder. The capacity to sanction and the resources on which the sanctions are based are *part* of power analysis, but are in themselves insufficient to attribute power, since what counts as a sanction in the specific power relation is itself dependent on the specific values and preferences in the minds of the people involved.

To sum up the critique of the dual causal link from resources to outcomes and from outcomes to political order: if power cannot be objectively measured for its lacking fungibility, we know neither when it is "balanced" nor when it has been "maximized". If power is inferred from effects, the concept is circular; if it is not inferred, because no direct causality exists, power is indeterminate, and hence not centrally relevant. If it is used in the explanation of outcomes, its relational and multidimensional character makes it specific to issue areas and even to particular historical situations in which the different preferences of actors may affect what resource can count as a power base in the first place. With the link from resources to outcomes broken, there is no further link to the understanding of the world polity which can be based on it. Indeed, the empirical non-equivalence of money and power makes it impossible for realists to use it as a fundamental assumption for their theoretical enterprise.

Coherence across meta-theories and the domains of social and political theory

Another way to use conceptual analysis for critiquing the internal consistency of theories consists in checking for theoretical and meta-theoretical coherence when new ideas have to be accommodated within a theory, or when concepts with their theoretically embedded meanings are transferred from one theory into a different one. For instance, "habit" is an idea which is not so easily accommodated within a neo-utilitarian or rational-choice approach, since it refers to a different logic of action (see e.g. Hopf, 2013). Conversely, social theories of action that stress structural components have more problems when dealing with "creativity" (but see Dalton, 2004). As a result, conceptual transfers can reach limits of meta-theoretical coherence and may produce significant theoretical paradoxes. I will try to illustrate this here with the realist use of power.

When faced with the conceptual conundrum of needing but lacking a measure of power, realists could decide to retreat back to political theory and leave explanatory theory to others – at the risk of conceding to their scientific critics by preferring not to engage them (for a more detailed critique on this line, see Guzzini, 2004). Another possible reaction is to stay in the scientific context and elaborate on the concept of power. This is where realists in international political economy (IPE), such as Robert Gilpin, Stephen Krasner and Susan Strange, have made their most important contributions to the analyses of power. Yet, as this section shows, their expansion runs into another paradox: either they keep the importance of the analysis of power but then need to alter the individualist and materialist meta-theoretical framework which underlies most realist explanatory theories, or they keep the latter but then see power analysis escape the confines of realism. I will illustrate this via Lukes' well-known three dimensions of power, since his discussion shows how the concept of power, while becoming increasingly wider, ended up facing internal tensions.

To move beyond Dahl's conception of power, which undergirds most realist understandings of power, many realist scholars have widened the concept. They follow Bachrach and Baratz' analysis of non-decision-making (Lukes' second dimension of power), in that many important issues are decided before they reach the bargaining stage – indeed, often because they never reach it. This *indirect institutional power* refers to the conscious manipulation of the institutional setting within which bargaining relations take place. It has been theorized in Krasner's (1985) concept of "meta-power", and in Caporaso's (1978) and Strange's (1988) concepts of "structural power". Such an approach is still perfectly coherent with a rationalist and individualist analysis, since power is still about the individual capacity to achieve intended ends. As shown by Dowding's (1991) discussion of "social power", the only difference is the indirect channel to do so. Also, Strange's insistence on conceptualizing power to include unintended effects, i.e. *non-intentional power*, can be accommodated in such a framework (as shown, for example, by Elster, 2007).

The issue becomes more interesting with the further widening of Lukes' third dimension, which is inspired by Gramsci. For Lukes teases out an ambiguity in Bachrach and Baratz' approach in which non-decision-making refers to both "ante-decisions" and "systematic bias" (Guzzini, 1993: 462; for an earlier pointer to this ambiguity, see Debnam, 1984: 24). The latter refers to an *impersonal "mobilization of bias"* whereby social structures systematically favour certain agents. It is here that Lukes defends power as a version of "false consciousness" in which actors come to misconceive of their own interests in such a way as to pre-empt conflicts breaking out in the first place.

But for the social theorist, Lukes' approach produces a certain tension: how can we simply add up Gramsci to a "Dahl-plus-Bachrach-and-Baratz approach"? Their underlying meta-theories are divided by the antinomies of the agency–structure debate: "add some Gramsci and stir" will simply not do, since it contradicts the meta-theoretical assumptions of the other approaches. As such, it is not surprising that IR scholars are open to the analysis of such *impersonal power*, but outside a more structuralist tradition, tend to reduce it back to an agency concept (Caporaso, 1978) or stay uncertain in their theoretical set-up (Strange, 1988). In fact, Lukes' analysis is also a prime example of the tensions and possible contradictions when moving between the two domains of power analysis (see Table 2.1) – the explanatory domain of the social sciences and the domain of political theory. By proposing a third dimension of power as the impersonal power that affects social relations through the mobilization of unconscious biases, Lukes writes in a social science tradition to which he responds (Dahl and the community power debate). The conception of power is surely structuralist and the reference to Gramsci consistent (the top-right quadrant). But then, the social scientist Lukes also meets the liberal/radical philosopher Lukes. There, his interest in power is ultimately driven by his interest in a more radical idea of autonomy and freedom (lower-left quadrant). As a result, and in clear tension with, if not contradiction to, his Gramscian take, structure and power are not connected, but suddenly antithetical (Lukes, 1977).

A similar mixing between the two domains and between a micro and macro approach to power can also be seen in the debate around the "benefit fallacy" of power (Barry, 1989 [1975]: 315; Polsby, 1980: 208). Seen from an individualist approach, power as systematic bias has been criticized for overstretching the concept by deducing power from rewards. A free-rider who systematically profits from a certain structure but otherwise remains at its mercy is usually not called powerful, but, at best, described as having "systematic luck" (Dowding, 1991: 137).[5] Yet the benefit fallacy exists only within a causal and individualist framework itself, where outcomes only count when they can be traced back to an action which caused them. To say that a society is arranged such as to systematically benefit certain people is inspired by more structuralist theories that do not tie power to action. For their understanding of power in a social system, and for anyone interested in understanding systems of rule and domination, it seems odd not to take into account the effects of that system which can systematically advantage some actors: the "tacit power of the strong". In this theoretical context, the benefit fallacy does not apply.

These illustrations show that widening the meaning of concepts needs to be consistent with the theoretical context in which this takes place. This applies to meta-theoretical strictures like the agency–structure debate, but also to the passage between the explanatory and philosophical domain, as seen with Lukes. On returning to our case of realist power analysis, which includes more and more structural factors, it requires making a theoretical choice. If the individualist and rationalist set-up of realism does not allow for such a wider analysis, then one side must give. Either realists will exclude such power concerns, as Knorr (1973: 77–8) did when calling Perroux's concept of "dominance" incidental, or they will have to re-arrange their meta-theoretical assumptions to integrate and account for them – an invitation

[5] Dowding (1996: 94ff.) later included systematic luck not in a *concept* of power but at least in a wider *analysis* of power, without really elucidating the exact link.

I issued some time ago when, following Richard Ashley's lead, I proposed Bourdieu's theory of domination to translate the concerns of Foucault into an explanatory theory (Guzzini, 1993: 471–4). This dilemma exposes a basic tension in realism: realist political philosophy cannot let the central importance of power go, yet attempts to translate it into an explanatory theory tend to reduce it to a "currency" of world politics with which to realize "influence" – a far cry from the concerns of Weber and Morgenthau, for instance.

The need for coherence between concepts and (meta-)theories also implies that recent typologies which simply add new qualifiers to power are not very helpful, since they suggest that one can simply add new facets to one and the same approach. Adding Foucault to Lukes without any translation into a coherent meta-theory and social theory, as Barnett and Duvall (2005) do, makes for no coherent typology of power. For one, treating Foucault's approach as just another social theory of power misses one of the key contributions of Foucault, which is clearly about understanding the nature of "government" in its old sense, i.e. about political philosophy. And, more importantly, the typology takes the sting out of the conceptual critique: if one takes the analysis of power seriously, an individualist approach will end up excluding facets of power analysis a priori, allegedly irrelevant, reducing them to instances of luck, as seen above. It is not enough to show that wider concepts allow more or other phenomena to be seen – one also needs to provide a common meta-theory for analysis *across the existing power concepts* to account for such wider phenomena in a theoretically coherent manner, something a good conceptual analysis of power can prepare the ground for.

A Performative and Reflexive Analysis of Power: The Power Politics of Power Analysis

In a disarmingly candid manner, Bull (1977: 113–14) conceded that power cannot be "precisely quantified", but "the conception of overall power is one we cannot do without". But who cannot do without it? The fact that there is no consistent overall measure of power has posed perhaps more problems to the (realist) observer than to the (realist) diplomat. Whereas scholars are still searching for a measure that would help fix their analysis, diplomats do not deduce power in any objective way, but understand it from the way practitioners understand it. Since power as a measurable fact appears crucial in the language and bargaining of international politics, measures of power are agreed to, and constructed as, a social fact: diplomats must first agree on what counts before they can start counting (Guzzini, 1998: 231). This moves the analysis of power away from the quest for an objective measure to the political battle over defining the criteria of power, which in turn has political effects. Concepts of power are not merely external tools with which to understand international politics; they intervene in it. After all, some concepts, such as power, play a special role in our political discourse. This means that besides understanding what they *mean*, their analysis has to assess what they *do* (for a more detailed account, see Guzzini, 2005). This moves the analysis onto constructivist ground, since it is interested in how knowledge reflexively interacts with the social world.

Two issues stand out for our present discussion. First, in our political discourse, power is connected to the assignment of responsibility. Second, power definitions have a reflexive "looping effect" (Hacking, 1999: 34), with the shared understandings and hence workings of power in international affairs. By not making this reflexive component visible, traditional power analysis overlooks one of the most salient links between "power" and world politics. And by analyzing the performative and reflexive side of "power", this last section illustrates a third way of applying conceptual analysis in which the concept of power becomes itself an object of empirical investigation.

What does power do?

A central characteristic of power is its relationship with responsibility. Such an appeal to responsibility, in turn, calls for justification: "For to acknowledge power over others is to implicate oneself in responsibility for certain events and to put oneself in a position where *justification* for the limits placed on others is expected" (Connolly, 1974: 97, original emphasis). This link with responsibility and justification turns power into a concept that is closely connected to the definition of political agency, or politics *tout court*. The traditional definition of power – getting someone to do something he/she would not have otherwise done – invokes the idea of counterfactuals. The act of attributing power (re)defines the boundaries of what can be done. In the usual way we conceive of the term, this links power inextricably to "politics" in the sense of the "art of the possible/feasible". Lukes rightly noticed that Bachrach's and Baratz's conceptualization of power sought to redefine what counts as a political issue. To be "political" means to be potentially changeable; that is, not something natural, objectively given, but something that has the potential to be influenced by agency. In a similar vein, Frei argued long ago that the concept of power is fundamentally identical to the concept of the "political": in other words, to include something in one's calculus as a factor of power means "politicizing" it (1969: 647). Attributing power to an issue brings it into the public realm, where action (or non-action) must justify itself.

Conversely, "depoliticization" happens when, by common acceptance, no power was involved. In such instances, political action is exempted from further justification and scrutiny. Such depoliticization can happen, for example, when what is considered power by one party is simply the outcome of luck for someone else. You do not need to justify your property or action if you were just lucky. No power and hence no further politics is involved or needed. Here, the discussion links up with the last section, in which power as impersonal effects or a system of rule was reduced to "systematic luck", a quintessential move of depoliticization.

The politics of "power": looping effects of power analysis

A conceptual analysis that focuses on the performative character of some concepts implies a series of reflexive links (this section relies on Guzzini, 2006: 128–32). A conceptual analysis of power in terms of its meaning is part of the social construction of knowledge; moreover, defining and assigning power is itself an exercise of power, or "political", and hence part of the social construction of reality. As the following illustrations show, the very definition of power is a political intervention. And having a broader concept of power requires more issues to be factored into political decisions and actions.

The link between power and agency/responsibility in our political discourse has been the main inspiration of Strange's conceptualization of structural power, but also of some neo-conservative and liberal understandings of power. Strange (1985, 1987) developed the concept of structural power in the context of a perceived US decline in the early 1980s, in which scholars saw the US as unable to manage the international economy and hence as not responsible for its effects. Strange argued that this had less to do with the United States' alleged declining power than with US interests, which had shifted in a way that was not causally tied to power. To make this argument, she reconceptualizes power so as to make non-intentional effects and structural biases visible: whether the US Federal Reserve intended to hurt anyone with its high-interest-rate politics, as it did Mexico, was less important than the fact that it did (and, indeed, that only the Fed could have a similar effect). This perspective comes with significant political implications. Making actors aware of the unintended structural consequences of their actions raises the expectation that they will change their actions in the future or, at the very least, requires them to justify why they do not.

In a neo-conservative twist to this conceptual link between power, responsibility and justification, the power-holder no longer downplays its power to keep aloof of criticism, but heavily insists on its power-thus-responsibility so as to justify its worldwide interventionism. If it were true that the US enjoys very great power and superiority, so the argument goes, then it is only natural that it assumes a greater responsibility for international affairs. Insisting on the special power of the US triggers and justifies a disposition for action. US primacy means that it has different functions and responsibilities to other states. From there, the final step to a right or even a duty to undertake unilateral and possibly preventive interventions is not far removed. Its role as the world's policeman is no longer a choice, but actually a requirement of the system (see e.g. Kagan, 1998). Being compelled to play the world leader means, in turn, that the rules that apply to everyone else cannot always apply to the US. The US becomes an actor of a different sort: its special duties exempt it from the general norms. This is the basis of its tendency towards US "exemptionalism", where rules apply to all others but itself (Ruggie, 2005).

The political implications are clear. The more observers stress the unprecedented power of the US, the more they mobilize the political discourse of agency and responsibility, tying it to the US and the US alone, and the more they can exempt US action from criticism, since such action responds to the "objective" (power) circumstances of our time (Krauthammer, 2002–3). Even if the US failed, it did the right thing in responding to its special duty, and the only way forward is to do more of the same, the US being the only game in town. The logic is a kind of Microsoft theory of security: the problem is not that there is too much Windows, but that there is still not enough. As a result, debates about how best to understand power are not politically innocent. By stressing US soft power and its potential decline, analysts can advocate a much more prudent and varied foreign policy strategy that is sensitive to claims of legitimacy and cultural attraction (Nye Jr., 2004, 2007, 2011). Obviously, the more observers see the "special responsibility" or exceptionalism as part of the problem for, not the solution to, US security concerns (and international order in general), the more they may be inclined to double-check the alleged unipolarity. Inversely, neo-conservative writers tend to strongly stress US primacy and thereby legitimate, for example, the Bush administration's security doctrine. Their definition of power "empowers" this type of policy.

If the international community were eventually to share this assessment, it would actually create a social fact. The insistence with which Joseph Nye tours China to plead for a softer definition of power – where countries compete in their attractiveness to others, in their model character, and hence in "resources" like movies – is not just an expression of his understanding of world politics, it is an intervention in it. For if China understood international status as defined by that very attractiveness, unnecessary military escalation could be avoided and the nature of world order changed towards a more peaceful setting. Similarly, the neo-conservative understanding of the world would actively change the world, not just respond to it. Here, it is hard not to be reminded of the by now (in)famous words of a senior adviser to President George W. Bush, as reported by Suskind. The adviser insisted that people like Suskind were part of the "reality-based community" which thinks about solutions in terms of the existing reality: "That is not the way the world works anymore ... We're an empire now, and when we act, we create our own reality" (Suskind, 2004). This also implies that foreign policy acts are not only about marking a country's power, but are active interventions in the shared understanding of power and status that may turn out to be far more consequential than the individual acts per se.

Conclusion

Conceptual analysis is an unavoidable core moment of theorizing itself – and of its critique. Every definition provides an ontological component and decision, and, as such, concepts are the central building blocks in our theoretical languages. At the same time, concepts allow the possibility of translations between languages. This chapter has shown that their implicit multivalences allow us to move across theories and philosophies – while the latter provide checks for the move. As for power, both as a concept and in its empirical application, this chapter has argued that power analysis has gone a long way from its early conceptualizations, even if this rarely shows in publications in the discipline of IR. In exploring some of the wider conceptualizations of power, this chapter has focused more on the theoretical work that can be done with conceptual analysis. It has argued that analyzing the meaning of power can neither be neutral nor instrumental. It then checked the theoretical coherence both of "lump" concepts of power, which assume a concept of overall power that cannot be, and of the eclectic lumping of different concepts of power across meta-theories and philosophies. In a performative twist, the chapter showed that power analysis is not only a critique of power politics, but that there is a power politics in power analysis itself when certain negotiated views of power interact with a reality of power they allegedly only describe. Power is co-constitutive with IR theory well beyond realism and with power politics beyond *Realpolitik*.

Acknowledgements

I am indebted to the many insightful comments on earlier versions of the chapter at the ISA workshop in Toronto in 2014 and the panel at the ISA in New Orleans in 2015, as well as to Cas Mudde and an anonymous referee. I wish in particular to thank the ISA panel discussant Jens Bartelson and, above all, Felix Berenskoetter for his very close reading and many helpful suggestions, which I tried to honour as much as I could.

Suggested Readings

Baldwin, David A. (1989) *Paradoxes of Power*. Oxford: Blackwell.

A collection of Baldwin's articles on power that develops Dahl's tradition in IR and, in particular, a relational understanding of power, the issue of fungibility and the use of positive sanctions in world affairs.

Barnett, Michael and Raymond Duvall (2005) 'Power in International Politics', *International Organization*, 59 (1): 39–75.

A reference article providing an overview of the different conceptualizations of power in IR, including Lukes' three dimensions and Foucault.

Berenskoetter, Felix and Michael J. Williams (eds) (2007) *Power in World Politics*. London, New York: Routledge.

The best collection of articles on power in IR since it provides both breadth of different conceptualizations and usages and depth by showing the theoretical premises and implications of different power concepts.

Guzzini, Stefano (2013) *Power, Realism and Constructivism*. London, New York: Routledge.

A collection of Guzzini's articles on power that shows the connections and tensions between different power concepts and their underlying theoretical assumptions, as applied to both social theories and IR theories.

Lukes, Steven (2005) *Power: A Radical View*. 2nd enlarged edition. Houndmills: Palgrave Macmillan.

An indispensable *locus classicus* for power conceptualization which, in its enlarged version, engages Foucault and Bourdieu and answers his many critics.

Strange, Susan (1988) *States and Markets: An Introduction to International Political Economy*. New York: Basil Blackwell.

A representative theorization from IPE that reconceptualizes power to take account of structural origins and/or effects of actions, and that uses this to re-think world order in terms of four power structures.

Bibliography

Aron, Raymond (1962) *Paix et guerre entre les nations*. Paris: Calmann-Lévy.

Bachrach, Peter and Baratz, Morton S. (1970) *Power and Poverty: Theory and Practice*. New York: Oxford University Press.

Baldwin, David A. (1979) 'Power Analysis and World Politics: New Trends versus Old Tendencies', *World Politics*, 31 (1): 161–194.

Baldwin, David A. (1989) *Paradoxes of Power*. Oxford: Blackwell.

Baldwin, David A. (1993) 'Neoliberalism, Neorealism, and World Politics', in David A. Baldwin (ed.), *Neorealism and Neoliberalism: The Contemporary Debate*. New York: Columbia University Press, pp. 3–25.
Baldwin, David A. (2002) 'Power and International Relations', in Walter Carlsnaes, Thomas Risse and Beth A. Simmons (eds), *Handbook of International Relations*. London: Sage, pp. 177–191.
Barnett, Michael and Duvall, Raymond (2005) 'Power in International Politics', *International Organization*, 59 (1): 39–75.
Barry, Brian (1989 [1987]) 'The Uses of Power', in *Democracy, Power and Justice*. Oxford: Clarendon Press, pp. 307–321.
Berenskoetter, Felix (2007) 'Thinking about Power', in Felix Berenskoetter and Michael Williams (eds), *Power in World Politics*. London, New York: Routledge, pp. 1–22.
Bobbio, Norberto (1981) 'La teoria dello stato e del potere', in Pietro Rossi (ed.), *Max Weber e l'analisi del mondo*. Torino: Einaudi, pp. 215–246.
Bull, Hedley (1977) *The Anarchical Society: A Study of Order in World Politics*. London: Macmillan.
Caporaso, James A. (1978) 'Dependence, Dependency and Power in the Global System: a Structural and Behavioural Analysis', *International Organization*, 32 (1): 13–43.
Collier, David and Gerring, John (eds) (2009) *Concepts and Method in Social Science: The Tradition of Giovanni Sartori*. London: Routledge.
Collier, David and Mahon, James (1993) 'Conceptual "Stretching" Revisited: Adapting categories in comparative research', *American Political Science Review*, 87 (4): 845–855.
Connolly, William E. (1974) *The Terms of Political Discourse*. Oxford: Martin Robertson.
Dahl, Robert A. (1957) 'The Concept of Power', *Behavioural Science*, 2 (3): 201–215.
Dahl, Robert A. (1961) *Who Governs? Democracy and Power in an American City*. New Haven, CT: Yale University Press.
Dahl, Robert A. (1968) 'Power', in David L. Sills (ed.), *International Encyclopedia of the Social Sciences, Vol. 12*. New York: Free Press, pp. 405–415.
Dahl, Robert A. (1976) *Modern Political Analysis*. Upper Saddle River, NJ: Prentice Hall.
Dalton, Benjamin (2004) 'Creativity, Habit, and the Social Products of Creative Action: Revising Joas, Incorporating Bourdieu', *Sociological Theory*, 22 (4): 603–622.
Debnam, Geoffrey (1984) *The Analysis of Power: A Realist Approach*. London: Macmillan.
Dowding, Keith (1991) *Rational Choice and Political Power*. Cheltenham: Edward Elgar.
Dowding, Keith (1996) *Power*. Minneapolis: University of Minnesota Press.
Elster, Jon (2007) *Explaining Social Behavior: More Nuts and Bolts for the Social Sciences*. Cambridge: Cambridge University Press.
Frei, Daniel (1969) 'Vom Mass der Macht. Überlegungen zum Grundproblem der internationalen Beziehungen', *Schweizer Monatshefte*, 49 (7): 642–654.
Gerring, John (2001) *Social Science Methodology: a Criterial Framework*. Cambridge: Cambridge University Press.
Gilpin, Robert (1986 [1984]) 'The Richness of the Realist Tradition', in Robert O. Keohane (ed.), *Neorealism and its Critics*. New York: Columbia University Press, pp. 301–321.
Goertz, Gary (2006) *Social Science Concepts: a User's Guide*. Princeton, NJ: Princeton University Press.
Guzzini, Stefano (1993) 'Structural Power: the Limits of Neorealist Power Analysis', *International Organization*, 47 (3): 443–478.
Guzzini, Stefano (1998) *Realism in International Relations and International Political Economy: the Continuing Story of a Death Foretold*. London, New York: Routledge.
Guzzini, Stefano (2000) 'The Use and Misuse of Power Analysis in International Theory', in Ronen Palan (ed.), *Global Political Economy: Contemporary Theories*. London, New York: Routledge, pp. 53–66.

Guzzini, Stefano (2004) 'The Enduring Dilemmas of Realism in International Relations', *European Journal of International Relations*, 10 (4): 533–568.

Guzzini, Stefano (2005) 'The Concept of Power: a Constructivist Analysis', *Millennium: Journal of International Studies*, 33 (3): 495–522.

Guzzini, Stefano (2006) 'From (alleged) unipolarity to the decline of multilateralism? A power-theoretical critique', in Edward Newman, Ramesh Thakur and John Tirman (eds), *Multilateralism under Challenge? Power, International Order and Structural Change*. Tokyo et al.: United Nations University Press, pp. 119–38.

Guzzini, Stefano (2007) Re-reading Weber, or: the three fields for the analysis of power in International Relations. *DIIS Working Papers*. Copenhagen: Danish Institute for International Studies.

Guzzini, Stefano (2011) 'Power and International Relations', in Bertrand Badie, Dirk Berg-Schlosser and Leonardo Morlino (eds), *International Encyclopedia of Political Science*. London: Sage, pp. 2109–2114.

Guzzini, Stefano (2013) *Power, Realism and Constructivism*. London, New York: Routledge.

Hacking, Ian (1999) *The Social Construction of What?* Cambridge, MA: Harvard University Press.

Haugaard, Mark (2010) 'Power: a "Family Resemblance" Concept', *European Journal of Cultural Studies*, 13 (4): 419–438.

Hopf, Ted (2013) 'The Logic of Habit in International Relations', *European Journal of International Relations*, 16 (4): 539–561.

Kagan, Robert (1998) 'The Benevolent Empire', *Foreign Policy*, 111: 24–35.

Knorr, Klaus (1973) *Power and Wealth: The Political Economy of International Power*. London: Macmillan.

Krasner, Stephen D. (1985) *Structural Conflict: The Third World against Global Liberalism*. Berkeley, CA: University of California Press.

Krauthammer, Charles (2002–3) 'The Unipolar Moment Revisited', *The National Interest*, 70: 5–17.

Lukes, Steven (1977) 'Power and Structure', in Steven Lukes (ed.), *Essays in Social Theory*. New York: Columbia University Press, pp. 3–29.

Mearsheimer, John J. (2001) *The Tragedy of Great Power Politics*. New York: W.W. Norton.

Merrit, Richard L. and Zinnes, Dina A. (1989) 'Alternative Indexes of National Power', in Richard J. Stoll and Michael D. Ward (eds), *Power in World Politics*. Boulder, CO: Lynne Rienner Publications, pp. 11–28.

Morgenthau, Hans J. (1948) *Politics Among Nations: The Struggle for Power and Peace*. New York: Knopf.

Morriss, Peter (2002 [1987]) *Power: a Philosophical Analysis*. Manchester: Manchester University Press.

Nagel, Jack H. (1975) *The Descriptive Analysis of Power*. New Haven, CT; London: Yale University Press.

Nye Jr., Joseph S. (2004) *Soft Power: the Means to Success in World Politics*. New York: Public Affairs.

Nye Jr., Joseph S. (2007) 'Notes for a Soft Power Research Agenda', in Felix Berenskoetter and M.J. Williams (eds), *Power in World Politics*. London, New York: Routledge, pp. 162–172.

Nye Jr., Joseph S. (2011) *The Future of Power*. New York: PublicAffairs.

Oppenheim, Felix E. (1981) *Political Concepts: A Reconstruction*. Oxford: Basil Blackwell.

Polsby, Nelson W. (1980) *Community, Power and Political Theory*. New Haven, CT: Yale University Press.

Ruggie, John Gerard (2005) 'American Exceptionalism, Exemptionalism and Global Governance', in Michael Ignatieff (ed.), *American Exceptionalism and Human Rights*. Princeton, NJ: Princeton University Press, pp. 304–338.

Sartori, Giovanni (1970) 'Concept Misformation in Comparative Politics', *American Political Science Review*, 64 (4): 1033–1053.

Sartori, Giovanni (1984) 'Guidelines for Concept Analysis', in Giovanni Sartori (ed.), *Social Science Concepts: A Systematic Analysis*. London: Sage, pp. 15–88.

Sartori, Giovanni (2009 [1975]) 'The Tower of Babel', in David Collier and John Gerring (eds), *Concepts and Method in Social Science: The Tradition of Giovanni Sartori*. London: Routledge, pp. 61–96.

Strange, Susan (1985) 'International Political Economy: The Story So Far and the Way Ahead', in W. Ladd Hollist and F. Lamond Tullis (eds), *The International Political Economy*. Boulder, CO: Westview Press, pp. 13–25.

Strange, Susan (1987) 'The Persistent Myth of Lost Hegemony', *International Organization*, 41 (4): 551–574.

Strange, Susan (1988) *States and Markets: An Introduction to International Political Economy*. New York: Basil Blackwell.

Suskind, Ron (2004) Faith, Certainty and the Presidency of George W. Bush. *The New York Times Magazine*, 17 October.

3

Security

Holger Stritzel and Juha A. Vuori

Questions of "security" have been at the heart of international relations (IR) since its inception as an academic discipline (Carr, [1939] 1981; Morgenthau, [1948] 1978; Wolfers, 1952). Yet while there have always been competing reflections, concerns and understandings of the term ever since, conceptual investigations into security started only in the early 1980s and intensified with the end of the Cold War, which questioned many of the academic, political and theoretical givens of international politics. As such, increased interest in security as a concept is a fairly recent development and has been particularly pronounced in Europe (Buzan, [1983] 1991; Haftendorn, 1991; Lipschutz, 1995; Baldwin, 1997; Huysmans, 1998; Buzan, 1999; Smith, 1999; Buzan/Wæver, 2008; Buzan/Hansen, 2009). These investigations revolve around several questions serving as central axes of debate: what constitutes a threat, who is to be secure and from whom? What is the object of security about, what quality does it produce, is security objective or subjective, is security positive or negative? How is security currently practised and with what effects? (Williams, 2008; Buzan/Hansen, 2009; Wæver, 2012). Often, scholarly discussions on these questions, such as the literature on securitization, now use the concept of security as their pivotal intellectual starting point (Buzan et al., 1998; see also Dillon, [1996] 2001; Krause/Williams, 1997; Huysmans, 2006).

The purpose of this chapter is to review these reflections and histories in an attempt to outline some of the different meanings, usages and implications of security as a central concept in international relations. While it can be argued that security has a logic and rationale of its own, contemporary debates are often expressed in terms of "common", "global", "cooperative" and, more recently, also "comprehensive" or "human" security, although the understandings underpinning these terms go back at least to the establishment of early peace societies after the end of the Napoleonic Wars (see Dean, 2008). As noted in the introduction to this volume, it is important to examine what various attributes do to notions of "security" and what "security" does to such attributes. However, looking at each of these (and other) attributes is beyond the scope of this chapter. So the focus here will be on security conceptions that carry the attribute of the national. This may appear overly traditional, yet "national security" arguably still is the most influential notion of security for both the practices and theories of international politics, which is why we concentrate our discussion on it here.

The approach to conceptual analysis we deploy in this chapter is closest to the approach of Quentin Skinner (2002). Historical conceptions of security, then, are viewed here as sets of techniques "concerned with exploiting the power of words to underpin or undermine the construction of our social world" (Skinner, 2002: 5). This approach allows for the analysis of continuity and change in the "grammar" of security notions: studies of speech acts and language in a more general sense are important tools to identify conceptual changes at certain moments, or over periods of time (Brauch, 2008b: 67; cf., Skinner, 2002; Wæver, 2008: 100). As such, methodologically this chapter is not limited to Skinner but combines the traditions of conceptual history and conceptual analysis with a critical reading of the genealogy of security as a key concept in international affairs. The chapter starts by analyzing systematic aspects of the etymology of "security" as well as the distinct historical origins and ambivalences of security as "national security" in the early post-Second World War discourse. The chapter then turns to the more recent fragmentation of the concept after the end of the Cold War and examines the "broadening and deepening" of the notion in the form of "comprehensive" or "new" security.

Systematic Aspects of a Conceptual History of Security

Our starting point in the tradition of conceptual history is that any meaning (of security) is historically contingent and changeable, as well as closely tied to social relations of power and their alterations. For Skinner, this suggests that historians of concepts generally have to take the stated beliefs of people (i) as being conventionally truthful, (ii) at face value, and (iii) as part of a broader network of other conventionally held beliefs (Skinner, 2002: 40–3). Such stated beliefs can be examined as speech acts, as utterances that have performative functions in language and communication (Austin, 1975). People do things with words – for example, they make promises and issue threats. Concepts of security and how security is spoken about can be approached in this manner too. With the aid of speech act analysis, it is possible to infer what speech acts do and, thereby, it can be used to deduce what they mean (Vuori, 2008, 2011). When this general approach to conceptual history is applied to study conceptualizations of security, it provides a means to analyze conceptual change as regards security rationales in different time periods as well as between different socio-political contexts. And it shows that what speaking in terms of security has done has varied from time to time and from place to place (Buzan et al., 1998; Vuori, 2011; Stritzel, 2014).

The approach thus reveals that the meaning of concepts is not permanent. Indeed, a number of scholars have noted that "security is a political construction in specific contexts" (Dalby, 2002: xxii), which leads to a question about "the conditions under which it is possible to think, speak, and make authoritative claims about" security

(Walker, 1997: 61). The view that "security has to be brought into question" (Dillon, [1996] 2001: 12) may once have been held only at the critical fringes of the discipline, but this is no longer the case. In contemporary security studies, it has become common to recognize security as an "essentially contested concept" (Buzan, [1983] 1991; Buzan et al., 1998; Fierke, 2007). According to Gallie (1962), essentially contested concepts generate debates about their meaning and applications that cannot be resolved because they "contain an ideological element which renders empirical evidence irrelevant as a means of resolving the dispute" (Little, 1981: 35). William Connolly (1983) took this argument a step further by arguing that there are no sets of secure basic concepts at all to guide practical judgements, that any attempt to construct such sets depends on the exercise of socio-political power, and that any claim of incontestability is itself contestable. While some concepts arguably have a more stable temporary understanding than others due to the exercise of political or social power, others seem to be under constant struggle or deliberately kept vague or intangible, as this allows them to be used for political purposes, i.e. to mean what is expedient for a political speaker. From a discourse theoretical viewpoint, security is an example of a notion that can be considered to be an "empty" (Laclau/Mouffe, [1985] 2001) or a "floating" (Barthes, 1977: 38) signifier, a notion which can be filled with politically useful contents when needed.

Many scholars, at least implicitly, refer to security as something good, as being or feeling safe from harm or danger, which corresponds with its everyday meaning as something positively value-loaded (Enskat et al., 2013: 11; Williams, 2008: 8). For example, Arnold Wolfers (1952: 484–5) argued that "a nation is secure to the extent to which it is not in danger of having to sacrifice core values" and that "security, in an objective sense, measures the absence of threats to acquired values, in a subjective sense, the absence of fear that such values will be attacked". This positive connotation is also reflected in the origins of the word "security" in the English language derived from the Roman word *securus*, where *se* means "without" and *cura* means "worry", "care", "concern" or "anxiety" (Markopolous, 1995: 745; Chilton, 1996; Wæver, 1997, 2008). *Securitas* is the Roman version of the Greek *ataraksia* (άταραξία, impassiveness, calmness), which also begins with a negation; without its negation, *tarasso* (ταράσσω) means "to stir, trouble the mind, agitate, disturb" (Markopolous, 1995: 745; Arends, 2008: 264). Arends (2008: 264–5) however argues that the most important Greek root of security is *asphaleia* (άσφάλεια, steadfastness, stability, assurance from danger, personal safety) that was widely used both in Homer and by Thucydides, and transported to English political philosophy by Thomas Hobbes who translated Thucydides. Michael Dillon ([1996] 2001: 123–4) too considers *asphaleia* as the main root of security, but through the meaning of not falling (negative of *sphallo*, to fall, to trip). The Greek double negative of security then is "not insecure" and means "to make something stand, steadfastness, assured from danger, safe, steady, fortified, to be furnished with a firm foundation, to be certain, or sure" ([1996] 2001: 124).

There are two principal avenues to interpret *securus* then (Mesjasz, 2008: 46): in the first, the term is understood as a state of being secure or of being free from danger, while in the second, the term is understood as being without unease or without cares or worries. These two aspects have been given different emphasis historically, which today seems to be reflected in the objective versus subjective dimensions of security discussed further below. Indeed, during its conceptual development, security has shifted on the axis of objectivity and subjectivity several times.[1] For example, Cicero viewed security as an absence of distress on which happy life depends (Cicero, [45 BC] 1971, V. 14, 42, 466–7); for him, security was a negation, the absence of worry. As such, he would most likely disagree with an understanding of security as something objective, something of which one can have correct or illusory subjective perceptions (Jervis, 1976). Yet, in contemporary understandings, security is often viewed as a quality that we either have or do not have. Security here appears as a measurable mass, or a "container" with an inside (which is safe, but where there has to be surveillance of the enemy within) and an outside (which is dangerous and has to be guarded against) (Chilton, 1996).

While security has generally been viewed as something positive and sought-after, this has not always been so. With the fall of Rome, the use of "security" as a term diminished (Conze, 1984: 834). For Medieval Christians, only God could provide certainty in matters of salvation, so the concept remained ambiguous, even hinting at mortal hubris (Markopolous, 1995: 746; Rothchild, 1995: 61); *securitas* became the "mother of negligence" for some time in slackening the struggle against sin (Schrimm-Heins, 1991: 147). This negative side of security was again emphasized with the protests of Luther and Calvin, when *certitudo*, the certitude of faith, replaced the use of *securitas* in most contexts (Schrimm-Heins, 1991: 169). This usage was similarly evident in 16th-century English, in which the words secure and security could even be used pejoritatively in the sense of "careless" or "carelessness" (Chilton, 1996: 77), as illustrated by Shakespeare's ([1611] 1993: 788) Macbeth: "you all know, security is mortals chiefest enemie". As Der Derian (1995: 28) notes, these pejorative connotations were still evident in mid-19th-century Britain. According to Wæver (2004: 55, 2008, 2012) security then split into two separate concepts in English, but not in all languages, namely safety and surety/security. Safety has a different etymological root than security: *salvus* ("uninjured, healthy, safe"), and to be safe has been understood as not being exposed to danger. The split and later fusion of the concepts produced the "objective" understanding of security which eventually led to probabilism.

As Wæver (1995) argues, in the 20th century, orientation towards the future has been central to the concept of security. That is, security is understood to be about future bads and the probability of their occurrence, and concerned with the possibility of their prevention. Indeed, during the Cold War, and largely also after it, security was viewed more as an objective state, not of mind, but of being: the probability of states posing a threat or being able to deter enemies on the basis of their material capabilities (Buzan/Hansen, 2009: 33). Paul Chilton (1996: 86) already finds this kind of shift from the state of mind of security into an understanding of security as a "container" or a "link" in Hobbes' ([1651] 1999) *Leviathan*. The mental state of being without care is replaced in Hobbes' treatise with an understanding of both physical protection and a psychological confidence in the future – a confidence of being able to avoid or counter future bads.

The principal tension between the objective and subjective dimensions of security was also a central line of demarcation for conceptualizing matters of security during the Cold War. While objective conceptions of security typically defined security in material terms as the probability of states posing a threat, subjective approaches typically

[1] For 14 developmental steps in the conceptual history from 200 BC until today, see Wæver (2012).

emphasized various distorting psychological factors such as (mis)perceptions, negative group dynamics, or fear and panic (Buzan/Hansen, 2009: 33). Yet, the subjective dimension was often not seen as a different conception of security, but as a challenge for measuring security as an objective state of being. Wolfers, for instance, acknowledged that it is never possible to truly measure security objectively because subjective evaluations, influenced by numerous domestic factors, including national character, tradition, prejudices as well as ideological and moral convictions or inclinations of individual policy makers, always play a part in threat assessments. Nevertheless, he claimed that in hindsight it may sometimes be possible to tell how far a threat assessment has deviated from a "rational reaction" to the actual state of danger existing at a particular point in time (Wolfers, 1952: 485).

Interestingly, though, for Wolfers, the subjective aspects had an explicitly interactional connotation. He argued that any level of security which a nation practises results from a process of negotiation between a leader/the decision makers and the people. The decision makers are in a position to choose the *values*, which deserve protection, the *level* of security that is thought to be needed, and the *means* and the *sacrifices*, which the choice of means implies (Wolfers, 1952: 502). The people in turn give their *consent* to any additional efforts for security which they necessarily experience as a burden due to the cost in taxes, reduction in social benefits, or "sheer discomfort" (Wolfers, 1952: 487–8).

After the end of the Cold War, distinctly intersubjective dimensions, such as culture, social norms or historical memory, were added to conceptualizations of security. Security was presented as a relational concept (Buzan, [1983] 1991), where it did not make sense to speak only of the security of one particular actor. Furthermore, those approaches focused on the politics of security have emphasized that security should be investigated as an intersubjective status function rather than as a subjective feeling, or an objective state of affairs (Buzan et al., 1998). More recently, IR scholars have returned attention to the subjective and mental dimension through the notion of ontological security, a concept taken from psychology and designating a "stable sense of Self", usually juxtaposed with more common readings of security that emphasize material referent objects and threats (Huysmans, 1998; Mitzen, 2006; Steele, 2008).

This leads us to another relevant systematic vantage point, namely the question of the level of analysis, or "whose security" is under discussion (Wæver, 2008: 102; Williams, 2008: 7–8). For IR scholars, the state was for a long time, and arguably still remains, the most central referent of security. Yet, again, this has not always been the case: for most classic philosophers of politics, the state is a means to an end, that end being the survival and security of the individual (Rothchild, 1995; Wæver, 2008). For example, for Hobbes ([1651] 1999), the Leviathan was the way to self-preservation of the individual. He emphasized that the right of self-preservation and defence was the only right that could not be given away. In today's IR scholarship, the liberal emphasis on the individual as not only the holder of rights, but also as the referent object of security is visible in debates on "human security" (Kaldor, 2007).[2] Here we encounter the fundamental question of how state and individual relate in terms of security, or

[2] Notably, the two main concerns of human security (freedom from fear and want) are a limited set of President Roosevelt's (1941) four freedoms (of speech, of worship, from want, and from fear).

more precisely, whose and what kind of security should be prioritized and how this security is provided. Such questions lead to the issue of whether "security" is discussed in positive or negative terms.

For instance, we might say that understandings of security in everyday use and in international politics differ. In an everyday, non-expert understanding, security, like safety, tends to be considered a positive: the more security the better. Yet, Wæver (1995, 2004, 2008) prominently argues that for states (and security experts too), security is ultimately always a negative concern: to repel threats imbues costs and entails dangers. Indeed, connotations of security include fastening or tying down, rather than free movement; security is a conservative value. This approach to the value of security by Wæver is similar to other critical security scholars who often see security as potentially "anti-democratic" and therefore as a negative (see e.g. Lipschutz, 1995; Krause/Williams, 1997; Weldes et al., 1999; CASE Collective, 2006). Perhaps most explicitly, Jef Huysmans (2014: 180), in this sense, defines "security as a practice enacting limits of democracy". The usual reasoning here is that more security means less freedom, and vice versa – that liberty and security are a trade-off as the enactment of security allows for authoritarian practices; yet, one cannot have liberty without security, or security without liberty (Huysmans, 2014).

From such viewpoints, the logic of considering the negative of a negative, i.e. not being insecure, to be a positive is considered to be faulty. Rather than a good for all, the increase of security for some means its sacrifice for others (Bigo, 2008: 124). Insecurity and unease produce inequalities and suppression. Accordingly, from this viewpoint, security does not have a fixed normative value, i.e. a general good for all, independent of actors that enunciate security claims in their contexts, i.e. referents of security, historical trajectories, as well as practices of violence and coercion in the name of protection (Bigo, 2008: 123–4). Security is politics, not only in bureaucratic terms but also as a classificatory practice (Bigo, 2002; Huysmans, 2006): to speak and to enact security have social and political consequences (Buzan et al., 1998).

The problem of viewing security as something positive when the measures put in place to provide this security often entail a negative form of politics is confounded by the image of effectiveness which security arguments often convey. Indeed, to present something as a security concern suggests that the proposed means will effect an increase in security, which makes it a very powerful tool to galvanize an audience behind the measures the speaker proposes (Buzan, [1983] 1991). However, as security speech identifies vulnerabilities, this process also gives the impression that to decline the proposed path of action will bring about a loss of security, i.e. security is in this sense bound to insecurity. Accordingly, the way security is spoken and security policies presented tends to promise more than can actually be delivered (Hietanen/Joenniemi, 1982: 35–6): the (non-expert) everyday understanding of security suggests a sense of certainty that cannot actually be achieved with any security measures; security discourses are designed to provide safety and the defeat of danger, something which can never be totally accomplished given the limits of human life. Security discourses thus conceal this unavoidable deferral of surety by producing the referents of security as stable, knowable and, in effect, securable (Stern, 2006: 193). As security arguments contain a threat, they, in effect, reproduce insecurities. Thus, Anthony Burke (2002: 20) notes that security can never escape insecurity as its own meaning depends on the production of images of insecurity. This association between security and insecurity represents an aporia (Dillon, [1996] 2001: 78).

One approach to bypass this is to target the assumption of survival as the primary objective of being. Such a radical position would adopt Friedrich Nietzsche's view that survival is merely the most common result of the will to power, that death cannot be escaped, and that, therefore, it makes no sense to recreate and reify fantasies of perfect control and order. For these critical scholars, creative "Nietzschean" politics, without the fear of death, would be preferable to the conservative and repressive nature of security issues and policies intended to ensure survival. As death will collect us all in the end, people should dare to live and embrace their "insecurity" rather than focus their energies on forestalling death.[3]

National Security and the Cold War Context

This section focuses on national security as the primary way for conceptualizing security in international relations both as a field of scholarship and as a political practice. As the political prevalence of this concept emanated and mainly gained its prominence from the US discourse, our discussion will focus on this context. It is perhaps surprising, in view of its political prevalence today, that security was not a key concept in international relations before the mid-20th century. As Yergin (1977: 193–4) has illustrated in some detail, security only came to its (perhaps temporary) fruition when it was considered useful to explain the US relationship with the rest of the world in an evolving Cold War context (Yergin, 1977: 193–4). Until the end of the Second World War, "defence" was the preferred term used by the military. Defence has a distinct opposite, which security lacks, namely attack; through this lack, security allowed the promotion of "defence" against intangible threats. This new kind of war effort required the combination of civilian and military activities. In such a situation, a shift in terminology was expedient, as security blurred the distinction between military and civil issues, and between the domestic and the international, even though "defence" was never fully replaced by "security".[4] Arguing with and through security made the Cold War effort more palatable: defence was usually understood as following geopolitical lines, whilst security was freed from this constraint. National security could be defined more broadly according to the needs of "national interests", a defining referent for security in the 1940s (see Lippmann, 1943). By the 1950s, this emphasis had shifted towards what Wolfers (1952) has prominently coined "core values", those values which are the fundamental principles a political order is based on (e.g. "freedom" in the US).

The change in terminology did not come out of the blue. It was supported by a number of social and value developments that are reflected in other conceptual shifts

[3] Dillon's (2008) biopolitical viewpoint on security emphasizes that "events" rather than "will" dominate life that is uncalculable, contingent and transactional; human actions cannot control such events.

[4] This is reflected in various US and other Western security documents after World War II; see Freiberger (2013: 48–94); also Dockrill (1996); Bowie and Immerman (1998); Hogan (1998); and Gaddis (2005).

too. For example, with President Roosevelt's reforms, "social security" became a widely used concept (Neocleous, 2006; Rana, 2012). On the international scene, "collective security" was a term used in the inter-war years to legitimate various international policies (Carr, [1939] 1981), while realists highlighted the national interest as the goal of international politics (Morgenthau, [1948] 1978). As Emily Rosenberg (1993) suggests, national security seemed a fitting compromise in this conceptual space. The idealism of "collective security" was discredited by the developments of the 1930s. At the same time, "national interests" had also gained negative undertones with the militant rise of Nazism in Europe. National security then allowed the combination of two positive values, the national and security, although notions of "collective" and cooperative/common security never disappeared, not even in the early Cold War context of the US national security discourse.[5]

Specifically, for the Truman administration, national security, as outlined in the famous National Security Act of 1947, provided a means to retain a form of radical *ragione di stato* (state reason) policies of absolute (but now limited) state authority/preservation in an era when democratic ethics seemed to be making such a way of thinking increasingly unacceptable.[6] First the national interest, and now national security, were thus ways to address the "democrat's dilemma" of how to combine democratic values in domestic politics with a perceived amoral and anarchic international system. As such, national security could justify drastic measures including military intervention, political assassinations and war. For example, in the US before the 1940s, "reasons of state" combined with sovereign immunity meant that any state documents could be deemed secret without any need for legitimation beyond reasons of state, and there was no possibility of suing the state. With the passing of the Federal Tort Claims Act of 1946, US citizens gained the right to sue the state, yet with the National Security Act of 1947, the state *limited* its general state secrets privilege to that of security issues. In other words, before the act, all state documents could be deemed secret, but after it, "reasons of national security" were necessary to limit citizens' access.

This limitation and specification of security, and thereby of what it did politically, was crucial for the political uses of security as a concept. To speak security began to do things it had not done before, while "necessity" and "national interests" no longer worked efficiently as sources of political justification (Wæver, 2012). Domestically, the notion of security became a useful and prominent tool to curtail the traditional mistrust of standing armies in the US. It was first Secretary of Defence Forrestall who used national security to legitimate a strong military establishment to fight a perceived "future enemy", which was then also reflected in the National Security Act of 1947 (Yergin, 1977: 209–10, 339–40). The consequences of this new line of peacetime military development were quite apparent in Eisenhower's (1961) famous farewell address, in which he lamented the necessity to build a massive standing army, and warned against the likelihood of unwarranted decision-making power shifting to the "military-industrial complex" (see Hogan, 1998). Internationally, national security henceforth worked as a "package legitimizer" in

[5] See previous footnote.

[6] This is at least according to Yergin's (1977) prominent study. For more nuanced readings of the complexities and ambivalences of post-World War II US security discourse, see Freiberger (2013); also Dockrill (1996); Bowie and Immerman (1998); Hogan (1998); and Gaddis (2005).

the Cold War competition with the Soviet Union and the "Communist threat"; it became one of the watchwords in the evolving threat narratives of the era.

The use of national security as a new political concept was not limited to the political space of the US but spread to other parts of the world. For example, in Japan, anzen hoshô (the securing of safety) replaced kokubô (armed national defence) after the Second World War (Sato, 2000). Eventually, it also arrived in the People's Republic of China. Although the exceptionalist logic of security has been in operation throughout the 20th century (Vuori, 2011), the notion of national security only became institutionalized in the 1980s and 1990s, for example when the Central Investigation Department was renamed as the Ministry of State Security in 1983, and the counter-revolutionary penal code was changed to that of crimes that jeopardize national security in 1997 (Vuori, 2014: 56). By the end of the Cold War, counter-revolution was too limited and specific for the Chinese threat register.

Indeed, in the US and elsewhere, the success of the notion of national security laid in it being more flexible, encompassing and blurry in regard to the distinction between war- and peace-time than the notion of national defence, which was mainly concerned with foreign military aggression. For example, as Field Marshal Castelo Branco, the President of Brazil (1964–1967), noted, "[t]he concept of national security is much more complete" (than national defence). For him, it included the global defence of institutions, took into account psycho-social aspects, the preservation of development, and internal political stability, which could be jeopardized by infiltration, ideological subversion and guerrilla movements. For the president, "All of these forms of conflict are much more likely to occur than foreign aggression" (quoted in Huysmans, 2014: 51).

Thus, already during the Cold War, the understanding of "national security" was quite broad and varied in use, and was situated within different clusters of concepts, competing logics and alternative reflections on security (Fierke, 2007: 43; see also Bubandt, 2005). Yet, in the academic study of security, a prominent manifestation of different understandings has been the portrayal of a stark dichotomy between "peace" and "security" and, correspondingly, the development of "peace studies" as opposed to "strategic studies" (Buzan, 1983; see also Chapter 7, this volume). Peace scholars were seen as focusing on non-violent means as opposed to purely military means and claimed to analyze "world problems" from "a world perspective" (Lawler, 2008). At the same time, strategic studies was viewed to overlap with the type of security thinking that prevailed among political elites, and was portrayed to be narrowly interested in the threat, display and use of military force in international politics.

While this portrayal is not entirely wrong, several military strategists such as Liddell Hart recognized that "grand strategy" should always take into account and apply the power of diplomatic, commercial and "not least" ethical pressure (Hart, 1967: 322). Similarly, American officials such as Eisenhower and Dulles also thought of national security in comprehensive terms (Freiberger, 2013: 48–94). For example, for President Eisenhower, "the theory of defense against aggressive threat" had to comprise something "far more constructive than mere survival" and "comprehend more than simple self-preservation" (PDDE, 1970, XII, Doc. 329: 488). Crucially, for him, it included "moral leadership", "the defense of a way of life" rather than just (national) territory, a comprehensive unity of the "free nations" and domestic and world opinion (Ferrell, 1981: 210; see also Dulles, 1950: 16). Internal documents show the US concern that allies should be "genuinely convinced that our strategy is one of *collective security*"

(FRUS, 1952–54, II, NSC 162/2: 178; emphasis added), which, in this context, meant "cooperative/common security". When read in the context of the liberal outlook which has long characterized US policy, it shows that thinking about "national security" was embedded in what is today referred to as "liberal internationalism" (see e.g. Melanson, 1987) or "liberal order building" (Ikenberry, 1989, 2011), and, thus, always took on a more comprehensive form than that which the term may at first suggest.

The ambiguity of the concept of national security was recognized by classical realists and also generated some concern. Wolfers (1952: 487) explicitly rejected a radical *ragione di stato* reading of national security practices, including the claim that nations completely subordinate all other values to the maximization of their security (see also, for example, Meinecke, [1957] 1997). This was also the very essence of Thucydides' actual argument in *The History of the Peloponnesian War*, one of the key historical references in the realist tradition and often misleadingly reduced to the Melian dialogue. For Thucydides, it was Pericles' prudent and comprehensive security policies that represented the ideal-type of a good statesman and strategist, whereas the Melian dialogue was deliberately portrayed by him as the climax of a *strategic aberration* that contributed to Athens' decline as a great power (Enskat, 2014: 70–4). For Wolfers (1952: 499), a glance at history showed that a practice of radical *ragione di stato* only rarely reflects the reality of actual security practices (see also Lebow, 2008). In his still highly readable article "National Security as an Ambiguous Symbol", Wolfers notes that the extreme view that "every sacrifice [...] is justified provided it contributes in any way to national security" assumes "national security" to constitute "an absolute good to which all other values must be subordinated". Wolfers argues that such a position is rarely taken because "if [one] subscribed to a nationalistic ethics of this extreme type [one] *would probably go beyond security* – the mere preservation of values – and insist that the nation is justified in conquering whatever it can use as *Lebensraum* or otherwise" (Wolfers, 1952: 500; emphasis added). Thus, Wolfers, like most realists, suggests that there is a limit to what can justifiably be done in the name of national security and warns against the political abuse of the concept.

Securitization and the Post-Cold War Context

It was the Cold War experience that prompted peace researchers in Europe to criticize the rigidity and self-fulfilling consequences of "national security" discourses and the threat images they contained, and to explore the conception of security as a political tool of legitimation. This analytical angle, including the normative agenda and emphasizing the relationality and intersubjectivity of security, was then introduced to the academic field of IR most prominently through the notion of "securitization" (Buzan et al., 1998). Crudely put, the securitization approach captures the performative power politics of the concept and traces how issues obtain the status function of security through intersubjective socio-political processes.

In the context of late Cold War détente, the purpose of conceptualizing the social construction of security issues as speech acts was that they could also be dismantled through "desecuritization". Thus, the aim was to make security speech unable "to function in the harmonious self-assured standard-discourse of realism" (Wæver, 1989a: 38) and to alter "security" from the inside by unmasking its operative logic and stripping away its innocent appeal. "More and more trans-national activities should become purely 'economic', 'social' and 'political'" (Wæver, 1989b: 314), rather than issues of security where states claim the right to use any means necessary to hinder a development which goes against its interests. Wæver argued that the pitfalls of previous understandings could be avoided by focusing not on what security means, but on what security does or, more exactly, on what is done by "speaking" or "doing" security (Wæver, 1989a: 43). From this viewpoint, security is not objective or subjective, but intersubjective; security is a socio-political status function among political actors.

As dominant practices in international politics changed towards the end of the Cold War, conceptions of security too became more malleable once more. Starting in the 1980s, an increasing number of security scholars started to question a narrow military and exclusively inter-state focus prevalent in "traditional security studies" (Booth, 1991; Krause and Williams, 1997). Often ignoring more complex traditions within realism, military strategy, and actual reflections and practices of officials outlined earlier, in the discipline of IR, security was typically defined as the absence of (or protection against) (i) an existential threat (ii) to the state (iii) by other states; and security policy as identifying and employing the means to protect against threats thus defined (Brauch, 2008a: 29). This narrow understanding changed significantly with the new debates on security that emerged in the 1980s and 1990s in both academic and political discourse: an agenda of "new security challenges" was promoted that eventually dominated reflections on security (Sheehan, 2005: 43–63). Importantly, these perceived new security challenges, such as ethnic conflicts in Africa or the Balkan Wars, but also regional security dynamics in East and Central Asia or the Middle East, were seen as having important domestic components or were predominantly "internal". Still other perceived security challenges seemed to fall completely outside the immediacy and severity of the military realm of traditional security studies: economic and environmental threats, people's movements, transnational organized crime, and international terrorism, or, more recently, cyber-security (Williams, 2008).

Proponents of international terrorism as a "new threat" that would differ profoundly from the "traditional terrorist threat" of the 1970s (Hoffman, 2006) typically stress the much stronger hybridity of the perceived threat in the current environment. Security against terrorism is practised as a concern with "internal" security, policing and surveillance, in addition to traditional "external" security in the context of wars against "safe havens" and/or "state sponsors of terrorism". Sophisticated military technology is today often used in policing operations, and to secure state borders; and military operations in turn incorporate aspects of policing, good governance, and development, which redefine the traditional concepts of "soldier" and "policeman" in security affairs (Guillaume et al., 2015). For some scholars, these "new threats" erode not only inter-state understandings of security, but also a previous demarcation of "internal" and "external" in security affairs (Bigo, 2000, 2001; Huysmans, 2006; Eriksson/Rhinard, 2009), while the general perception of a broader, more comprehensive and complex security agenda has typically been articulated analytically as suggestions to both *broaden* and *deepen* the concept of security (Buzan/Hansen, 2009: 187–225; see also Booth, 1991, 2005, 2007; Wyn-Jones, 1999).

The broadening of the concept and/or its use in academia and, especially, among practitioners has consequently increased the analytical playing field for securitization research. This includes exploring how the enactment of security has become much more dispersed and concerned with a broader range of issues of governance. As Huysmans (2014: 186) points out, in addition to the perennial issues that pertain to military and state threats, assemblages of diverse security practices and techniques are engaged in areas such as migration, environmental protection, disaster management, human development, and so on. For Huysmans (2014: 9–10), contemporary security practice and techniques operate through two logics: the rationale of security can be applied to some issues through exceptional security speech, which "works through the creation of existential threats and emergencies", while more diffuse practices can bring about and disseminate security rationales through the dispersed governance of uncertainties, "surveillance, and political economies of data transfer and risk knowledge". For him, security is a technique that simultaneously "renders insecurities and politics" (2014: 13); it is both a rationality and the practical enactment of this rationality (2014: 18). Exceptional security speech as a technique intensifies political situations, while diffuse security practices circulate a sense of both unease and suspicion. From this perspective, security has thus become a part of the everyday governance of insecurities, where it retains beyond the world of high politics its negative effects of unease, suspicion, technocracy and authoritarianism through modes of procedures, training, routines, practical skills, knowledge, and artefacts of security experts who enact security (Huysmans, 2006: 9).

As a result of developments in both the politics and academic study of security, the study of security has become more pluralistic and less coherent than during the Cold War. There is currently no unifying theme or theory other than a series of debates and sub-debates; and a predominant concern with "the international" during the Cold War seems to have been replaced by a greater awareness of the dynamics of various regional, national and local particularities (Stritzel, 2014). In light of this, contemporary security scholarship tends to be more inclusive than during the Cold War, and now explicitly incorporates military and non-military, state and human security concerns, as well as peace and military security aspects under a broader, multidimensional rubric of International Security Studies (Buzan, 1984; Collins, 2007; Williams, 2008; Buzan/Hansen, 2009). Yet as a result of this openness, scholars are also more divided than ever on the question of what the study of security is and should be about. Accordingly, choosing one analytical approach rather than another has major implications for what is considered to be relevant in the investigation of "security" and its politics (Vuori, 2014).

Conclusion

The conceptual analysis of security has come a long way. Among academics, there arguably is today a much greater awareness of the history, nuances and implications of security as a basic concept and of the political stakes it involves. And the ongoing scholarly and political discussions surrounding the meaning of "security" highlight its enduring relevance and contestedness. While for some this complexity is frustrating, for others it makes the concept a particularly fascinating object, or subject, of analysis (Walker, 1997). Despite repeated attempts to conclude these deliberations, for example through conceptual categorization and specifications (Baldwin, 1997), many scholars, particularly in the critical branch, celebrate this diversity as a major strength. Indeed, if security is seen as an inherently political value, its meaning perhaps "*should be* a matter of disagreement and debate" (Jarvis, 2013: 247). Students of world politics certainly should expect such disagreements and debates to continue, and the need to understand them highlights the very usefulness and importance of conceptual analysis.

Suggested Readings

Buzan, Barry and Hansen, Lene (2009) *The Evolution of International Security Studies*. Cambridge: Cambridge University Press.

A useful book that provides a comprehensive intellectual history of international security studies.

Chilton, Paul A. (1996) *Security Metaphors: Cold War Discourse from Containment to Common House*. New York: Peter Lang.

A thorough linguistic analysis of security metaphors, discourses and conceptual underpinnings of international relations theory.

Stritzel, Holger (2014) *Security in Translation: Securitization Theory and the Localization of Threat*. London: Palgrave.

This study offers a detailed engagement with the concept of security as it travels between different discursive contexts.

Vuori, Juha A. (2014) *Critical Security and Chinese Politics: The Anti-Falungong Campaign*. London and New York: Routledge.

The book places three critical approaches to security into a comparative perspective and examines their implications for research design and conceptual travel.

Wolfers, Arnold (1952) '"National Security" as an Ambiguous Symbol', *Political Science Quarterly*, 67, 4, pp. 481–502.

A classic article that has influenced and inspired much of the critical study of security from a conceptual perspective.

Bibliography

Arends, J. Frederik M. (2008) 'From Homer to Hobbes and Beyond', in: *Globalization and Environmental Challenges*, Hans Günter Brauch et al. (eds). Berlin: Springer, pp. 263–277.

Austin, John L. (1975) *How to Do Things with Words*. Oxford: Clarendon Press.

Baldwin, David (1997) 'The Concept of Security', *Review of International Studies*, 23, 1, pp. 5–26.

Barthes, Roland (1977) *Image – Music – Text*. New York: Hill and Wang.

Bigo, Didier (2000) 'When Two become One: Internal and External Securitisations in Europe', in: *International Relations Theory and the Politics of European Integration: Power, Security and Community*, Morten Kelstrup and Michael C. Williams (eds). London: Routledge, pp. 171–204.

Bigo, Didier (2001) 'Internal and External Securit(ies), the Mobius Ribbon', in: *Identities, Borders, and Orders*, Mathias Albert, David Jacobsen and Yosef Lapid (eds). Minneapolis: University of Minnesota Press, pp. 91–116.

Bigo, Didier (2002) 'Security and Immigration', *Alternatives*, 27, 1, pp. 63–92.

Bigo, Didier (2008) 'International Political Sociology', in: *Security Studies*, P. D. Williams (ed.), London: Routledge.

Booth, Ken (1991) 'Security and Emancipation', *Review of International Studies*, 17, 4, pp. 313–326.

Booth, Ken (2005) *Critical Security Studies and World Politics*. Boulder, CO: Lynne Rienner.

Booth, Ken (2007) *Theory of World Security*. Cambridge: Cambridge University Press.

Bowie, Robert R. and Richard H. Immerman (1998) *Waging Peace*. Oxford: Oxford University Press.
Brauch, Hans Günther (2008a) 'Introduction', in: *Globalization and Environmental Challenges*, Hans Günther Brauch et al. (eds). Berlin: Springer, pp. 27–44.
Brauch, Hans Günter (2008b) 'Conceptual Quartet', in: *Globalization and Environmental Challenges*, Hans Günter Brauch et al. (eds). Berlin: Springer, pp. 65–98.
Bubandt, Nils (2005) 'Vernacular Security', *Security Dialogue*, 36, 3, pp. 275–296.
Burke, Anthony (2002) 'Aporias of Security', *Alternatives*, 27, 1, pp. 1–27.
Buzan, Barry (1984) 'Peace, Power, and Security', *Journal of Peace Research*, 21, 2, pp. 109–125.
Buzan, Barry ([1983] 1991) *People, States and Fear*. London: Harvester Wheatsheaf.
Buzan, Barry (1999) 'Change and Insecurity Reconsidered', *Contemporary Security Policy*, 20, 3, pp. 1–17.
Buzan, Barry and Hansen, Lene (2009) *The Evolution of International Security Studies*. Cambridge: Cambridge University Press.
Buzan, Barry and Wæver, Ole (2008) 'After the Return to Theory', in: *Contemporary Security Studies*, Alan Collins (ed.). Oxford: Oxford University Press, pp. 383–402.
Buzan, Barry, Ole Waever and Jaap de Wilde (1998) *Security: A New Framework of Analysis*. London: Lynne Rienner.
Carr, Edward Hallett ([1939] 1981) *The Twenty Years' Crisis, 1919–1939: An Introduction to the Study of International Relations*. London: Papermac.
CASE Collective (2006) 'Critical Approaches to Security in Europe', *Security Dialogue*, 37, 4, pp. 443–487.
Chilton, Paul A. (1996) *Security Metaphors*. New York: Peter Lang.
Cicero, Marcus Tullius (1971 [45BC]) *Tusculan Disputations*. Trans. J. E. King. London: William Heinemann.
Collins, Alan (2007) *Contemporary Security Studies*. Oxford: Oxford University Press.
Connolly, William E. (1983) *The Terms of Political Discourse*. Princeton, NJ: Princeton University Press.
Conze, Werner (1984) 'Sicherheit', in: *Geschichtliche Grundbegriffe*, Otto Brunner, Werner Conze und Reinhart Koselleck (eds), Bd. 5. Stuttgart: Klett-Cotta, pp. 831–862.
Dalby, Simon (2002) *Environmental Security*. Minneapolis, MN: University of Minnesota Press.
Dean, Jonathan (2008) 'Rethinking Security in the New Century', in: *Globalization and Environmental Challenges*, Hans Günter Brauch et al. (eds). Berlin: Springer, pp. 3–6.
Der Derian, James (1995) 'The Value of Security', in: *On Security*, Ronnie D. Lipschutz (ed.). New York: Columbia University Press, pp. 24–45.
Dillon, Michael ([1996] 2001) *Politics of Security*. London: Routledge.
Dillon, Michael (2008) 'Underwriting Security', *Security Dialogue*, 39, 2–3, pp. 309–332.
Dockrill, Saki (1996) *Eisenhower's New-Look National Security Policy 1953–61*. London: Palgrave.
Dulles, John Foster (1950) *War or Peace*. New York: Harrap.
Eisenhower, Dwight D. (1961) 'Military-industrial Complex Speech', in *Public Papers of the Presidents of the United States*, pp. 1035–1040.
Enskat, Sebastian (2014) 'Strategie', in: *Internationale Sicherheit*, Sebastian Enskat and Carlo Masala (eds). Wiesbaden: Springer, pp. 61–98.
Enskat, Sebastian, Carlo Masala and Frank Sauer (2013) 'Internationale Sicherheit', in: *Internationale Sicherheit*, Sebastian Enskat and Carlo Masala (eds). Wiesbaden: Springer, pp. 9–18.
Eriksson, Johan and Mark Rhinard (2009) 'The Internal–External Security Nexus', *Cooperation and Conflict*, 44, 3, pp. 243–267.
Ferrell, Robert H. (1981) *The Eisenhower Diaries*. New York: W. W. Norton.
Fierke, Karin M. (2007) *Critical Approaches to International Security*. Cambridge: Polity Press.

Foreign Relations of the United States (FRUS) (1952–54) II, NSC 162/2. Washington, DC: Government Printing Office.

Freiberger, Thomas (2013) *Allianzpolitik in der Suezkrise 1956*. Göttingen: V&R Unipress.

Gaddis, John Lewis (2005) *Strategies of Containment*. Oxford: Oxford University Press.

Gallie, Walter Bryce (1962) 'Essentially Contested Concepts', in: *The Importance of Language*, Max Black (ed.). Englewood Cliffs, NJ: Prentice-Hall, pp. 121–146.

Guillaume, Xavier, Rune S. Andersen and Juha A. Vuori (2015) 'Paint it Black: Colours and the Social Meaning of the Battlefield', *European Journal of International Relations* [online].

Haftendorn, Helga (1991) 'The Security Puzzle', *International Studies Quarterly*, 35, 1, pp. 3–17.

Hart, Basil Henry Liddell (1967) *Strategy*. New York: Meridian.

Hietanen, Aki and Pertti Joenniemi (1982) 'Varustelu, kieli ja maailmankuva', *Rauhaan Tutkien*, 11, 1, pp. 18–44.

Hobbes, Thomas ([1651] 1999) *Leviathan*. Cambridge: Cambridge University Press.

Hoffman, Bruce (2006) *Inside Terrorism*. New York: Columbia University Press.

Hogan, Michael J. (1998) *A Cross of Iron*. Cambridge: Cambridge University Press.

Huysmans, Jef (1998) 'Security! What Do You Mean?', *European Journal of International Relations*, 4, 2, pp. 226–255.

Huysmans, Jef (2006) *The Politics of Insecurity*. London: Routledge.

Huysmans, Jef (2014) *Security Unbound*. London: Routledge.

Ikenberry, John G. (1989) 'Rethinking the Origins of American Hegemony', *Political Science Quarterly*, 104, 3, pp. 375–400.

Ikenberry, John G. (2011) *Liberal Leviathan*. Princeton, NJ: Princeton University Press.

Jarvis, Lee (2013) 'Conclusion', in: *Critical Approaches to Security*, Laura Shepherd (ed.). London: Routledge, pp. 236–247.

Jervis, Robert (1976) *Perception and Misperception in International Politics*. Princeton, NJ: Princeton University Press.

Kaldor, Mary (2007) *Human Security*. Cambridge: Polity.

Krause, Keith and Michael C. Williams (eds) (1997) *Critical Security Studies*. London: Routledge.

Laclau, Ernesto and Chantal Mouffe ([1985] 2001) *Hegemony and Socialist Strategy*. London: Verso.

Lawler, Peter (2008) 'Peace Studies', in: *Security Studies*, Paul D. Williams (ed.). London: Routledge, pp. 73–88.

Lebow, Richard N. (2008) *A Cultural Theory of International Relations*. Cambridge: Cambridge University Press.

Lippmann, Walter (1943) *US Foreign Policy: Shield of the Republic*. Boston: Little, Brown & Co.

Lipschutz, Ronnie D. (1995) *On Security*. New York: Columbia University Press.

Little, Richard (1981) 'Ideology and Change', in: *Change and the Study of International Relations*, Barry Buzan and R. J. Jones (eds). London: Pinter, pp. 30–39.

Markopolous, M. (1995) 'Sicherheit', in *Historiches Wörterbuch der Philosophie*, Vol. 9. Basel: Schwabe Verlag, pp. 745–750.

Meinecke, Friedrich ([1957] 1997) *Machiavellism*. New Brunswick, NJ: Transaction.

Melanson, Richard A. (1987) 'The Foundations of Eisenhower's Foreign Policy', in: *Reevaluating Eisenhower*, Richard A. Melanson and David Mayers (eds). Urbana, IL: University of Illinois Press, pp. 31–64.

Mesjasz, Czeslaw (2008) 'Security as Attributes of Social Systems', in: *Globalization and Environmental Challenges*, Hans Günther Brauch et al. (eds). Berlin: Springer, pp. 45–62.

Mitzen, Jennifer (2006) 'Ontological Security in World Politics', *European Journal of International Relations*, 12, 3, pp. 341–370.

Morgenthau, Hans J. ([1948] 1978) *Politics among Nations*. New York: Knopf.

Neocleous, Mark (2006) 'From Social to National Security', *Security Dialogue*, 37, 3, pp. 363–384.
Rana, Aziz (2012) 'Who Decides on Security?', *Connecticut Law Review*, 44, 5, pp. 1417–90.
Roosevelt, Franklin Delano (1941) Annual Message to Congress on the State of the Union: 6 January 1941. Available at: www.fdrlibrary.marist.edu/pdfs/fftext.pdf (accessed 28.07.15).
Rosenberg, Emily S. (1993) 'Commentary', *Diplomatic History*, 17, 2, pp. 277–284.
Rothchild, Emma (1995) 'What is Security?', *Daedalus*, 124, 3, pp. 53–98.
Sato, Seizaburo (2000) 'Why the Shift from Kokubô (National Defense) to Anzen Hoshô (Security)?', *Asia-Pacific Review*, 7, 2, pp. 12–32.
Schrimm-Heins, Andrea (1991–2) 'Gewißheit und Sicherheit', in: *Archiv der Begriffsgeschichte*, 34, pp. 123–213; 35, pp. 115–213.
Shakespeare, William ([1611] 1993) 'Macbeth', in *The Illustrated Stratford Shakespeare. All 37 Plays, All 160 Sonnets and Poems*. London: Chancellor Press, pp. 776–789.
Sheehan, Michael (2005) *International Security*. Boulder, CO: Lynne Rienner.
Skinner, Quentin (2002) *Visions of Politics*. Cambridge: Cambridge University Press.
Smith, Steve (1999) 'The Increasing Insecurity of Security Studies', *Contemporary Security Policy*, 20, 3, pp. 72–101.
Steele, Brent J. (2008) *Ontological Security in International Relations*. London: Routledge.
Stern, Maria (2006) '"We" the Subject', *Security Dialogue*, 37, 2, pp. 187–205.
Stritzel, Holger (2014) *Security in Translation*. London: Palgrave.
The Papers of Dwight D. Eisenhower (PDDE) (1970) XII, Doc. 329. Baltimore, MD: Johns Hopkins University Press.
Vuori, Juha A. (2008) 'Illocutionary Logic and Strands of Securitisation', *European Journal of International Relations*, 14, 1, pp. 65–99.
Vuori, Juha A. (2011) *How to Do Security with Words*. Turku: University of Turku Press.
Vuori, Juha A. (2014) *Critical Security and Chinese Politics*. London and New York: Routledge.
Wæver, Ole (1989a) 'Security the Speech Act', in: *Working Paper* 1989/19. Copenhagen: Centre for Peace and Conflict Research.
Wæver, Ole (1989b) 'Conflicts of Vision – Visions of Conflict', in: *European Polyphony*, O. Wæver, P. Lemaitre and E. Tromer (eds). London: Macmillan.
Wæver, Ole (1995) 'Securitization and Desecuritization', in: *On Security*, Ronnie D. Lipschutz (ed.). New York: Columbia University Press, pp. 46–86.
Wæver, Ole (1997) *Concepts of Security*. Copenhagen: University of Copenhagen.
Wæver, Ole (2004) 'Peace and Security', in: *Contemporary Security Analysis and Copenhagen Peace Research*, Stefano Guzzini and Dietrich Jung (eds). London: Routledge, pp. 51–65.
Wæver, Ole (2008) 'Peace and Security', in: *Globalization and Environmental Challenges*, Hans Günter Brauch et al. (eds). Berlin: Springer, pp. 99–111.
Wæver, Ole (2012) 'Security: A Conceptual History for International Relations', paper presented at the History of the Concept of 'Security' conference, 26–28 November, organized by the Centre for Advanced Security Theory.
Walker, R. B. J. (1997) 'The Subject of Security', in: *Critical Security Studies*, M. C. Williams and K. Krause (eds). London: UCL Press.
Weldes, Jutta, Mark Laffey, Hugh Gusterson and Raymond Duvall (eds) (1999) *Cultures of Insecurity*. Minnesota, MN: University of Minnesota Press.
Williams, Paul D. (ed.) (2008) *Security Studies*. London: Routledge.
Wolfers, Arnold (1952) '"National Security" as an Ambiguous Symbol', *Political Science Quarterly*, 67, 4, pp. 481–502.
Wyn-Jones, Richard G. (1999) *Security, Strategy, and Critical Theory*. Boulder, CO: Lynne Rienner.
Yergin, Daniel (1977) *Shattered Peace*. Boston, MA: Houghton Mifflin.

4

Rationality

Annette Freyberg-Inan

The concept of rationality – and the challenges raised against it – have been central to key debates in International Relations (IR). It is ingrained in the "rational actor" assumption underpinning mainstream IR theories, like realism and liberalism, and the basic tenet underpinning "rational choice" models imported from economics. As such, it has even served to mark out a fundamental difference between those IR theories that adopt the assumption and the specific form of knowledge generation associated with it, and those that do not (Keohane 1988). Its meaning may, at first glance, seem straightforward: individual actors pursue their own goals with the aim of maximum gain at minimum cost. And yet, as discussed in this chapter, rationality is one of the more complicated concepts of the discipline, for two main reasons: first, because it borders on and even overlaps with other terms, which need to be distinguished from it, the most prominent of these being the concept of *reason*; second, the concept of rationality is complicated because it can serve very different functions in thinking about the world. It serves a descriptive function – when we use it to describe how we think people *do* behave – and a normative one – when we use it to describe how they *should* behave. As such, it is used to both predict and judge behaviour. This makes it a politically charged and problematic concept, especially as rational thinking and acting are still often considered an achievement of Western civilization and an attribute of educated males.

This chapter will discuss both how "rationality" gains meaning through links to related terms and how the concept is used in – and how it has shaped – our thinking about international politics. To this end, I set up two juxtapositions and problematize them through the moves of "deconstruction" and "reconstruction": one between rationality and reason and one between rationality as a descriptive and rationality as a normative assumption. This will reveal that the resilience of the concept of rationality in our discipline is to a large extent accounted for by its in-built tensions, which allow the concept to function in multiple, even contradictory roles. In the terms of the analytical framework laid out in the introduction to this volume, the following pages explore a semantic field, or web of concepts, including qualifiers, such as "thin", "thick" and "enlightened" rationality, as well as neighbouring and overlapping concepts, most importantly "reason". Indeed, it will be suggested that the enduring popularity of "rationality" owes a great debt to its relation with "reason".

The discussion also locates the concept in historical, theoretical and socio-political contexts and draws to some extent on all three approaches discussed in the introduction: it employs the historical approach to reveal the variability and evolution of the concept's meaning and relevance for IR. It also draws on the critical approach to show how the concept not merely describes what is real or desirable, but in fact helps shape the way we see and act in the international world. Inter alia, it can serve as an excuse for unbridled and short-sighted selfishness in pursuit of our goals; it exhorts against what are perceived as irrational motives guiding our actions, such as dogmas or emotions; and it has increasingly come to counter and delegitimize appeals to the human capacity for insight and progress, as informed by the concept of reason. Lastly, the analysis here also hints at the scientific approach in that it seeks to reveal how the concept has been imbued with concrete meanings and how it has been used in IR scholarship. In addition to showing how the concept has been constructed and "performed", the chapter tries to clarify and to distill the meaning it currently bears for our field of study.

The chapter unfolds as follows: I first introduce the notion of rationality as it is used in contemporary IR and provide a first explanation of its popularity. I show that, when it comes to the categories of concepts covered in this book, rationality clearly belongs to the group of "fundamental human claims". While in its "thin" variant it contains claims about traits only, in "thick" variants it also carries ideas about actors' goals. I then distinguish the concepts of rationality and reason and trace their relationship from Hobbes and Kant to today's distinction between mainstream positivist and idealist IR theory. This reveals how the concept's meanings and roles have never been fixed but instead evolved over time; most notably, they have been affected profoundly by Enlightenment philosophy and by the evolution of economic thought. In the fifth part of the chapter, I present the most important critiques that have been levied against reliance on the concept of rationality. I reveal how the concept benefits by being able to travel across theoretical contexts in IR, while losing some traction and becoming problematized beyond the modern–postmodern divide. The constructivist and post-structuralist critiques of rationality presented in part five also serve to locate the concept in a socio-political context by showing how it helps naturalize political order. The concluding section summarizes how the importance and resilience of the concept of rationality in our discipline is in fact based on its in-built tensions: the appeal of rationality owes to its being associated with reason, and its alter ego as a normative concept has helped prevent its being discarded via empirical refutation.

What is Rationality?

In contemporary IR, we are most familiar with the concept of rationality appearing as a descriptive assumption about human nature, that is, as a way of characterizing the reality of how actors behave in the world of international politics. These actors can be individual human beings, but to the extent that IR theory treats collectives like, for example, states *as if* they were individuals, the assumption is also applied to these collectives.[1] As noted, many theories – though far from all – build on the assumption that states and other agents of international politics generally act "rationally".

The assumption of rationality consists of two basic elements: it holds, first, that human beings will attempt to achieve their goals – they are goal-oriented – and, second, that they will try to use the most efficient means to achieve their goals. This includes the ideas that human beings can define their goals and rank them, that is, that they can determine their own interests in any situation which requires a decision, and that they will pursue the interests which they have identified as their own in a way that maximizes the benefits and minimizes the costs of doing so. Thus, human beings are portrayed as self-interested and efficiency-oriented goal-seekers. Since rationality is either given or not – there are no gradations – it introduces a binary between the rational (which, as we will see, is usually considered normatively desirable) and the irrational (which is not).

Rationality as a quality can be ascribed to agents themselves or to their behaviour. For example, we can think of someone as *being* rational, or as *acting* in a rational way, based on making rational choices. The second way of applying the assumption is less demanding and therefore usually considered more convincing: it merely states that actors in international politics mostly *appear* to act rationally, not that they *are* essentially rational beings. While we cannot directly ascertain the latter, the former may be claimed to be observable.

The assumption of rationality serves an important purpose: it allows us to predict behaviour. In IR, for example, it is used by different schools of thought to explain and predict both conflict and cooperation (Glaser 2010). Once we know, or think we know, what an actor's interests are in a given situation, if we assume she is rational, we can try to predict what that actor will do. If we did not believe her to be rational, such predictions would be difficult to make. And the other way around – if the behaviour of actors can be observed, we can employ the so-called "rational calculus" to infer their goals from their behaviour: whatever interest an actor appears to be maximizing must be what it has chosen as its primary goal.[2] As long as goals remain stable, this information can then be used to predict future behaviour.

The manner in which it allows us to link goals with behaviour in predictable ways makes the assumption of rationality potentially very useful for theorizing international politics and for increasing the policy relevance of IR research. But it has also received considerable criticism, as we will see below. Recently emerged approaches to understanding world politics have attempted to steer away from it. Yet, doing so raises its own problems, and so it is still fair to say that, in spite of the many criticisms raised against the concept, the idea of rationality remains a key ingredient of much of IR theory.

However, while the assumption of rationality tells us that actors are self-interested goal-seekers, in its narrow sense it does not tell us what their goals are. The literature

[1] The "as if" logic, which maintains that assumptions are justified if reality functions as if they were true, was defended for economics by Friedman (1953) and transferred to collective actors in international politics by Verba (1961: 95).

[2] The "rational calculus" is clearly described in Morgenthau (1955[1948]). Another early statement of the logic can be found in Harsanyi (1966: 139).

speaks of "thin" rationality when the concept is employed without added ideas about the goals that actors will attempt to achieve. "Thick" rationality, by contrast, adds some ideas about what it is that actors want (Ferejohn 1991). By itself, "thin" rationality cannot explain or predict behaviour without additional information about actors' goals. Whenever we call behaviour rational, we in fact purport to know what it is the actor we are observing wants. Otherwise, we would not be able to say whether she has acted rationally to obtain her goals or not. The problem with assuming "thick" rationality, however, is that this incorporates a notion of the values which actors are expected to maximize. Such a notion may be incorrect. It may serve to justify the pursuit of goals we find morally questionable. It may also be problematic for a third reason, namely when the substantive assumptions about what actors want are not expressly specified in the theory but only implied. That creates a situation in which the theory smuggles in substantive ideas about what actors (should) want through the backdoor, thereby protecting them from critical scrutiny.

Whenever the rationality assumption is employed in IR theory, it necessarily becomes "thick" rationality. But, notably, it is the IR theory and not the concept of rationality that contributes the information about actors' goals and thus the substance of their utility calculations.[3] For example, a realist account may emphasize the importance of relative power or security, while a liberal account may emphasize the goal of economic benefits from cooperation. An important reason why the rationality concept is so powerful in IR is that it is in principle compatible with any IR theory which assumes that actors have interests and are goal-oriented.[4] That being said, certain goals appear to ally more frequently with rational actor accounts than others. In liberal economic theory, as I will explain further below, the interest is routinely profit-making; this has translated into a bias in liberal as well as in Marxist IR theory, in favour of stressing the importance of economic interests. In realist IR theory, on the other hand, interest is typically defined in the first place as survival of the state as a sovereign entity (or even of its specific regime), and in second place as security through a position of relative power, seen as a prerequisite for survival. That said, the enduring popularity of the rationality assumption in IR is not merely the result of its simplicity and openness to combination with different substantive theories of international relations, but is also indebted to its philosophical roots in European enlightenment philosophy, which I will get to now.

Rationality and Reason: So Far and Yet So Close

It is impossible to put a firm date on the emergence of the notion of rationality. The idea that human beings pursue their self-interests is fairly universally present

[3] Utility calculations weigh up the pros and cons of different behavioural options and thus allow actors to make their decisions. They are expressed by formal rational choice and game theory in the form of mathematical functions – so-called utility functions.

[4] As we shall see, that excludes theories which are radically constructivist or poststructuralist.

throughout what we know of human history, although often alongside other, more powerful ideas which emphasize the social and moral aspects of humanity. The notions of rationality and reason have been intertwined ever since they emerged in the history of thought in Europe in full force in the 17th century at the dawn of the Enlightenment. Many dictionaries today suggest that they are synonyms, and in common usage they might indeed be used interchangeably. But in the social sciences rationality has taken on a distinct meaning, as laid out above, and it will be important to see both how this distinct meaning has evolved and how the two concepts still connect. Both concepts gained prominence in the context of the birth of liberalism and bear the key liberal message that progress is possible if human beings realize what is good for them. However, they are the respective key terms of two different strands of thought – both relevant for IR – that continue to develop contrasting implications to this day. The tradition of rationality can be traced, inter alia, to Thomas Hobbes and has had a profound effect on the discipline of economics as well as on mainstream positivist IR. The tradition of reason, via, for instance, Immanuel Kant, continues to inspire idealist approaches in the field.

Hobbes (1588–1679) began his intellectual development in the context of the newly emerging culture of positivist science (Skinner 1996). He reacted, especially in his early works, against the view of the Tudor rhetoricians that the findings of reason require reinforcement through eloquence in order to persuade. Instead, he held that science should rely as much as possible on concrete evidence gathered through observation. This would become a central tenet of positivism. However, Hobbes himself was not yet a positivist. Especially in his *Leviathan*, it is quite evident that he himself purposefully employed rhetoric in the service of propagating his ideas (Latour 1993: Ch. 2; Skinner 1996). The concept of rationality, while implicit in Hobbes' argument, was beset from the start by this tension between the attempt to present an objective truth based on empirical evidence and a recognition of the need to persuade. As a result, until this day, the concept of rationality can serve in IR theory both as an empirical claim (actors are indeed rational) and as a normative one (it would be better if they were).

Hobbes presented lack of rationality as the key problem of social life. In *Behemoth or The Long Parliament*, he discussed the civil war which devastated his native England between 1640 and 1660. In his introduction to one of the editions of the book, Stephen Holmes (1990[1682]: xlix) writes that "the general impression left by ... [Hobbes's] dialogues on the civil war is that many human beings are, first of all, incapable of calculative reasoning and, second, stupidly indifferent to self-preservation". *Behemoth* leaves no doubt that "civil war broke out because key actors were bewitched by irrational passions and tragically misled by doctrinal errors" (Holmes 1990[1682]: viii). Hobbes thus illustrated in *Behemoth* what he perceived to be the major problem underlying political disorder: the limits of rationality and the reign of passions. From this diagnosis, he derives a cure, which is presented at length in his *Leviathan*: human beings should be more rational.

David Gauthier (1969) has explained the Hobbesian logic as follows: for Hobbes, human beings' primary motive is the fear of violent death and, thus, their primary desire is to preserve themselves. Every action aimed at self-preservation is therefore a means to the highest end and in accordance with human nature. In Gauthier's (1969: 21) words: "From premises of the form X is a necessary means to self-preservation",

Hobbes can derive conclusions of the form "a man must do X to secure what he wants". Hobbes defines rational actions – as we still do today – as those which represent the best means to achieve a given end. This means that "we can then derive from 'a man must do X to secure what he wants', the further conclusion 'a man, if rational, will do X'" (Gauthier 1969: 21). Not being fully rational and tending to misjudge his own ends as well as the most rational means to achieve them, he will however not always do X. Therefore, "from the claim 'a man, if rational, will do X', it seems possible to derive the imperative of advice 'Do X!' For any man has sufficient reason to do whatever he would do, were he fully rational, and what he has sufficient reason to do is what he is best advised to do" (Gauthier 1969: 21). The advice "Do X!" does in fact not follow logically from the statement "a man, if rational, will do X". However, it is justified through it, because it is plausible "that a man who accepts the statement is behaving irrationally if he rejects the imperative" (Gauthier 1969: 22).

Hobbes contributed to the history of thought in IR and beyond a vision of rationality as the pursuit of self-interest tied to the desire for self-preservation. By appealing to human beings to act rationally in this way, and creating a context in which they could do so by assuring law and order, the shared goods of relative stability and prosperity for all could be achieved. This idea helped shape the belief in pluralism which came to characterize political liberalism: the idea that individuals should be free to organize to pursue their various interests in society, and that this would be good for society on the whole. Gaining hold through the thinkers of the Scottish Enlightenment in the 18th century, notably Adam Smith (1723–1790), it also formed the core of liberal economic theory, which sought to harness the potential of the profit-seeking of each to maximize the economic welfare of all. As Albert Hirschman (1977: 32) has shown, both political realism, for which Hobbes was a great inspiration, and economic liberalism emerged from the 17th-century strategy of "opposing the interests of men to their passions and of contrasting the favorable effects that follow when men are guided by their interests to the calamitous state of affairs that prevails when men give free reign to their passions".

Meanwhile, the German philosopher Immanuel Kant (1724–1804) became a key figure in shaping the tradition of reason. Reason also appeals to the human mental faculties to make us comprehend the appropriate course of action. However, the appropriate course of action is here not determined by what we understand to be our own self-interest only. Rather, it is determined by a process of aligning our self-interest with a logic that transcends us, a logic that encompasses a *collective* mission. There is something outside the individual human being – a system of substantive norms – which provides guidance, and reason is our ability to perceive and act on this guidance. In this way, a collective interest is served by the individual's capacity for reason. Inasmuch as we are part of this collective, it is also our individual self-interest, but, importantly, individual self-interest does not serve as the standard for behaviour.

While in the rationality tradition the common interest might be served as a by-product of individual selfishness, in the tradition of reason it is served by our mental ability to comprehend that the common interest is in fact our own. An example for the first logic would be individuals gaining access to medication as pharmaceutical suppliers compete over market shares by lowering prices. Here, the good of all is served as a by-product of the pursuit of economic self-interest by firms. An example for the second would be citizens perceiving a shared human need for access to medication and boycotting patent-hording pharmaceuticals to pressure them to produce cheaper, generic drugs. Here, action is taken by individuals to achieve a goal which is perceived as collective and simultaneously their own. A classic example for the second logic with particular prominence in IR is Kant's (2003[1795]) own road-map towards "perpetual peace", which advocates a system of norms which may *reasonably* be expected to further this collective good.

A third notion stands in between the two previous notions of rationality and reason and connects them in a manner which has come to shape much of international political practice in particular Western ways: this is the concept of "enlightened rationality", which was formed by, among others, the Swiss Jean-Jacques Rousseau (1712–1778) and stands between the realist and idealist traditions of thought also in other respects. Rousseau contributed the idea that the development of the human capacity for rationality, as called for by Hobbes and others, is in fact contingent on civilization. The necessary ability to delay instant gratification of all sorts of impulses to pursue more complex and longer-term goals is seen as the hallmark of the civilized human being.[5] Civilization is what teaches actors that it is ultimately better for them not to pursue their narrow short-term self-interests, which may easily conflict with those of others and with other values, but rather a version of self-interest that takes into account their own interdependence with others and their reliance on values worth protecting in the longer run.

The notion of "enlightened self-interest", which is also often framed as long-term as opposed to short-term interest, typically fills the "thin" notion of rationality with liberal (Enlightenment) content and in this way seeks to purge the pursuit of self-interest from its association with both selfish immorality and self-defeating short-sightedness. To compare with our above examples, the "enlightened rational" pharmaceuticals company would sell vital drugs at the lowest sustainable prices in the recognition that access to such drugs is a shared human need. It would thereby profile itself as a moral actor, in the process harnessing the image benefits that brings. At the same time, it would aim to maximize profits elsewhere in its portfolio, both to maintain economic viability (maximize self-interest) and to enable its continuing operation as a moral actor. It would also be aware that if large numbers of people died due to lacking access to vital drugs, it would lose customers. The pursuit of values and self-interest have here merged, in a manner which is typical for actors self-styling themselves in an Enlightenment tradition. In IR such actors include major international organizations like the IMF or the World Bank, which merge appeals to reason and rationality in both their policy interventions and in their self-image construction. This benefits both the defence of Enlightenment values – by cloaking them in a widely accepted instrumentalist logic – and the pursuit of self-interest – by draping it with widely accepted values.

While it may appear normal, even desirable, for international actors to pursue their instrumental goals and values in this manner, it is not difficult to see that it is also problematic. This is due to the manner in which civilization, as the prerequisite for enlightened rationality, has so often been attributed to the global north or the Western world, while the remainder of the planet has been framed as a place where people have

[5] To understand this notion better, see also Chapter 5, by Lebow, in this volume.

to be taught by others what their interests should be and how to pursue them. The Western bias in the notion of rationality, the racism it supports, and the political consequences are problematized by growing literatures in postcolonial and otherwise critical IR, International Political Economy, and development studies (e.g. Chabal 2012). Similarly, feminist scholarship has drawn attention to the masculinist bias of rationalism and to how women have frequently been depicted as suffering from inferior capacities for rationality, and patronized or dominated on those grounds (e.g. Sjoberg and Tickner 2012). In short, we need to critically scrutinize the biases which are inevitably attached to appeals to rationality as well as reason, and we can understand IR as having evolved in a field of tension between these concepts, their logics and the substantive biases they transport.

Legacies of the Incomplete Split between Rationality and Reason

The tension between rationality and reason also left its mark on IR because they can be seen as linked to different approaches to the generation of knowledge. Simply put, the tradition of reason has fed, and continues to feed, idealist approaches in our field, while the tradition of rationality dominates positivist approaches.[6] Positivist approaches in IR set out to reveal the realities of international politics, to maintain an exclusively empirical focus and to avoid taking a normative stance. This commitment distinguishes them both from idealist approaches, which take an explicit normative stance, and from radical constructivist and post-structuralist approaches, which reject the positivist idea that human beings can be impartial judges of empirical evidence. I will lay out the first distinction now, while the second will be clarified in the next section.

While there is no logical reason why positivist approaches should have to rely on an assumption of rationality, in IR they generally do. This is due to the strong influence of behaviouralism since the 1930s and more specifically of behavioural models inspired by the discipline of economics after World War II.[7] The latter incorporated into positivist IR the idea that actors' behaviour could generally be expected to comply with the model of homo œconomicus: the rationally self-interested being populating mainstream theories of economics. In response, rational choice and game theory approaches evolved in IR, which explicitly employ this view of rationality as a theoretical axiom. But also beyond these formal approaches, positivist IR by and large came to accept the idea of rationality. Its association with behaviouralism and with economics, as well as its advantages for parsimonious theorizing, as discussed above, have granted the rationality assumption a strong scientific appeal from which approaches using it benefit to this day.

---

[6] The label "naturalist" is also often used for what I here termed "positivist". See e.g. Moses and Knutsen (2012).

[7] In the so-called Second Great Debate in the discipline of IR, novel, behaviouralist approaches began to displace so-called traditionalist approaches to re-create IR according to a natural science template. See Hollis and Smith (1990).

As noted earlier, it is possible for rationality to function simultaneously as a descriptive and a normative concept in one and the same theory. Yet, for the positivist tradition embracing both at the same time poses a logical problem: either actors really are rational, in which case it makes no sense to demand that they should be – why would one need to demand that? Or they are not, in which case it makes little sense to demand that they should be – how could they be? Moreover, positivist approaches generally avoid taking an openly normative stance, so it seems odd for them to embrace rationality as a norm. As a result, positivist IR tends to explicitly employ rationality in the descriptive vein, as a useful simplification of a reality. However, whenever such scholarship moves from the empirical mode of describing and explaining world politics to the prescriptive mode of giving advice to decision-makers, we can see the normative function come through. In those instances, the view is that rational behaviour can be taught and learned and that rational decisions are the most prudent and thereby the best. A good example was the occasion when 33 prominent IR scholars working on international security intervened in the debate preceding the Iraq War in 2002 by calling on the US government not to start the war, arguing that foreign policy should be based not on desires for revenge or dogmatism but on the rational pursuit of national interest.[8] From their perspective, the decision to go to war was irrational and, thus, wrong (see also Mearsheimer and Walt 2003).

Its normative function has helped the concept of rationality to maintain its centrality even where it seemed to be contradicted by behaviour. In such cases, actors going against what a rational choice model would predict are diagnosed as misguided, blinded by ideology or otherwise delusional and, thus, in need of enlightenment. The fact that the concept allows scholars to flexibly transfer between its descriptive and prescriptive functions helps explain the continuing attraction of the "rationality" assumption in mainstream IR, as comprised of realist theory and post-World War II variants of liberalism.[9] It allows theorizing actors in international politics to behave rationally and to simultaneously frame any failure to behave accordingly as a problem and as evidence for the need to further promote rationality as a norm.

What I term "idealist" IR theories instead rely more on reason than rationality. And in contrast to the treatment of rationality as a simplifying descriptive assumption and an argumentative tool for problem solving, reason functions more like an article of faith; it involves the belief that agents are capable of doing the right thing in a way that aligns the self with the social. As such, it can become the foundation for ethical practice and for idealist theory. Idealist approaches in IR today mainly comprise classic liberal, liberal constructivist and, broadly speaking, Marxist-inspired variants. All belong to the tradition of reason in the sense that they appeal to human beings to see what is in the interest of humanity, to identify that larger interest with their own and to align their own behaviour with it. Whether they prioritize interdependence, cooperative problem-solving, multilateralism, international socialization, social justice, cosmopolitanism or solidarity as key principles, they all

[8] *New York Times*, 26 September 2002.

[9] Their shared reliance on rationality is one reason why the competition between neo-realist and neo-liberal institutionalist IR theory has also been referred to as a "neo-neo-synthesis". See e.g. Lamy (2013).

contain the hope that progress might be made in international affairs, based on the universal human capacity to use reason.

In the 20th century, Jürgen Habermas and other adherents of the Frankfurt School of critical theory criticized the rise of positivism for having brought about a split of "reason" into an instrumental and a moral notion, and the triumph of the former over the latter.[10] In the context of the rise of positivism since World War II, we can indeed see that idealist approaches in IR have become marginalized, as their normative content makes them appear "unscientific". In the process, the concept of reason has become marginalized. In Foucauldian terms, the ideas inspired by the concept of reason have become "subjugated knowledge": "meanings/uses that are ignored because they do not fit established discourses [...] validated by science" (Chapter 1, this volume). Enlightenment notions of reason have become subjugated by the rise of rationality as a concept ostensibly devoid of normative content and thus amenable to positivist scientific inquiry.

However, while the notions of rationality and reason have developed away from each other, they have in fact never been fully de-coupled. Indeed, the enduring appeal of rationality is in part owed to its continuing implicit association with reason. Hirschman (1977) has explained how the notion of rational market behaviour could become entrenched in liberal economic theory due to its foundation in Enlightenment values. A parallel development took place in liberal IR theory. Also here, the reliance on rationality is justified by its intrinsic link to notions of "enlightened self-interest" and the resulting collective benefits of actors behaving in predictable and risk-averse ways and becoming able to realize shared gains. While owing to "civilization" (Linklater 2011) it may by now be widely considered unpalatable to base policy decisions on unabashed selfishness, the reign of rationality keeps being rehabilitated by its lingering association with liberal values, which is a heritage of the Enlightenment. And even while the debt owed by rationality to reason is not generally recognized in scholarship that employs the rationality assumption, it has primed both realist and liberal IR scholarship to expect a decline in rationality to go along with a reassertion of the destructive sides of human nature and thence to implicitly embrace rationality as a behavioural norm.

The incomplete split of rationality from reason has also meant that in the context of contemporary IR scholarship the concept of rationality itself is not "essentially contested" (Gallie 1956). Rather, a broad consensus has emerged around its narrow meaning, as sketched in the introductory part of this chapter. Not only has a large scientific community – referred to as rationalists or rational choice scholars – been constructed around this meaning, it is also largely accepted by critics of the rationality assumption, who disagree only on the desirability of using it. This does, however, not mean that disputes about the link of rationality to reason and broader questions about the aims which actors do and should pursue have disappeared. Rather, they have become ontological and normative disputes, rather than conceptual ones. Realists, liberals, Marxists, constructivists and others argue about these questions, but they do so at the level of theory, using their entire arsenals of concepts and empirical and normative propositions. In the following section, I turn to the most important challenges that have been raised against a reliance on the concept of rationality.

[10] For important attempts to rehabilitate a more substantive notion of reason, see Morgenthau (1946) and Alker (1990, 1996).

Challenges to Rationality in the Praxis of Science and Politics

In the introductory section, I explained that the rationality assumption can serve as a vehicle for surreptitiously smuggling potentially erroneous substantive assumptions about actors' goals into our theories. Several other important criticisms have been leveled against the assumption that the actors of international politics are, or should be, by and large, acting rationally (Renwick Monroe 1991; Green and Shapiro 1994). I will first present the less fundamental of those criticisms, as they tend to be expressed even from within mainstream rationalist IR. Further on, I will present the more fundamental critiques by social constructivist and postmodernist approaches. The critiques are, first, that the informational and cognitive prerequisites for rational behaviour are not usually given; second, that the rationality assumption promotes selfishness; third, that it leads to the neglect of important other aspects of human psychology; fourth, that it is incompatible with a social ontology such as would be more appropriate for our field; and, fifth, that in its guise as a scientific concept it actually serves the political function of social control.

First, critics have pointed out that making rational choices requires full information about all possible choices that can be made, along with their likely consequences and payoffs. In addition, it requires the cognitive capacity to process all that information in a cost-benefit analysis and to do so quickly enough to be able to act in a timely manner. It is quite clear that these prerequisites are usually not met, especially not when decisions have to be made in times of crisis, on complicated policy issues or on questions affected by attempts to obfuscate and dissimulate, all of which is common in the world of foreign policy decision-making. Defenders of the rationality assumption admit that conditions for making perfectly rational decisions hardly ever obtain,[11] yet maintain that rationality is still frequently enough approximated closely enough to make the assumption useful (Elster 1989).

A second criticism that has been raised against assuming rationality is that it exaggerates the self-centered, even selfish aspects of human psychology and that, in so doing, it can create a self-fulfilling prophecy. This critique recognizes that in describing a certain way of behaving as "normal", a theory can also be seen to excuse, perhaps even advocate such behaviour. As Felix Berenskoetter reminds us in the introductory chapter, quoting Foucault, "concepts don't just make [...] things intelligible, they actually *make* things, that is, they 'systematically form the objects of which they speak'". For the concept of rationality, as perceived in contemporary mainstream economics, this has been vividly illustrated by Robert H. Frank et al. (1993) in a famous study which showed that students' exposure to rational choice thinking made them more prone to base their own decisions on narrow self-interest.

A third broad cluster of critique points out that the assumption neglects aspects of human psychology which appear to counteract rationality, such as emotionality and sociality. To start with the former, rationality is in fact often explicitly juxtaposed to emotionality, the latter being seen as generating irrational behaviour. It is of course difficult to deny that human beings have emotions and that those are likely to influence behaviour in some way. If we do not take that into account, are we not distorting reality

[11] This has led to a host of work on "bounded rationality", pioneered by Simon (1982).

and risking making unwarranted predictions? One response of defenders of the rationality assumption is that analysts of international relations are usually concerned with the behaviour of political elites, that is, "professionals" who would likely not be where they are if their behaviour tended to be driven by emotions more than by the cool calculation of how to maximize their states' or organizations' interests. Ordinary people, especially in masses, may be driven by emotions, but these are then manipulated by rationally thinking elites. As more recent IR scholarship on the role of emotions affecting government-level decision-making pokes some holes in this defence (see e.g. Renshon and Lerner 2012), a second response shifts the discussion from an empirical to a normative level to hold that it would be better for the world if decision-makers behaved rationally. Although this may sound like a cheap defence, this normative argument is a powerful one and, as noted, has helped to maintain the popularity of the concept.

The critique that the rational actor assumption neglects the sociability of humans has been more difficult to counter. Although the rationality assumption does not outright deny the social nature of reality, it portrays human beings as essentially atomistic individuals who define and then pursue their own individual self-interest. The social world figures into their decisions only via strategic cost-benefit calculations, and is not seen as having an impact on goals or interests themselves. And even though goals or interests may coincide with those of others, they are "owned individually" and conceptualized as prior to making decisions. The actor first knows what she wants, by herself, and then acts to obtain it in the social environment. These ideas have been disputed by social constructivists, who emphasize that human beings construct their identities as well as their interests dynamically in interaction with others, that is, in social context. They argue that the assumption of rationality abstracts too much from social context and fails to take into account that and how identities and interests change through interaction. While the "rational calculus" requires actors' preference structures to remain stable, in fact they are dynamic. As opposed to being prior to, or exogenous to, behaviour, interests are as much a product of, as an input into, the processes that constitute international politics; they also can be shared with others at a level much deeper than the mere co-incidence of individual preferences.[12] The social constructivist critique does not rule out that actors might appear to be acting rationally at any given time, but it makes any model based on the assumption considerably more complicated, as interests themselves are in flux alongside the environmental features which condition their satisfaction. Also, inasmuch as agents perceive themselves as social beings dependent on others, it makes room for other considerations determining choices, such as a desire for social acceptance, which cannot easily be subsumed under the concept of rational self-interest.

The social constructivist critique of rationality has proven particularly effective and has been a major factor behind its popularity in the field of IR. The split between the two schools of thought, famously captured by Keohane (1988) in terms of "rationalism" versus "reflectivism", may even be considered the most significant in contemporary international relations theory (Wæver 1996). Constructivists have however already moved to transcend this dichotomy by incorporating rational choices in

[12] The growing literature on ontological security concerns is particularly pertinent here. See e.g. Mitzen (2006).

broader behavioural logics. A notable example is the inclusion of a logic of consequences shaping actors' behaviour in line with expectations of rationality with a logic of appropriateness, leading actors not only to ask "will this choice help me realize my goal x?" but also "will this choice be acceptable to my relevant others?" (Schimmelfennig and Sedelmeier 2005; Checkel 2007; see also March and Olsen 2009).

Last, but not least, an even more fundamental critique sees rationality as a performative concept in the service of social control. At the end of the 19th century and in the context of the development of the modern state and its bureaucracy, Friedrich Nietzsche forcefully expressed the idea that "rationality" could also become a repressive homogenizing logic applied by government to stifle the potentially disruptive impulses stemming from individual freedom. The insight that rationality operates as a norm, and therefore as a possible instrument of control, was further developed inter alia by Max Weber, the so-called Stanford School of philosophers of science, and the sociologist John W. Meyer. Particularly influential for its uptake in IR were Michel Foucault and his concept of "governmentality", which profoundly affected postmodernist approaches in our field. "Governmentality" might be defined as the structures and processes through which political power has come to be exerted in the form of modern government and which rely strongly on certain forms of knowledge and routines which have been granted the difficult-to-challenge status of governmental rationality: seemingly "neutral" rules and "technical" procedures that make sense from the perspective of the current order (Joseph 2012). While critiques of governmentality tend nowadays to be mostly directed against neo-liberally inspired models of control, they are just as applicable to the realist notion of *raison d'état*. The latter concept emphasizes that the statesman must do what is perceived to be in the interest of his state, without being distracted by personal concerns, including those of a moral nature. While the French word "raison" sounds like the English "reason", the correct translation of *raison d'état* is, however, "rationality of state", because what is emphasized here are not Enlightenment ideals but rather the need to set all (other) ideals aside for the sake of Realpolitik – in the interest of safeguarding or buttressing existing power structures.

This more radical critique of the concept of rationality and its use as a performative device – acting out particular normative ideas in opposition to other normative ideas – allows us to see more clearly which other ideas about international politics are marginalized by the power of the rationality concept, and with what consequences.[13] For example, the reign of rationality supports a lasting marginalization of non-state actors in world politics, because they appear disconnected from and might even challenge the "rationality of state". In consequence, they are framed as less rational and less worthy interlocutors for foreign policy elites. In the so-called Global War on Terrorism, for instance, the mantra "we do not negotiate with terrorists" appeared motivated by a form of Orientalism (Said 1979) that mixed ugly stereotypes of the excessively emotional and therefore dangerous Muslim and Middle Easterner with a structural disinclination to deal with non-state actors, even in contexts in which approachable state actors were, for all intents and purposes, absent. In the context of the armed conflicts between state actors and various other organized groups in Syria,

[13] For a powerful critique of the consequences of the dominance of rational choice theory, among other elements of a mainstream IR ontology and epistemology, see Smith (2004).

Iraq, and elsewhere in North Africa and the Middle East after the "Arab Spring", Western governments have tended to frame non-state actors as less rational and, in consequence, also as less useful partners for external intervention. In this manner, they have helped to abort struggles for popular emancipation and to entrench power elites.

Conclusion

This chapter has discussed the concept of rationality through the moves of deconstruction and reconstruction by establishing and then problematizing two juxtapositions: one between rationality and reason and one between rationality as a descriptive and rationality as a normative concept. The meaning of the concept is effectively constructed and its enduring popularity largely explained by the tensions between these paired notions. To borrow from this volume's introduction, the concept of rationality clearly has the descriptive function "to grasp a fundamental feature of our socio-political system", yet it simultaneously has an "aspirational outlook" and contains a "promise of progress" (Chapter 1, this volume). We can only understand its appeal and endurance if we understand that rationality is not only an analytical assumption but also a very powerful norm. We usually don't like to be called irrational. This is the result of the concept's history, in which the notions of rationality and reason became intertwined in such a way that "thick" notions of rationality became filled with dominant values. Due to the tensions it incorporates, the concept of rationality remains a potent analytical and political tool. Despite its vagueness and evident shortcomings, actors in international politics very often consciously strive to (appear to) behave rationally, and use the concept as a basis for judging and engaging others. And so, while there is much in world politics that cannot be explained with a reference to "rationality", the concept continues to shape interpretations, expectations and behaviour in international relations and remains central to political analysis.

Acknowledgements

Next to the editor and fellow contributors to this volume, I want to particularly thank Juliet Kaarbo for her useful feedback on an earlier version of this chapter.

Suggested Readings

Chabal, Patrick (2012) *The End of Conceit: Western Rationality after Postcolonialism*. London: Zed Books.

Explores the failure of Western social thought to address pressing social and economic issues and prejudices about the rationality of the human and social sciences. Chabal argues that challenges from Asia, Africa, Latin America and the Middle East, as well as the influence of citizens of non-Western origins living in the West, expose the limits of Western rationality and the theories and concepts we currently use to understand and act on the world.

Glaser, Charles L. (2010) *Rational Theory of International Politics: The Logic of Competition and Cooperation*. Princeton, NJ: Princeton University Press.

A theoretically sophisticated application of a rationalist approach to understanding international relations, explaining patterns of cooperation and conflict from a realist perspective.

Green, Donald and Shapiro, Ian (1994) *Pathologies of Rational Choice Theory: A Critique of Applications in Political Science*. New Haven, CT: Yale University Press.
An important text dissecting rational choice approaches in political science and IR and providing a comprehensive overview of arguments against them.

Hirschman, Albert O. (1977) *The Passions and the Interests: Political Arguments for Capitalism before its Triumph*. Princeton, NJ: Princeton University Press.
Explains in clear language how liberal (and also realist) philosophy, as the foundation of capitalism, became based on the idea that the rational pursuit of self-interest is the best recipe for societal order and prosperity. One of the most important books published in the social sciences.

References

Alker, Jr., Hayward R. 1990. 'Rescuing "Reason" from the "Rationalists": Reading Vico, Marx, and Weber as Reflective Institutionalists', *Millennium: Journal of International Studies* 19/2: 161–184.

Alker, Jr., Hayward R. 1996. *Rediscoveries and Reformulations: Humanistic Methodologies for International Studies*. Cambridge: Cambridge University Press.

Chabal, Patrick. 2012. *The End of Conceit: Western Rationality after Postcolonialism*. London: Zed Books.

Checkel, Jeffrey T., ed. 2007. *International Institutions and Socialization in Europe*. Cambridge: Cambridge University Press.

Elster, Jon. 1989. *Nuts and Bolts for the Social Sciences*. Cambridge: Cambridge University Press.

Ferejohn, John. 1991. 'Rationality and Interpretation: Parliamentary Elections in Early Stuart England', in Kristen R. Monroe (ed.), *The Economic Approach to Politics*. New York: HarperCollins.

Frank, Robert, Thomas Gilovich, and Dennis Regan. 1993. 'Does Studying Economics Inhibit Cooperation?' *Journal of Economic Perspectives* 7/2: 159–171.

Friedman, Milton. 1953. *Essays in Positive Economics, Part I: The Methodology of Positive Economics*. Chicago: University of Chicago Press.

Gallie, W.B. 1956. 'Essentially Contested Concepts', *Proceedings of the Aristotelian Society* 56: 167–198.

Gauthier, David P. 1969. *The Logic of Leviathan: The Moral and Political Theory of Thomas Hobbes*. Oxford: Clarendon Press.

Glaser, Charles L. 2010. *Rational Theory of International Politics: The Logic of Competition and Cooperation*. Princeton, NJ: Princeton University Press.

Green, Donald P. and Ian Shapiro. 1994. *Pathologies of Rational Choice Theory: A Critique of Applications in Political Science*. New Haven, CT: Yale University Press.

Harsanyi, John. 1966. 'Some Social Science Implications of a New Approach to Game Theory', in Kathleen Archibald (ed.), *Strategic Interaction and Conflict*. Berkeley, CA: University of California Press.

Hirschman, Albert O. 1977. *The Passions and the Interests: Political Arguments for Capitalism before its Triumph*. Princeton, NJ: Princeton University Press.

Hollis, Martin and Steve Smith. 1990. *Explaining and Understanding International Relations*. Oxford: Clarendon Press.

Holmes, Stephen. 1990[1682]. 'Introduction', in *Thomas Hobbes, Behemoth or The Long Parliament*. Chicago: University of Chicago Press.

Joseph, Jonathan. 2012. *The Social in the Global: Social Theory, Governmentality and Global Politics*. Cambridge: Cambridge University Press.

Kant, Immanuel. 2003[1795]. *To Perpetual Peace: A Philosophical Sketch*. Indianapolis, IN: Hackett Publishing.

Keohane, Robert O. 1988. 'International Institutions: Two Approaches', *International Studies Quarterly* 32/4: 379–396.

Lamy, Steven L. 2013. 'Contemporary Mainstream Approaches: Neo-realism and Neo-liberalism', in John Baylis, Steve Smith and Patricia Owens (eds), *The Globalization of World Politics: An Introduction to International Relations*, 6th edn. Oxford: Oxford University Press.

Latour, Bruno, 1993. *We Have Never Been Modern*, transl. Catherine Porter. Cambridge, MA: Harvard University Press.

Linklater, Andrew. 2011. 'International Society and the Civilizing Process', *Ritsumeikan International Affairs* 9: 1–26.

March, James G. and Johan P. Olsen. 2009. 'The Logic of Appropriateness', in Robert E. Goodin, Michael Moran and Martin Rein (eds), *The Oxford Handbook of Public Policy*, online, DOI:10.1093/oxfordhb/9780199548453.003.0034.

Mearsheimer, John J. and Stephen M. Walt. 2003. 'An Unnecessary War', *Foreign Policy*, Jan/Feb: 50–59.

Mitzen, Jennifer. 2006. 'Ontological Security in World Politics: State Identity and the Security Dilemma', *European Journal of International Relations* 12/3: 341–370.

Morgenthau, Hans J. 1946. *Scientific Man vs. Power Politics*. Chicago: University of Chicago Press.

Morgenthau, Hans J. 1955[1948]. *Politics among Nations: The Struggle for Power and Peace*, 2nd edn. New York: Alfred A. Knopf.

Moses, Jonathon and Torbjørn Knutsen. 2012. *Ways of Knowing: Competing Methodologies in Social and Political Research*, 2nd edn. London: Palgrave Macmillan.

Renshon, Jonathan and Jennifer S. Lerner. 2012. 'Decision-Making: the Role of Emotions in Foreign Policy', in Daniel J. Christie (ed.) *The Encyclopedia of Peace Psychology*. London: Blackwell Publishing.

Renwick Monroe, Kristen, ed. 1991. *The Economic Approach to Politics: A Critical Reassessment of the Theory of Rational Action*. New York: HarperCollins.

Said, Edward W. 1979.*Orientalism*. London: Vintage.

Schimmelfennig Frank and Ulrich Sedelmeier, eds. 2005. *The Europeanization of Central and Eastern Europe*. New York: Cornell University Press.

Simon, Herbert A. 1982. *Models of Bounded Rationality*. Cambridge, MA: MIT Press.

Sjoberg, Laura and J. Ann Tickner. 2012. 'Feminist Perspectives on International Relations', in Walter Carlsnaes, Thomas Risse, and Beth A Simmons (eds), *Handbook of International Relations*. London: Sage.

Skinner, Quentin. 1996. *Reason and Rhetoric in the Philosophy of Hobbes*. Cambridge: Cambridge University Press.

Smith, Steve. 2004. 'Singing Our World into Existence: International Relations Theory and September 11', *International Studies Quarterly* 48/3: 499–515.

Verba, Sidney. 1961. 'Assumptions of Rationality and Non-Rationality in Models of the International System', in Klaus Knorr and Sidney Verba (eds), *The International System: Theoretical Essays*. Princeton, NJ: Princeton University Press.

Wæver, Ole. 1996. 'The Rise and Fall of the Inter- Paradigm Debate', in Steve Smith, Ken Booth and Marysia Zalewski (eds), *International Theory: Positivism and Beyond*. Cambridge: Cambridge University Press, pp. 149–85.

5

Identity

Richard Ned Lebow

This chapter offers a critical discussion of the concept of identity by combining parts of the historical, scientific and critical approaches outlined in the introduction to this volume. Identity is a concept that developed in early modern Europe and took on new meanings in the nineteenth century. In the twentieth century, it has been the subject of sustained investigation by philosophers, psychologists and political scientists. There is a general agreement that much of modern life revolves around questions of identity and the internal, social and political conflicts they engender. The concept of identity has been coined to describe and study this phenomenon. In what follows, I describe the origins of the concept and how it is the secular descendant of the soul and serves the same purposes: providing uniqueness and consistency to individuals. Like other basic concepts, it was coined to advance political or psychological goals but is also used for analytical purposes. In the study of international relations, identity has become the foundational concept of many constructivists who give it the same kind of ontological priority that realists give power.

The analytical use of concepts coined for other purposes, in this case for serving a socio-psychological function, is as unavoidable as it is problematic. These concepts are invariably imprecise, lending themselves to varying, if not contradictory uses. This is, of course, true of all concepts in the social sciences, as they are composed of other concepts and rarely refer to anything "real". Many can nevertheless be operationalized in a way to make them useful analytically. They can be measured as in the case of power, although different metrics lead to widely varying results. Or, their presence (or absence) can be determined by looking for a specific set of markers. Brubaker and Cooper (2000) note that identity fails the first test. I contend that it does not meet the second because it can be used retrospectively to explain almost any behavior but not to predict it in advance. A concept that is used to explain everything explains nothing (Lebow, 2012: Ch. 1). Equally problematic is the tendency among social scientists to treat identity as a "variable" that can be operationalized (Abdelal et al., 2009). At best, "identity" should be considered a heuristic that encourages us to think about the ways in which identifications, interests and behavior interact. As Felix Berenskoetter (2010: 3607) puts it, we might think about it as an "eye opener".

More importantly, basic concepts like identity, democracy or hegemony have strong political resonance and it is difficult to build a firewall between their political and analytical use. This can become all but impossible when scholars who coin or use these concepts are themselves partisans of political projects. Consider the democratic peace thesis. As much ideology as science, its controversial claims have been hailed by American politicians as evidence of the superiority of their form of government and offered as justification for the invasion of Iraq (Bush, 2007). Princeton professors G. John Ikenberry and Anne-Marie Slaughter have joined policy advocates in calling for a concert of democracies to run the world (Daalder and Lindsay, 2007; Ikenberry and Slaughter, 2006; see also Chapter 13, this volume). Likewise, the concept of hegemony was coined to describe a situation in which one state is so dominant that it is able to order the system and more or less impose its preferences on others (see also Chapter 12, this volume). Prominent realist and liberal scholars have for some years asserted that the US is a hegemon, that this is essential to maintain global security and the international order and that people around the world recognize these truths and welcome American leadership. There is little empirical support for any of these claims (Reich and Lebow, 2014); what is clear, however, is that concepts like the democratic peace and hegemony are used to advance American foreign policy goals.

The concept of identity faces similar and different challenges. On the collective level, identity is inseparable from nationalism and on the individual level, it serves the long-standing striving for personal autonomy. It is difficult for scholars to employ "identity" as an analytical category without inadvertently legitimizing these projects. I say inadvertently because those constructivist IR scholars who use identity – unlike their realist and liberal counterparts who invoke hegemony – are not writing in support of nationalism. They attempt to detach themselves from what they study, or in some instances – recent works on geopolitics and stigma, for example – attribute negative consequences to the resulting identities (Badie, 2014; Guzzini, 2012; Zarakol, 2011). However, constructivist scholars are open to the risk of assuming the existence of identities and their determining, or at least, important, consequences for shaping interests and behavior. But as the existence of identities is arguably more illusion than reality, it is inappropriate to attribute it ontological standing or behavioral consequences.

In this chapter, I begin with a brief account of the modern concept of identity and the project with which it became associated. I draw on recent philosophical writing and psychological research to show just how questionable the concept of identity is and propose the use of self-identification in its stead. Most research on identity has focused on individual identities, and only recently on collective identities, especially nationalism. However, constructivists are primarily interested in national identities; their core research program on identity – ontological security – assumes that states have identities and that they serve similar purposes to individual ones. I explore the differences between national and individual identities and argue that the concept of identity is even more difficult to defend at the national level. In the process, I elaborate some of the key similarities and differences between individual and national self-identifications. I conclude with some general comments about the implications of my analysis for concepts in our field.

The Emergence of Identity the Concept

Identity is the secular descendant of the soul and coined for much the same reason. Christians were forced to confront identity in ways that pagan Greeks and Romans were not because of their belief that heaven was the reward for a lifetime of piety and suffering. If people are responsible for their behavior, their continuity and uniqueness must somehow be established. The soul serves both needs; it provides uniqueness because each one is different, and continuity in this world and the next by virtue of its assumed unchanging nature and ability to survive death (Augustine of Hippo, 1950: 248). The soul found its fullest theoretical development in the writings of Thomas Aquinas, who described it as God's creation and the first principle of being. Drawing on Aristotle, he considered it to be incorporeal and to operate separately and independently from the body. As the soul was not made of matter, it could not be destroyed by any natural process and therefore guaranteed immortality (Aquinas, 2002: Question 75).

There is no consensus among historians of political thought about when a discourse about the self emerged; René Descartes' *Passions of the Soul* (1649), Thomas Hobbes' *Leviathan* (1651) and John Locke's *Essay Concerning Human Understanding* (1690) are reasonable starting points. All three philosophers began the process by which the soul became an increasingly problematic category in early modern Europe. Descartes used the word mind (*mens*) in lieu of soul (*anima*), and attempted to return to a Platonic understanding of the latter. Hobbes differentiated artificial from natural selves. Locke (1975: Book II, Ch. 27) introduced the concept of the person and the self, the latter defined as "that conscious thinking ... which is sensible or conscious of pleasure and pain, capable of happiness or misery, and so is concerned for itself, as far as that consciousness extends". Locke also invoked memory as the quality that provided continuity and distinctiveness to individual selves. He reasons that human beings enter the world as blank slates and become persons as a result of their life experiences and reflections on them. Selfhood is a complicated concept because, contra Locke, our understanding of ourselves is incomplete due to our imperfect and punctuated memories. We are selves to others, but even more imperfectly, as they know less about us and have no recourse to our reflections about ourselves. Only God understands us perfectly, he avers, and holds out the hope that at some point might make us more transparent to ourselves (1975: Book II, Ch. 27). Locke's understanding of identity is not about uniqueness, but about the supposed "identicality" that provides continuity to our lives (Wahrman, 2004: 191).

David Hume (1998) dismisses soul and self as comforting "fictions". The mind, he argues, is best conceived of as "a bundle or collection of different perceptions which succeed one another with an inconceivable rapidity and are in perpetual flux and motion". It follows that "there is no impression constant and invariable", and no continuous self (Hume, 1999: I, 1.3). To posit such a creature would require us to deny its existence during all the hours when we sleep and are insensible of ourselves. Hume nevertheless describes people as generally predictable in their behavior, without which it would be impossible to sustain a society. This stability, he believes, derives from a set of universal internal motives (e.g. ambition, avarice, vanity, friendship, generosity) that are constantly moderated and channeled by external constraints and opportunities (Hume, 1998: VIII, 1.7–8). These motives were all social in origin and dependent on society for their satisfaction. This understanding reflects eighteenth-century Britain's belief that people were fundamentally alike and could effectively be described in terms of archetypes. In contrast to Hume, Kant is convinced of the epistemic legitimacy of a persisting self-identical object and of the passage of time without change. His defense is too complex to elucidate here but rests on the assumption that space and time are not discursive concepts but pure intuitions and that there is a fundamental isomorphism between our minds and the universe (Kant, 1998: A271–B327). Following Kant, German Idealism treats persons as continuous by virtue of their identity.

The other great eighteenth-century influence on modern conceptions of identity is Jean-Jacques Rousseau. His *Discourse on the Origin and Foundation of Inequality* lays out an historical account of the emotional and cognitive development of humankind. In his original, savage state, man – I use Rousseau's gendered language – is driven by *amour de soi* [love of self] and *identification* [pity and sympathy]. *Amour de soi* is a pre-rational instinct for survival, tempered by pity for the suffering of others (Rousseau, 1964: 115–16). Primitive man is distinguished from animals by his ability to think and reflect. Comparative modifiers enter his vocabulary; he not only compares himself to other people but recognizes that others make comparisons to him. Recognition and esteem are conferred on those who excel in the various comparative categories. Public standing now becomes his dominant goal, and *amour propre* – the passion to be regarded favorably by others – his principal motive for acting (1964: 147–60). Civilized man is also moved by *amour propre*, but a subtle yet important transformation occurs. His cognitive faculties increase and his calculations and goals become more complex. He is driven to postpone gratification for long periods of time in the pursuit of affluence. Whereas savage man sought esteem directly, civilized man seeks it indirectly, through the attainment and display of material possessions (1964: 174–5). In the modern world, Rousseau insists, people are doubly enslaved: they are politically subjugated, and more troubling still, are in thrall to the artificial material and ego needs generated by modern society. This self-enslavement is the source of major social ills, from exploitation and domination of others to low self-esteem and depression. Liberation can only be achieved through self-education and self-discovery, both with the goal of recapturing the virtues dominant in the state of nature. Identity is not a personal project but a political one.

Rousseau's emphasis on authenticity was taken in a different direction by nineteenth-century German philosophers. Early in the century, German Idealists and Romantics emphasized the importance of personal and national identity, a quest that stressed uniqueness, originality and self-realization. Following Rousseau, they understood personal and collective identities as inextricably connected. The former, while unique, could only find healthy and creative expression within a larger, national community. Such communities, Herder (1969) insists, have organic identities that had to be nurtured, developed and expressed within a wider community of nations. Building on this approach, Hegel created an elaborate philosophical framework in which states were envisaged as the highest stage of historical development and one in which the human spirit finds its fullest expression. For these thinkers, it is impossible to separate individual from collective identity or the personal from the political. They differed from Rousseau in making individual identity dependent on a collective one. At the end of the nineteenth century, Nietzsche returned to Rousseau's emphasis on the individual, but embedded it in a darker vision. He accuses bureaucracies, educational systems and science of crushing human freedom and making it difficult for people to develop their creative impulses. These parallel but opposed strands of philosophical development provide the intellectual underpinnings for nationalism, the dominant social identity in the twentieth century, and individual authenticity, the principal individual psychological goal in the postwar era.

Identity Interrogated

My brief genealogical account highlights three questionable assumptions on which scholarly understandings of identity rest. Starting from the belief that we have a self, the first assumption is that we are somehow able to sustain a continuous identity even though our personalities, affiliations and roles change in the course of our lives. The second assumption is that our identities are unique. Third, there is the belief in our potential to remake ourselves, or at least to discover our "true" selves. These beliefs are deeply ingrained in the modern Western psyche and scholarly literature.

The continuity assumption, so central to Locke's construction of identity, has been described as realistic and essential to our wellbeing. Erik Erikson, arguably the most influential postwar author on the subject, maintained that "The conscious feeling of having a personal identity is based on two simultaneous observations: the immediate perception of one's selfsameness and continuity in time; and the simultaneous perception of the fact that others recognize one's sameness and continuity" (Erikson, 1959: 22). Clifford Geertz (1983) describes the Western self "as a bounded, unique, more or less integrated motivational and cognitive universe, a dynamic center of awareness, emotion, judgment, and action". French philosopher Paul Ricoeur (1995) maintains that identity is little more than a continuously reconstructed biography. Similar claims are made by Charles Taylor (1989) and Alasdair MacIntyre (1981), who equate our identities with our "unity of life", which is created by a coherent life story. In the same vein, Anthony Giddens (1991) maintains that a person's identity "is not to be found in behaviour … but in the capacity *to keep a particular narrative going*". This narrative cannot be "wholly fictive" but must draw on real-world events to create a "'story' about the self". Whereas for Erikson (1950) and Ricoeur (1995) self-narratives are a resource we frequently reshape to meet psychological and social needs, Giddens insists that autobiographies must be to some degree based on fact. He represents a tradition that extends back to Rousseau and his belief that individual uniqueness is rooted in diverse life experiences. But if our life narratives evolve a response to social cues and needs, it is difficult to maintain that they are either continuous or reality-based. This is also true for organizations and states, whose identities are equally unstable as their pasts are continually rewritten to accommodate present needs.

Unity of consciousness was invoked by Locke to justify the person, however psychological research indicates that nothing like it exists because memory is a highly selective, abstract recording, ordering and reordering of experiences. It misrepresents experience in three fundamental ways; we process only part of the stimuli received by our sense organs, remember only a fraction of those experiences, and only a sharply declining percentage of them over time. There are, moreover, distinct biases in what we remember, and we do not necessarily recall events accurately or in proper sequence. Research on all three kinds of memory highlights their subjective and labile character and leads prominent researchers to question the epistemological status of "original events". Derek Edwards and Jonathan Potter (1992) suggest that historical reality is not something out there that can be used to validate memories, but a mental configuration created by memories (see also Gergen, 1994). What we call identity is maintained through illusion and frequent updating of past memories.

The second assumption, of uniqueness, also finds little empirical support. The most compelling critique builds on the pioneering work of Maurice Halbwachs, a French sociologist and student of Durkheim, who, like his mentor, maintains that memory is socially constructed (Halbwachs, 1925). It is created through communications with other members of society. It is heavily stylized and reflects dominant discourses. It helps people find meaning in their lives and create bonds of solidarity with others. Collective memory and its ritualization form the core of communities (Durkheim, 2001). At the neurological level, our ability to store, recall and reconfigure verbal and nonverbal stimuli is mediated by patterns that we learn from our social and cultural environments (Schacter, 1965, 1969). So, too, are the language and narratives we use to describe memory and make it plausible and significant to others. Memory adapts itself to the conventions of the age. In the process, more general memories are typically simplified and condensed in their representation. Their detail is reduced and aspects emphasized that are more readily assimilated to widely used narrative schemes (Conway, 1992; Collins et al., 1993). The problem of recall aside, psychologists have discovered multiple "remembered selves", whose evocation depends on the nature of the trigger and the social milieu in which the person is situated at the time (Neisser and Fivush, 1994).

The third questionable assumption about identity is our ability to find our "true" selves. It was a goal of Rousseau and the Romantics. In the nineteenth century, it dominated European and American literature, the latter most notably in the writings of Emerson and Thoreau. It also underpins emancipatory projects. Perhaps most famously, it is central to the Marxist notion of "false consciousness", which assumes there is a true, class-based consciousness around which workers' identities must form. In the twentieth century, prominent psychiatrists took up the project of self-fashioning and reached a wide audience through best-selling books. Carl Jung (1928) called for individuals to assert themselves against society. Abraham Maslow (1954, 1968) popularized the concept of "self-actualization", which holds people responsible for discovering and developing their inner selves. There is a large literature on "authenticity" in philosophy and psychology that emphasizes the supposed self-shaping powers of the self and our potential to commit ourselves to value-based action. Its advocates claim Rousseau, Herder, Schiller, Kierkegaard and Sartre as their intellectual forebears (Ferrara, 1998; Vannini and Williams, 2009). Some insist that authenticity is more important than ever, given the "toxic levels of inauthenticity" that constantly barrage us in ads, emails and blogs (Gilmore and Pine, 2007: 43).

Socialization is undeniably imperfect, and leaves room for agency. Even strong social ontologists like Durkheim acknowledge its importance. This "flexibility", often attributable to the passions, is responsible for positive changes in society and pathologies like suicide (Durkheim, 1982). Agency, as Durkheim understands it, necessarily implies freedom, but not authenticity. There are also logical objections to self-actualization. If we can reshape our identity, we are no longer the same people we were previously and our continuity is questionable. Gradual changes in character and projects may not represent sharp ruptures but do bring about major transformations over time. The very possibility of transformation suggests some deeper layer of mind that inspires and helps us accomplish this change by overcoming the identifications fundamental to our current identity. If so, identity cannot represent our core essence. The existence of multiple identities points to the same conclusion. Some of our identifications are mutually supporting, but others are not, and all of them rise and fall in salience, depending on the context. The concept of a unitary identity requires something superordinate to our internal heterogeneity. In its absence, the struggle between or among competing identifications indicates that we are deeply divided beings.

Self-identifications

Rather than using a concept of identity that proposes the existence of a continuous, unique and "true" Self, analysts should focus on processes of identification, because what people think of as "identity" is really a composite of numerous self-identifications. We are multiple, fragmented and labile selves, at least some of which are in conflict. Self-identifications in turn are largely a function of our roles, affiliations and relationships with our bodies. This holds true for political units as well. States pioneer roles, or are assigned them by regional and international societies, such as great power, neutral, regional power, and so on. These political units have bodies in the double sense of population and territory; and they tell stories about themselves, generally flattering ones intended to support claims of distinctiveness and superiority.

Roles prescribe certain ways of behaving. Societies use them to sustain hierarchies and order the lives of their members. Roles in turn help define who we are, and all the more so when we internalize these identifications (Mead, 1962). Some roles are clearly defined, but many allow considerable leeway in their enactment. If not socially assigned, they must be socially validated. We cannot be recognized as fire fighters without some training and professional experience, and better yet, association with a fire department. Most institutions encourage members to develop positive emotional attachments, and some roles, like spouse, only function effectively when they develop. States also require recognition for the roles they fulfill. International relations is marked by the phenomenon of rising powers seeking recognition as great powers, and great powers seeking recognition as dominant powers or hegemons.

Affiliations to people, groups and institutions are another important source of self-identification (Tajfel and Turner, 1986). They are found at every level of social aggregation; people identify with partners, families, clans, social and professional groups, organizations, communities, religions, nations, regions and the human race. All affiliations are markers of selfhood and, like roles, achieve deeper meaning for actors when they are repeatedly enacted in practice. Affiliations can be independent of roles. People feel strong attachments to collectivities like sports teams, religions and ethnic groups, without those feelings being recognized, reciprocated or validated. However, roles also often generate affect. Strong attachments to roles, especially those with high status, or those that require time, intellectual resources, courage or emotional commitment to perform, significantly influence our understanding of ourselves. To the degree that roles generate positive affect, roles and affiliations become mutually reinforcing pillars of self-identification. Being the dominant power in the world has become important to many Americans as a source of self-esteem, just as it did in earlier eras for the French and the British. When dominant powers decline in relative power or standing, leaders and peoples can confront an "identity crisis". Arguably, the US currently confronts such a crisis (Reich and Lebow, 2014).

The third source of self-identifications is the relationship we develop to bodies (Seigel, 2005). Science fiction stories aside, we cannot live without bodies, and those we possess shape our identities in the most fundamental ways as they determine our gender and physical and mental capabilities and handicaps. These features shape how others see and respond to us, and thus how we understand ourselves. Tensions develop when people develop different relationships with our bodies that others expect or mandate. While we may speak about the 'body politic', states bodies are often more problematic because of internal political and ethnic divisions and territorial irredenta. Nationalists invoke the language of the body when they talk about "making the state whole" by incorporating land they claim and feel attached to. People may also identify with individuals whose bodies they see as representing the state, reflected in political leaders' concern about their physical appearance.

Affiliations, roles and bodies account for most of the selfhood we feel, conceived as the sum of our self-identifications, and they do much of the analytical work for which the concept of identity is mobilized. And unlike the concept of identity, they are useful in explaining, possibly even predicting, behavior. They have the additional advantage of lending themselves to definition and measurement in ways identity does not. Importantly, they can also be reinforcing or in conflict. We are sometimes forced to choose between or among roles or affiliations, but just as often we learn to negotiate the tensions and conflicting responsibilities they generate. As our affiliations and roles change, as does their practice, self-understandings also evolve. One way we cope with this fluidity is by the construction of retrospective narratives that minimize change and inconsistency and create a false, but useful, sense of ontological security.

Social versus Self-Construction

Thinkers have always attributed individual identity to both socialization and self-fashioning, but they disagree about the relative strength of the two processes. British liberals like Boswell, Hume and Mill give precedence to self-fashioning. They regard the tension between society and individuals as productive; society offers role models, allowing people to emulate them or mix and match the qualities of different people to fashion new selves. Society and individuals evolve in a parallel and reciprocal process. Continental romantics and their postmodernist successors condemn society as corrupting and totalizing; it coerces people into assuming pre-determined identities and renders the prospect of self-fashioning all but illusory. Marx, Weber, Mead and Foucault stress the social determinants of identity and characterize society as a steel cage and source of discipline. The literature in social psychology acknowledges some prospect of self-fashioning, but on the whole emphasizes the social construction of identity.

I contend that the reality of identity construction is somewhere between these extremes, although just where varies considerably across societies and within them. It is an empirical question, not a theoretical assumption, and thus is subject to research. Perhaps the most insightful attempt to explore the possibilities and limits of self-fashioning is the work of the nineteenth-century American pragmatist philosopher George Herbert Mead. He conceives of the self as the organization by the individual of a set of attitudes toward its social environment and itself. These attitudes are generated by imagining what it would be like to perform the roles of others and regarding oneself from their perspective. To build this understanding, a person must have considerable social experience; experience and reflections on it are the core of the self. Reflection for Mead is also a source of freedom and spontaneity. Reflections builds the "I", which is the source of attempted self-fashioning. Toward this end, we require a general, rather than a purely personal, perspective on society. In evaluating our performance, as say partner or parent, we must view ourselves from the vantage point of the partnership or family. The "I" can be severely constrained when people are exposed to, and possibly assimilate, a strongly negative "Me" from their society (Mead, 1962: 174–8). Research indicates that negative stereotypes can cause inner tension, low esteem and low achievement (Heatherton, 2000).

For individuals, the construction of selves is a social and personal process. For states, it is political. States have no "I" or reflexive self. They lack the kind of internal agency people have, as they are institutions or, more properly speaking, assemblages of them. To the extent that power is diffused through the system, as it most certainly is in democratic and federal states, there is no conscious center able to develop its own identification and resist, assimilate or reformulate those imposed from the outside. States are not passive as officials everywhere produce or encourage the narratives that support identities consistent with their political, and often psychological, goals. However, there are often multiple and conflicting official narratives that have been sponsored by different governments, or groups and institutions within the same government. The state might be analogized to a refrigerator on which family members use small magnets to attach snapshots, postcards, lists, notes and other objects. By doing so, they personalize the appliance and make it reflect their interests, needs, commitments and hopes. The refrigerator has no say in the matter. Many families have refrigerators with large enough doors to accommodate many different magnetized objects. By this means, the family refrigerator receives an identity, really multiple identities, as there is rarely anything coherent or consistent about this process. There may be some controversy within families about what goes on the fridge. In states, this process is much more conflicted because it has more serious purposes and consequences and many more actors are attempting to stick identifications on the body politick. States do have self-identifications, but these identifications are imposed from inside and outside the state. Much of politics consists of efforts to propagate these identifications and embed them in collective memory.

National Identities: Three Tensions

While individual and state autonomy are parallel projects, we must be careful in the analogies we draw between them. As noted above, states are not persons and have neither emotions nor psychological needs. Their leaders and citizens do. They attempt to impose identities on states to foster instrumental goals and psychological needs. Mead's formulation of identity does not capture this process because there is no state "I" to step back, reflect on these identifications, modify or resist them and attempt to engage in self-fashioning. States are composed of multiple institutions that perform diverse functions and are related to one another in complicated ways. These institutions and their leaders and bureaucracies are likely to have different self-identifications, or different hierarchies of them. National leaders may attempt to order these preferences, but rarely succeed in doing so effectively. State identities are accordingly more varied, local and conflictual than their individual counterparts.

With individuals, we can properly use the term "self-identifications" because many, if not most, of these identifications are accepted by or originate with them. People are unhappy about negative attributions and stereotypes that others make or foist on them. In the case of states, it is political leaders and citizens who accept or reject the attributions made by others. This difference is critical for identity formation and its consequences at the national level. At the domestic level, numerous actors attempt to impose identifications on their state. At the international level, where states interact with one another and with other members of international society, the distinction between them and individuals is at least partially blurred. If we treat states as units, they have identifications that are in part self-chosen in the sense that they are created from within. Other identifications are external and originate with other actors or are negotiated by states. National leaders exercise some choice regarding state identifications, but this does not make states persons, and it is important to acknowledge this difference and its consequences.

The formulation of national identities is characterized by three tensions. The first is that between socially imposed and internally generated identifications. It is more pronounced for states because their identity construction takes place at multiple levels. At the sub-state level, diverse actors devise and attempt to impose identifications on their states. At the state level, officials do the same, and there are not infrequently conflicts among them about the nature and importance of these identifications. At the international level, other states and actors enter this process. Consider, for example, efforts by Japan's neighbors to push it into acknowledging and apologizing in a meaningful way for the crimes it committed in the Second World War. Symbolic gestures of this kind and changes in school textbooks would encourage Japanese to think of themselves and their nation differently (Dower, 2012).

A second tension concerns similarity and difference. As noted, our self-identifications derive largely from our roles, affiliations and relationship to our bodies. We identify with those who perform the same roles, share the same kinds of affiliation and relate to their body in the same ways. And yet, identity formation has long been conceived of in terms of separation and distinction from others. It is commonly thought to require, or at least be assisted by, the negative stereotypes of those from whom we are differentiating ourselves. Research in social and child psychology calls this assumption into question. Contrary to the assertions of social identity theory, negative stereotypes in international as well as inter-personal relations appear to be something of a special case, most often arising when groups compete for the same scarce resources (Lebow, 2012: Chs 3 and 8). Much more commonly, identifications of self and other develop through a combination of similarity and difference, by drawing closer to those from whom we are separating in a dialogical process.

This is most evident in the case of countries that were once conjoined: Belgium–Holland, Norway–Sweden and the Czech Republic–Slovakia are cases in point. Although the breakup of Yugoslavia involved much violence, its successor states may in due course develop more intense and positive relationships that facilitate national stability and identity. This has been the case for ex-colonies and their former metropole, including the US, Ireland, India and the UK, the successor states of Austria–Hungary, and many of the countries of Latin America and Spain. The postcolonial identities of former metropoles were in turn shaped in part by their relations with their former dependencies. So, too, were these identities very much affected, if not shaped, by their interactions with their colonies in the age of empire (Clark, 2005: 35; Keene, 2002). The dialectic of distancing and drawing closer is usually a complicated non-linear process, often characterized by initial hostility, followed by periods of partial rapprochement, and possibly by additional irruptions of hostility, or at least strained relations. Anglo-American relations are a case in point. To some degree, post-independence conflicts between these countries arose from substantive issues. They were also connected to identity issues, and were only resolved when both, but especially the Americans, were able to recognize what they shared in common without feeling that this somehow lessened or devalued them or their independence.

The third tension arises from the multiple identifications that constitute our sense of self. Here, too, there is a double dynamic at work. The more roles we perform, the more likely we are to feel cross-pressured because of their different, even competing, commitments and behavioral expectations. We are frequently pulled in opposite directions by social requirements and personal preferences, and by different roles established for ourselves in different relationships. States are not reflexive and cannot become alienated from themselves, but policymakers confront this dilemma when domestic identifications require them to respond in a manner at odds with personal preferences or foreign policy needs. For instance, US President Lyndon Johnson had a gut feeling that large-scale military intervention in Vietnam would not achieve its intended goal, but did not feel confident enough in his command of foreign policy to resist the nearly uniform pleas of his advisors to commit to the policy.[1] President Obama appears to have had similar misgivings about Afghanistan (Shanker, 2014).

The three tensions outlined above cut across sub-national, national and international levels of society. And through these tensions, assemblages of self-identification are created, challenged and changed. Analyses of identity politics must deal with the reality that states have multiple selves stemming from multiple identifications, which evolve, rise and fall in importance over time. To some extent, this evolution is a product of behavior as people tend to remake their understandings of themselves – and their states – to make them consistent with their behavior (Bem, 1972). Behavior at odds with a particular self-image can change conceptions of state and self. Consider the transformation of the US from an isolationist power into a self-proclaimed hegemon and the ways in which discourses developed to justify this transition (Reich and Lebow, 2014: Chs 1 and 3). At the end of the Cold War, there was a lively debate over America's role in the world. Neoconservatives described the US as an empire and urged Americans to recognize this "reality" and act accordingly. Liberals rejected this characterization as empirically unwarranted and ethically offensive (Ferguson, 2009; Kagan, 2003; Nexon and Wright, 2007). The neoconservative depiction of America's role in the world was not entirely inaccurate in the light of how Washington behaved toward less powerful states, especially in Latin America. It sought to bring into harmony self-definition and practice by defining the country in a way that justified the unilateral and unrestrained use of force against other states and political groups. Liberal objections represented an attempt to defend a more benign characterization of national identity and use it to restrain imperial practices.

---

[1] Personal communication from McGeorge Bundy, New York City, 24 April 1992.

At any given moment, a state's "identity" is an uneasy composite of multiple, sometimes nested and often competing identifications, each of which is associated with one or more narratives. Individuals possess a phenomenological self, which allows them to adjudicate among their multiple self-identifications and attempt to reconcile them, even if these reconciliations are often more illusory than real. States find this more difficult to do, although those who control the government attempt to do it through the vehicle of official discourse. Orwell's *1984* and Stalin's Soviet Union provide graphic examples of how this is done. We may consider such action as a reprehensible exercise of power, yet it parallels the process which occurs within our psyches, where phenomenological selves rewrite the past and repress memories of inconvenient persons, events, beliefs and self-identifications. To the extent that we find totalitarian efforts at identity construction abhorrent, we ought to develop a greater commitment to monitor and control them, and to stress the political and ethical benefits of greater acceptance of the fragmented, conflicting and labile nature of our self-identifications (Lebow, 2012: Ch. 8).

Conclusion

Ted Hopf (1998) warns that a world without identities would be one of "chaos, a world of pervasive and irremediable uncertainty, a world much more dangerous than anarchy". His fear reflects the widespread, but questionable, belief that identities are anchors for individuals and social collectivities and that without them they would be cast adrift. Only with a clear identity, so the assumption goes, are we able to act, as individuals or collectives. Sociologist Anthony Giddens and political philosophers Leo Strauss, Alasdair MacIntyre and Charles Taylor propagate similar understandings of identity, as do many IR scholars focusing on the concept of ontological security. Yet the relationship between behavior and identity is a complex one. Self-identifications, based on affiliations, roles and our relationship to bodies, are only one of many factors that determine how we behave and what we consider ethical, appropriate or obligatory. Different self-identifications generate different, sometimes conflicting, ethical imperatives or policy directives; they rise and fall in importance as a function of context and timing. Self-identifications are neither a source of unity and continuity nor a steady ethical and behavioral compass. If they provide ethical or policy guidance, it is of the most arbitrary kind.

The problems we encounter when taking a closer look at the concept of identity point to a more fundamental problem noted by Max Weber (1968): As soon as we attempt to reflect about the way in which life confronts us in immediate concrete situations, it presents an infinite multiplicity of successively and coexistently emerging and disappearing events. The social world is not naturally divided into categories whose members can be considered comparable in all meaningful ways. It is neither lawful nor rational; it is rendered this way – in appearance only – by our own transcendental faculties (Lebow, 2014: Ch. 1). Conceptualization and causal inference in the social world, including assumptions about "identities" and what they "do", are pure reification. They do not ultimately capture anything that could be described as real. We must construct and choose among them on the basis of their utility. Identity as an analytical concept is difficult to defend by this metric, so long as our purpose is to understand social and political behavior. If anything, this chapter affirms that concepts do much more than provide frameworks for research; they provide justifications for political and psychological projects and paradigms. This is unavoidable but it should make alarm bells go off in the heads of students and scholars. Before using concepts, we must consider the context in which they were created and mobilized and the projects for which they are being used. Good scholarship requires awareness and sensitivity to the interactions between concept and context and recognizes the subjective nature of our research and findings, and its ethical implications. This is particularly important for an existential label like "identity".

Suggested Readings

Brubaker, R. and Cooper, F. (2000) 'Beyond "Identity"', *Theory and Society*, 29 (1): 1–37.
This article offers a recognized epistemological and political critique of the concept of identity.

Gallagher, S. (ed.) (2011) *The Oxford Handbook of The Self*. Oxford: Oxford University Press.
This is the best overview of the concept of identity from a philosophical perspective.

Lebow, R. N. (2012) *The Politics and Ethics of Identity: In Search of Ourselves*. Cambridge: Cambridge University Press.
This text draws on psychology, philosophy and literature to explain why identity became important in the modern era and describes four generic identity projects.

Lebow, R. N. (2016) *National Identifications and International Relations*. Cambridge: Cambridge University Press.
A study of the role of national identifications and a critique of current constructivist understandings of identity.

Neisser, U. and Fivush, R. (1994) *The Remembering Self: Construction and Accuracy in the Self Narrative*. Cambridge: Cambridge University Press.
This is the most sophisticated use of psychological research to show the unreliability of memory and the way it serves our social and psychological needs.

Seigel, J. (2005) *The Idea of the Self: Thought and Experience in Western Europe since the Seventeenth Century*. Cambridge: Cambridge University Press.
This is the best account of the history of the self in philosophy.

Bibliography

Abdelal, R., Herrera, Y. M., Johnston, A. I. and McDermott, R. (2009) *Measuring Identity: A Guide for Social Scientists*. Cambridge: Cambridge University Press.
Aquinas, T. (2002) *Summa Theologica*. Trans. Richard J. Regan. Indianapolis, IN: Hackett.
Augustine of Hippo (1950) *City of God*. Trans. Marcus Dods. New York: Modern Library.
Badie, B. (2014) *Temps des Humiliès: Pathologie des Relations Internationales*. Paris: Odile Jacob.
Bem, D. J. (1972) '"Self-Perception" and "Self-Perception Theory"', in Berkowitz, L. (ed.), *Advances in Experimental Social Psychology*. New York: Academic Press. pp. 1–62.
Berenskoetter, F. (2010) 'Identity in International Relations', in Robert A. Denemark, *The International Studies Encyclopedia*, IV. New York: Wiley-Blackwell, pp. 3595–3611.
Brubaker, R. and Cooper, F. (2000) 'Beyond "Identity"', *Theory and Society*, 29 (1): 1–37.

Bush, G. W. (2007) Transcript of President Bush's Address to the Nation on US Policy in Iraq, 11 January, www.nytimes.com/2007/01/11/us/11ptext.html?pagewanted=all
Clark, I. (2005) *Legitimacy in International Society*. Oxford: Oxford University Press.
Collins, A. E., Gathercole, S. E., Conway, M. A. and Morris, P. E. M. (eds) (1993) *Theories of Memory*. Hillsdale, NJ: Lawrence Erlbaum.
Conway, M. (ed.) (1992) *Theoretical Perspectives on Autobiographical Memory.* Dordrecht: Kluwer.
Daalder, I. and Lindsay, J. (2007) 'Democracies of the World, Unite', *The-American-Interest.com*, Jan.–Feb.
Dower, J. (2012) *Ways of Forgetting, Ways of Remembering: Japan in the Modern World.* New York: The New Press.
Durkheim, E. (1982) *Rules of Sociological Method.* Ed. Steven Lukes, trans. W. D. Halls. New York: Free Press.
Durkheim, E. (2001) *Elementary Forms of the Religious Life.* Trans. Carol Cosman. Oxford: Oxford University Press.
Edwards, D. and Potter, J. (1992) 'The Chancellor's Memory: Rhetoric and Truth in Discursive Remembering', *Applied Cognitive Psychology*, 6: 187–215.
Erikson, E. H. (1950) *Childhood and Society*. New York: Norton.
Erikson, E. H. (1959) *Identity and the Life Cycle*, Vol. 1. New York: Norton.
Ferguson, N. (2009) *Colossus: Rise and Fall of American Empire*. New York: Penguin.
Ferrara, A. (1998) *Reflective Authenticity*. London: Routledge.
Gallagher, S. (ed.) (2011) *The Oxford Handbook of the Self.* Oxford: Oxford University Press.
Geertz, C. (1983) '"From the Native's Point of View": On the Nature of Anthropological Understanding', in *Local Knowledge: Further Essays in Interpretive Anthropology.* New York: Basic Books, pp. 55–70.
Gergen, K. (1994) 'Mind, Text, and Society: Self-Memory in Social Context', in U. Neisser and R. Fivush (eds) *The Remembering Self: Construction and Accuracy in the Self Narrative.* Cambridge: Cambridge University Press, pp. 78–103.
Giddens, A. (1991) *Modernity and Self-Identity: Self and Society in the Late Modern Age.* Cambridge: Polity Press.
Gilmore J. and Pine, J. (2007) *Authenticity: What Consumers Really Want.* Cambridge: Harvard Business School Press.
Guzzini, S. (2012) *Return of Geopolitics in Europe?* Cambridge: Cambridge University Press.
Halbwachs, M. (1925) *Les Cadres sociaux de la memoire*. Paris: Alcan.
Heatherton, T. F. (ed.) (2000) *Social Psychology of Stigma*. New York: Guilford.
Herder, J. G. (1969) *Herder on Social and Political Culture*. Trans. F. M. Barnard. Cambridge: Cambridge University Press.
Hopf, T. (1998) 'The Promise of Constructivism in International Politics', *International Security*, 23: 171–200.
Hume, D. (1998) *An Inquiry Concerning the Principles of Morals*. New York: Oxford University Press.
Hume, D. (1999) *An Enquiry Concerning Human Understanding*, ed. Tom L. Beauchamp. Oxford: Oxford University Press.
Hume, D. (2000) *Treatise of Human Nature*, David Fate Norton and Mary Norton, eds. Oxford: Oxford University Press.
Ikenberry, G. J. and Slaughter, A.-M. (2006) *Forging a World of Liberty Under Law: US National Security in the 21st Century*. Princeton, NJ: Princeton University Press.
Jung, C. G. ([1928] 1971) 'The Spiritual Problem of Modern Man', in Joseph Campbell, ed. *The Portable Jung*. New York: Viking, pp. 456–79.
Kagan, D. (2003) *Of Paradise and Power*. New York: Knopf.

Kant, I. (1998) *Critique of Pure Reason*. Trans. Paul Guyer and Allen W. Wood. Cambridge: Cambridge University Press.

Keene, E. (2002) *Beyond the Anarchical Society: Grotius, Colonialism and Order in World Politics*. Cambridge: Cambridge University Press.

Lebow, R. N. (2012) *The Politics and Ethics of Identity: In Search of Ourselves*. Cambridge: Cambridge University Press.

Lebow, R. N. (2014) *Constructing Cause in International Relations*. Cambridge: Cambridge University Press.

Lebow, R. N. (2016) *National Identifications and International Relations*. Cambridge: Cambridge University Press.

Locke, J. (1975) *An Essay Concerning Human Understanding*. Oxford: Oxford University Press.

MacIntyre, A. (1981) *After Virtue: A Study in Moral Theory*. Notre Dame, IN: University of Notre Dame Press.

Maslow, A. H. (1954) *Motivation and Personality*. New York: Harper & Row.

Maslow, A. H. (1968) *Toward a Psychology of Being*. New York: Van Nostrand.

Mead, G. H. (1962) *Mind, Self and Society*. Chicago: University of Chicago Press.

Neisser, U. and Fivush, R. (1994) *The Remembering Self: Construction and Accuracy in the Self Narrative*. Cambridge: Cambridge University Press.

Nexon, D. and Wright, T. (2007) 'What's at Stake in the American Empire Debate?', *American Political Science Review*, 2: 253–71.

Reich, S. and Lebow, R. N. (2014) *Good-Bye Hegemony! Power and Influence in the Global System*. Princeton, NJ: Princeton University Press.

Ricoeur, P. (1995) 'Narrative Identity', *Philosophy Today*, 35 (1): 73–102.

Rousseau, J.-J. (1964) *The First and Second Discourses*. Trans. Roger Masters. New York: St. Martin's Press.

Schacter, D. (1965) *Searching for Memory: The Brain, the Mind and the Past*. New York: Basic Books.

Schacter, D. (1969) *Cognitive Neuropsychology of False Memory*. New York: Psychology Press.

Seigel, J. (2005) *Idea of the Self: Thought and Experience in Western Europe since the Seventeenth Century*. Cambridge: Cambridge University Press.

Shanker, T. (2014) 'Obama Lost Faith in Afghan Strategy, Book Asserts', *New York Times*, 8 January. Available at: www.nytimes.com/2014/01/08/world/asia/obama-lost-faith-in-his-afghan-strategy-memoir-asserts.html?hp

Tajfel, H. and Turner, J. (1986) 'The Social Identity Theory of Intergroup Behavior', in S. Worchel and W. Austin (eds), *Psychology of Intergroup Relations*. Chicago: Nelson-Hall, pp. 7–24.

Taylor, C. (1989) *Sources of the Self: The Making of Modern Identity*. Cambridge, MA: Harvard University Press.

Vannini, P. and Williams, J. P. (2009) *Authenticity in Culture, Self, and Society*. Padstow: Ashgate.

Wahrman, C. (2004) *Making of the Modern Self: Identity and Culture in Eighteenth-Century England*. New Haven, CT: Yale University Press.

Weber, M. (1949) '"Objectivity" in Social Science and Social Policy', in E. A. Shils and H. E. Finch (eds), *Max Weber: The Methodology of the Social Sciences*. New York: Free Press.

Weber, M. (1968) 'Objektivität', in M. Weber, *Gesammelte Aufsätze zur Wissenschaftslehre*, 3rd ed. (ed. Johannes Winckelmann). Tübingen: J. C. B. Mohr (Paul Siebeck, pp. 170–72.

Zarakol, A. (2011) *After Defeat: How the East Learned to Live with the West*. Cambridge: Cambridge University Press.

Conditions

6
War

Antoine Bousquet

No phenomenon is arguably more central to the study of international relations (IR) than war. The history of armed conflict is deeply intertwined with the formation of virtually every nation-state and it was the very superiority of the modern territorial polity's mobilization of the war machine that ensured its historical dominance over other types of units. The exercise of armed force is still viewed today by states as their singular prerogative and the greatest calling they can make on their populations and, as realist scholars keep reminding us, the ever-present possibility of war always lurks in the background of international relations. Yet for all its centrality, the concept of war itself was until relatively recently rarely submitted to sustained scrutiny within IR scholarship. This is a paradox given the importance accorded to war within the modern academic discipline of IR at its foundation. Back then, figures such as E. H. Carr (2001) and Hans Morgenthau (1948) insisted on a clear-eyed recognition of the inherent propensity of states to employ bellicose means to further their interests as the surest way to avert, or at least mitigate, the evils of war. The original emphasis on war is hardly surprising given that the field established itself in the shadow of two world wars and a tense confrontation between American and Soviet superpowers. But it is precisely the weight of these historical conditions that gave scholars little reason to probe the concept of war in any great depth, so self-evident did it appear to them that it primarily referred to the kind of large-scale inter-state conflict that had so dominated recent world affairs.

Today we can scarcely hold to such certainties any longer. While inter-state war may not have disappeared, its overall occurrence has been much reduced and a direct confrontation between major powers appears improbable for the foreseeable future. In its place has burgeoned a multiplicity of armed conflicts ever more difficult to reconcile with the classical coordinates of war that informed both state policy and early IR scholarship. Commentators have proliferated the number of prefixes attached to the term of "war" in an attempt to capture its proteiform manifestations, a non-exhaustive list which would contain "nontrinitarian war" (Van Creveld 1991), "postmodern war" (Gray 1997), "new war" (Kaldor 1999), "netwar" (Arquilla and Ronfeldt 2001), "asymmetric war" (Thornton 2007), "chaoplexic war" (Bousquet 2008) and "hybrid war" (Hoffman 2009). Simultaneously, the rhetorical invocation of war in public discourse is more ubiquitous than ever, brandished whenever a heightened state of urgency or threat needs to be conveyed. Campaigners and political leaders have declared wars on poverty, disease, crime, drugs and any social blight deemed to require domestic or international mobilization. Political discourse is likewise replete with high-pitched accusations of wars being waged on women, working families, religious freedom or Christmas, implying a wanton attack on cherished values in need of robust defence. While these metaphorical references do little to clarify the concept of war, they do however reveal the enduring hold that its idea exerts on our collective imaginaries.

It is therefore all the more striking that states have concurrently largely disavowed the unilateral pursuit of war as a legitimate act of sovereign power and are today more likely to refer to their employments of military force as collective self-defence, counter-insurgency, humanitarian intervention or stability operations. Even the so-called "war on terror" that has defined world politics in the early twenty-first century and mandated the engagement of armed forces across the globe has not involved a single formal declaration of war of the kind that were a regular feature of international intercourse in the nineteenth century, nor does it appear to have any definable end-point that would bring it to a close. The terminology of the "war on terror" was eventually disowned by the Obama administration after 2008, preferring to it that of "overseas contingency operations", a label that downplays the conflict's military character while only further highlighting its open-endedness. If the rhetoric of war is still a powerful means of denoting a heightened state of collective life, it has visibly waned as a juridico-political category that was for so long central to the exercise of international politics. This is probably less an indication that war per se "has almost ceased to exist" (Mueller 2009) than of the twilight of a specific framing and apportioning of political violence that gave war its particular meaning within the modern state system.

This chapter will first consider the task of providing a formal definition of war that might pare down the phenomenon to its essential traits, thereby underlining the inherent limitations of any purely abstract conceptualization. In a second step, it will examine the specific conception of war that emerged alongside the Westphalian international order and informed the practice of armed conflict between states for several centuries. Despite its predominance, this state-centric bounding of war has not been without historical tensions and challenges that the chapter will then turn to. Finally, it will consider the present, and perhaps terminal, crisis of the Westphalian understanding of war in the face of the complex contemporary manifestations of armed conflict.

Conceptualizing War

While it is possible to devise a social scientific definition of war as organized violence perpetrated for political ends, such a conception remains decidedly broad and indeterminate until it is related back to the specific usages and meanings invested in it within the sociocultural practices of armed conflict. Central to these practices are the delineations and attendant legitimations that draw distinctions between various manifestations of political violence and set the parameters of conduct of the activity referred to as war. Or, as Michael Walzer puts it:

> War is not usefully described as an act of force without some specification of the context in which the act takes place and from which it derives its meaning [...] the social and historical conditions that "modify" war are not to be considered as accidental or external to war itself, for war is a social creation [...] What is war and what is not-war is in fact something that people decide. (2006: 24)

The conceptualization of war is thus inevitably intertwined with its own practice and enmeshed within a wider constellation of significations and material forces. It is therefore necessary for us to pay particular attention to the specific institutionalization of war as a regulated means of punctuated intercourse between sovereign peers that was historically realized under the Westphalian state system, since it is that to which we still owe our dominant mental conceptions of armed conflict. Only then can we grasp the ways in which new expressions of organized violence have rendered this conventional understanding of war increasingly untenable, opening up its concept to renewed intellectual scrutiny.

When looking for a definition of war, IR scholars have long been tempted to adopt the one proposed by David Singer and Mel Small (1972) for the purpose of cataloguing its historical occurrence. The Correlates of War (COW) database sets a threshold of 1,000 battle-related deaths within a 12-month period for a sustained conflict involving organized armed forces to qualify for inclusion as a war. A further typology of wars (inter-state, extra-state, intra-state, non-state) is then overlaid on the basis of the nature of the belligerents. COW and other databases such as that of UCDP/PRIO are frequently referred to in IR literature to support arguments about general trends in the manifestation of war and, notwithstanding the pitfalls involved in handling military statistics of often dubious reliability, it would be unwarranted to deny them any empirical value. More problematic is the manner in which the chosen definitions of war are primarily dictated by the twin imperatives of populating the databases while broadly conforming to prevailing common-sense identifications of conflict. The inclusion of the 1982 Falklands War within the COW database, despite its fatality count falling short of the required threshold, is illustrative of the fact that the boundaries of the empirical phenomena under study are rather less scientific than its proponents would like us to think. A rigorous interrogation of the concept of war must therefore pass through a much more fundamental inspection of its elementary features and tendencies.

Hedley Bull's definition of war as "organized violence carried on by political units against each other" (2002: 178) remains a popular starting point for many discussions of armed conflict in international affairs. Although it does not provide a definition of violence, a philosophically contested category in itself (Thomas 2011), Bull's formula does usefully highlight the organized and political qualities it manifests in the activity of war. War is purposefully waged by and in the name of social groups against other groups as a means of settling disputes or competing claims between them. As such, it is a collective endeavour submitted to the prevailing rules and customs that govern the use of force within a given group. So while it may plausibly be argued that war draws on an innate human propensity, or at least potentiality, for aggression, it nevertheless constitutes a particular form of violence that is both socialized and culturally imbued with significance. For one, it represents a particular institutionalization and codification of violence that rationalizes and even mandates acts that inflict death and injury on members of another collective which are otherwise prohibited or severely circumscribed. And if war necessarily entails the cessation or curtailment of other modes of interaction between political groupings such as trade or diplomacy, its conduct also still frequently obeys certain conventions and norms shared by the belligerents.

If organized violence is to be a necessary constituent of war, it may follow, as Barkawi and Brighton have suggested, that fighting is "the basic element of the ontology of war" (2011: 136). To be sure, the invocation of war first brings to mind scenes of large-scale combat pitting opposing armies against each other. A war that did not involve any violent struggle would hardly seem to merit the label other than as a loose metaphor. And yet it must be that war cannot be reduced to the strict temporality of the battle but also covers a wider condition of hostility that includes the actions of preparation, observation and manoeuvre that separate actual clashes of arms. The attribution of such a "state of war" can be readily applied to the period bookended by official declarations of the opening and cessation of hostilities that states have traditionally engaged in, but becomes more fraught where such usages have lapsed and deeply problematic when considering such phenomena as the Cold War or the War on Terror.

Some observers have gone on to propose that, insofar as polities maintain a persistent military capability and exhibit a readiness, however reluctant, to engage in armed conflict, there exists between them an ever-present condition of latent war. Indeed, this was already Thomas Hobbes' judgement in the seventeenth century:

> In all times, Kings, and Persons of Soveraigne authority, because of their Independency, are in continuall jealousies, and in the state and posture of Gladiators, having their weapons pointing, and their eyes fixed on one another; that is, their Forts, Garrisons, and Guns upon the Frontiers of their Kingdomes, and continual Spyes upon their neighbours, which is a posture of War. (1986: 18)

This contention has famously been embraced by the realist school in international relations, with its insistence on the anarchical nature of international relations and innate disposition of states to resort to force to either enhance their standing or simply ensure their survival. In his well-known inquiry into the causes of war, Kenneth Waltz (2001: 238) would conclude that "war will be perpetually associated with the existence of separate sovereign states" since "force is a means of achieving the external ends of states" in the absence of a "consistent, reliable process of reconciling the conflicts of interest that inevitably arise among similar units in a condition of anarchy".

War in this view is entirely understood in terms of an instrumental action undertaken by states for the purpose of attaining their political goals, be they of aggrandizement or mere survival. Such a conception would appear to find support from the nineteenth-century military theorist Carl von Clausewitz in the form of his much-cited dictum according to which "war is merely the continuation of policy by other means" (1989: 87). As a political instrument available to state leaders alongside the other tools of their craft, war is hence likely to be employed when and only insofar as it appears suited to achieve specific political objectives. As soon as the costs of its use appear too great relative to the gains that it might be expected to deliver, it will be forsaken. The appeal of such a conception to policy-makers and analysts of international affairs is evident. Indeed, an entire field of academic study was founded on this very premise under the name of strategic studies, predominantly concerned with a practically oriented knowledge of military affairs that could best inform and guide the decisions of military officers and political leaders. By tethering it to a rational means–end calculus, war is made intelligible, limited and largely predictable. And to a degree it can be said to yield real explanatory value. States do go to war for deliberate purposes, estimating that their interests are thereby best served. However, by taking the above maxim in isolation from the rest of his writings, we risk ignoring the full richness of Clausewitz's thinking on the matter, which reveals a much more sophisticated handle on the phenomenon of war that deeply problematizes and constrains any purely instrumental conception of it, while simultaneously establishing both the benefits and limits of any purely abstract theorization of war.

For one, Clausewitz never intended his dictum to be a purely descriptive statement to which all wars would perfectly conform. He insisted just as much on its prescriptive character – that wise statesmanship would consist in according military efforts with that which could be gained through them. That war might exceed the designs of policy-makers had however more to do with the very nature of war itself. In his efforts to conceptualize war, Clausewitz was careful to distinguish between what he referred to as the "absolute" and "real" forms of war. The former conception was derived from a purely logical and abstract deduction of war as a clash of wills striving to impose themselves on each other. Clausewitz submitted that such a struggle would, in principle, escalate in intensity and commitment through the reciprocal actions of the respective parties until the complete disarming, if not annihilation, of one side by the other: "War is an act of force, and there is no logical limit to the application of that force. Each side, therefore, compels its opponent to follow suit; a reciprocal action is started which must lead, in theory, to extremes" (1989: 77). In such a conflict, the belligerents might well have initiated the war with limited political goals, but these would eventually be entirely subsumed by the demands of an all-encompassing struggle to the death.

Yet Clausewitz observed that, much as this logic of escalation was an inherent tendency to the phenomenon of war, in practice absolute war was never attained (although he believed it had been most closely approached in his own lifetime during the Napoleonic wars). Because war is "never an isolated act", abstracted from its particular historical and political context, that it "does not consist of a single short blow" which would definitively decide the outcome, and that it never yields a "final result" that forever precludes a future reversal of fortune for the defeated side (1989: 78–80), "real" war necessarily falls short of its ideal conception. It is thus precisely because concrete conflicts fall short of the abstract and logical concept of war that the "political object" is allowed to govern the conduct of the conflict throughout, determining military objectives and the amount of effort to be expended on their achievement. If we appear here to be back to the original dictum of war as the continuation of policy, the conditions laid out for it by Clausewitz now inherently restrict its applicability. The political instrumentality of war and the rational calculations imposed on the employment of forces are always liable to be undercut by both the elemental passions of sheer enmity and the inescapable role of chance attached to any military action. The intrinsic unpredictability of war acts as a persistent constraint on the political designs of its would-be masters who neglect these uncertainties at their own peril. As Clausewitz sums it up:

> War, therefore, is an act of policy. Were it a complete, untrammeled, absolute manifestation of violence (as the pure concept would require), war would of its own independent will usurp the place of policy the moment policy had brought it into being; it would then drive policy out of office and rule by the laws of its own nature ... In reality war, as has been shown, is not like that. Its violence is not of the kind that explodes in a single discharge ... War moves on its goal with varying speeds; but it always lasts long enough for influence to be exerted on the goal and for its own course to be changed in one way or another ... Policy, then, will permeate all military operations, and, in so far as their violent nature will admit, it will have a continuous influence on them. (1989: 87)

In carefully distinguishing between the "pure" concept of war and its actual realization in the world, Clausewitz opens up a space within which is articulated the complex and uneasy interplay of politics and organized violence, a relationship that threatens to collapse altogether as war approaches the plenitude of its ideal form. While Clausewitz determined that the absolute form of war could never be attained in reality, it has appeared dangerously approximated by the all-out thermo-nuclear war threatened during the Cold War. If good fortune played its part in averting its outbreak, political leaders were also forced to recognize the impossibility of reconciling the prospect of mutual annihilation with rational statecraft. It is this concern with nuclear apocalypse that prompted President Eisenhower (1956) to declare that "war in our time has become an anachronism".

So, although it is possible to approach war in the abstract as a logical concept outside of space and time, the phenomenon of war also has to be apprehended in the concrete and always particular historical circumstances of its individual manifestations. Any purely formal conceptualization of war will be of limited empirical purchase unless it is attentive to the wider contextual frames that permeate its conduct. Indeed, the societies that wage armed conflict at any given time do so by reference to their own conceptualizations of war, not least through their delineation and regulation of the violent practices permitted within it. The concept of war will hence be from here on addressed as a social and historical construct that hinges on particular understandings of the functions of violence and status of the actors engaged in it. Whereas realist observers are wont to treat the dominant characteristics of war in the modern era as givens, reflecting a fundamental and largely fixed feature of international relations, the following sections will seek to provide an account of the constitution and development of the normative Westphalian model that defined war in Europe and beyond for several centuries, but which now appears increasingly ill-suited to manifestations of organized violence in the twenty-first century.

The Westphalian Institution of War

Notwithstanding the extremities to which it may tend, the practice of war can be thought of as a codified mode of interaction between social groups who ascribe cultural meaning and purpose to the manner of its conduct. While some of these significations may be determined unilaterally for one side, many of them are also the outcome of intersubjective negotiation between belligerents. In this sense, war is not altogether different from the other forms of interaction that can take place between discrete groups, such as diplomacy or trade. Anthropology has indeed long pointed to the rich variety found in human societies in terms of expressions of organized violence and the cultural bounds placed on them (Haas 1990). The underlying point is that the very practice of war necessarily rests on an understanding of war according to which forms of violence are determined to be war or not-war and certain actions permitted or prohibited.

Our main focus here will be on the particular codification of war concomitant to the rise of the Westphalian state system in the modern era, since it is that which lies at the heart of the discipline of international relations, even as it frays ever more visibly. This is not to say, of course, that the Westphalian framing is any truer to a putative "essence" of war than other conceptions. But it is that framing which continues to anchor the coordinates of dominant understandings of war today and in relation to which various claims about the new manifestations of conflict are formulated. It is this conception of war that has served as a veritable institution of international society in political modernity (Bull 2002).

To label this specific institutionalization of violence as 'Westphalian' does not require that one thereby subscribe to any simplistic attribution of epochal change to that treaty from 1648 or that one deny the extent to which trumpeted principles of sovereignty have been inconsistently enforced and have constituted a form of "organized hypocrisy" (Krasner 1999). Nor can it be ignored that this order was, at its inception and throughout most of its existence, intended to apply solely to European (eventually Western) polities, and that other societies were conspicuously excluded from it, with all the implications that had for the ruthlessness with which they were frequently fought and stripped of their autonomous governance. The notion of a Westphalian compact does however provide a convenient shorthand for a regulative ideal that undeniably guided relations between states for several centuries. At the heart of the establishment of that ideal was a desire to ward off the generalized strife fuelled by the bitter theological disputes that erupted with the Protestant Reformation and whose convulsions reached their paroxysm in the Thirty Years War (1618–1648). If, following Bull, "the historical alternative to war between states was more ubiquitous violence" (2002: 179), this bounding of organized violence would hinge on the realization of new conceptions of territory and legitimate authority.

In Max Weber's enduring formulation, the modern state consists in a monopoly of the legitimate use of physical force within a given territory. As various scholars have shown (Giddens 1985; Tilly 1992; Porter 1994), this monopoly was achieved in Europe over several centuries through a bureaucratic centralization of political power supported by an effective taxation of nascent capitalist economies. Intense competition between rival polities and a revolution in military technology and tactics (Parker 1996) saw a dramatic decrease in the number of independent centres of power and the emergence of the nation-state form we are familiar with today. Simultaneous to this was a gradual disarming and disqualification of non-state actors as autonomous wielders of violent means (Thomson 1994).

The Westphalian norms that were established in this period played a vital role in this process. The key principle of sovereignty entailed recognition of the exclusive political authority of states over their territories and formal legal equality between all states (see also Chapter 11, this volume). Along with that came a specific understanding of the forms of violence that could be legitimately understood as war and the circumstances under which they could be deployed. This codification of violence and of the institutions that can yield it rests above all on the partition of an essentially pacified domestic realm and an international sphere of intense armed rivalry.

Since the sovereign is endowed with an exclusive right over the governance of domestic territory, any unsanctioned acts of violence conducted therein are deemed illegitimate. In the typical conditions of low-level threat to the state's monopoly of violence that these acts constitute, they are to be dealt with by police institutions in accordance with domestic law. The state will characteristically resist recognizing perpetrators of non-mandated violence in its territory as other than criminal since it can only grant them any legitimacy to the same extent that it undermines its own. Only where levels of internecine violence come to significantly challenge its monopoly will the state eventually be forced into acknowledging, at least tacitly, a condition of war. Of course, the characterization of certain conflicts as "civil" is only intelligible in a world in which violence perpetrated between certain political groupings (states in this instance) is conceptually distinguished from that occurring within these groupings. A spectral presence haunting each and every state, civil war effectively marks the breakdown of the sovereign power capable of deciding between legitimate and illegitimate forms of violence. As such, determining the legal status of civil wars and the appropriate response to bring to them has unsurprisingly proven a persistently contentious issue within the international state system.

Counterposed to the domestic realm is an international sphere which, in the absence of any higher sovereign power, recognizes in each and every state the right to employ armed force to protect and advance its interests. Within the Westphalian international order, European states would face each other as peers with an equality of status, if not necessarily of power. Freed from responsibilities for the coercion of their domestic societies, military institutions could be dedicated to the clashes that would be expected to periodically break out between sovereign states. Although liable to result in formidable expenses in wealth and manpower for their pursuit, inter-state wars came to take on a highly codified and regulated form that can be seen most clearly in the practices of the nineteenth century. Hostilities were to be preceded by formal declarations of war that constituted an official "state of war" between belligerents and to be eventually concluded by a peace treaty that brought that state of conflict to an end. The conduct of war itself became increasingly subject to numerous conventions and rules governing the legitimate applications of force or the treatment of non-combatants and prisoners.

Consideration of both the grounds on which war could be permitted (*jus in bello*) and the principles that should guide its prosecution (*jus ad bellum*) was of course not new. A long established body of ethical thinking known as "just war" theory existed within the Christian tradition, as it did in other faiths. The Westphalian compact did however mark a fundamental break with this tradition in abandoning appeals to divine sanction to determine the justness of a cause for which war could be initiated. Anxious to avoid competing claims to theological rectitude of the kind that had fuelled the devastating Thirty Years War, the new secular order recognized in all states the right to determine for themselves when they wished to employ armed force.

While political leaders naturally never ceased to claim the moral high-ground for their actions, it was understood that to be sovereign was to hold an exclusive decisionary power over matters of war and peace. No appeal other than to national interest or *raison d'état* were ultimately required, a principle that finds its most naked expression in the unabashed adoption of *Realpolitik* in the nineteenth century. At the same time, entering into a war with another state signified the application of an international legal regime that formally recognized it and regulated its modalities. Quincy Wright (1964: 7) accordingly deemed war to be nothing else but "the legal condition which equally permits two or more hostile groups to carry on a conflict by armed force". From the second half of the nineteenth century onwards, customary restrictions on the conduct of war were thus increasingly codified into a burgeoning body of international law. The Hague Conventions of 1899 and 1907 and the Geneva Conventions of 1864, 1906, 1929 and 1949 notably sought to determine the types of weapons and munitions that could be employed, the protections that civilians should benefit from, and the protocols overseeing the treatment of prisoners.

Westphalian War and its Discontents

The institutionalization of norms regulating the practice of war had therefore arguably less to do with the moral advancement of the Western societies that promoted them than with principles of reciprocity and mutual recognition as formally equal members of a state system. Wherever these same states encountered in their colonial expansions peoples to whom this status was not extended, such restraints were rarely considered to apply. Wanton brutality and indiscriminate violence characterized many of the military adventures in these territories, at times begetting veritable wars of extermination against indigenous groups. For Wright (1964: 18), such conflicts did not even merit the term of war due to the absence of intergroup or international standards regulating them, since one cannot speak of war "where the participants are so self-centred that each fails to recognize the other as a participant but treats it merely as an environmental obstacle to policy, as men treat wild animals or geographical barriers". From this perspective, war can only exist as an intersubjective activity that entails some mutual recognition by the belligerents that they at least minimally share in the same kinds of motives and social practices. This is the basis on which it is possible for reciprocal rules constraining military conduct to accrete and diffuse.

But even between signatory states the actual conduct of war frequently fell short of the standards set by the laws of war, not least because these same laws inevitably lagged behind the latest developments in military technology and practice. Indeed, the 'Westphalian institution' was severely tested by the dramatic intensification that inter-state war underwent in the first half of the twentieth century. Industrialism and modern technique (Bousquet 2009) combined with unprecedented degrees of social control over their populations to grant nation-states unparalleled human and material resources, which they hurled into war-making in two major global conflagrations. During the two world wars, the established boundaries between military and civilian spheres blurred under the mass social mobilization that saw war become "total", exemplifying the escalatory logic of conflict outlined by Clausewitz. Non-combatants and vast areas behind the front-lines were increasingly targeted as a means to destroy the capacity for an adversarial state to continue the fight. Fierce ideological enmities loosened many of the established restraints, with defeat in those conflicts becoming generally synonymous with the comprehensive collapse of the vanquished societies and the demise of their political regimes. The historian Johan Huizinga (1949: 89) would thus task total war with having extinguished the "play-element" that had previously granted war a "cultural function", highlighting the limiting rules that regulated its exercise among antagonists who regarded each other as equals.

In fact, the Westphalian bounding of war had not remained unchallenged prior to the twentieth century even at the very heart of its Eurocentric order. The revolutionary war that erupted out of France in 1792 was motivated by fervent ideological belief in ideals of liberty and equality that rejected the prevailing constraints of limited war and sought nothing less than the complete overthrow of hostile regimes. War was, in this view, to be the means to both safeguard the revolution at home and export it beyond with the prospect of a definitive end to political tyranny and with it to conflict of any kind. Yet, after several decades of upheaval, the coalition of states pitted against the French Republic and then Empire succeeded in reasserting the principles of formal sovereign equality and limited competition that then largely prevailed throughout the nineteenth century.

Revolutionary war, and with it counter-revolutionary war that sought to buttress the existing order, would eventually resurface in 1917 with the Bolshevik seizure of power in Russia. For Lenin and his comrades, inter-state war was merely the outgrowth of imperial rivalries between capitalists that masked the more fundamental class war that divided humanity into exploiters and exploited. Since global revolution and the triumph of the world proletariat were their ultimate political goals, any accommodation between communist and capitalist states could necessarily only be a temporary prelude to a final showdown. As Mikhail Frunze, a leading Red Army commander during the Russian Civil War (1917–1922) would put it, "between our proletarian state and the rest of the bourgeois world there can only be one condition – that of long, persistent, desperate war to the death" (Kipp 1992: 77). Indeed, for Schmitt (2004), war in the name of humanity and the "absolute" forms of enmity attendant to it could only culminate in the annihilation of one side by the other. This character of irreconcilable ideological struggle would come to impress itself on many of the conflicts of the twentieth century, notably through the related rise of the fascist and Nazi movements. Its influence would be further amplified with the break-up of the European empires and its accompanying armed struggles in which wars of national liberation frequently blurred into revolutionary war.

Yet the Westphalian institution proved quite resilient, even if the crippling human and material costs entailed by the pursuit of all-out industrial war did lead to sustained international efforts to revise the grounds on which armed conflict could be permitted. Through the 1928 Kellogg-Briand Pact and the 1945 United Nations Charter, "aggressive war" for the purpose of advancing a state's interests became firmly proscribed. If in the nineteenth century war had been widely admitted as an essential and legitimate tool of statecraft for the deliberate enhancement of state power, now only in self-defence or under the strict mandate of the United Nations could military action ever be justified. Although not a formal requirement of the UN Charter, the new juridico-political framing of armed conflict it presupposed resulted in the virtual disappearance post-1945 of the legal condition of the "state of war" (Greenwood 1987). Thus, neither the US nor the UK has issued any declarations of war since the Second World War, notwithstanding the numerous military operations they have engaged in thereafter. Similarly, Ministries of War have given way to Ministries of Defence across the world. Although not entirely prohibited, the state conduct of war is now tightly circumscribed and framed in terms of the protection of the interests and values of the "international community".

Yet the more war in its traditional Westphalian guise has been restricted, the more the persistence of armed conflict in other forms has prompted an extensive interrogation of the concept(s) of war apposite to these manifestations. A recurrent feature of such discussions has been the noted blurring of criminality and policing with war, categories which had all acquired a particular meaning through the Westphalian ordering of the modalities of violence. There is therefore a sense in which we can speak of a twilight of war as predominantly conceived of in the modern era and which may well prove to be tantamount to the proliferation of war as a generalized, if fragmented, condition.

From the End of "War" to War without End?

If the ideological enmities of the twentieth century loosened war from its Westphalian moorings, it is in fact with the end of the Cold War and the ascendancy of a system of global governance underpinned by American hegemony that these ties have come close to being decisively severed. One particularly salient feature of this present era has been the increasing rationalization of the employment of military force as a form of policing of the world order (Dean 2006; Holmqvist 2014), the most visible expressions of which have been those actions labelled as "humanitarian interventions", most notably in Yugoslavia (1999) and Libya (2011). As we have seen above, the Westphalian compact rested on a delineation of domestic and international spheres which were the respective domains of police and military institutions with their particular missions and modes of operability, this distinction between inside and outside permitting the articulation of "a logical and political distance between enemy and criminal, peace and war" (Galli 2010: 161). Inconsistent and schematic as such a partition may have been in practice, it is nonetheless being subjected today to unprecedented levels of strain. To underline the contemporary "elision of police and military violence" (Caygill 2001) is not simply to recognize that the tasks undertaken by military organizations in the realm of peacekeeping and state-building come to resemble in certain aspects those of police bodies. At a more fundamental level, the exercise of armed force is being increasingly justified and framed as merely a moment in the continuous governance of a global polity (Neumann and Sending 2010). Thus, for Hardt and Negri (2000: 12) as for others, war has been "reduced to the status of police action". Such deployments of military violence in the name of human rights, democracy or civilization see those held to be standing against such values relegated to the status of international outlaws, if not enemies of humanity itself (see also Chapter 16, this volume). Where the offenders are state entities, they are labelled "rogue" and in need of "regime change". Where they are non-state actors, they find themselves in a juridical no man's land, denied the status of legitimate combatants under the laws of war but liable to being killed or indefinitely imprisoned outside of the framework of criminal law.

Of the conflicts that see the indeterminably amidst decaying state apparatuses and constitute prime candidates for global policing operations, scholars (Kaldor 1999; Münkler 2005) have proposed that they should be labelled "new wars", with the qualifier not so much denoting new practices than differentiating them from those subsumed under Clausewitzian understandings of war. Fought over the control of natural resources and profitable global traffics by a motley array of armed groups and habitually characterized by large-scale violations of human rights, in the protracted new wars "often it is difficult to distinguish between criminal and political violence" (Kaldor 1999: viii). In direct contrast to Clausewitz's celebrated formula, we are told that war has simply become "a continuation of economics by other means" (Keen 2000: 27), the perpetuation of which frequently serves the material interests of all the belligerents. In the absence of conclusive military outcomes that might lay the ground for a reconstitution of state authority, these low-intensity conflicts simmer on indefinitely, reputedly breeding multifarious threats to international security. Much commentary has been expounded on the globalized character of the new wars, in terms of the transnational reach of both their causal complexes and spill-over effects. However, to view these conflicts as being essentially driven by economic motives would risk occluding their political character, albeit expressed through modes of governance unfamiliar to us. Thus, for Mark Duffield, the new wars are to be understood as "a form of non-territorial network war that works through and around states" and participate in the emergence of "new forms of authority and zones of alternative regulation" (2001: 3).

Those processes of globalization that have as their correlate the erosion of the state's centrality in war further manifest themselves in the marked reconfiguration of the spatio-temporalities of organized violence. Frédéric Mégret (2011) pointedly notes the disappearance of the battlefield as both a temporally and geographically delineated space where combat takes place and a normative space in which the particular laws of war apply. The setting in which opposing sides traditionally clashed in their quest for a decisive victory, the battlefield was also a social construction that supported the idea that war, in contrast with other forms of violence, "unfolds in discreet spaces insulated from the rest of society, confining military violence to a confrontation between specialized forces whose operation should minimally disrupt surrounding life" (2011: 4). Through their extension of the reach and scale of hostilities, total war and the advent of nuclear weapons would however render entire continents into theatres of conflict. The post-1945 proliferation of guerrilla wars and insurgencies in turn diminished the role of decisive battlefield encounters and further blurred the distinction between civilians and combatants. But it is perhaps the War on Terror, initiated at the turn of the new century, that best exemplifies the present crisis of the notion of the battlefield. On one side, we see a "terrorist" adversary that eschews any direct military confrontation, dissimulates itself within the enemy's society and embraces a maximalist definition of the legitimate target. On the other is a fluid coalition of states led by the US that arrogates itself the right to take the fight to wherever it perceives a sufficient threat, deploying an array of conventional troops, special operations forces

(Niva 2013) and drone strikes (Chamayou 2015) to neutralize it. To speak of a global battlefield in this context, as analysts are increasingly wont to, is to simultaneously concede the obsolescence of the very notion of the battlefield and with it of a certain conception of war itself.

The proclamation of a War on Terror by the George W. Bush administration was in itself highly ambiguous, asserting that the carnage of September 11 was on a scale that called for a full military response, while simultaneously refusing its perpetrators any of the legitimacy normally afforded to participants in a war through their labelling as terrorists. Subsequent invasions of Afghanistan and Iraq may have temporarily succeeded in locating the conflict within more familiar inter-state coordinates, but it soon became apparent that the term covered a much wider range of operations conducted across multiple geographies and against a nebulous and endlessly shape-shifting adversary. Scholars (Bigo 2005; Huysmans 2006) have further underlined the manner in which the expansive framing of the War on Terror has increasingly submitted domestic societies to processes of "securitization" that blur the established boundaries of internal and external security (see also Chapter 3, this volume).

Hence, for Carlo Galli (2010), global war "is a war without frontiers, without advances or retreats, consisting only of acts into 'precise' spaces, and in real time, the logics of war, economics and technology" (p. 162) and that signals "the collapse of the categories of modern political thought" (p. 183). Vivienne Jabri similarly refers to a "global matrix of war" in which "it is now always problematic to claim distinctions between the inside and outside, the domestic and the international, the zone of civic peace and the zone of war, the sovereign state and the anarchic outside" (2007: 2). In place of the traditional concept of war that rested on those categories, Frédéric Gros (2010: 260) refers to "states of violence" that involve the "moments of pure laceration caused by the terrorist act in the public spaces of great urban centres, the mathematic calculations of a missile trajectory in high-tech conflicts or the indefinite wasting brought about by civil wars in failed states". The unity of the concept of war that prevailed in the Westphalian imaginary and was principally achieved through the exclusion of a much more disparate set of violent practices from its understanding, has manifestly been shattered. The neatly partitioned manifestations of violence and delineated spatio-temporalities of war and peace previously held have become decidedly untenable, confronting us with a new landscape of conflict that presently confounds our attempts to circumscribe it and render fully intelligible its workings.

Conclusion

As an approach to concept analysis, this chapter has sought to keep in tandem the formulation of a general abstract conception of war as organized violence for political purposes with a historically grounded treatment of the ways in which the socially embedded practices of armed conflict entail specific understandings of war. A formal conceptualization of war is absolutely necessary to bring rigour to a term that is so widely and loosely employed in public discourse and to outline the broad features of a phenomenon to which we seek to ascribe some consistency across time. And yet such a general concept of war as we can arrive at in this manner remains wholly indeterminate outside of the specific cultural frames within which its practice takes place.

Indeed, if the notion of war is to refer to certain uses of violence and not others, it cannot be apprehended without engaging the web of related concepts and significations on the basis of which such discriminations are made.

While the Westphalian international order provided a certain stability to the meaning of armed conflict and the regulation of its conduct, there is today a growing sense that such understandings are no longer apposite to the new manifestations of war. The extent to which we are facing truly unprecedented types of violent conflict rather than their occurrences merely being more visible in the context of a decline of major interstate war, remains an open question. It is clear however that any novel conceptions of war are inevitably intertwined with new sets of martial practice and contests over the legitimacy of violent actions.

For a discipline of international relations founded in the last century on the central *problematique* of the recurrence of war and the means to reduce, if not completely arrest, its incidence, the task of reconceptualizing war is likely to be essential to any meaningful contribution to this laudable goal in the twenty-first century. That most efforts so far have insisted on the manner in which contemporary conflicts depart from an established Westphalian-Clausewitzian model tells us that we are still largely unable to apprehend the novel constellation of war on its own terms. It is perhaps more fitting than ever then that the etymology of "war" leads us back to an Old Germanic verb that means "to confuse" or "to perplex". The present conceptual anomie may however have one great virtue in disclosing to us what war was all along – a dynamic and unstable ground that is both shaped by and constitutive of wider struggles over power, authority and legitimacy.

Suggested Readings

Clausewitz, Carl von (1989 [1832]) *On War* (Princeton, NJ: Princeton University Press).
Arguably the foundational text of the modern study of war. Devises a philosophical approach to the subject and offers an array of related conceptualizations still relevant today to both scholars and practitioners.

Gros, Frédéric (2010) *States of Violence: An Essay on the End of War* (London: Seagull Books).
Offers a philosophical examination of the essential historical features of war to argue that war, as we have known it, is increasingly being replaced by new forms of violence that no longer conform to those customary characteristics.

Jabri, Vivienne (2007) *War and the Transformation of Global Politics* (Basingstoke: Palgrave).
By reference to the ways in which the uses of armed force are legitimized today, Jabri discusses the blurring of notions of war and peace and the breakdown of the conventional delineation between domestic and international spheres of interaction.

Kaldor, Mary (1999) *New and Old Wars: Organized Violence in a Global Era* (Oxford: Polity).
Influential formulation of the concept of "new wars" to capture a transformation in the character of armed conflicts in an era of globalization. Although the object of considerable criticism and qualification, the label was widely adopted in the period following the end of the Cold War.

Wright, Quincy (1964 [1942]) *A Study of War* (Chicago: University of Chicago Press).
A classical liberal study of the phenomenon of war. Its attempt to provide a definitive scientific understanding may appear inadequate today in light of the changing expressions of conflict, but it remains instructive in highlighting where the conventional understanding of war presently flounders.

Bibliography

Arquilla, John and David Ronfeldt (2001) *Networks and Netwars: The Future of Terror, Crime, and Militancy* (Santa Monica, CA: RAND).

Barkawi, Tarak and Shane Brighton (2011) 'Powers of War: Fighting, Knowledge, and Critique', *International Political Sociology* 5(2): 126–43.

Bigo, Didier (2005) 'Globalized (in)Security: The Field and the Ban-Opticon', in N. Sakai and J. Solomon (eds), *Translation, Biopolitics, Colonial Difference* (Hong Kong: Hong Kong University Press).

Bousquet, Antoine (2008) 'Chaoplexic Warfare or the Future of Military Organization', *International Affairs* 84(5): 915–29.

Bousquet, Antoine (2009) *The Scientific Way of Warfare: Order and Chaos on the Battlefields of Modernity* (New York: Columbia University Press).

Bull, Hedley (2002) *The Anarchical Society: A Study of Order in World Politics* (New York: Palgrave).

Carr, E. H. (2001) *The Twenty Years' Crisis, 1919–1939: An Introduction to the Study of International Relations* (Basingstoke: Palgrave).

Caygill, Howard (2001) 'Kosovo and the Elision of Police and Military Violence', *European Journal of Social Theory* 4(1): 73–80.

Chamayou, Grégoire (2015) *A Theory of the Drone* (New York: The New Press).

Clausewitz, Carl von (1989) *On War* (Princeton, NJ: Princeton University Press).

Dean, Mitchell (2006) 'Military Intervention as "Police" Action', in Markus D. Dubber and Mariana Valverde (eds), *The New Police Science: The Police Power in Domestic and International Governance* (Stanford, CA: Stanford Law Books).

Duffield, Mark (2001) *Global Governance and the New Wars: The Merging of Development and Security* (London: Zed Books).

Eisenhower, Dwight D. (1956) Address at the Annual Dinner of the American Society of Newspaper Editors, Philadelphia, PA, 21 April.

Galli, Carlo (2010) *Political Spaces and Global War* (Minneapolis, MN: University of Minnesota Press).

Giddens, Anthony (1985) *The Nation-State and Violence: A Contemporary Critique of Historical Materialism, Vol. 2* (Cambridge: Polity).

Gray, Chris Hables (1997) *Postmodern War: The New Politics of Conflict* (New York: The Guilford Press).

Greenwood, Christopher (1987) 'The Concept of War in Modern International Law', *International and Comparative Law Quarterly* 36(2): 283–306.

Gros, Frédéric (2010) *States of Violence: An Essay on the End of War* (London: Seagull Books).

Haas, Jonathan (ed.) (1990) *The Anthropology of War* (Cambridge: Cambridge University Press).

Hardt, Michael and Antonio Negri (2000) *Empire* (Cambridge, MA: Harvard University Press).

Hobbes, Thomas (1986) *Leviathan* (Harmondsworth: Penguin Books).

Hoffman, Frank G. (2009) 'Hybrid Warfare and Challenges', *Joint Force Quarterly* 52: 34–9.

Holmqvist, Caroline (2014) *Policing Wars: Military Intervention in the Twenty-First Century* (Houndmills, Basingstoke: Palgrave Macmillan).

Huizinga, Johan (1949) *Homo Ludens: A Study of the Play-Element in Culture* (London: Routledge & Kegan Paul).

Huysmans, Jef (2006) *The Politics of Insecurity.* London: Routledge.

Jabri, Vivienne (2007) *War and the Transformation of Global Politics* (Basingstoke: Palgrave).

Kaldor, Mary (1999) *New and Old Wars: Organized Violence in a Global Era* (Oxford: Polity).

Keen, David (2000) 'Incentives and Disincentives for Violence', in Mats Berdal and David M. Malone (eds), *Greed and Grievance: Economic Agendas in Civil Wars* (Boulder, CO: Lynne Rienner).

Kipp, Jacob W. (1992) 'Lenin and Clausewitz: The Militarization of Marxism, 1915–1921', in Willard C. Frank and Philip S. Gillette (eds), *Soviet Military Doctrine from Lenin to Gorbachev, 1915–1991* (Westport, CT: Greenwood Press).

Krasner, Stephen D. (1999) *Sovereignty: Organized Hypocrisy* (Princeton, NJ: Princeton University Press).

Mégret, Frédéric (2011) 'War and the Vanishing Battlefield', *Loyola University Chicago International Law Review* 9(1): 131–55.

Morgenthau, Hans (1948) *Politics among Nations: The Struggle for Power and Peace* (New York: Alfred A. Knopf).

Mueller, John (2009) 'War Has Almost Ceased to Exist: An Assessment', *Political Science Quarterly* 124(2): 297–321.

Münkler, Herfried (2005) *The New Wars* (Cambridge: Polity Press).

Neumann, Iver B. and Ole Jacob Sending (2010) *Governing the Global Polity: Practice, Mentality, Rationality* (Ann Arbor, MI: University of Michigan Press).

Niva, Steve (2013) 'Disappearing Violence: JSOC and the Pentagon's New Cartography of Networked Warfare', *Security Dialogue* 44(3): 185–202.

Parker, Geoffrey (1996) *The Military Revolution: Military Innovation and the Rise of the West, 1500–1800* (Cambridge: Cambridge University Press).

Porter, Bruce (1994) *War and the Rise of the State: The Military Foundations of Modern Politics* (New York: Free Press).

Schmitt, Carl (2004) 'A Theory of the Partisan', *CR: The New Centennial Review* 4(3): 1–78 (trans. A. C. Goodson).

Singer, J. David and Melvin Small (1972) *The Wages of War, 1816–1965: A Statistical Handbook* (New York: John Wiley & Sons).

Thomas, Claire (2011) 'Why Don't We Talk About "Violence" in International Relations?', *Review of International Studies* 37(4): 1815–36.

Thomson, Janice E. (1994) *Mercenaries, Pirates, and Sovereigns: State-building and Extraterritorial Violence in Early Modern Europe* (Princeton, NJ: Princeton University Press).

Thornton, Rod (2007) *Asymmetric Warfare: Threat and Response in the Twenty-First Century* (Cambridge: Polity Press).

Tilly, Charles (1992) *Coercion, Capital, and European States, AD 990–1992* (Cambridge, MA & London: Blackwell).

Van Creveld, Martin (1991) *The Transformation of War* (New York: Free Press).

Waltz, Kenneth (2001) *Man, the State and War: A Theoretical Analysis* (New York: Columbia University Press).

Walzer, Michael (2006) *Just and Unjust Wars: A Moral Argument with Historical Illustrations* (New York: Basic Books).

Wright, Quincy (1964) *A Study of War* (Chicago, IL: University of Chicago Press).

7

Peace

Oliver P. Richmond and Felix Berenskoetter

Peace clearly is of great importance for societies and states around the world, yet the concept has been widely ignored in the academic discipline of International Relations (IR) as a site of close interrogation and detailed theorization. Given that peace has been regularly declared as both the justification for, and aim of, IR scholarship, its marginality is somewhat perplexing. Some scholars have, of course, examined the concept, ranging from the work of David Mitrany and Kenneth Boulding to Johan Galtung, Dieter Senghaas and Michael Banks. Nevertheless, despite their contributions, and despite having its own journal, such as the highly-ranked *Journal of Peace Research* and newer entrants such as *Peacebuilding*, the concept of peace seems to be missing from mainstream theorizing. In a discipline shaped by the Cold War context and long dominated by realist assumptions of survival as the primary goal of states and war as an ever-present possibility, the focus was on understanding the causes of war and how to maximize national security. Thinking about peace was seen as something for idealists and in close proximity to pacifism, dismissed as an ideological stance lending itself more to activism than scientific research.[1] Thus, security studies came to dominate over peace studies in IR, confining the latter to a niche (Buzan and Hansen, 2009).

Yet, just as security and peace are not necessarily contrasting concepts, it would be incorrect to say that the latter concept was confined to peace studies. Notions of peace remained implicit in mainstream debates such as the realist concern with "stability" and liberal thinking about "cooperation". If anything, one might say it was assumed that the question of peace had been settled: peace was seen as an agreement between states (the term "pact" derives from *pax*), depending on state and international law, and, at a stretch, human rights. While most scholars and practitioners, certainly in the West, have embraced a liberal conception of peace as their orthodoxy, in practice

[1] The invited prominence of quantitative methods in the *Journal of Peace Research* (Urdal, Ostby and Gleditsch 2014) can be seen as an attempt to counter this perception.

many of the elements have been mediated by different voices across time: from Augustine to the Magna Carta (1215), to Tolstoy, Gandhi, Russell and Einstein, Eleanor Roosevelt and the doctrines of human rights (1947), to Boutros-Ghali's Agenda for Peace (1992), the postcolonial subaltern, and Responsibility to Protect (2005).[2] Even now, progress can be seen in the breadth of documents such as the High Level Panel Report on UN Peace Operations (2014) and the Sustainable Development Goals (2015), among others.

The increase and investment in multinational "peacebuilding" operations since the end of the Cold War has given the concept new prominence in practical terms. And carving out the understanding(s) of "peace" among practitioners involved in the planning and implementation of such missions would offer valuable insights into the political performance of the concept (Richmond 2005). This chapter takes a different route. Instead of focusing on how the concept is used by political actors, supported by a growing body of literature addressing practical issues of peacebuilding, the following offers an overview of prominent understandings of peace embedded in different theoretical approaches to world politics. Of course, the theoretical and the practical inform each other, *especially* when it comes to a basic concept like peace, and the chapter reflects this. Peace is, ultimately, an ideal, a desirable condition, and its deeply normative character motivates action aimed at creating such a condition. However, analyses of practice must be complemented with a critical understanding of how the concept gains and maintains its meanings through its place in particular theories, not least because theories carry these meanings into the heads of practitioners.

The chapter proceeds in three broad steps. Following a brief reminder of the reality and stakes involved in plural conceptions of peace, the first part outlines some prominent readings of the concept in Western thought to highlight its core features. The second part shows how these conceptions of peace are embedded in and dealt with by established "mainstream" theories of international relations, and the third part presents a critical and *eirinist* angle on the subject.

Many Peaces or One?

For social scientists and political practitioners, peace is understood not simply as a subjective mental state ("peace of mind") but as a particular kind of relationship and form of social interaction. And, of course, it has a strong normative connotation in that "peace" is unequivocally considered a good thing. But when it comes to specifying the meaning of peace, or peaceful relations, there is no unity. Scholars tracing understandings of the concept across historical and cultural contexts have found that there are "many peaces" (Dietrich 2012) or multiple forms of peace (Richmond 2008). This pluralism is also visible in the case of the Nobel Peace Prize, awarded annually to a person or institutional body. Despite being selected by an established institution whose voting members are all of the same nationality (Norwegian) and guided by general criteria laid out in Alfred Nobel's will, it is difficult to find a common

[2] For a comprehensive history of peace movements and ideas, see Cortright (2008).

ground among the roughly 100 recipients of the prize to date (see also Bulloch 2008). The existence of "many peaces" is in line with the general point made in the introduction to this volume that basic concepts are vague and that their concrete meaning(s) vary with context(s). And yet, there is something intriguing, if not disturbing about it, when American sociologist C. Wright Mills notes:

> Peace is such an altogether "good" word that it is well to be suspicious of it. It has meant and it does mean a great variety of things to a great variety of men ... Everybody agrees upon peace as the universal aim – and into it each packs his own specific political fears, values, hopes, demands. (cited in Chernus 2002: 4)

The plural reading generates practical dilemmas that are perhaps unique to the concept of peace. While even warring parties are likely to agree on peace as a desirable goal, their disagreement about its concrete manifestation may be a decisive factor behind the continuation of the conflict. In a slightly different context, the failure to recognize and address different conceptions of peace also hampers cooperation among actors involved in the same peacebuilding mission, leading to what various UN reports decry as inefficient and uncoordinated practices. Conversely, an attempt to impose a particular reading of peace on others can be seen as a hegemonic exercise of violence, as highlighted in the critical literature on Western-led peacebuilding practices (Richmond 2005).

The crucial question arising here is, ultimately, whether and how "world peace" can be pursued on the basis of respecting multiple readings of peace. For practitioners, any attempt to find a shared meaning requires pragmatic and political negotiations. This "negotiated peace" can take various forms, and the intuitively most useful starting point is the reading of peace as "not-war", namely a cease-fire-like situation and an absence of killing.[3] Yet this conception is not sufficient if peace is something to be built once the fighting stops, and so scholars as well as practitioners have always been trying to establish a more substantial reading. That is, rather than defining peace by stating what it *is not*, the ambition has been to establish what peace *is*, or rather, how we should think about it in positive terms. Methodologically speaking, it involves moving away from reading peace simply through its contrasting concept of war and, instead, to think more carefully about the broader conceptual web out of which the meaning of peace can, or should, be woven.

Peace as Order and Process

In Western thought and practice, the notion of peace has historically evolved to comprise a victor's peace aimed at security (as with the Roman treatment of Carthage), an institutional peace to provide international governance and guarantees (as with the Congress system in Europe from 1815, or the UN since 1945), a constitutional peace to ensure democracy and free trade (as with the development of the liberal democratic–capitalist constitutional framework since the 18th century in Europe and North

[3] Although it still needs to come to terms with pluralist readings of war (see Chapter 6, this volume).

America) and a civil peace to ensure freedom and rights (drawing on a range of global social movements for human rights, voting rights, workers' rights, self-determination and independence, security and disarmament, and environmental sustainability, since at least the 18th century).[4] While these perspectives are often shaped and limited by understandings of geopolitics, global capital and governance, they are also inspired by, or have inspired, scholarly ideas on "peace".

In Europe an political philosophy, the social contract theories of Hobbes, Locke, Rousseau and Kant provide sophisticated ideas for how a peaceful society ought to be organized. The most influential attempt to imagine peace in the liberal tradition is Immanuel Kant's *Perpetual Peace [Zum Ewigen Frieden]*. In this succinct text published in 1795, Kant criticized the Treaty of Basel signed between Prussia and France in April that year as "a mere truce, a suspension of hostilities, not *peace*" (Kant 1917 [1795]: 107). As Kant saw it, the treaty put an end to war for the moment, "but not to the conditions of war which at any time may afford a new pretext for opening hostilities" (1917 [1795]: 133). For him, "true" peace was something sustainable. It was not simply the opposite of war, but the suspension of the very possibility of war.

There is an extensive literature on Kant's ideas of how such a peace might be achieved within and among nations, some of which is referenced later in this chapter, so there is no need to engage them here in detail. It suffices to say that Kant presents this vision in terms of a fictional contract which serves as a roadmap grounded in core themes of Western enlightenment thinking, such as equality, rights, emancipation, progress and universality. At the heart of it is the argument that people, given their natural interest in self-preservation and the good life, will consider going to war as an unreasonable thing to do: recognizing that war is destructive and entails more costs than benefits, people will choose peace if given the option. In other words, peace is the rational choice of enlightened beings.[5] And so, according to Kant, perpetual peace is guaranteed through the human ability to reason and, hence, "by no less a power than the great artist nature" (Kant 1917 [1795]: 144). More precisely, it is guaranteed if the socio-political conditions are created which allow the people to reason and decide freely, which, for Kant, requires a republican constitution, complemented by the spirit of hospitality, commerce and cosmopolitan law. Thus, Kant's notion of peace rests on a particular human capacity and on a social order which both springs from and supports this capacity.

In contemporary Western debates about the character of a peaceful order, Johan Galtung makes an important contribution by scrutinizing what peace "as the absence of violence" (Galtung 1969: 168) might mean. Galtung's starting point is that the meaning of "peace" is conceptually dependent on the meaning of "violence", which consequently requires careful thinking about the latter. In his reading, violence is a form of power exercised in a relationship that prevents the realization of someone's potential through a denial of "input" (e.g. food, water, information) or a denial of "output" (e.g. health, growth, learning). In short, "violence is the cause of the difference between the potential and the actual" (Galtung 1969: 168). Galtung then makes

---

[4] For a discussion of these components, see Richmond (2005), especially the conclusion.

[5] For a discussion of the concepts of rationality, see Chapter 4, this volume.

four distinctions, of which the first two are the most important: (1) between *physical* and *psychological* violence, that is, violence that works on either the body or the mind; (2) between *personal (direct)* violence and *structural (indirect)* violence, exercised either through a conscious act/actor or through oppressive structural forces. Supplementing these two, he distinguishes (3) between *intended* and *unintended* violence and, finally, (4) between *manifest* and *latent* violence. The latter distinction highlights that violence can either be more overt and easily observable, which tends to be the case in the form of physical and personal violence, or operate more covertly, hidden in the order of things and surfacing only in particular moments, as tends to be the case with forms of structural violence.

This extended conception of violence allows Galtung to formulate a more nuanced conception of peace and, in particular, put forward the famous distinction between *negative peace* as the absence of personal violence (physical or psychological) and *positive peace* as the absence of structural violence (physical or psychological). While Galtung holds that neither conception of peace can be prioritized in temporal, logical or evaluative terms, it is clear that he considers positive peace a higher form of development: whereas negative peace is a condition of social injustice, positive peace is characterized by a socially just order in which potentials can be fully realized. Yet creating such a condition is a challenging task. Because structural violence operates indirectly and can be unintentional, it is more difficult to address and easily overseen by systems directed against personal and intended violence. Indeed, Galtung points out, systems of "law and order" often still designate a form of negative peace (Galtung 1969: 172).

Another important angle is added by Michael Banks (1987) who distinguishes between four conceptions of peace. The first is the notion of peace as harmony. Banks dismisses this reading because it ignores the notion that disagreement and conflict are facts of the human condition. In his words, "the idea of 'peace' as a life without any conflict at all … is at best irrelevant and at worst a badly misleading conception" (1987: 260).[6] Next, he considers the understanding of peace as order and stability. Banks concedes that this is a persuasive and, hence, popular conception among IR scholars, yet he criticizes it as conservative and unimaginative, failing to provide an opening for progressive change (1987: 265). Instead, third, like Galtung he favourably discusses the notion of peace as justice. He agrees that this conception is important as it requires recognizing the need for 'wrongs [to] be set right', such as tackling poverty, racism, political inequality, or any form of oppression and marginalization. And yet, for Banks, the concept of justice is also too vague and too political to ground the concept of peace. It leads peace researchers to become emotionally involved and take sides in a given conflict/claims over justice, which he argues is problematic, not so much because it goes against the modern ideal of the objective scientist, but because it makes it difficult for the analyst to show a path forward and contribute to the resolution of the conflict (Banks 1987: 286).

Thus, Banks proposes a fourth reading of peace as conflict management. This not only contrasts with the first two conceptions of peace as harmony and stability, but more generally guards against the temptation to see peace as a fixed condition

[6] For more sympathetic readings of peace as harmony, see Dietrich (2012).

by reading it as an ongoing process instead. In Banks' words, "peace is not a state of general tranquillity, but rather a network of relationships full of energy and conflict ... kept under societal control ... a process, a dynamic" (Banks 1987: 269). Banks presents this process-oriented perspective as a liberal progressive alternative to the conservative notion of peace as order, yet there is a tension between his emphasis on the practical aim of conflict *resolution* and his conception of peace as a conflict *management*. The progressive nature is better captured in Galtung's notion, developed in a later work, of peace as "creative conflict transformation" that takes place non-violently (Galtung 1996; see also Senghaas 2007). Either way, the reading of peace as a process of managing, transforming or solving violent conflict suggests that treating "peace" and "conflict" as conceptual opposites is misleading. It reminds that "building peace" is often practically intertwined with "ending a war" and, consequently, requires a connection between the concept of peace and an understanding of the causes and consequences of war. It even leads Banks to conclude that "the serious business of peace research ... is conflict research" (Banks 1987: 270). The danger here is that the latter comes to overshadow the former, that is, that conflict research diverts conceptual attention away from "peace" towards "violence", prompting a (re)turn to the study of war (see also Gleditsch, Nordkvelle and Strand 2014).

These brief extracts illustrate the conceptual webs in which dominant understandings of peace are embedded. They highlight links to contrasting and supporting concepts like violence, conflict, order, stability, freedom, development and justice, whose meanings are interwoven with and, thus, affect, how "peace" is understood and practised. Underpinning these webs are the temporal and the socio-political dimension of "peace", the two features of the concept core (see Chapter 1). The temporal dimension is tied to the normative element and expressed in the notion of peace as a desirable condition, captured in Kant's search for "true" peace and Galtung's conception of "positive" peace. This ideal is usually formulated as an aspiration and, thus, raises expectations about the future, making peace a forward-looking concept. Although, it should be noted, ideals of peace can also be projected into the past through nostalgic memories of bygone "golden ages". In either case, imagining peace as a possibility in time has an important aesthetic element. As John-Paul Lederach notes, "Aesthetics helps those who attempt to move from cycles of violence to new relationships and those of us who wish to support such movement to see ourselves for whom we are: artists bringing to life and keeping alive something that has not existed" (Lederach 2005: 73). The vision of what a peaceful condition would, or could, look like and its aesthetic expression is thus an integral feature of the concept. The ability of such visions to shape political agendas, mobilise resources and guide practices point to the socio-political dimension of the concept.[7]

The temporal and socio-political dimensions also inform the reading of peace as process. It captures peace as something dynamic that unfolds over time and reminds that such reconceptualizations tend to go along with a concern of how to achieve it, which directly links them to the practical agenda of peacebuilding. Understanding peace as a progressive movement away from relations of violence

[7] On the 'pull' factor of visions and their political nature, see Berenskoetter (2011).

also highlights the emancipatory thrust contained in the concept. As discussed later, this emancipatory aspect often gets downplayed in hegemonic attempts to formulate and establish a framework of socio-political relations in which movement is possible. Such frameworks and related views about the degree to which progress is possible depend not only on a diagnosis of the existing condition of violence but also on a reading of human nature. Crudely put, for those who see aggression as a fundamental trait of human nature, peace is provided through a system that oppresses or tames these destructive drives. In contrast, those who believe in the human ability to foster positive traits of empathy and solidarity into dominant characteristics of human behaviour emphasize frameworks that empower rather than constrain. The following outlines their expressions in theories of international relations.

Peace in Mainstream IR Theory

This section reviews how the concept of peace, in its different forms, is embedded in major schools of thought in IR, namely realism, idealism and liberalism, Marxism, the English School and social constructivism.

Realist IR theory assumes that human nature is violent, or driven to violence in a competitive struggle for survival, and that states reflect this in their institutional design, even if imperfectly so. War between states is perceived to be an ever-present possibility, reflecting the forces which drive international relations, whether a lust for power or an anarchical structure, and their permanence. The tragedy of realist approaches lies in their unitary internal assumptions of a shared peace within political units based on common interests and values, as well as an enforceable social contract, and the difficulties in maintaining peaceful relations with other external polities (states) that have their own interests, values and notions of peace (Waltz 1959; Buzan 1996; Brown 2007). In this condition, peace is assumed to be temporary and can only be a negative peace. In the words of classical realist Raymond Aron, peace is "the more or less lasting suspension of violent modes of rivalry between political units" and, thus, designates relations which "do not involve the military forms of struggle" (Aron 2003 [1966]: 151). Peace thus understood is often a victor's peace that has Darwinian, exclusive and unreflexive qualities. It is only available to the powerful and a "commonwealth" they may want to create.

More generally, realists see peace as the (temporary) stability of relations structured by the same principle that guides all state behaviour, namely the distribution of power in the international system. Consequently, realist forms of peace take on different expressions, depending on the kinds of power relations at play in a given setting. Crudely put, there are two types: a state-centric balance of power, whereby each camp might be dominated by a hegemon, and an overarching, system-wide hegemonic power, which takes on the form of an empire (see also Aron 2003 [1966]: 151). The "balancing peace" is based on self-constraint upheld by the logic of deterrence and effectively replaces the concept of peace with "security". Realists have debated whether a bipolar or a multipolar world is more stable – "less war-prone" and thus more "peaceful" – and what role nuclear weapons have in this logic. This is not the place to rehash this debate (see Grieco 2007), but it is worth noting that those favouring bipolarity draw on a deep tradition of viewing equilibrium as a form of natural harmony (see also Little 2007).[8] The notion of an "imperial peace" builds on the view that one superior power is able to control and order relations among all other actors in the system, as expressed in the notion of a *pax romana* or *pax britannica*. In the realist literature, this kind of peace has been discussed in terms of "hegemonic stability" (Kindleberger 1973; Grunberg 1990; see also Chapter 12, this volume).

Even if we accept the notion of peace as stability, the obvious problem with the realist account is that it suffers from a great power bias in which peace is measured by the ability to rule and maintain order without any consideration of the violence intrinsic to an imperial system. More generally, for both balancing and imperial conceptions of peace, the logic of strategy dominates the realist mode of thinking and "pervades the upkeep of peace as much as the making of war". War can even be seen as the origin of peace by exhausting opponents and their resources (Luttwak 1987: xi, 57).

Opposed to this negative view of peace and humanity, idealism and liberalism claim a future possibility of a universal peace in which states and individuals are free, prosperous and unthreatened. The idealist aspect of the first "great debate" in IR realism and offered an ambitious, ethically oriented account of peace through liberal internationalism and governance, and based on human rights and a positive reading of the potential of human nature (Wilson 1998; Ashworth 2006). It advanced conceptualization of peace that highlighted international-level ethics, interdependence and transnationalism. Idealists called for disarmament, the outlawing of war, and adopted a positive view of human nature and the international capacity to cooperate. In the tradition of Kant, idealist thinking about international relations held on to the hope that war could be eradicated eventually, the right of self-determination of all citizens, and the possibility of world government or a world federation. And although idealist conceptions of peace were regarded by realist contemporaries as hopelessly utopian, their representatives saw these propositions and plans as eminently practical (Angell 1910; Zimmern 1936; Carr 2001 [1939]; Osiander 1998). They maintained that there was a human and social potential for a more sophisticated peace, resting on the normative foundations offered by liberal thought and which might be engineered in a pragmatic manner.

Arguably the most prominent liberal conception of peace in IR is found in the "democratic peace" thesis, brought to popularity with Michael Doyle's adaptation of Kant's aforementioned text (Doyle 1983). An extensive literature exists debating the theoretical logic and empirical validity of this thesis, as well as its ethical and political implications.[9] The accepted view among proponents is the familiar reading of peace as the belief among political actors that war (the use of military force) ceases to be a viable option in dealing with each other. Adopting Kant's logic, Doyle argues that such a peace is possible amongst societies based on a liberal order, with

[8] That said, in realist logic no balance is perfect and always contains seeds of instability due to the dynamic of the security dilemma.

[9] For a selection, see Brown et al. (1996); Bohman and Lutz-Bachmann (1997); Barkawi and Laffey (2001); Ish-Shalom (2013).

adherence to democratic institutions, principles of free trade, and human rights enshrined in cosmopolitan law as the three pillars of the "democratic peace" (Doyle 2005). Importantly, whereas in the theory these factors are discussed as the necessary conditions for, or causes of, the liberal peace, in the consciousness of practitioners, as well as in much of Western scholarly discourse, they have mutated into the markers of the very ontology of peace. In other words, the argument that two states governed by liberal ideas of order do not consider war as an option to solve their conflicts/disputes has generated the seductively simple image of democracy = peace, often with significant implications for Western foreign policy (Ish-Shalom 2013). Even outside the cloud of the "democratic peace" paradigm, the liberal emphasis on internationalism, functionalism, constitutionalism, as well as on norms, regimes and global governance, provided fertile ground for thinking about peace. It infers an ontology in which state institutions and international organizations can be used to develop peace as a common good for all, through which a specific epistemology and methods can be practically deployed towards an ideal of peace. This peace is represented as both process and outcome defined by a grand theory, which works in a linear and rational fashion through Western frameworks claiming universality (Paris 2004).

Marxism offers a conception of peace envisioning the absence of structural violence related to economic distribution and class domination (Rosenberg 1996). As such, it seeks to advance the notion of a positive peace in Galtung's terminology. According to Marxist thinkers, the global economy, world trade and global economic relations are structured to the advantage of small elites and social classes and their control of state and international institutions, leading to global injustice and the disempowerment of much of the world's population. Peace as social justice cannot exist while such structures exist and so revolutionary forces are deemed necessary to overcome injustice (Kubalkova and Cruickshank 1985; Maclean 1988). For Marx, capitalist property relations must be abolished in order to remove the exploitation that occurs between "nations", which intertwines the communist vision of a classless society with the necessity to transform existing conditions and, hence, links the conception of peace to an agenda of fundamental change (Padover 1971). The class framework enables a transnational view of international relations in which a struggle over the nature of order takes place not just between states, but also between mobilized classes aiming at economic justice and equality (by taking control of the means of production and removing private property). It is concerned not only with developing a form of peace in the form of a classless society, but also with a transnational organization of the masses who would take discursive and practical action to resist and overcome elite structures of exploitation. This emancipatory discourse is one of Marxism's most important contributions to IR's approaches to peace, which has brought into view the significance of peripheries and "grassroots actors", the processes by which they are marginalized and how resistance occurs. We will return to some of these aspects below.

The English School (ES) debates surrounding the concept of international society offer another take on peace. In this school of thought, "international society" is based on shared values and interests between states as a framework for peace and follows a narrow path between a balance of power and stable social relations. Although the concept of peace was never closely developed, it underpins a core theme in ES literature, perhaps most famously in the work of Hedley Bull (1977), regarding the meaning of and relationship between order and justice. There is no consensus among ES scholars as to which of the two – the pursuit of order or the promotion of justice – should take priority in the formation and maintenance of international society, with arguments moving from "pluralist" (more realist) to "solidarist" (more liberal) positions. Crudely put, peace is seen in the identification, development and expansion of international society, extended by the debate on human rights (Vincent 1986), one of the core components of the liberal notion of peace. Yet, as this expansion is limited by the norms of sovereignty and non-intervention, human rights would be merely the luxury of those whose political conditions seem to be more conducive to them (Bull 1977: 292). As the English School developed, there was a movement away from seeing human rights as subservient to power and interest, to the point where it became one of its core assumptions and driving dynamics. This was a step towards a liberal understanding of peace. Such arguments were extended in various ways via normative (Beitz 1979), cosmopolitan (Held 2003) and institutional (Keohane 1984) approaches, which later connected with the notion of just war (Walzer 1977; Wheeler 2000).

Mainstream social constructivist approaches have been concerned with how states moderate anarchy and engage in processes of socialization. A core argument of such approaches is that state behaviour and interactions are guided by (concerns over) their identities. Consequently, the construction of peaceful relations is also dependent on, or occurs through, the construction of identities. Building on the work of Karl Deutsch (1957), Adler and Barnett (1998) developed the idea of "security communities" in which states act in groups to establish a community with its own institutions aimed at providing a stable peace amongst its members. In such a transnational community, states retain their own sense of identity while sharing a "meta-identity" with other members. The fabric of this community is composed of shared knowledge, especially ideas, and dense interactions, which are seen as generating forms of (positive) mutual identification and, with it, "dependable expectations of peaceful change" (Adler and Barnett 1998: 6ff., 34). The same logic is at play in Wendt's theory, which sees states moving from enmity to friendship by changing the culture of anarchy and recasting their images of Self and Other from enemies to friends (Wendt 1999; see also Kupchan 2010).

These social constructivist attempts of outlining a path away from a realist world towards regional "security communities" or global international "friendship" entertain a process-oriented conception of peacebuilding and have an unmistaken liberal undertone. The envisioned endpoint, also, is rather familiar, namely a relationship in which there is "neither the expectation of, nor the preparation for organized violence as a means to settle internal disputes" (Adler and Barnett 1998: 34). The emphasis on a shared normative order underpinning this expectation links up with both English School and democratic peace scholarship and is sometimes combined with Deutsch's view of "integration" as a force for peace (see also Chapter 17, this volume). The reluctance of constructivist literature to theorize peace in more substantive ways could be attributed to the view that peace is what you make of it. At the same time, the emphasis on collective identity formation opens an important door towards thinking about the construction of a positive peace. There is little place for structural violence within friendship, one might say. Such intuitive claims can also be the source of complacency, however, as they allow constructivists to benefit from the rhetorical affiliation with concepts of "community" and "friendship" and, more generally, to rest their head on the idea that a shared "identity" is a source of peace. The problem is not only that the literature often treats these associated concepts in vague terms, but also that processes of collective identity formation are compatible with, and often the source of, violence vis-à-vis others.

The frameworks offered by Marxism, the English School and social constructivism challenge realist and liberal approaches on ontological and methodological grounds. However, any alternative conceptions of peace they did offer were sidelined by or assimilated into the conviction that Western ideas of order won the Cold War, in which the liberal peace emerged as the main blueprint approach and widely accepted standard. As a seemingly objective point of reference, the liberal conception enables the diplomat, politician, official of transnational organizations or transnational agencies, to judge what is right and wrong in terms of aspirations, processes, institutions and methods. Within this frame, even notions of peace as process operate with the idea of a stable order developed and controlled through systems of governance run by state elites and the rationalist bureaucratic and administrative power which goes with statehood. More recently, a neo-liberal and technocratic version of the liberal peace has emerged, focused on security and institutional design, framed by global capital rather than norms and rights. Although often infused with notions of development and images of the good life, this peace largely remains negative in character: a treaty between competitive states best ensured through strong national and international institutions and law, as well as globalized capital, which are supposed to minimize the violence inherent in society and between states.

Peace in Critical IR Theory

The emergence of a critical impulse has perhaps been one of the most important developments in IR theory over the last generation. Different strands rest partially on a rejection of the object–subject divide and on a linguistic turn, bringing to the fore power relations, including those affecting constructions of identities, to critique the liberal orthodoxy and the increasingly neo-liberal overtones of mainstream IR theory. Through doing so, critical approaches have also advanced a more sophisticated conceptualization of peace (Cox 1987; Linklater 2007).

A general point of departure is the critique of the (neo)liberal conception of peace as Eurocentric in origin and often top-down in practice. It targets the very attempt to clearly define peace on an abstract level and to ground conceptions in Western philosophical traditions and experiences, as well as the subsequent practice of measuring and building such "peace" in other parts of the world. As such, the critique is both theoretical and practical. Given the immediacy of the politics of everyday life, as well as the complexities of global and historical injustice and inequality, critical perspectives consider the (neo)liberal peace as not responsive enough to the demands made on it by states, officials and communities, particularly in the sphere of social welfare, justice, culture and identity. It is also not designed with the structural limitations of conflict-affected societies and states in mind, resulting in resistance and a contradiction between institutions, capital, security and expanded notions of rights.

In response, critical perspectives advance the notion of what might be called a post-Westphalian peace, in which territorial sovereignty and its ontology no longer characterize the global normative landscape and political cartography. It is a complex and pluralist concept of peace, relating to a discursive, emancipatory project, reflecting the everyday life of all, men, women and children, in varied contexts around the world. It points towards a postcolonial understanding of peace as hybrid, representing an encounter between claims of the subaltern and existing power structures relative to state and global governance (Richmond 2015).

Critical perspectives emphasize emancipation as an integral element of a conceptualization of peace, opening up broader questions of justice. This form of peace is based on, and revolves around, forms of communication designed to facilitate emancipation from violence in direct and structural forms, both for the individual and for groups, leading to empathy and commensurate equality between them (Balibar 2002: 4). It offers an account of a systemic process of emancipation built into the communicative institutions of world politics, as well as an attempt to show how individuals can achieve emancipation within such moral communities. It implies a negotiated but pluriversal peace attainable though dialogue in various fora. This materialist and "discourse ethic" requires that principles be established through a dialogue that does not exclude any person or moral position. All boundaries and systems should be examined through this process to avoid exclusion and facilitate a recognition of the inter-subjective nature of knowledge, even in instrumental areas such as the workings of the global political economy. This would be made possible through the evolution of social learning towards a post-conventional morality where actors and individuals seek norms that have universal appeal and consequently lead to a universal moral community (Linklater 2007). The positive epistemology of peace advanced by critical theorists thus holds that emancipation is both plausible and pragmatic, and an epistemic basis and methodology to realize this is possible, despite the age-old problems related to entrenched understandings and discourses of interests and difference. Although it requires that the inherent contradictions of capitalism, of the nation-state, self-determination and identity, and the requirements for free universal communication, are engaged with (Allan 2006: 91; see also Gilligan 1993).

A position that emphasizes emancipation inevitably has to skirt between the twin dangers of relativism and universalism, and grapple with the difficult question what this higher form of freedom looks like (Laclau 1996: 18–19). A universalism which recognizes that individuals create their world – or in this case, their particular forms of peace – may well be a sufficient response to this problem. But the liberal impulse constrains this authorship which should entail emancipations rather than a singular form of emancipation (Laclau 1996: 122). A conception of peace offered through critical approaches thus is not unproblematic, if it relies on a specific and claimed universal set of human norms and discourse ethics, which does not deal with technology, the environment or agency outside of the Enlightenment framework of autonomous and individual rationality. Although critical approaches have brought a much richer set of issues and dynamics to the debate (Rengger and Thirkell-White 2007), they are in danger of falling back into the familiar territory of liberal thinking about peace and its dependence on rational states, markets and institutions that progressively provide emancipation from above, with only limited engagement with those being emancipated according to their historical and material positionality.

Post-structuralism offers an alternative critical approach to those based on universalism, by explicitly taking an anti-foundationalist stance against Enlightenment meta-narratives of progress, structural determinism or realist tragedy. It holds that rational theory effectively reifies a (neo)liberal empire that rests on the residue of historical imperialism and capitalism, as well as maintaining a range of discriminatory frameworks and "truths" that are in effect simply the interests of the powerful. Given its resistance to meta-narratives, post-structuralism does not offer a single concept of peace. Instead, it opens up radically new possibilities for ontologies of peace, by exploring the relationship between knowledge and power. Yet, while post-structuralist approaches are effective in exposing power relations, they offer little in the way of suggestions for how to deal with oppressive direct and structural forms of power beyond resistance. In the best case scenario, agonistic forms of peace will co-exist, especially at the everyday level where critique and resistance to power and injustice will continue, but there is no universal utopia waiting to be uncovered or organized.

One fruitful perspective on how an ontology of peace may be thought of is derived from the postcolonial notion of hybridity (Bhabha 1994). This implies the overlay of multiple identities and ideas, and their transmission without necessarily resulting in the domination of one core identity or idea, though power relations are inevitably present. Adjusting Galtung's typology, a negative hybrid peace would see existing power structures remaining dominant. A positive hybrid peace would result from thinking through the possibility of a positive peace from the 'bottom up', in which power structures would be shaped in favour of the subaltern, the local and the everyday. How this would happen is a debate that often turns to discussions of empowerment in terms of intervention and the developmental state, or the agency of civil society actors able to operate in an open up alternative spaces that are not necessarily delineated or patrolled by states (Walker 1994).

From this perspective, much of IR's orthodoxy is anti-peace, at least in positive hybrid form, and at best leads to a negative peace. The accounts outlined earlier favour a discursive and hegemonic framework derived from Western ontologies and interests, where everyday life is rationalized within a universal knowledge system, which is biased towards specific, normally Western, localities and their historical privileges. They cannot escape the "othering" impact of Western categories and their tendency of discursively dominating and dehumanizing the non-liberal, non-Western subject (Said 1978; Chan et al. 2001; Muppidi 2012). An appropriate response, from this perspective, is to "decolonize" peace as a concept and the structure in which it is practised (Fontan 2012). Such a move would require not only a deconstruction of and distancing from mainstream conceptions of peace, but also refraining from even attempting to formulate a particular meaning. It would require humility and taking "not knowing" what peace might mean as a point of departure. Combined with an *eirinist* perspective aimed at opening up a critical discussion about forms of peace found in existing peacebuilding praxis and with a commitment to a pluralist perspective on who peace is for, it would aim at letting meanings of peace emerge in an inclusive dialogue that gives preference to subaltern voices (Richmond 2009).

Here the notion of a positive hybrid peace and the possibility of a mutual mediation of ideas and identities it denotes could still be useful. Inspirations in this regard can be found in work on aesthetic approaches to IR (Bleiker 2009), on development (Sylvester 2006), and more generally in work that identifies a range of power relations and injustices across time and space, and which identifies or rescues alternative modes of governance and legitimacy. An important contribution to such moves has been encapsulated within feminist approaches and their critiques of wealthy, male-dominated views of power and their priorities embedded in the international system. The feminist project (or projects) seeks not only to understand the power relations that attempt to objectify and marginalize voices and perspectives, but also to offer various routes to recognize the inter-subjectivity identities, not least through a reflexive methodology and an emphasis on listening (Tickner and Sjoberg 2011). Feminist theorizing makes clear the need to engage with everyday life, and indeed that there is an "everyday realm to international relations" where "empathetic cooperation" has potential (Sylvester 1994). This implies a subtler form of emancipation, incorporating an understanding of the politics of resistance, solidarity and indigenous movements, rather than following the conceptualizations offered through elite intellectual and interventionary practices and action in top-down hegemonic institutions.

Ultimately, the more critical the approach, the more the positive form of peace has to encompass a range of actors, issues, claims and demands, resulting in a hybrid form bringing together different identities and values into a common relationship of difference, which may often be agonistic. Positive and hybrid forms of peace also need to address underlying structural and material issues if they are to move from being negative to positive. And yet, supporting the emancipatory promise of "peace" by formulating a positive reading through the notion of hybridity also must recognize that direct, structural or governmental forms of power can severely limit its potential. As discussed in postcolonial theory, as well as the work of Foucault, such forms of power can turn hybridity into domination and complicity, which are hardly plausible conditions for positive forms of peace to emerge.[10] This is not a reason to relinquish the ambition. But it illustrates the dilemma for critical approaches of how to advance an intuitively benign concept like "peace" and prevent it from becoming part of the very power structure it aims to overcome.

Conclusion

Peace is a deeply normative concept that necessarily combines idealism, materialism and pragmatism. Thinking about "peace" is thus never simply an academic undertaking – indeed, we might say conceptualizing it is inevitably linked to the practice of building it. And when we do think about it, we see that peace is both an ideal and a process variously related to conceptions of security, violence, power, emancipation, cooperation, development, identity, justice, and so on. While this chapter has focused primarily on how the concept is treated in different theoretical contexts, it is clear that visions of peace and the practical frameworks created in its name are politically consequential, enabling states, international architecture, and markets.

For both theorists and practitioners it is important to keep alive the emancipatory thrust of the concept and to keep in mind that, whatever form it takes, peace is not

[10] For a critical discussion of the notion of hybrid peace, see Nadarajah and Rampton (2015).

therapeutic and discursive but is connected to the harder materiality of conditions. It should provide social, economic and political resources sufficient to meet the demands made on it by its local constituencies and an international community of which it should be a stakeholder. And while we must guard against the attempt to conceive of a universal concept of peace encompassing the world in its totality, peace should also not become a paradox of oppositional forces or concepts. It should not be utopian and unobtainable, but it should also not be dystopian and lack legitimacy amongst those who are subject to it. Any version of peace should cumulatively engage with everyday life as well as institutions from the bottom up. It should rest on uncovering a relational ontology, on empathy and emancipation, and recognize the fluidity of peace as a process, as well as its constant renegotiation on the international level. In other words, scholars and practitioners of peace should endeavour to see themselves as agents of empathetic emancipation, whereby their role is to mediate the global norm or institution with the local before it is constructed. This involves an exploration of different and more hybrid ontologies of peace than those found in mainstream IR theory.

Suggested Readings

Boulding, Elise (2000) *Cultures of Peace: The Hidden Side of History*. Syracuse, NY: Syracuse University Press.

An ambitious book that brings together the author's life work and provides a cogent description of the cultural dimensions of peace.

Kant, Immanuel (1795) *Zum Ewigen Frieden: Ein Philosophischer Entwurf* (On Perpetual Peace: A Philosophical Essay). Königsberg: Nicolovius.

A classic and highly influential text, easy to read and richer than many contemporary discussions of it may suggest.

Lederach, John-Paul (1997) *Building Peace: Sustainable Reconciliation in Divided Societies*. Washington, DC: US Institute of Peace.

Explains why and how grassroots peacebuilding is important.

Mitrany, David (1944) *A Working Peace System: An Argument for the Functional Development of International Organization*. Oxford: Oxford University Press.

Explains how international institutions can be established to build peace after the Second World War.

Richmond, Oliver (2005) *The Transformation of Peace*. London: Palgrave.

Discusses the limitations of contemporary liberal peacebuilding and points to the emergence of hybrid forms of peace.

Bibliography

Adler, Emmanuel and Michael Barnett (eds) (1998) *Security Communities*. Cambridge: Cambridge University Press.

Allan, Pierre (2006) 'Measuring International Ethics', in Pierre Allan and Alexis Keller, *What is a Just Peace?* Oxford: Oxford University Press.

Angell, Norman (1910) *The Great Illusion*. London: Heinneman.
Aron, Raymond (2003 [1966]) *Peace and War*. New Brunswick, NJ: Transaction Publishers.
Ashworth, Lucien (2006) 'Where are the Idealists in Interwar IR?', *Review of International Studies* 32(2): 291–308.
Balibar, Etienne (2002) *Politics and the Other Scene*. London: Verso.
Banks, Michael (1987) 'Four Conceptions of Peace', in S. Sandole and I. Sandole (eds) *Conflict Management and Problem Solving*. New York: New York University Press, pp. 259–273.
Barkawi, Tarak and Mark Laffey (eds) (2001) *Democracy, Liberalism and War*. Boulder, CO: Lynne Rienner.
Berenskoetter, Felix (2011) 'Reclaiming the Vision Thing: Constructivists as Students of the Future', *International Studies Quarterly* 55(3): 647–668.
Beitz, Charles (1979) *Political Theory and International Relations*. Princeton, NJ: Princeton University Press.
Bhabha, Homi K. (1994) *The Location of Culture*. London: Routledge.
Bleiker, Roland (2009) *Aesthetics and World Politics*. London: Palgrave Macmillan.
Bohman, J. and M. Lutz-Bachmann (eds) (1997) *Perpetual Peace: Essays on Kant's Cosmopolitan Ideal*. Cambridge, MA: MIT Press.
Brown, Chris (2007) 'Tragedy, "Tragic Choices" and Contemporary International Political Theory', *International Relations* 21(1): 5–14.
Brown, Michael, Sean Lynn-Jones and Steven E. Miller (eds) (1996) *Debating the Democratic Peace*. Cambridge, MA: MIT Press.
Bull, Hedley (1977) *The Anarchical Society*. New York: Columbia University Press.
Bulloch, Douglas (2008) 'For Whom Nobel Tolls? An Interpretative Account of the Migration of the Concept of Peace as Perceived through the Solemn Eyes of Norwegian Lawmakers', *Millennium: Journal of International Studies* 36(3): 575–595.
Buzan, Barry (1996) 'The Timeless Wisdom of Realism', in Steve Smith et al. (eds) *International Theory: Positivism and Beyond*. Cambridge: Cambridge University Press, pp 47–65.
Buzan, Barry and Lene Hansen (2009) *The Evolution of International Security Studies*. Cambridge: Cambridge University Press.
Carr, Edward H. (2001 [1939]) *The Twenty Years' Crisis, 1919–1939*. Basingstoke: Palgrave.
Chan, Stephen, Peter G. Mandaville and Ronald Bleiker (eds) (2001) *The Zen of IR*. London: Palgrave.
Chernus, Ira (2002) *Eisenhower's Atoms for Peace*. College Station, TX: Texas A&M University Press.
Cortright, David (2008) *Peace: A History of Movements and Ideas*. Cambridge: Cambridge University Press.
Cox, Robert W. (1987) *Production, Power, and World Order*. New York: Columbia University Press.
Deutsch, Karl (1957) *Political Community and the North Atlantic Area*. Princeton, NJ: Princeton University Press.
Dietrich, Wolfgang (2012) *Interpretations of Peace in History and Culture*. Basingstoke and New York: Palgrave Macmillan.
Doyle, Michael (1983) 'Kant, Liberal Legacies, and Foreign Affairs', *Philosophy and Public Affairs* 12(3/4): 323–353, 1151–1169.
Doyle, Michael (2005) 'Three Pillars of the Liberal Peace', *American Political Science Review* 99(3): 463–466.
Fontan, Victoria (2012) *Decolonising Peace*. Doerzbach: Dignity Press.
Galtung, Johan (1969) 'Violence, Peace and Peace Research', *Journal of Peace Research* 6(3): 167–191.
Galtung, Johan (1996) *Peace by Peaceful Means*. London: Sage.
Gilligan, Carol (1993) *In a Different Voice*. Cambridge, MA: Harvard University Press.

Gleditsch, Nils P., Jonas Nordkvelle and Havard Strand (2014) 'Peace Research – Just the Study of War?, *Journal of Peace Research* 51(2): 145–158.
Grieco, Joseph (2007) 'Structural Realism and the Problem of Polarity and War', in F. Berenskoetter and M. J. Williams (eds) *Power in World Politics*. London: Routledge, pp. 64–82.
Grunberg, Isabelle (1990) 'Exploring the "Myth" of Hegemonic Stability', *International Organization* 44(4): 431–477.
Held, David (2003) 'Cosmopolitanism: Globalisation Tamed', *Review of International Studies* 29(4): 465–480.
Ish-Shalom, Piki (2013) *Democratic Peace: A Political Biography*. Ann Arbor, MI: University of Michigan Press.
Kant, Immanuel (1917 [1795]) *Perpetual Peace: A Philosophical Essay* (trans./intro. Mary Campbell Smith). London: George Allen & Unwin.
Keohane, Robert O. (1984) *After Hegemony*. Princeton, NJ: Princeton University Press.
Kindleberger, Charles (1973) *The World in Depression, 1929–1939*. Berkeley, CA: University of California Press.
Kubalkova, Vendulka and Albert Cruickshank (1985) *Marxism and International Relations*. Oxford: Clarendon Press.
Kupchan, Charles A. (2010) *How Enemies Become Friends*. Princeton, NJ: Princeton University Press.
Laclau, Ernesto (1996) *Emancipation(s)*. London: Verso.
Lederach, John Paul (2005) *The Moral Imagination*. Oxford: Oxford University Press.
Linklater, Andrew (2007) *Critical Theory and World Politics*. London: Routledge.
Little, Richard (2007) *The Balance of Power in International Relations*. Cambridge: Cambridge University Press.
Luttwak, Edward N. (1987) *Strategy: The Logic of War and Peace*. Cambridge, MA: Harvard University Press.
Maclean, John (1988) 'Marxism and International Relations: a Strange Case of Mutual Neglect', *Millennium: Journal of International Studies* 17(2): 295–319.
Mitscherlich, Alexander (1968) *Die Idee des Friedens und die menschliche Aggressivität*. Frankfurt am Main: Suhrkamp.
Muppidi, Himadeep (2012) *The Colonial Signs of International Relations*. London: Hurst & Co.
Nadarajah, Suthaharan and David Rampton (2015) 'The Limits of Hybridity and the Crisis of Liberal Peace', *Review of International Studies* 41(1): 49-72.
Osiander, Andreas (1998) 'Rereading Early Twentieth Century IR Theory: Idealism Revisited', *International Studies Quarterly* 42(3): 409–432.
Padover, Saul K. (ed.) (1971) *The Karl Marx Library: On Revolution*. New York: McGraw Hill.
Paris, Roland (2004) *At War's End*. Cambridge: Cambridge University Press.
Rengger, Nicholas and Ben Thirkell-White (eds) (2007) 'Critical IR Theory after 25 Years', *Review of International Studies* 33, Special Issue.
Richmond, Oliver (2005) *The Transformation of Peace*. London: Palgrave.
Richmond, Oliver (2008) 'Reclaiming Peace in International Relations', *Millennium: Journal of International Studies* 36(3): 439–470.
Richmond, Oliver (2009) 'A Post-liberal Peace: Eirenism and the Everyday', *Review of International Studies* 35(3): 557–580.
Richmond, Oliver (2015) 'Dilemmas of a Hybrid Peace: Negative or Positive?', *Cooperation and Conflict* 50(1): 50–68.
Rosenberg, Justin (1996) 'Isaac Deutscher and the Lost History of International Relations', *New Left Review* (Jan.–Feb.): 3–15.
Said, Edward (1978) *Orientalism*. London: Penguin.
Senghaas, Dieter (2007) *On Perpetual Peace: A Timely Assessment*. Trans. Ewald Osers. New York: Berghahn Books.

Sylvester, Christine (1994) 'Empathetic Cooperation: A Feminist Method for IR', *Millennium: Journal of International Studies* 23(2): 315–334.

Sylvester, Christine (2006) 'Bare Life as Development/Postcolonial Problematic', *The Geographical Journal* 172(1): 66–77.

Tickner J. Ann and Laura Sjoberg (2011) *Feminism and International Relations*, London: Routledge.

Urdal, Henrik, Gudrun Ostby and Nils Petter Gleditsch (2014) 'Journal of Peace Research', *Peace Review: A Journal of Social Justice* 24(4): 500–4.

Vincent, John (1986) *Human Rights and International Relations*. Cambridge: Cambridge University Press.

Walker, R. B. J. (1994) 'Social Movements/World Politics', *Millennium: Journal of International Studies* 23(3): 669–700.

Waltz, Kenneth (1959) *Man, the State and War*. New York: Columbia University Press.

Walzer, Michael (1977) *Just and Unjust Wars*. New York: Basic Books.

Wendt, Alexander (1999) *Social Theory of International Politics*. Cambridge: Cambridge University Press.

Wheeler, Nick (2000) *Saving Strangers*. Oxford: Oxford University Press.

Wilson, Peter (1998) 'The Myth of the First Great Debate', *Review of International Studies* 24(5): 1–16.

Zimmern, Alfred (1936) *The League of Nations and the Rule of Law*. London: Macmillan.

8

Anarchy

Alex Prichard

Steven Walt recently argued that if you had to explain an International Relations (IR) degree in five minutes, the number one concept you should understand, the concept that distinguishes IR as a social science, is anarchy. "You don't have to be a realist", he said, "to recognize that what makes international politics different from domestic politics is that it takes place in the absence of central authority" (Walt 2014). The absence of central authority between states is indeed the basic working definition of anarchy in IR. But the confidence with which anarchy's centrality to IR was proclaimed by Walt cannot be said to be matched by everyone. John Mearsheimer (2005) laments that realists, like Walt, are in fact fighting a rear-guard action from the "idealists", who have more or less taken over the field in the UK, and increasingly in North America too. This latter (somewhat amorphous) group, he argued, does not prioritise states as the primary actors, nor do they place them at the heart of their analysis. For Mearsheimer, by contrast to Walt, it seems you might indeed need to be a realist to think that anarchy is IR's core concept.

In fact, Mearsheimer is probably right, and Walt wrong. When we survey the rest of the discipline, we see that the centrality of the concept of anarchy to explaining world politics is routinely rejected on normative grounds, as well as empirical, ontological and methodological ones. Liberal theorists have long complained that an analytical focus on anarchy occludes more than it illuminates (Milner 1991). Many theorists point out that while anarchy may be a formal structure of world politics, it does not help us explain why states cooperate or how institutions emerge or why domestic politics shapes states' preferences and actions (Donnelly 2015). Feminists have rejected the centrality of anarchy to the analysis and practice of world politics because to prioritise it sustains the informal hierarchy of states, and a public/private distinction within them, and therefore the domination of women by men globally (Sjoberg 2011). Marxists have consistently argued that anarchy is only a structural feature of late-modern capitalism. Modern states were formed to manage the structural contradictions and inequalities precipitated by the institution of private property, and the anarchic state system is a function of underlying economic inequalities, not of states per se (Rosenberg 1994, cf. 2013). Constructivists have sought to show that anarchy is indeterminate, and that the mutual constitution of identity explains outcomes in international relations more effectively than anything else. Indeed, it has become something of a new orthodoxy to claim that "anarchy is what states make of it" (Wendt 1992). Finally, though this is by no means an exhaustive list, postcolonial and poststructuralist theorists have shown how a political discourse and de jure defence of anarchy in fact sustain a very clear "standard of civilization", in other words, a de facto hierarchy between states and races (Hobson 2014).

My approach in this chapter is somewhat different. I will explore the legacy of the social contract tradition in IR's empirical account of anarchy, in other words the way ideal social contract theory has shaped and in some instances acted as a stand in for empirical reality. I also want to explore the ways and means by which IR theorists have rejected this move. The social contract tradition stretches back at least to Hobbes, and what we in IR are contending with today are a range of responses to, and interpretations of, his writings (Tuck 2001; Armitage 2012: 59–74). I will argue that within this tradition the invocation of anarchy acted as a justification of state power, which became a bulwark against the many and highly politicised threats 'out there'. The existence of anarchy became, therefore, a justification for the state and a European notion of international right. It was not, at its inception, a *description of* world politics (Jahn 2009). By re-embedding the genealogy of anarchy, as used in IR, in these much wider moral and philosophical arguments, we can show what is at stake when we invoke the concept of anarchy, why the debate has been so heated and how definitions of anarchy delimit what is deemed possible and permissible in world politics.

I argue that the concept of anarchy is used in four ways. There are those who (1) extol the *virtues* of anarchy; (2) those who have sought to *tame* anarchy; (3) a group that has sought to *transcend* anarchy; and (4) a final, more radical and admittedly smaller and more recent group that has sought to *rethink* anarchy's virtues. It will become clear that each group of writers defines the concept in subtly different, but far-reaching ways, each with identifiable links back to a very parochial European tradition of political theory. Each group of writers, indeed, different individuals within the same group, are also responding to very different historical circumstances and proposing very different visions of politics and the good life. It is the relationships between these factors – internal conceptual genealogy, intellectual debate, world-historical context, and normative vision – that have shaped the evolution of the concept of anarchy.

"The Virtues of Anarchy"

It was Kenneth Waltz who argued that anarchy had distinct "virtues" (1979: 111), but this stands in stark contrast to standard understandings of the term. Anarchy derives from the Greek αναρχία. Written as *an-arkhos*, this denotes the absence (*an*) of a leader (*arkhos*). In ancient Greece, leaders of all sorts were known as *archon*, today rendered as *archontas*. For Plato, anarchy was synonymous with democracy, the rule of the plebeians, usually by lot (sortition). Democracy, the rule of the many or demos, was contrary to nature, and, he believed, it even infected animals with a sickness (Gordon 2006; Rancière 2006). It was from this latter understanding of anarchy that it came to be associated with chaos and disorderliness, contrary to nature. It is only recently, through the anarchistic tendencies of the Occupy movement, that the link between anarchy and democracy has been reclaimed in political discourse more widely, and I discuss this further in the final section of the chapter.

The conventional use of anarchy in IR theory relates to a quite different set of social relations. But the first thing to note is that the IR scholars that championed the use of the term were never particularly interested in the internal makeup of states. It became a matter of disciplinary autonomy for IR to focus efforts on understanding the relations *between* states. Anarchy was said to reside 'out there', not within modern states. The problem of anarchy has now been pushed outside, where states refuse to bow to a superior power. As noted, in this context, anarchy is defined simply as "the absence of centralised authority" (Wendt 1999: 249). The challenge, then, was to understand why (if at all) anarchy is pathological in world politics instead, and what to do about it.

By contrast to Plato, most mainstream, predominantly American IR scholars note that in spite of the absence of centralised authority in world politics, there are still identifiable patterns and regularities in the conduct of states that would seem to be the antithesis of chaos and disorder. Somewhat counter-intuitively perhaps, during the Cold War, key IR theorists such as Kenneth Waltz (1979) argued that anarchy imparts order to the international system. He challenged the discipline to answer the following question: "how to conceive of an order without an orderer and of organizational effects where formal organisation is lacking" (1979: 89)? His answer started from the assumption that "[f]ormally, each [state] is the equal of all the others. None is entitled to command; none is required to obey. International systems are decentralised and anarchic" (1979: 88). Throughout history, Waltz argued, anarchy has forced states into remarkably similar patterns of self-help behaviour, which precipitate balances of power between them, and these balances are generally stable and enduring and are dependent on nothing more than the changing distribution of material capabilities in the system.

Transhistorical claims such as these are eminently amenable to a broadly neo-positivist approach to world politics, to game theory and other sorts of modelling and statistical analysis. This dominant approach in IR takes descriptive or explanatory hypotheses drawn from theories such as these, and tests them against the available evidence. The development of the explanatory power of the concept of anarchy (for example) takes place when the evidence is incongruent with the theory. But what is most interesting about Waltz is that this was not his method. As he put it, "I consider myself to be a Kantian, not a positivist" (Halliday and Rosenberg 1998: 379). Exploring Waltz's writings a little further helps us uncover this little appreciated aspect of his theory, and will begin to illustrate IR's deep roots in political theory.

Following Kant, Waltz believed that anarchy was not only something to observe, but also something to uphold. It had distinctive "virtues". "The prospect of world government", he argued, "would be an invitation to prepare for world civil war", (Waltz 1979: 112) and the greater the need to defend this world state, the more concentrated power would become at the centre and the greater the prize for any would-be revisionist states. Thus, "the virtues of anarchy" revolve around the defence of the autonomy of states, the freedoms people secure within them and the means by which they choose to do so. Inter-state anarchy is the precondition of the liberty of states vis-à-vis one another. Anarchy also permits the fullest freedom of action at the international level. But this freedom precipitates a security dilemma, since all states can also resort to war. The threat of violent conflict compels states to build up their internal military capacities, and the most successful at modernising, in such a way that can pull people into that process, will be those best equipped to respond to the structural pressures imposed by a condition of self-help. We may not like the fact that there is no world government, but, he concludes, "[i]f freedom is wanted, insecurity must be accepted" (ibid).

In the context of Cold War détente, Waltz had very particular policies and processes in mind when he developed this defence of the virtues of anarchy. His particular object of attack was an emerging full-throated liberalism that saw the defeat of Soviet Russia as the manifest destiny of the US. Waltz deployed a Hobbesian reading of Kant (Waltz 1962; see also Tuck 2001), one which was both more pessimistic and more conservative, to counter the transcendental universalism so common in more radical-liberal Kantian politics, for example contemporary democratic peace theory.

Waltz explicitly rejected the interpretation of Kant that justified the transcendence of anarchy and the institutionalisation of a global commonwealth of like-minded republics (Kant 1991). Waltz's conservative Kantianism is an explicit echo of the criticisms of the messianic expansionism that animated Prussian, and later twentieth-century German, foreign policy (Shilliam 2009). Here, our protagonist was the liberal historian of the Prussian unification of Germany, and the early twentieth century's arch-militarist, Heinrich Gotthard von Treitschke (1916). Von Treitschke developed a thin Kantian or conservative republicanism into a much thicker, Hegelian and Hobbesian account of an organic state. Whereas for Waltz the state is a means to an end, for von Treitschke the state is the epitome of political reason, and a people without a state is a people without reason. Following Hegel, the state is an end in itself. The state's legal personality is key, demarcating it as distinct from its neighbours, having quelled the anarchy within. The myth of the Peace of Westphalia, so central to IR's self-identity, was central to von Treitschke's account of German unification and statehood, the defining moment in the ascendency of the unified and sovereign German state, and was instrumental in justifying the unification of Germany under the influence of Prussia and its prime minister, Otto von Bismarck. With Bismarck's success, the centre of gravity in the intellectual world shifted from France to Germany, with students and scholars of strategy, history, political science and administration flocking there to continue their education.

It should be no surprise that this account of politics was to become so central to US political science, when we consider that Woodrow Wilson's professors at Princeton, like many other first-generation US political scientists, were students of von Treitschke (Schmidt 1998: Ch. 2). Their aim, as Brian Schmidt and others have so aptly shown, was to justify and make sense of US colonial responsibilities in the aftermath of the wars with Spain and the internal colonisation and unification of North America, and give both a defence of state-building internally and of expansionism externally. For theorists writing at a time when the establishment of the state was so precarious, it seemed anarchy threatened from without and within and only overwhelming state power, slowly spreading outwards, could remedy this. It is this that Waltz rejected, but it was to become more entrenched in Anglo-American political science as the decades passed.

Central to the political or practical purchase of this expansionism was the rhetorical force of Hobbes' great thought experiment, the state of nature, in which the absence of authoritative force left individuals in a state of constant fear and insecurity. But, as he put it: "though there had never been any time, wherein particular men were in a condition of warre one against the another; yet in all times, Kings, and Persons of Soveraigne authority, because of their Independency, are in continual jealousies, and in the state and posture of Gladiators ... which is a posture of War". What he says following this is equally important for our purposes. He continued: "But because they uphold thereby the Industry of their Subjects; there does not follow from it, that misery, which accompanies the Liberty of particular men" (Hobbes 1996: 90). Anarchy is fine for states but not for peoples. Hobbes had two types of peoples in mind with this metaphor. The first were the warring noblemen of the English Civil War, the second the stateless people of the New World. Hobbes' holdings in the Virginia Company, a key coloniser of the Eastern seaboard of the Americas, is also highly relevant in this context (Tuck 2001: 119). It was sentiments such as these that were picked up by von Treitschke, who argued that the forces at the borders were irrational for as long as they lacked a powerful state and could rightly be defeated in war. So, as Hobbes makes clear here, anarchy has distinct virtues: it protects the sovereignty of peoples that thereby makes them free, but it creates a tension between the need to consolidate state power and reduce insecurity at home, and the potentially limitless scope of the state needed in order to do so, threats being ubiquitous in a state of anarchy.

This tension is part of what John Mearsheimer calls *The Tragedy of Great Power Politics* (2001). The structure of anarchy itself imposes imperatives on states that militate against a defensive posture. More closely following von Treitschke than Kant or Waltz, Mearsheimer (2001: 2) argues that "A state's ultimate goal is to be the hegemon in the system". In such a competitive environment, states are compelled to pursue offensive strategies, which prompts them in others, entrenching anarchy and the security dilemma in turn. The tragedy of great power politics is arguably allegorical, because we think and act as though politics can be a domain of progress, believing that what we achieve domestically must be defended and even extended overseas. But it is precisely in this attempt that the revisionist and hegemonic states alike reveal the war-prone, cyclical and unchanging anarchy of world politics. While Mearsheimer doesn't put it quite like this, if we understand tragedy in this way (Lebow, 2003), anarchy can be understood as virtuous precisely because it is educational. At the very least, for Mearsheimer, the recognition of the structural imperatives of anarchy counters the moralisation of politics, a tendency he is most prone to identify in the theories of the "idealists" to which we will now turn.

Taming Anarchy

I have of course begun by presenting a stylised, realist account of anarchy, an account that, depending on the inflection, can lead to both revisionist or conservative, or offensive and defensive realist policy at once. This section will unpack variations of the liberal account of anarchy. It may surprise the reader to know that the term "international anarchy" was coined by Goldsworthy Lowes Dickinson, a radical liberal, in his

1916 title *The European Anarchy*. What did he mean by this? The book opens with the following words: "In the great and tragic history of Europe there is a turning-point that marks the defeat of the ideal of a world-order and the definite acceptance of international anarchy. That turning-point is the emergence of the sovereign State at the end of the fifteenth century" (Dickinson 1916: 1). At this time, the medieval era began to give way to the rise of absolutist states. It was this absolutism, he argued, and the egoism of the unencumbered sovereign, that precipitated the state of war. Far from being a stable and progressive force, for Dickinson, this egoism ultimately precipitated the hated balance of power doctrine, and the European empires it rationalised and sustained. Like the "realists" that followed him, Dickinson's advance over the nineteenth-century liberals was to argue that it was not in the character of this or that state, or the fault of any one state, that the cause of war can be found, but rather, the "main and permanent offence is common to all States. It is the anarchy which they are all responsible for perpetuating" (1916: 10).

Anarchy is no more natural than a choice of tie, and for Dickinson, unlike defenders of *raison d'état*, it was within the powers of given states to change their behaviours and change the international order, namely via authoritative international institutions such as the League of Nations. The Enlightenment philosopher most likely to act as an intellectual buttress for this sort of institutionalism was the Genevan Calvinist, Jean-Jacques Rousseau. Rousseau was the single most important political theorist of the eighteenth and nineteenth centuries, if we gauge that importance in terms of his "impact" on practical politics. His writings were taken up by revolutionaries of all stripes across Europe, none more significant than Robespierre, the architect of the French Revolution, who treated his writings literally as gospel. Robespierre, like Rousseau, demanded a unified, culturally and politically homogenous republican state, governed by a unicameral parliament subservient to the rule of law. Only this, he argued, could ensure the flourishing of political order and justice. The converse, absolutism, particularly the divine right to rule, was the antithesis of order. For Rousseau, absolutist sovereigns, of the type that Hobbes defended, were illegitimate for being unencumbered by the law of nations. It is this *lawless* state that epitomises anarchy for liberals. As he put it, "[w]hen the state dissolves, any abuse of government whatsoever takes the general name of *anarchy*" (Rousseau, 1997: 108). Absolutism, anarchy and the state of war are synonymous precisely because the will of the sovereign is unencumbered, and the rule of force reigns. Like egoists in a state of nature, these states were the pathogens of order and politics. Unlike individuals in a state of nature, however, states are potentially limitless in size and it is this collective egoism that makes the state of war qualitatively different from relations between peoples. Rousseau therefore rejected the idea that states were people and, contra many realists, the idea that unconstrained superpowers could be relied on to bring order (let alone justice) in the absence of law. Rousseau also rejected the way in which Hobbes' state of war naturalised an unnatural and antisocial world order.

One classic misinterpretation of Rousseau's writings in IR is that of Kenneth Waltz and helps illustrate the points I have just made. According to his use of the analogy of a stag hunt, a single hunter might break away from the stag hunt to catch enough for himself, therefore sabotaging the hunt and leaving the larger group to go hungry (Waltz 1959). But Rousseau thought republican states, as opposed to selfish absolutist ones, would be less egoistic. In his advice to the Dietines (small principalities) of Poland, Rousseau argued that alongside abolishing money (for him, one of the most corrupting factors in society), and the development of republican constitutions, the unification of like-minded republican states in an ever-wider federation was indispensable to their historic destiny. Republican constitutions would make the Polish states "indigestible", he famously argued, while a republican federation would make them invincible.

We see similar sentiments to these in the writings of the liberal Member of Parliament and industrialist Richard Cobden. He was a vocal critic of the way a defence of the balance of power doctrine defended the absolutist tendencies of states. He too believed the rule of law and trade would lead to the taming of anarchy. Unlike Rousseau, however, he believed in the power of money to pacify, and was instrumental in crafting The Cobden-Chevalier Treaty (1860), establishing free trade agreements with the French, the old rival of the British, as an attempt at ever closer union, in the aftermath of their mutual campaign against the Russians in the Crimea. At the turn of the twentieth century, Norman Angell would articulate similar ideas, arguing that the interdependence of European powers was structured by the mutual credit agreements between states and private enterprises, and that these could one day be strong enough to enlighten European statesmen to their true interests in peace and the mutually disastrous costs of war. The utility of war, or anarchy, as a guarantor of peace was the "great illusion" of the time. Angell's views on the enlightened self-interest of bankers moved leftwards in the post-1919 world order, much as have ours post-2008 (Ashworth 2014: 116–121).

None of those we have surveyed thus far believed states would or should disappear anytime soon. But they each believed that there were ways and means of institutionalising the relations between states, thereby taming anarchy. By the second half of the twentieth century, principally in reaction to the perceived failures of the earlier generation of "idealists" to end either the first or the second World War, the second generation, or of *neo*-liberal IR scholars were even more circumspect about anarchy, reverting to a more minimalist progressivism. When the study of international relations developed into a more self-consciously positivistic discipline, anarchy returned, this time as a key independent variable for explaining international order. As formal modelling and game theory took over in parts of the field, the instrumental use of a minimalist definition of anarchy precluded any philosophical reflection around its meaning. The concept might have been abandoned altogether, were it not for the fact that the new liberals were able to demonstrate the possibility of cooperation between self-regarding individuals-cum-states *in* anarchy.

The strongest version of this argument was that cooperation in anarchy was not only possible, but an evolutionary norm or necessity. International anarchy was understood to be akin to a primordial gloop in which states, like bacteria and genes, compete to ensure genetic reproduction. Axelrod and Hamilton's (1981) modelling of this process, developed from a computer programme developed by Anatole Rappaport, suggested that by following simple tit-for-tat strategies of reciprocity, stable patterns of cooperation emerge, practically from nothing. Robert Keohane (1984) argued that minimal reciprocal altruism of this sort not only could, but did routinely develop into stable cooperative strategies in international relations too, within, for example, powerful multilateral and multinational organisations. Like Rousseau, Keohane took sociality to be primordial, but without the right institutions it would always be threatened.

This was a powerful argument in the early 1980s, a period of renewed superpower rivalry, which corresponded with a growing concern that the US was in relative decline. Keohane wanted to explain the persistence of order and build confidence in the stability and durability of the liberal international architecture at a time when conventional wisdom suggested conflict was imminent. The collapse of the Bretton Woods institutions, the Iranian Revolution, the oil shocks and the end of the gold standard in the 1970s, all pointed to renewed superpower rivalry. But because the international order had been moderately institutionalised, while anarchy was still very much present, order was explicable with reference to complex interdependence *in* anarchy.

A similar take on the issue was proposed by the Australian academic Hedley Bull (1977), who was, like most, worried about the prospect of global annihilation as a consequence of nuclear war. He not only wanted to account for the persistence of order in world politics, but he also wanted to give a defence of its uniquely liberal character. Interestingly, he deployed a reading of Edmund Burke, the preeminent conservative and reactionary critic of Robespierre and the French Revolution, to this end. Burke argued that the revolutions ignited by the radical republicanism of Rousseau's social contract theory threatened the historic moral fabric of Europe, which was Christian and Monarchical, and which rested on the cultured interchange of ideas by European elites. The French Revolution, the regicide and the Terror, all promised to shatter this ancient order. Bull developed a version of this theory as Cold War allegory. He saw Cold War international anarchy as deeply layered and structured by historical and moral social relations, from the practices of diplomacy to the multi-lateral institutions of great power politics, international law and sovereignty, indeed even the right of war. Anarchy was the indispensable precondition of all the other institutions that we take for granted in world politics, since without the autonomy of states, guaranteed by the right of war, none of the others would be necessary or possible. Thus, if we valued the autonomy of peoples and wanted to promote restraint in a nuclear age, it was in these primary institutions that the prospects for peace were to be found. Not only were the US and Soviet Union threatening this social order with their mutually apocalyptic vision of universal sovereignty, but, more contentiously, Bull argued, the Anti-Apartheid movement was putting justice before order in its demands for self-rule for black South Africans, and thereby threatening Cold War bipolarity (Bull 1977: 83–94). Bull's was a conservative or realist (il)liberalism, one that sought to show how anarchy could be both virtuous and tamed, but it was deeply problematic for huge swathes of the next generation of liberal and left-leaning scholars who saw the unflinching defence of the liberal order as precisely the problem to be overcome. While Bull did devote some attention to how this order may be transcended by a future new-medieval world order, he was not particularly hopeful. It was down to the next generation of scholars to show how anarchy could be transcended rather than tamed.

Beyond Anarchy

One of the key realist claims about the structure of anarchy was its ahistorical nature. As Waltz put it: "[t]he enduring anarchic character of international politics accounts for the striking sameness in the quality of international life throughout the millennia"

(1979: 66). When the Cold War ended, a cacophony of critical voices demanded a theory of international politics that could account for change, and the standard account of anarchy seemed routinely to get in the way of this.

One of the earliest and most important interventions in this debate was Barry Buzan, Charles Jones and Richard Little's *The Logic of Anarchy* (1993). Working with a basic realist definition of anarchy, their innovation was to point out that anarchy is conditioned by the specific form of the units of which it is composed. The particular order we observe in anarchy is not only attributable to the distribution of capabilities, as Waltz claimed, but also, if not more so, dependent on what functions the units in the system perform. Following Hedley Bull and Adam Watson, Buzan et al. argued that clusters of empires, cities and states generate quite different types of anarchical societies, precisely because the units deploy the use of force and structure their relations in ways that are atypical and historically conditioned. As the functions of the units change, for example, if cities agglomerate into states or empires collapse, then so too will the logic of anarchy – anarchy does not lead inexorably to self-help. Buzan and Little stated this more forcefully later, arguing that change and progress could only be properly theorised (in IR as well as "out there") if we as a field first ditch the "Westphalian straightjacket" (Buzan and Little 2001) and the corresponding "anarchophilia" (Buzan and Little 2000) that govern our conception of its core actors.

Alex Wendt's social constructivism adds a measure or two of Hegelianism to this account, but in so doing reanimates the Westphalian state (via another German state theorist, Max Weber) and anarchy. Even so, Wendt offers us a way beyond both. A detailed discussion of Wendt's theory of the state is beyond the scope of this chapter, but the upshot of his account is that states adapt to and change their environment. They do this because "states are people too" (Wendt 2004). Mirroring Hegel's account of the emergence of the liberal social contract, Wendt argues that state identities are mutually constituted, progressively over time. Just as the master and slave need one another for their mutual identities to make sense, so too do these relationships evolve and liberalise as the two realise that this mutual constitution demands a form of mutual recognition that compels them towards a recognition of equality.

Wendt therefore believes that states have identities prior to entering into relations with one another, and have evolved over time from a Hobbesian (warlike) to a Lockean or Groitian (law-governed) and ultimately a Kantian (revolutionary) "culture of anarchy", in which both states and the logic of anarchy are ultimately superseded by a world state (Wendt 2003). Ironically, on this account, anarchy does very little – states as people are the agents. Anarchy is not causal in the efficient or material sense, it is only causal formally or teleologically, which means that, like the working out of the plan of some super-deity, anarchy compels us towards a future *beyond* anarchy, in spite of ourselves, indeed, *because* states are self-interested. Enlightenment and secularised theodicy (rational explanations of how good can come of evil) echo throughout this theory, and, as I have argued elsewhere (Prichard 2013), this set of views was central to modern social contract theory too.

Marxists may reject social contract theory, but they end up in a similar place to Rousseau regardless. For example, E. H. Carr, perhaps a reluctant or crypto-marxist, argued that the historical inevitability of the rise of revisionist powers, like Hitler's Germany and then Stalin's Russia, ought to compel us to see that history is shaped by material and ideological power and weaker states are mostly powerless to resist. Carr criticised those who thought that "[r]eason could demonstrate the absurdity of the international anarchy; and with increasing knowledge, enough people would be rationally convinced of its absurdity to put an end to it" (2001: 28). Rather, in *Nationalism and After*, he suggested that the processes that were to take us beyond power politics would be nothing other than material power itself. A post-statist future could only be driven by the greatest agglomerations of power, and the state most likely to do this was the USSR (as he set out in detail in his 24-volume history of the Soviet Union). Morgenthau's scathing review of *The Twenty Years' Crisis* anticipated Carr's later trajectory by pointing out that Carr's materialism left him powerless to mount a moral critique of power itself, thus explaining Carr's predilection for appeasement (Morgenthau 1948). But neither Carr nor Morgenthau deployed the concept of anarchy to reach their conclusions. Anarchy was a concept deployed by liberals in the inter-war period and so not one that early realists had much use for.

Two important modern-day Marxist IR theorists, Justin Rosenberg (2013) and Benno Teshcke (2003), have somewhat contrasting views on anarchy and historical materialism. They agree that capitalism has generated unique constellations of political and social power, but they disagree about whether anarchy is a transhistorical structural force. For Teschke (and indeed the early Rosenberg (1994)), the anarchy of states emerged out of the transformation of dynastic property rights in the absolutist period (the seventeenth and eighteenth centuries). States arose to defend and entrench monarchical and dynastic title to property. However, in a recent thought-provoking piece, Rosenberg (2013) argued that anarchy may be a function of "inter-societal multiplicity", with capitalism one emergent form to deal with conflicts and cleavages within, as well as between, societies. If this is the case, then anarchy is as much a feature of social life as it is of international life, with difference and change (in general) generated by uneven and combined patterns of global development.

It is because it is so difficult for states to manage these complex social relations between social groups, and the structures of power that increasingly transcend state boundaries, that many Marxists are currently calling for a world state, to move us beyond both a realist anarchy of states and a liberal anarchy of the market, by institutionalising macro processes of rule and democratisation. Processes of transnational social, political and legal identification and integration exist, and there is no doubting this. But Marxists claim that we should start thinking more clearly about the virtues and vices of the EU or the UN, institutions many believe to be extant if primitive world states (Albert et al. 2012). Interestingly enough, the EU is a template for liberals too. Francis Fukuyama famously deployed Hegel's recognition theory to argue that the EU pointed to the "common marketization" of world order, or "the end of history" as it is better known (Fukuyama 1992), a position John Ikenberry (2009) has dubbed as "Liberal Internationalism 3.0", in which Westphalian sovereignty is abandoned once and for all and power and authority are networked, diffused and plural. For all of these writers, history and the progressive development of justice take us beyond anarchy.

Dan Deudney's (2007) republican security theory is an interesting interjection in these debates. His work explicitly charts a course between liberal, realist and Marxist theory. It is materialist in so far as it accounts for the material motors of history, realist in so far as states and nuclear capabilities feature prominently in the analysis, but liberal and republican in its recognition that the constitutionalisation of global order is vital. Deudney sees massive agglomerations of nuclear weaponry rendering us mutually vulnerable on a global scale. Deudney calls for the republicanisation of global institutions, to facilitate three-dimensional balances of power, between and within states. His neologism "negarchy" signifies a system where *archos* has a plethora of "negative" constraints placed on it. This would be a system of global order in which states and social groups mutually and constitutionally constrain each other, rather than that constraint being left to the whim of self-interest or the dictates of a supreme power.

A final group of omiarchists are avowedly normative and make no attempt to disguise the neo-Kantian grounds on which they develop their accounts of history and progress. Neo-Kantian normative international political theorists refute the idea that anarchy is a permanent condition of international politics that leads ineluctably to moral scepticism and the prioritisation of power politics. They do so on the grounds that a moral universalism exists a priori and that the state system sustains and is sustained by it. This neo-Kantian moral universalism is premised on the deontological position that all individuals are ends in themselves. It is from this prior commitment to the individual that states gain their legitimacy (Beitz 1979).

Like the maximalist Rousseau, and developing a radical liberal reading of Kant, writers in the more radical Frankfurt School tradition of critical theory claim that civilization entails the abandonment and transcendence of both anarchy *and* the state. Andrew Linklater, the current Woodrow Wilson Professor of International Politics at Aberystwyth University, argues that where the Kantians went wrong in the nineteenth century was in believing that it was in the entrenchment of the state that the transcendence of anarchy could be found. In the aftermath of the totalitarian catastrophes of the twentieth century, transcendence had to be found *beyond* both the state *and* anarchy. Linklater follows Bull in pointing towards a future neo-medieval order, in which multiple and plural systems of rule and governance overlap and intersect.

Feminist, poststructuralist and postcolonial theorists are both more pessimistic and more radical. These writers were among the first to openly criticise the distinctly ideological nature of the anarchy problematique in IR (a theme I have picked up here). For these writers, a focus on anarchy occluded the more salient hierarchies that structured world politics. Gender hierarchies and white supremacy are made possible, it is argued, through the defence of anarchy. When international anarchy is naturalised as a domain of war and high politics, this produces very specific cultural and political roles for women and for non-white peoples. The discourses that legitimate these hierarchies become objects of analysis and critique themselves, and anarchy no less so (Ashley 1988). Feminist scholars, for example, demonstrate that a focus on anarchy reified the personal power relationships between, for example, statesmen and their hostess wives, across global production chains mainly staffed by women, and in the bars and brothels surrounding US military bases (Enloe 1989). These gendered, racialised and cultural hierarchies are integral to sustaining world politics in its current form, and anarchy is a political discourse that naturalises them by imploring that practitioners reproduce the very states the theory of anarchy was only ever developed to describe. The concept of anarchy sets the boundaries of legitimate discourse and practice in world politics, setting out sensible policy against unrealistic policy, and in so doing it generates its own resistance and reactions that endlessly perpetuate the need for the "heroic practice" that is IR (Ashley 1988). The barriers to thinking beyond the cultural embeddedness of the mainstream anarchy problematique are gargantuan. I will now turn to a small group who are giving it a go.

Rethinking "the Virtues of Anarchy"

The standard account of politics has been well stated by Thomas Nagel (2005: 147). For him, the march of politics, history and morality is from "anarchy to justice". Nagel concedes that international anarchy sometimes remains preferable to the injustices which flow from state sovereignty, because, while the extension of institutions of global justice can mitigate injustices, this can only come at the cost of state sovereignty, and thereby the autonomy of peoples. Hence the paradox of liberal accounts of anarchy. But why do we see anarchy as something to transcend or tame? If anarchy defends autonomy of states, and this has its virtues, could we not extend this principle, and make anarchy a constitutional principle of politics as such? In this section I turn to the anarchists to develop what Waltz called "the virtues of anarchy".

One of the first to deploy anarchy as an analytical concept for understanding world ordering (without referring to "the international anarchy" explicitly) was the first self-professed anarchist, Pierre-Joseph Proudhon. In his first book, *What is Property?* (1994 [1840]), he argued the following: "As man seeks justice in equality, so society seeks order in anarchy". On his deathbed, some 25 years later, he dictated his final book on working-class politics to his friend Gustave Chaudey. Having spent the previous five years writing seven books on European international politics, it was inevitable that ruminations about international relations would make their way into this book. Here he argued that "[t]hat which is known in the particular as treaties [*le pacte de garantie*] between states is nothing else than one of the most brilliant applications of the idea of mutuality, which, in politics, becomes the idea of federation" (both cited in Prichard 2013: 4). Proudhon consistently argued that anarchy pervades all of social life and diplomats were only the most obvious examples of a general social phenomenon of mediated self-rule. In terms recently echoed by Rosenberg, Proudhon suggests that in the absence of a transcendent power, particular social relations always take place in anarchy, mutually constrained by other related powers and forces, some local, others transnational (cf. Deudney 2007). Proudhon argued that international politics and domestic politics are essentially the same thing. Neither has any natural form – both are constituted by people pursuing particular conceptions of the good. Force and right are central to order in both domains, and since there is no single, final point of authority, international and domestic politics take place in a far deeper anarchy than many analysts have been willing to recognise.

Proudhon argued that anarchy's virtues are far more expansive than simply defending the autonomy of states. Rather, anarchy ought also to be central to the freedom of all peoples (cf. Frost 2009).

Like contemporary critical IR theorists, Proudhon argued that the international domain has no *sui generis* properties, nor does it exist a priori. International relations take place in the micro contexts of our daily lives where we enact and reproduce global power structures through habit and conscious effort (Hutchings 1994; Rossdale 2010). Proudhon and contemporary anarchist theorists would probably agree with Robert Keohane that cooperation and institutionalisation are not only possible but the norm *in anarchy*. Adam Goodwin (2010) has shown that anarchists draw very different lessons from evolutionary theory. For Goodwin, the take-home lesson is that the state closes down the possibilities for innovation and adaptation, while a defence of anarchy presupposes it. Complexity theorists, like Hobden and Cudworth (2012), take this further, suggesting that the radical openness and non-linearity of social systems demands a rethink of the political structures developed for a conception of politics as consisting in natural unchanging forms. Contemporary anarchists would also likely agree with contemporary Marxists that capitalism and statism are directed in the interests of the few, and would also be sceptical of any argument that suggested this inequality was inevitable. But unlike Marxists, they would be sceptical of arguments for a world state, and equally of any notion of a universal "humanity" that might underpin a cosmopolitan world order.

The key object of attack is precisely what international anarchy, by conventional accounts, was designed to protect: European statism. It is no coincidence, therefore, that anarchist ideas chime with attempts to come to terms with and push forward the transformation of political community. Anarchist theories of asymmetric which we find in Proudhon and elsewhere, federalism look remarkably like contemporary versions of new medievalism, as Andrew Linklater (1998: 196) has recognised. Ken Booth summed up this argument in his E. H. Carr professorial lecture in 1991, and citing him at length helps bring our survey full circle:

> 'anarchy' or absence of government in the states system becomes less of a problem than the 'statism' – the concentration of all power and loyalty on the state – that has typified much of the twentieth century. To achieve security in anarchy, it is necessary to go beyond Bull's 'anarchical society' of states to an anarchical global 'community of communities'. Anarchy thus becomes the framework for thinking about the solutions to global problems, not the essence of the problem to be overcome. This would be a much messier political world than the states system, but it should offer better prospects for the emancipation of individuals and groups, and it should therefore be more secure. (Booth 1991: 540)

Thinking more expansively about the relationship between freedom, security and anarchy will not come naturally to a discipline that has historically seen anarchy as the problem. That said, with the rise of new anarchist and anarchistic social movements, the failure of Marxist-Leninism, and a broad turn away from statism in critical social theory, might it be that we could yet reconsider the virtues of anarchy in IR and political theory?

Conclusion

In a discussion of James C. Scott's *The Art of Not Being Governed*, Steven Krasner pointed out that, "[i]t is not just that the social contract is an analytic fiction, that human beings are social animals and have never lived as isolated individuals; it is also that the logic of the social contract is based on empirically incorrect assumptions" (2011: 82). Hobbes, he argued, is the wrong place to start thinking about order and justice in world politics. And yet, not only is Hobbes routinely the starting point for thinking about justice, order and anarchy, but the social contract tradition's ideal justification of states has morphed into a description of the actual distribution of power in world politics and the natural proclivities of humans. In this context, the minimalist definition of anarchy, as the absence of centralised authority, tells us as much about the unthinking assumptions of the vast majority of political scientists, as it does about the world in which we live. The absence of centralised authority presumes nothing. It is the intellectual, discursive and historical context in which such an account of politics is couched which tells us most. By opening up the concept of anarchy to this sort of critical scrutiny, and embedding it in wider modern debates, it is hoped that students of politics and international relations will be able to reconsider the virtues of anarchy for themselves.

Acknowledgements

I would like to thank Luke Ashworth, Felix Berenskoetter, Jonathan Havercroft, Charles Jones, Ana Juncos, Andreas Karoutas and Ruth Kinna for their comments on and suggestions for this chapter. It is far better thanks to their efforts.

Suggested Readings

Alker, Hayward R. 1996. The presumption of anarchy in world politics: On recovering the historicity of world society. In *Rediscoveries and Reformulations: Humanistic Methodologies for International Studies*, edited by H. R. Alker. Cambridge: Cambridge University Press. pp. 355–393.

The only discussion of the etymology and contrasting use of the concept of anarchy in neo-realist and English School IR theory.

Ashley, Richard K. 1988. Untying the sovereign state: A double reading of the anarchy problematique. *Millennium* 17 (2): 227–262.

The first article to point to the hole where a discussion of anarchy should have been in realist IR theory.

Donnelly, Jack. 2015. The discourse of anarchy in IR. *International Theory* 7 (3): 393–425.

The most recent argument for the rejection of the use of anarchy in neo-positivist IR theory. Worth contrasting with the argument presented in this chapter.

Milner, Helen. 1991. The assumption of anarchy in international relations theory: A critique. *Review of International Studies* 17: 67–85.

An important corrective to Weberian state theory in IR. Milner's comparative approach illuminates the parochialism of IR's theory of anarchy.

Wendt, Alexander. 1992. Anarchy is what states make of it: The social construction of power politics. *International Organization* 46 (2): 391–425.

Wendt's rethinking of the causal effects of anarchy set off an avalanche of writing on the social construction of world politics, but not on the concept of anarchy itself.

Bibliography

Albert, Mathias, Gorm Harste, Heikki Patomäki, and Knud Erik Jørgensen. 2012. Introduction: World state futures. *Cooperation and Conflict* 47 (2): 145–156.

Armitage, David. 2012. *The Foundations of Modern International Thought*, Cambridge: Cambridge University Press.

Ashley, Richard K. 1988. Untying the sovereign state: A double reading of the anarchy problematique. *Millennium* 17 (2): 227–262.

Ashworth, Lucian M. 2014. *A History of International Thought: From the Origins of the Modern State to Academic International Relations*. London: Routledge.

Axelrod, R. and Hamilton, W. D. 1981. The evolution of cooperation. *Science* 211: 1390–1396.

Beitz, Charles (1979) *Political Theory and International Relations*. Princeton, NJ: Princeton University Press.

Booth, Ken. 1991. Security in anarchy: Utopian realism in theory and practice. *International Affairs* 67 (3): 527–545.

Bull, Hedley. 1977. *The Anarchical Society: A Study of Order in World Politics*. London: Macmillan.

Buzan, Barry, Charles A. Jones, and Richard Little. 1993. *The Logic of Anarchy: Neorealism to Structural Realism*. New York: Columbia University Press.

Buzan, Barry, and Richard Little. 2000. *International Systems in World History: Remaking the Study of International Relations*. New York: Oxford University Press.

Buzan, Barry, and Richard Little. 2001. Why International Relations has Failed as an Intellectual Project and What to do About it. *Millennium: Journal of International Studies* 30 (1): 19–39.

Carr, Edward Hallett, 2001. *The Twenty Years' Crisis, 1919–1939: An Introduction to the Study of International Relations*, 2nd edn (reissued with a new introduction and additional material by Michael Cox, ed.). Basingstoke: Palgrave.

Cudworth, Erika, and Stephen Hobden. 2013. Complexity, ecologism, and posthuman politics. *Review of International Studies* 39 (3): 643–664.

Deudney, Daniel. 2007. *Bounding Power: Republican Security Theory from the Polis to the Global Village*. Princeton, NJ; Woodstock: Princeton University Press.

Dickinson, Goldsworthy Lowes. 1916. *The European Anarchy*. London: Allen & Unwin.

Donnelly, Jack. 2015. 'The discourse of anarchy in IR'. *International Theory* 7 (3): 393–425.

Enloe, C. H. 1989. *Bananas, Beaches and Bases: Making Feminist Sense of International Politics*. Berkeley, CA; London, University of California Press.

Falk, Richard. 1978. Anarchism and world order, in *Nomos XIX: Anarchism*, eds. J. Roland Pennock and John Chapman. New York: New York University Press, 63–87.

Frost, Mervyn. 2009. *Global Ethics: Anarchy, Freedom and International Relations*. London: Routledge.

Fukuyama, Francis. 1992. *The End of History and the Last Man*. New York: Free Press.

Goodwin, Adam. 2010. Evolution and anarchism in international relations: The challenge of Kropotkin's biological ontology. *Millennium: Journal of International Studies* 39 (2): 417–437.

Gordon, Uri. 2006. Αναρχία: What did the Greeks actually say? *Anarchist Studies* 14 (1): 84–91.

Halliday, Fred, and Justin Rosenberg. 1998. Interview with Ken Waltz. *Review of International Studies* 24: 371–386.

Hobbes, Thomas. 1996. *Leviathan*. Richard Tuck (ed.). Cambridge: Cambridge University Press.

Hobson, J. M. 2014. The twin self-delusions of IR: Why 'hierarchy' and not 'anarchy' is the core concept of IR. *Millennium: Journal of International Studies* 42 (3): 557–575.

Hutchings, K. 1994. The personal is international: Feminist epistemology and the case of international relations. In Lennon, K. and Whitford, M. (eds) *Knowing the Difference: Feminist Perspectives in Epistemology*. London: Routledge.

Ikenberry, G. John. 2009. Liberal Internationalism 3.0: America and the Dilemmas of Liberal World Order. *Perspectives on Politics* 7 (1): 71–87.

Jahn, Beate. 2009. Liberal internationalism: From ideology to empirical theory – and back again. *International Theory* 1 (3): 409–438.

Kant, Immanuel. 1991. Perpetual peace: A philosophical sketch. In *Kant: Political Writings*, ed. Hans Reiss. Cambridge: Cambridge University Press, 93–130.

Kazmi, Z. 2012. *Polite Anarchy in International Relations Theory*. New York: Palgrave Macmillan.
Keohane, Robert O. 1984 *After Hegemony*. Princeton, NJ: Princeton University Press.
Krasner, S. D. 2011. State, power, anarchism. *Perspectives on Politics*, 9: 79–83.
Lebow, Ned. 2003. *The Tragic Vision of Politics: Ethics, Interests and Orders*. Cambridge: Cambridge University Press.
Linklater, Andrew. 1998. *The Transformation of Political Community: Ethical Foundations of a Post-Westphalian Era*. Cambridge: Polity.
Mearsheimer, John J. 2001. *The Tragedy of Great Power Politics*. New York; London: W. W. Norton.
Mearsheimer, John. 2005. E. H. Carr vs. idealism: The battle rages on. *International Relations* 19 (2): 139–152.
Milner, Helen. 1991. The assumption of anarchy in international relations theory: A critique. *Review of International Studies* 17: 67–85.
Morgenthau, H. 1948. The political science of E. H. Carr. *World Politics*, 1, 127–134.
Nagel, T. 2005. The problem of global justice. *Philosophy & Public Affairs* 33 (2): 113–47.
Newman, Saul. 2012. Crowned anarchy: Postanarchism and international relations theory. *Millennium: Journal of International Studies* 40 (2): 259–278.
Prichard, Alex. 2010a. Deepening anarchism: International relations and the anarchist ideal. *Anarchist Studies* 18 (2): 29–57.
Prichard, Alex. 2010b. Introduction: Anarchism and world politics. *Millennium: Journal of International Studies* 39 (2): 373–380.
Prichard, Alex. 2012. Anarchy, Anarchism and International Relations. In *Continuum Companion to Anarchism*, ed. Ruth Kinna. New York: Continuum, 100–112.
Prichard, Alex. 2013. *Justice, Order and Anarchy: The International Political Theory of Pierre-Joseph Proudhon*. Abingdon: Routledge.
Proudhon, Pierre-Joseph. 1994 [1840]. *What is Property? Or, an inquiry into the principle of right and of government*. Trans. Donald. R. Kelley and Bonnie. G Smith. Cambridge: Cambridge University Press. Charleston, SC: Nabu Press.
Rancière, J. 2006. *Hatred of Democracy*. London: Verso.
Rosenberg, Justin. 1994. *The Empire of Civil Society: A Critique of the Realist Theory of International Relations*. London: Verso.
Rosenberg, Justin. 2013. Kenneth Waltz and Leon Trotsky: Anarchy in the mirror of uneven and combined development. *International Politics* 50 (2): 183–230.
Rossdale, Chris. 2010. Anarchy is what anarchists make of it: Reclaiming the concept of agency in IR and security studies. *Millennium: Journal of International Studies* 39 (2): 483–501.
Rousseau, Jean-Jacques. 1997. Of the social contract or principles of political right. In *Rousseau: The Social Contract and other Later Political Writings*, ed. Victor Gourevitch. Cambridge: Cambridge University Press, 39–152.
Schmidt, Brian C. 1998. *The Political Discourse of Anarchy: A Disciplinary History of International Relations*. New York: State University of New York Press.
Shilliam, Robbie. 2009. *German Thought and International Relations: The Rise and Fall of a Liberal Project*. Basingstoke: Palgrave Macmillan.
Sjoberg, L. 2011. Gender, the state, and war redux: Feminist international relations across the 'levels of analysis'. *International Relations* 25: 108–134.
Teschke, Ben. 2003. *The Myth of 1648: Class, Geopolitics, and the Making of Modern International Relations*. London: Verso.
Treitschke, Heinrich von. 1916. *Politics* (vols 1 and 2). Trans. Blanche Dugdale and Torben de Bille. New York: Macmillan.

Tuck, Richard. 2001. *The Rights of War and Peace: Political Thought and the International Order from Grotius to Kant*. Oxford: Oxford University Press.

Walt, Stephen M. 2014. How to get a B.A. in International Relations in 5 minutes. *Foreign Policy* May 19th. http://foreignpolicy.com/2014/05/19/how-to-get-a-b-a-in-international-relations-in-5-minutes/

Waltz, Kenneth Neal. 1959. *Man, the State and War: A Theoretical Analysis*. New York: Columbia University Press.

Waltz, Kenneth Neal. 1962. Kant, liberalism, and war. *The American Political Science Review* 56 (2): 331–340.

Waltz, Kenneth Neal. 1979. *Theory of International Politics*. Reading, MA; London: Addison-Wesley.

Weiss, Thomas G., David P. Forsythe, and Roger A. Coate. 2004. *The United Nations and Changing World Politics*. 4th edn. Boulder, CO; Oxford: Westview.

Wendt, Alexander. 1992. Anarchy is what states make of it: The social construction of power politics. *International Organization* 46 (2): 391–425.

Wendt, Alexander. 1999. *Social Theory of International Relations*. Cambridge: Cambridge University Press.

Wendt, Alexander. 2003. Why a world state is inevitable. *European Journal of International Relations* 9 (4): 491–542.

Wendt, Alexander. 2004. The state as person in international theory. *Review of International Studies* 30 (2): 289-316.

Wheeler, Nicholas J., and Tim Dunne.1996. Hedley Bull's pluralism of the intellect and solidarism of the will. *International Affairs* 72 (1): 91–107.

9

Society

Oliver Kessler and Benjamin Herborth

"There is no such thing as society". When the late British Prime Minister Margaret Thatcher made this now famous claim, she expressed the familiar neo-liberal credo highlighting the responsibility of the individual (and the family). Scholars of international relations (IR) are not quite as sweeping in dismissing the existence of "society", yet the concept has traditionally been kept at a distance. There are various reasons for this, some having to do with the history of the concept and some stemming from a methodological skepticism about conceiving of complex processes in terms of "society". Perhaps the main reason why the field of international relations has been at odds with the concept of society has to do with disciplinary identity. Crudely put, as a field of study, IR owes its relative independence to the idea that politics beyond the nation-state somehow works differently than politics within the nation-state. Wrapped within this idea is the view that we can think of everything that happens on the inside of the modern state in terms of society, while everything that happens on the outside of the modern state should be properly understood in terms of the absence of society. While the concept of society is seen as tied to the concept (and the 'ontology') of the state, discussions of state–society relations thus typically refer to relations occurring inside a particular state. By contrast, international relations has traditionally been construed as a world of anarchy characterized by the absence of a centralized, over-arching arbiter of conflict. Thus, society is not simply one of the core concepts of IR, but rather a concept that stands in a conflicted and antagonistic relation to the orthodox conception of world politics as relations between sovereign states existing under conditions of anarchy.

This traditional image of international relations is increasingly considered old-fashioned, an artefact of a mentality with roots in 19th-century balance of power thinking among European states, which survived into the late 20th century mainly because it offered a simple way to make sense of the Cold War, yet which has been on its way out for a number of decades. However, if anarchy is on its way out (see, however, Chapter 8, this volume), this does not mean that "society" is necessarily on its way in. Speaking about society raises suspicion not only among draconic privatizers like Thatcher, but also in an intellectual climate that views totalizing accounts, representations of the social whole, as unhelpful and obsolete. So while contestedness is characteristic of any core concept that comes under close enough scrutiny, it takes a particular form when it comes to the concept of society, because the very question of whether we – as students, scholars, or citizens – should bother having a concept of society is contested. Trying to make sense of the concept of society, then, requires crossing a hurdle of justification that is quite uncharacteristic in the context of a discussion of core concepts. We may disagree vigorously on concepts of state, war, or sovereignty, yet scholarly discussions on such matters can get down to business right away. It would seem obviously futile to be against efforts at conceptualization in the first place. The present chapter faces a bigger challenge, as before we can get to the business of mapping out a range of different uses of the concept of society we need to justify the conceptual effort as such. This, however, also makes conceptualizing society a most promising intellectual endeavor.

This chapter offers an attempt to render this promise and its implications transparent. In a first step, we will briefly review how global transformations observed within the discipline open the door to the concept of society. This section provides the "context" that allows for the concept "world society" to "emerge" in international theory. In a second step, we reconstruct the "use" of the concept by outlining three conceptualizations of world society by the English School, Stanford School and Bielefeld School respectively. Here, we show how these approaches *use* the concept to make sense of global transformations. In a final step, we circle back to the question of what is at stake in such a conceptual effort.

Observing Global Transformations: the Emergence of World Society in International Theory

Take any textbook on IR and you will find that, in spite of various theories, there is a fairly established consensus on what global order consists of. The traditional image of international relations is that of an apparently fixed and firm "Westphalian order" where international politics takes place between states. According to this image, states are the main actors forming an international system, with territoriality their playground, and diplomacy and, occasionally, war their rhythm. Questions about the political were related to the anarchical system-cum-nation-state and thereby were translated in a project of empirical/positivist social science (see Morgenthau 1944; Waltz 1979; King, Keohane, Verba 1994 for different variations on the theme; for a fundamental critique, see Ashley 1984; Walker 1991, 1993: Ch. 1). Positivism and anarchy gave IR its form, its topics, its arguments, and its boundaries; they enabled the claiming of disciplinary expertise and autonomy. While this kind of IR also created a negative foil against which proponents of various concepts of society could militate, it was neither political theory nor sociology and could not draw from the rich vocabulary we are familiar with from the domestic context.

Today's world is increasingly observed as complex, opaque and shot through with multiple forms of differentions (see Kessler 2012 for a discussion), which the traditional image fails to capture. In the face of global risks and transnational threats, classic IR debates about the extent and form of state cooperation under conditions of anarchy often have difficulties dealing with the most pressing questions of world politics. They fail to take seriously the variations of actors abound today: non-governmental organizations (NGOs), insurance companies, banks, transnational corporations, criminal networks and international organizations situated on the global, transnational, and regional levels. To privilege nation-states as primary actors in world politics increasingly appears to be an anachronism with a conservative bias. Furthermore, the complexity of IR's "object of study" makes it increasingly difficult to locate and demarcate the discipline: where does the study of the international begin if CCTVs in the remotest cities in mid-England are legitimized by the global war on terror? Where does it start if the war on terror not only makes a difference to the everyday lives of people in Afghanistan, but also to the everyday practices of the digital age? Where is the boundary between politics and the economy when risk models by private investors can carry financial turbulence that eventually leads to the collapse of an entire state? And where is the boundary between law and politics when, as David Kennedy (2006) pointed out, law is woven into the fabric of every modern practice of warfare and often enough does not constrain violence but rather legitimizes it?

Accepting that world politics cannot be reduced to "states" as actors and, hence, to sovereignty as the organizing principle raises demands for new analytical tools. Indeed, if contemporary world order is the product of the interplay between various actors, devices, and knowledge structures that constitute and perform spaces and temporalities, blurring previously constitutive boundaries such as public/private or national/international, these also cannot be taken for granted and "positioned" a priori to stabilize empirical inquiry. Rather, they need to subject themselves to historical and conceptual reconstruction.

The advent of *global governance* and *globalization* studies in the 1990s offered such an alternative discourse (see Chapter 18, this volume). At its core, the notion of global governance stresses the dual process of a horizontal decentralization of national systems and the emergence of new hierarchies in the international system. The classical bifurcation of world politics in national and international politics was abandoned and replaced by a recognition of the existing plurality of different political spaces. In particular, the *multilevel governance* approach points to the interplay and overlap of subnational, national, regional, transnational, and global spaces (see Hooghe/Marks 2001), which no longer fit the logic of the state system. Likewise, international rules, contracts, and conventions no longer stop at national borders, but impact on national polities. This moves the question of their democratic legitimacy to the center of IR theorizing, a question that could be excluded as long as the outside remains on the outside. More generally, this suggests that the international has to be conceived of as a net(work) of international rules, regulations, and agreements in which states still have an important function, but in which their sovereignty as the organizing principle of world politics is no longer sufficient to adequately explain or understand practices.

The challenge to sovereignty is flanked by a revived interest in transnational politics, epistemic communities, and private norm-entrepreneurs (see Keohane and Nye 1971: 329). In an attempt to capture this complexity, Michael Zürn, for example, suggested to distinguish between three configurations: *governance by government*, which refers to the classic image of how states regulate policy fields; *governance without governance*, which points to the constitution and self-regulation of transnational spaces (by definition, independent of the state system); and *governance with governments*, which stresses the important role of non-state actors and an apparently emerging global civil society (see Zangl and Zürn 2003). The latter is seen as a relatively autonomous sphere of transnational actors playing a crucial role in the agreement, monitoring, and enforcement of global legal rules such as the Convention on the Prohibition of the Use of Landmines or on the Protection of Species and Biodiversity (see Bartelson 2006 for a critique). Similarly, private types of regulations have become a fundamental element of global financial markets. For instance, the Basle Committee on Banking Supervision, as well as various rating agencies, fulfil public tasks related to bank supervision which lead to the development of hybrid regulation structures. The International Accounting Standard Board, which was founded by the auditing and consulting companies PriceWaterhouseCoopers, KPMG, Deloitte & Touche and Ernst & Young, develops and spreads standards for accountants/auditors that contradict and change national rules substantially (see Graz and Nölke 2008). In another realm, Risse and Sikkink describe a process in which states sign human rights conventions, and where the concomitant self-commitment subsequently enables local and transnational non-governmental organizations to highlight violations by governments, empowering civil society actors to bring about political transformation (Risse et al. 1999).

All these developments open up the study of global politics to the use of the concept of society. Once order, rule, and regulation are no longer situated strictly on the inside of the modern state, the international and the global are no longer referred to as social spaces subject to forms of politics that are categorically distinct from domestic ones. From such an angle, it becomes possible to descriptively accompany global transformations by recording governance projects and disseminating knowledge about their programs and procedures. Against the premise of the international being a traditionally anti-social space that cannot be governed, the insistence on using the term governance as an innovative feature further corroborates the nagging feeling that conceptual changes are afoot. And yet, the understanding of such global transformations remains undertheorized. Despite extensive research on governance in complex multi-level systems, what we know about such systems is little more than that they are complex due to the fact that they seem to operate on multiple levels. And accounts of how the transformation of the state system transforms the state remains wedded to the semantics of the state and its place as a vantage point of inquiries. It is the dissatisfaction with such a state of reflection that shifts attention to the concept of world society.

From this perspective, it is the problem of coming to terms with the observable complexity, as visible in the co-existence of multiple forms of rationalities or forms of differentiations, that make it increasingly plausible for IR scholars to take "society" out of the conceptual confines of the "domestic" and to rethink it on the global level under the notion of "world society". However, it should be clarified right at the outset that "world society" is not to be confused with any sense of "world community", the latter characterized by deeper integration that allows members to embrace an era of peace and democracy.[1] In its most general form, the concept of world society simply

[1] For a classic discussion of the society/community distinction, see Tönnies (1887).

means that relations, processes, and structures are to be conceived of in "social" terms. While the "social" could thus be seen as a supporting concept, in this chapter we treat society and the social interchangeably. To speak of world society is to establish from the very beginning an alternative conceptual frame of reference that does not take for granted a world of states, but instead starts from some conceptualization of global processes of ordering, regardless of who or what does the ordering in the first place: the state system represents only one mode of organizing politics. At the same time, world society de-couples politics from the state to locate political processes in the stabilization of temporal and spatial constructions, as discussed further below.

In the next section, we will reconstruct the use of the concept "world society" in IR. Even though the concept itself has emerged in sociological theory since the 1970s (for a discussion, see Heintz and Greve 2005), here we focus only on its use in IR scholarship where the concept has evolved relatively independently.[2] Crudely put, it is possible to distinguish three main intellectual traditions that have informed the use of the concept of world society in IR: approaches attached to what is known as the English School, the world culture approach of the Stanford School, and the Bielefeld School which builds on Niklas Luhmann's modern systems theory. As we cannot do justice to each of these complex literatures here, we limit ourselves to briefly highlight the different functions of the concept of world society in each of these theoretical contexts.

Uses of World Society: Three Schools

The English School gained its reputation within IR primarily by introducing the idea of an "anarchical society". Importantly, English School scholars argued that the concept of anarchy in itself does not imply the absence of the social, as realism's analogy to a Hobbesian state of nature suggested. Instead, Hedley Bull showed that the very concept of sovereignty actually fulfils Hume's criteria for a social order: promises are kept, property rights are secured and violence is limited (Bull 2002 [1977]: 3–4). Hence, international order can be understood in terms of an international society that operates on the basis of common values and rules. As Bull defines it:

> A *society of states* (or international society) exists when a group of states, conscious of common interests and common values, form a society in the sense that they conceive themselves to be bound by a common set of rules in their relations with one another, and share in the working of common institutions. (Bull 2002 [1977]: 13, emphasis in original)

Bull's examples of the rules making up the fabric of international society include respect for claims to independence, the honoring of agreements, and "certain limitations in exercising force against one another" (2002 [1977]: 13). Contrary to the concept of an international system, which is characterized merely in terms of anarchy

[2] Interestingly, the Stanford School has had an influence on IR theory, not in the context of world society but as "sociological institutionalism" and in its use by moderate constructivists.

and the relative distribution of capabilities, international society is characterized in terms of primary institutions. Buzan (2004: 167) defines primary institutions as "relatively fundamental and durable practices that are evolved more than designed". What is more, primary institutions are "constitutive of actors and their patterns of legitimate activity in relation to each other". While scholars writing in the tradition of the English School have put forth a variety of candidates for primary institutions, Bull's selection – state, diplomacy, war, balance of power, international law – remains the most influential one (see Buzan 2004: 174 for an overview).

However, from an English School perspective, the term "society" points not only to the institutional structure of international society, it has methodological implications as well: institutions cannot be derived from individual choice, they are social facts. Hence, institutions need to be understood and cannot be explained by positivist methods. Methodologically, English School theory thus comes with a commitment to interpretation and understanding as opposed to explanation and (linear) causality (Hollis and Smith 1990).

That said, the concept of international society retains core tenets of an orthodox approach to international relations, most notably its state-centrism. English School theorists like Barry Buzan thus subsequently introduced the concept of world society to distinguish a different kind of "global integration", cutting through the persistent state-centrism of an anarchical international society. Whereas the concept of "international society" conceptualizes the social in terms of states and the normativity of membership, i.e. the standards of civilization that each member of this society subscribes to, we move towards a world society as soon as the mode of integration moves from the state to sub-state levels and from state actors to non-state actors (Buzan 2004; see also Brown 2001; Bull 2002). This concept of world society thus ties in with the aforementioned scholarship on the "transformation of the state system", which sees the state system on the verge of being replaced by an order based on human rights (and hence the individual as international legal subject) and supported by global values. Buzan's account also echoes Wendt's influential discussion of Hobbesian, Lockean, and Kantian cultures of anarchy where the system is associated with the Hobbesian, the international society with the Lockean, and world society with the Kantian tradition (see Wendt 1999: Part II, as well as Buzan 2004). The concept of world society thus serves the purpose of both accounting for and directing processes of normative integration, moving beyond an anarchical society of states to an order where transnational actors assume an increasingly prominent role.

The Stanford School around John Meyer, sometimes also referred to as sociological neo-institutionalism, became a widespread source of inspiration for moderate constructivists in the 1990s. Like moderate constructivists, the Stanford School analyses the global dispersion of (Western) norms (scripts) and the theoretical and empirical consequences for the conceptualization of actorhood and social change. In a widely quoted article, Meyer and colleagues argued as early as the mid-1990s that the outlook of modern nation-states is actually part of a world culture in both its international and domestic affairs (Meyer et al. 1997; also Meyer 2010). Nation-states look surprisingly similar as they reproduce similar structures. For example, each state "has to have" a health system or an education system that is organized along global standards. While IR has been used to conceptualizing nation-states as unitary actors with specific interests, the Stanford School examines the cultural context that nation-states find themselves in. Global structures produce institutional isomorphisms, i.e. similar institutional forms re-appearing in different contexts and places. It is world society that "makes" actors and institutions in the first place.

By means of illustration, the Stanford School offers a thought experiment: imagine the discovery of an unknown civilization. Soon afterwards, this civilization would become a member of the international order. In order to do so, such a civilization would introduce reforms and develop structures that would mirror those of the other members: ministries and a government would be introduced, its population would be re-organized according to principles of citizenship, specific groups would be granted special rights (children, for example), and the economy would be re-organized to allow for innovation, companies, and financial markets (Meyer et al. 1997: 145). This civilization would find itself confronted with a thick cultural context with inscribed concepts of rationality and civilized conduct. It would be confronted with academics, consultants, and advisory bodies telling them what kind of actor they have to become (Meyer et al. 1997: 156; Meyer 2010: 7). On the other hand, these global scripts need to be translated into local contexts in which they have to work. Here, these global scripts do not construct or include actors fully as if actors were simply dummies following the script at play. In this recently discovered civilization, global norms would work differently than in a European state or the US. The same adherence and belief in the global good would be pursued differently with different practices. What can be observed is a conflict between the global values and the local practices, a de-coupling between the adherence to global norms and scripts, and the working level of local practices (Meyer et al. 1997: 154ff.). The Stanford School thus points to the fragmentedness of the multi-layeredness of agency (1997: 171) surrounded by an environment of rationalization and scientific knowledge.

In the context of the Stanford School, the concept of world society is not per se linked to non-state actors as the English School suggests. Instead, world society is defined in cultural terms of global scripts, rationalization, and processes of "scientification": world society is to analytically depart from the image of the self-interested rational actor to highlight how a common world culture legitimizes and constructs actors. These actors "function principally to make persons better actors, groups better organized actors, and nation states more complete rational actors. It is hard to imagine people, groups or countries living up to the advanced modern expectations for actorhood without the active assistance of all these people" (Meyer 2010: 7).

A third strand of literature in which the concept of world society features prominently is the Bielefeld School, inspired by the social systems theory of German sociologist Niklas Luhmann. Luhmann's account of world society most radically breaks with conventional presumptions of state-centrism and normative integration. Ironically enough, Luhmann developed all of this in the Westphalian town of Bielefeld, allowing us to continue to associate different conceptions of world society with their geographical point of origin. For Luhmann, society is to be understood as a social system. As systems are produced and reproduced by communication, society is defined in terms of the attainability of communication: within a society, communication is possible and everywhere where there is communication, there is a society, which makes communication possible. The term society is stripped of any substance or substantive values; it is also stripped of human beings. The idea that society is an aggregation of individuals that are integrated (normatively) into a society is discarded.

No human being per se is part of or makes up society. To illustrate the point here, one could think of Wendt's account of the first encounter, more specifically Wendt's argument that cultures of anarchy can be characterized by their particular way in which ego and alter are differentiated from each other. For the purpose of illustration, he proposes an imaginary first encounter between two strangers: what Wendt presupposes in his example is that ego and alter can already communicate, that there is a common signalling system on the basis of which information can be understood (Wendt 1999: 328ff). From a Luhmannian perspective, he assumes that they are able to select utterance, information, and understanding – and thus communication.

The notion of "world" used in systems theory derives from the phenomenological tradition as horizon of meaning. It is thus to be separated from and, indeed, strictly opposed to the concept of world as the sum of all things. The world is not simply the given reality of chairs, houses, streets, wires, and what else ponders on this earth. Instead, for system theorists the world encompasses all possibilities and, hence, imaginations, visions, and expectations that may or may not be realized. Meaning implies that in every moment, there are more alternatives and options available than can be realized. What "is" has meaning only by differentiating from "what was possible". Modern systems theory thus starts from differences and distinctions as opposed to identity and normative integration. A system is a system because it can be distinguished from the environment; meaning operates through the distinction between the actual and the possible. One crucial step in the Luhmannian tradition is to differentiate meaning into temporal, social, and factual dimensions: a temporal dimension of before and after; a social dimension of ego and alter (or self and other); and a factual dimension where objects and semantics are differentiated. For example, meaning changes in relation to an acceleration of practices (temporal dimension), in interaction with other actors (social dimension), or with a change in the technological infrastructure like computers or other "assembled objects". "World society" thus denotes a global horizon in the formation of expectations and the limits of communication based on a specific constellation of these dimensions (Luhmann 1971; Heintz and Greve 2005, for discussions in IR see Albert 2016; Albert et al. 2013; Kessler 2009, 2012).

This "constellation" is pursued in two research strands: the first strand focuses on how changes of these dimensions lead to structural changes: for example, how the acceleration of practices, the advent and decay of actors and their particular interplay, or changes due to the rise of the digital and technological infrastructure impact in complex ways on communication and, thus, society. Second, these changes do not impact the global complexity directly. Rather, world society is characterized by functional differentiation, i.e. the co-existence of different rationalities in world society and their mutual irritation: among others, there is a global economy, next to a global art, law, politics, health, science, or education system. Each of these systems creates its own perspective, rationality, and "way of world making"; each has its own temporalities, artefacts, range of identities. Hence, any single event will be processed differently (if at all) by different systems: the advent of the digital has very different impacts on, say, financial markets and legal proceedings.

The Bielefeld School's conception of world society thus differs in important ways from the previous two contexts: in contrast to the English School, world society is not opposed to or contrasted with the system or society of states. Rather, world society exists – and has already existed – as soon as the horizon of communication has achieved global reach (Luhmann 1984, 2007). For sovereignty to work, the concept has to be understood globally. That horizon of global understanding is world society. It may entail protracted conflicts just as well as prospects of cooperative evolution. Both, however, become possible only in terms of global structures of communication. The nation-state may still persist, but the state system would then simply represent a specific mode of the internal differentiation of world society into political units (see Albert et al. 2013, 2008; Albert 2008; Kessler 2009). Similarly, the concept of world society does not denote a new mode of integration, let alone a normative achievement of individuals connecting through human rights. Rather than characterized by common interests or the integration of states through common norms, the concept allows us to observe how functional and territorial borders and boundaries clash and produce new conflicts and ruptures (Albert 2008; Albert et al. 2008).

The idea of a functional differentiation of world society also points to important differences to the Stanford School. The theoretical background of the Stanford School is the agent–structure problem: it emphasizes how global scripts change the actorhood of states. The de-coupling of global scripts and practices gives the nation-state system a central theoretical position: functional differentiation takes place within nation-states whereas the nation-state is embedded in and confronted with a world cultural system. In contrast, Luhmann's systems theory considers functional differentiation to be prior to the state system. And so the meaning of the state cannot be de-coupled from the context we find ourselves in: legal proceedings, financial markets, arts, literature, sports, or education. It would seem rather naïve to presuppose a single, unified, and self-identical actor in all of these fields. In modern systems theory, the concept of world society thus allows us to think of a global horizon of communication, not in terms of an all-encompassing unity but in terms of an ensemble of differences constantly producing new challenges, paradoxes, and fault lines.

While we have highlighted differences in three concepts of world society, it is worth noting that each responds to a similar kind of problem: world society enters as soon as the presence of social categories beyond the nation-state is acknowledged. Social categories here simply refer to the sociological truism that social orders are not things of nature – and it is society that produces and disrupts social order. To understand world society in such a way has the advantage of not committing us to specific literatures or pre-established authorities who always already know the answer in advance and are fixated on global capital, neo-liberal governmentality, transnational justice, or some other master mechanism hypothesized to run the world. Instead, having a concept of world society is precisely about not knowing in advance and allows us to pose questions as to how the global, the international, and the transnational are being ordered, disrupted, and continuously transformed.

Is There Such a Thing as Society? The Politics of the Concept

We have suggested that engaging with the concept of society can be a helpful way for understanding the fundamental transformations in contemporary global politics. Let us now circle back to the question of what is at stake politically in the question of whether or not IR scholars should engage in explicit conceptualizations of society. The core argument here is that every form of social research always already presupposes *some* concept of society, some implicit understanding of where the conduct of social inquiry takes places and how it relates to its subject matter. To the extent that such understandings remain implicit, however, society continues to resemble the artefact of 19th-century thought so powerfully criticized by Charles Tilly (1984). Society is a thing apart; while it may be subject to change, such change is in itself directed; it follows a particular trajectory, a path, perhaps even a logic. And to the extent that the concept of society remains implicit, it remains intangible, out of reach from the point of view of political action.

To have or not to have a concept of society is thus not only a scholarly question in a discussion about how we can best think global politics, global order, and global transformation. It is also an immensely political question. If we give an account of ourselves in which the concept of society is absent, we will not be able to engage in a form of politics that addresses issues at the level of society. And while the concept of society may appear awkwardly abstract, what is at stake in having or not having a concept of society is very concrete in its political ramifications. Will we talk about failures at Lehman Brothers rather than power structures in the global economy and their effects? Will we lose sight of structural crises in financial markets and localize and territorialize economic problems when shifting our view from a financial market crisis to a Greek debt crisis in which the alleged culprits are more easily identifiable? (See Kessler 2015 for a discussion.) Similarly, did the West territorialize a new and complex set of security challenges after 9/11 by shifting the focus away from decentralized networks of terrorism to an identifiable target such as Iraq? More generally, are we tempted to locate structural changes and dynamics within or between states and remain blind for the dislocations and ruptures between and within structures of global order?

Often the answer is "yes", which highlights that in their everyday attempts to make sense of global politics, practitioners and analysts fall all too easily for a common pattern of abstraction. Politics is associated with state conduct rather than with the role of financial markets or legal systems because consequential "practice" is most easily associated with state behavior. Yet, as long as we do not make explicit our taken-for-granted conceptions of global ordering, we exclude them from the realm of political contestation. If we erect a taboo over the concept of capitalism (see Chapter 10, this volume), we will blame Lehman Brothers, "the Greeks" or some other culprit for a financial crisis. And as soon as a culprit is found and complexity is explained away, the root causes of the crisis can no longer be articulated.

The task of studying world society is not simply to replace a state-centric perspective with a focus on complex social systems, but to critically observe the forms, functions, and consequences of these common reductions in complexity. This points to an ethical reason for embracing the concept. Absent an explicit conceptualization of society, there is a continuous temptation to engage in some form of scapegoating. Rather than trying to tackle the complexity of the problem at hand, the unreflexive self will always find another other to blame. Such antagonistic fault lines between self and other, friend and enemy, are never necessary, but always tempting. Blaming the other is a paradigmatic example of reducing complexity, and the violence of antagonistic forms of othering can be read as an effect of surrogate concepts filling in the conceptual void. Again, the Greeks are much easier to blame than global finance.

Another problem is to conceive of society in all-encompassing terms that escape political inquiry. We find this problem, for instance, in the political thought of Hannah Arendt, which revolves continuously around the three closely related concepts of freedom, action, and politics. Each of these concepts can be contrasted with an oppositional concept. Freedom is opposed to necessity. Action, in the emphatic sense of being creative, is opposed to behavior, the mere enactment of a given script. And politics is opposed to the social, Arendt's pre-conceptual stand-in for society. In each of these oppositions, one side is marked as positive, as a site of proper political engagement, while the other stands in the way of any such engagement. While the social thus plays an important role, Arendt does not take the extra step of devoting conceptual attention to it, for instance in the form of a distinct conceptualization of society. As Hanna Pitkin aptly puts it, what the social does in Arendt's political theory is no different from what monsters from outer space do in 1950s science fiction movies:

> Arendt writes about the social as if an evil monster from outer space, entirely external to and separate from us, had fallen upon us intent on debilitating, absorbing, and ultimately destroying us, gobbling up our distinct individuality and turning us into robots that mechanically serve its purposes ... The particular film, which, it turns out, was called simply *The Blob*, concerned a monstrous, jellylike substance from outer space, which has a predilection for coating and then consuming human beings and grows with each meal. (Pitkin 1998: 4)

Pitkin actually follows through on the metaphor and calls her book-length discussion of Arendt's lack of a concept of the social *The Attack of the Blob*. The metaphor can help us to further clarify what is at stake in having or not having a concept of society. *The Blob* is conceptually inelegant. It has an onomatopoetic quality – the sound of the word already hints at the meaning it is supposed to convey. The blob quality of the social, sitting there, opaquely and oppressively on top of everyday practice and delimiting the scope of action, curtailing agency, is not merely the result of having no discernible concept of society whatsoever. It is also a consequence of conceptualizing the social in terms so rigid that literally no political questions remain to be asked. We have argued above that various traditions of using the concept of world society in IR revolve around a resistance to a naturalized understanding of social order. To emphasize that social order is social, that it is produced, maintained, transformed, and disrupted in and through social processes, begs the question of how we ended up with one order rather than another. To paint the social in the scary colours of *The Blob*, however, merely closes off questions that need to be unpacked.

The methodological punchline of our discussion of world society – unpacking practices of ordering and disordering, not knowing in advance – is thus also a political one. Consider another example of a concept of society that is all about knowing answers in advance. At the height of Marxism's dogmatic closure, and very much contrary to Marx's own vision of politics, Karl Kautsky declared that the German Social-Democratic Party was "a revolutionary, but not a revolution-making party". In the confidence that the official doctrine had in fact deciphered the laws of history, all that needed to be done was to wait for the forces of history to play out as anticipated. Fulfilling one's historical task as a non-revolutionary revolutionary then simply meant to be there at the right time, waiting for the great collapse that never happened. The more static and naturalized the concept of society, the lesser cause we see for political agency.

The alternative sketched here entails a methodological re-orientation in the conceptualization of society: the question is not only whether we – as social scientists, IR scholars, students of global politics – have a concept of society. The question is also whether society has a concept of society, i.e. whether structures and processes of global ordering become an explicit focus in the accounts we – as ordinary citizens – give of ourselves. From the point of view of such a reconstructive turn in the conceptualization of society, the conceptualization of society becomes a matter of self-observation (Luhmann 1984). More specifically, it involves observing how society as a social system differentiates itself from others by clarifying which communications belong to itself and which do not.[3] Such self-observation not only presupposes an acknowledgement of one's own contingent position and the limits of the concepts used. It would also reveal that society has not one but several concepts of itself: as capitalist, democratic, open, repressive, etc. Reductionist approaches would highlight one of these concepts, one particular aspect, and celebrate it as the crucial one. Refusing to engage in such a form of reductionism would mean to consider encounters between these different concepts of society as an important site of political contestation.

Conclusion

This chapter has discussed the emergence of the concept of world society and its uses in three steps. First, we identified the problems to which conceptualizations of world society respond. This conceptual challenge is part of a broader realization that the analysis of contemporary world politics demands the development of a new vocabulary (see Kessler 2009). On a par with literature emphasizing the concepts of "international organization" and "global governance/globalization", the concept of world society offers a third and distinct avenue to conceptualize global order and, thereby, also the boundaries of IR as a discipline. Taking world society seriously calls for a reconsideration of sociological approaches. Yet, as Justin Rosenberg and Jens Bartelson have reminded us, the classic sociological theories and their concepts were developed with the nation-state in mind, which makes it difficult to simply project them onto a global scale (see Bartelson 2001, 2006, 2009; Rosenberg 2006). This poses a challenge for IR scholars, yet it also opens the door for a creative discussion about how analysts of world politics should think about world society.

The second section identified the English School, the Stanford School and the Bielefeld School as three literatures where the concept of world society has been used. Even though these literatures are very distinct in both their outlook and their

[3] For instance, which distinctions make it possible to differentiate what kind of communications are considered "economic", "religious" or "legal" – and which one not. Society acquires the capacity to observe itself through these distinctions, which are the result of an evolutionary process, rather than human will or reason.

conceptualization of world society, they are united insofar as they use the concept to reach beyond the world we already know: it highlights change, openness and contingency, not fixation, laws and static "forces". The upshot of these various conceptualizations is thus in part a methodological one. Efforts at conceptualizing world society are efforts at forging a conceptual lens through which transformations of global politics can be observed. As the third section pointed out, what is at stake in such efforts, however, is not merely methodological or theoretical. It also allows us to identify political processes, for instance at the level of the fixation and stabilization of spaces and temporalities. To identify such processes is not merely an exercise in analytical stock-taking but renders them visible as potential sites of political contestation.

Suggested Readings

Albert, Mathias (2016) *A Theory of World* Politics. Cambridge: Cambridge University Press.
A helpful discussion of different concepts of world society, focusing in particular on their understanding of conflict.

Buzan, Barry (2004) *From International to World Society? English School Theory and the Social Structure of Globalization*. Cambridge: Cambridge University Press.
An important discussion of the concept of world society from an English School perspective.

Luhmann, Niklas (1997) 'Globalization or World Society: How to conceive of modern society?', *International Review of Sociology* 7(1): 67–79.
An accessible introduction to Luhmann's concept of world society.

Meyer, John, John Boli, George M. Thomas, and Francisco O. Ramirez (1997) 'World Society and the Nation State', *American Journal of Sociology* 103(1), 144–81.
One of the classical statements of the Stanford School perspective on world society.

R. B. J. Walker (1993) *Inside/Outside: International Relations as Political Theory*. Cambridge: Cambridge University Press.
A classic text on the implications of drawing a distinction between inside and outside, thus crucial for an understanding of how and why it is important to start with difference rather than identity, which may be important in IR.

Bibliography

Albert, Mathias (2008) 'Conflict in World Society Theory', *Distinktion: Scandinavian Journal of Social Theory* 9(2): 57–75.
Albert, Mathias (2016) *A Theory of World* Politics. Cambridge: Cambridge University Press.
Albert, Mathias, Barry Buzan, and Michael Zürn (eds) (2013) *Bringing Sociology to International Relations*. Cambridge: Cambridge University Press.
Albert, Mathias, Oliver Kessler, and Stephan Stetter (2008) 'On Order and Conflict: International Relations and the "Communicative Turn"', *Review of International Studies* 34 (Supplement S1): 43–67.
Ashley, Richard K. (1984) 'The Poverty of Neorealism', *International Organization* 38(2): 225–86.

Ashley, Richard K. (1988) 'Untying the Sovereign State: A double reading of the anarchy problematique', *Millennium: Journal of International Studies* 17(2): 227–62.
Bartelson, Jens (2001) *The Critique of the State*. Cambridge: Cambridge University Press.
Bartelson, Jens (2006) 'Making Sense of Global Civil Society', *European Journal of International Relations* 12(3): 371–95.
Bartelson, Jens (2009) *Visions of World Community*. Cambridge: Cambridge University Press.
Brown, Chris (2001) 'World Society and the English School: an "International Society" Perspective on World Society', *European Journal of International Relations* 7(4): 423–41.
Bull, Hedley (2002 [1977]) *The Anarchical Society: A Study of Order in World Politics*. London: Palgrave.
Buzan, Barry (2004) *From International to World Society? English School Theory and the Social Structure of Globalization*. Cambridge: Cambridge University Press.
Graz, Jean Christophe, and Andreas Nölke (eds) (2008) *Transnational Private Governance and its Limits*. London: Routledge.
Heintz, Bettina, and Jens Greve (2005) 'Die Entdeckung der Weltgesellschaft', *Zeitschrift für Soziologie Sonderheft*. Stuttgart: Lucius und Lucius.
Hollis, Martin, and Steve Smith (1990) *Explaining and Understanding in International Relations*. Oxford: Oxford University Press.
Hooghe, Liesbet, and Gary Marks (2001) *Multi-Level-Governance and European Integration*. London: Rowan & Littlefield.
Kennedy, David (2006) *Of Law and War*. Princeton, NJ: Princeton University Press.
Keohane, Robert, and Joseph S. Nye (1971) 'Transnational Relations and World Politics: An Introduction', *International Organization* 25(3): 329–49.
Kessler, Oliver (2009) 'Toward a Sociology of the International? International Relations between Anarchy and World Society', *International Political Sociology* 3(1): 87–108.
Kessler, Oliver (2012) 'World Society, Differentiation and Time', *International Political Sociology* 6 (1): 77-94.
Kessler, Oliver (2015) Contingency of Constructivism, unpublished manuscript (under review).
King, Gary, Robert O. Keohane, and Sidney Verba (1994) *Designing Social Inquiry: Scientific Inference in Qualitative Research*. Princeton, NJ: Princeton University Press.
Kratochwil, Friedrich V. (1991) *Rules, Norms, and Decisions: On the Conditions of Practical and Legal Reasoning in International Relations and Domestic Affairs*. Cambridge: Cambridge University Press.
Luhmann, Niklas (1971) 'Die Weltgesellschaft', in Luhmann, Niklas (ed), *Soziologische Aufklärung 2: Aufsätze zur Theorie der Gesellschaft*. Opladen: Westdeutscher Verlag.
Luhmann, Niklas (1984) *Soziale Systeme*. Frankfurt/Main: Suhrkamp.
Luhmann, Niklas (1992) 'The Concept of Society', *Thesis Eleven* 31(1): 67–80.
Luhmann, Niklas (1993) *Gesellschaftsstruktur und Semantik: Studien zur Wissenssoziologie der modernen Gesellschaft*. Vol. 2. Frankfurt/Main: Suhrkamp.
Luhmann, Niklas (1997) *Die Gesellschaft der Gesellschaft*. 2 vols. Frankfurt/Main: Suhrkamp.
Meyer, John (2010) 'World Society, Institutional Theories, and the Actor', *Annual Revue of Sociology* 36(1): 1–20.
Meyer, John W., John Boli, George M. Thomas, and Francisco O. Ramirez (1997) 'World Society and the Nation State', *American Journal of Sociology* 103(1): 144–81.
Morgenthau, Hans (1944) *Scientific Man vs Power Politics*. Chicago: Chicago University Press.
Onuf, Nicholas Greenwood (1989) *World of our Making: Rules and Rule in Social Theory and International Relations*. London: Routledge.
Pitkin, Hannah (1998) *'The Attack of the Blob': Hannah Arendt's Concept of the Social*. Chicago/London: University of Chigago Press.

Risse, Thomas, Stephen C. Ropp, and Kathryn Sikkink (1999) *The Power of Human Rights*. Cambridge: Cambridge University Press.

Rosenau, James N., and Ernst-Otto Czempiel (eds) (1992) *Governance without Government: Order and Change in World Politics*. Cambridge: Cambridge University Press.

Rosenberg, Justin (2006) 'Why is there no International Historical Sociology?', *European Journal of International Relations* 12(3): 307–40.

Rosenberg, Justin (2007) 'International Relations – the "Higher Bullshit": a Reply to the Globalization Theory Debate', *International Politics* 44(4): 450–82.

Tilly, Charles (1984) *Big Structures, Large Processes, Huge Comparisons*. New York: Russell Sage Foundation.

Tönnies, Ferdinand (1887) *Gemeinschaft und Gesellschaft: Abhandlung des Communismus und des Socialismus als empirische Culturformen*. Leipzig: Fues.

Walker, R.B.J. (1991) 'State Sovereignty and the Articulation of Political Space/Time', *Millennium: Journal for International Studies* 20(3): 445–61.

Walker, R.B.J. (1993) *Inside/Outside: International Relations as Political Theory*. Cambridge: Cambridge University Press.

Waltz, Kenneth (1979) *Theory of International Politics*. Reading, MA: Addison-Wesley.

Wendt, Alexander (1999) *Social Theory of International Politics*. Cambridge: Cambridge University Press.

Zangl, Bernhard, and Michael Zürn (2003) 'Frieden und Krieg', *Sicherheit in der nationalen und postnationalen Konstellation*. Frankfurt/Main: Suhrkamp.

10

Capitalism

Benno Teschke and Frido Wenten

It is perhaps not surprising that a concept's repressed history re-enters public consciousness and academic debate when the phenomenon it seeks to capture is in fundamental crisis (Streeck 2009; Kocka 2010; Neal and Williamson 2014a, 2014b; Piketty 2014; Adelman 2015). This is the case for the concept of capitalism in the wider social sciences and, specifically, in the field of IR/IPE, which, as we will argue, excised the term throughout much of its short disciplinary history during the 20th century. This elision, we further argue, is deeply embedded in mainstream IR/IPE's theoretical reliance on neoclassical economics, which had divested the term capitalism of its analytical significance by replacing it with a more restrictive, technical and socially disembodied category of "the market". Capitalism as a concept disappeared therefore from much of mainstream IR/IPE until the last decade or so.

A clarification of the concept of capitalism is hence confronted with its academically and politically contested nature and its consequent conceptual ambiguity. We proceed from the suggestion in the introductory chapter to this volume that singular concepts receive their meanings only within wider conceptual webs, which form an analytical vocabulary that is specific to distinguishable theoretical traditions. The meaning of the concept of capitalism is intrinsically polyvalent and receives a degree of semantic stability only within particular theoretical registers. Yet, these paradigms do not offer themselves as free-floating presences in the academic marketplace, but result from long-standing conceptual conflicts over the scope of diverse disciplines, manifest in the restriction of the concept to a narrower set of ideal-typical *economic* properties, which inform its replacement by categories like "the market" or "the economy", against the expansiveness of capitalism as an epochal and historically specific set of *social relations*. Broadly speaking, this analytical rift across the academic field corresponds to the contemporary disciplinary divide between economics and the wider social sciences. Yet, even within this divide, capitalism is more widely used as a suggestive and explicitly political *Kampfbegriff* (polemical term) of both the political right and left, whose contending definitions indicate the intellectual positionality of its respective defenders with direct implications for policy advice and politics.

Accordingly, this chapter reconstructs and unravels the amalgamation of the analytical and the political in the term by tracing its conceptual development from its emergence to its refinement, refusal and replacement within a contested history of discipline construction. The central thesis is that the conceptual history of capitalism is characterised by a progressive shift away from conceiving "the economic" in socio-political terms towards its de-socialisation and de-politicisation, captured in a restrictive and technical equation of the economic with "the market" as a detached object of investigation. We show that the progressive emancipation of the disciplines of political economy (PE) and, later, economics from an earlier, more holistic field of social philosophy left little room for wider conceptions of capitalism found in Classical Political Economy (CPE), Marxism and parts of sociology. In a second step, we argue that the analytical decoupling of abstract economic principles from their social underpinnings had profound implications for the main paradigms of IR and IPE. Due to their overwhelming reliance on the narrower conception imported from "economics", both disciplines were constructed without one of the social sciences' most fundamental concepts – capitalism.

This vanishing act poses a particular challenge for this chapter. It requires that a conceptual history of capitalism tracks the making of a conceptual absence through the successive crafting of place-holders, like "the market", "the economy" and "utility maximisation". We conceive these as counter-concepts forged to dissolve a wider conception of capitalism and to reserve the narrower one to the discipline of economics (Milonakis and Fine 2009: 91–118). In short, the chapter adopts a specific kind of conceptual history, which does not rely on the recovery of the textuality and intertextuality of capitalism's historical semantics, but rather retrieves its changing meanings – in tandem with, especially, the "market" – within a contested history of multiple discipline constructions. This strikes at another fundamental intellectual problem in concept analysis. Whereas the above reflections problematise the relation between history and concept formation, the chapter also interrogates the relation between social-scientific concepts and their historical-empirical referents. Classically, this question has produced two methodological answers. We can either pursue a strategy of general concept formation, generating firm definitions, general abstractions or ideal-types. These tend to reduce the points of contact between a historical phenomenon and its conceptualisation, yielding ideality. Alternatively, we can pursue a strategy of historicisation that tries to minimise the distance between conceptual abstraction and the phenomenon it tries to track. These two opposing methods are visible in Marxism as in many other social science traditions, as discussed in the introductory chapter to this volume.

However, if, as many Marxists would agree, capitalism is a contested social relation, grounded in differential access to property, then this relationality needs to be tracked in historically concrete ways. Thus, this chapter envisions capitalism not as a definitionally fixed theoretical category – identical with itself over time – but as an open-ended and lived historical praxis. It follows that we conceive of history neither as mere illustration nor as expression of a deeper conceptual logic, but as the primary terrain on which capitalism as a social relation is constructed – requiring conceptual reconstructions that capture specificity. Historicisation is therefore advocated not only against the replacement of the term capitalism by that of "the market" in mainstream economics, but also against counter-attempts – within Marxism and without – to stabilise an essentialised notion of capitalism in spatio-temporally indifferent general abstractions as ideal-types.

Social reality, we contend, is not unaffected by its conceptualisation and therefore is dependent on *how* we conceptualise it. Hence, a specific conceptual register calls a specific experience into consciousness by providing a common language designed to act on it. Few concepts lend themselves better to an examination of this relation between word and world than capitalism. Broadly speaking, our approach to analysing changes in the conceptual meanings of capitalism/market is informed by a critical historical sociology of concept formation, which emphasises the politics of concept construction – both in the sense of indicating what socio-political contexts and interests generate what kinds of conceptual changes, and in the sense of how these altered concepts inform policy changes. Inversely, we suggest that concept formation needs to be oriented towards specificity to avoid reification – a task whose exposition is largely beyond the scope of this chapter. The chapter employs therefore a Political-Marxist approach which rejects an economistic and systemic interpretation of capitalism left intact at an abstract conceptual level, replacing it with a social-relational and historicist understanding that emphasises the politics and geopolitics of social reproduction, grounded in social conflicts and differential market power (Wood 1981; N. Wood 2002). This approach, which has some affinities with concept history in the tradition of both Koselleck and the Cambridge School, rejects both generic and supra-historical definitions of "capitalism" and also its exclusive study through the retrieval of its semantic meaning articulated by contemporaries.

For our understanding of conceptual historicism also differs from either *Begriffsgeschichte* or the Cambridge School. *Begriffsgeschichte* was originally invented in dialogue with but over time increasingly in opposition to "social history" by insisting that the recovery of the past needs to proceed through the textual reconstruction of the changing semantics of selected social and political core concepts linguistically articulated by past contemporaries (Koselleck, 2002: 23). Accessing history through this procedure was declared as a "methodologically irreducible final instance" (Koselleck, 2006: 99). Yet, the privileging of intra- and inter-textual semantic shifts in the meanings of concepts systematically suppressed their pre-verbal and extra-linguistic empirical sources of evidence, which are routinely available to historians to assess the difference between concept and its referent. *Begriffsgeschichte* also elided the question "why" concepts changed their meanings in favour of "how" they did so, and remained restricted to the classical canon of political thinkers, the so-called *Höhenliteratur* (high road literature) to the exclusion of everyday language. Similar problems beset the Cambridge School. Its linguistic contextualization of political theory remains insufficient in its historicist method by understanding contexts primarily as wider traditions of contemporary political discourse. By suggesting to read "texts as contributions to particular discourses, and thereby to recognise the ways in which they followed or challenged or subverted the conventional terms of those discourses themselves"(Skinner, 2002: 125), wider socio-political contexts remain, as a rule, a passive background (N. Wood, 2002).

While we agree that all concepts are "essentially contested", we are missing methodological guidelines in the volume's three suggested modes of concept analysis of how socio-political conflicts inform concept formation, rather than how concepts perform and constitute reality. Ideally, this desideratum requires a critical sociology of knowledge, different from *Begriffsgeschichte*, concept analysis and discourse analysis (for a guiding critique, see Steinmetz 2008).

The chapter interrogates the conceptual history of capitalism through the prism of three distinct questions: (1) How are capitalism and its counter-concepts defined? (2) What understandings of theory and social science sustain these conceptualisations? (3) What are the implications of adopting either the concept of capitalism or the market, imported from the classical canon of economics, into contemporary IR/IPE for theorising international relations? We also draw out, where appropriate, the political implications of accepting a specific conceptualisation of the term capitalism. The first part of this chapter reviews how the economic came to be conceived – oscillating between "the market" and "capitalism" – across key traditions in the pre-Second World War social sciences and in the emerging sub-discipline of Political Economy.[1] The second part draws out how the absence or presence of conceptions of capitalism informs the analysis of global political dynamics in IR and IPE. That is, it not merely presents how different IR/IPE approaches conceive of capitalism, but also how the adoption of certain conceptions of the economic allows for certain options of modelling international relations. We exemplify this for neo-realism, neo-liberal institutionalism and two neo-Marxist traditions. We suggest that precisely because mainstream IR theories tend to conceive of the economic in terms of a de-socialised and de-politicised abstraction, imported uncritically from neoclassical assumptions of "the market", "the logic" of international relations is conceived independently of – but in analogy to – the alleged "logic" of competitive markets. The conclusion discusses the broader implications of such moves.

Capitalism versus the Market before IR/IPE

From Classical Political Economy to Karl Marx: 'The System of Natural Liberty' vs. capitalism as a social relation

The conflict over the conceptualisation of capitalism in terms of either "the market" or a distinct set of social relations reaches right back to CPE. Systematically grounding the workings of the economy in secular and rational principles, Adam Smith's notion of "the system of natural liberties" allows for two readings: one grounded in an abstract notion of "homo oeconomicus" and one grounded in the acceptance of specific social classes that configure capitalism as a social relation. Smith's *Wealth of Nations* conceives of "the economy" in terms of a natural "harmony of interests" among self-regarding individuals mediated by market transactions. An anthropological notion of the freely exchanging individual, driving an ever-widening division of labour, constitutes the phenomenon of the market as the ideal and naturalised mechanism for the allocation of resources, productivity improvements through specialisation, and the growth of the wealth of nations. Competitive price formation by the "invisible hand" of supply and demand turns egoistic behaviour spontaneously into aggregate social benefits. And, if left undisturbed by politics and social conflict

[1] Our argument in section 1 is indebted to the works of Hodgson (2001), Clarke (1991) and Milonakis and Fine (2009).

(and other unnatural obstacles), the dynamic of a widening and intensifying division of labour would drive history through successive stages of subsistence to the emergence of "commercial society".

However, this macro-dynamic theory of development, grounded in an elementary methodological individualism, is complemented by a theory of income distribution, premised on individuals differentially located in the structure of property ownership, and captured in the supra-individual category of three classes: landlords, workers and capitalists own different factors of production (land, labour, capital) and receive in turn rents, wages and profits. Smith developed these categories through an inquiry into the co-operative production of the (natural) price of a commodity, which he attributed to the respective factor of production each class added to its value. The differential forms of ownership determine differential kinds of interest, revenues and social relations. In this sense, Smith's naturalised economic theory receives not only historical specificity and social content, but it is here conducted in structural, collective and aggregate terms. Rather than an abstract science of economics, Smith devises a social theory premised on an emerging capitalist society, breaking free from "unnatural" feudal and mercantile privileges, conceived as obstacles to the full flowering of market principles, and anchored in a distinct and novel class structure. The economy was not an autonomous realm but coterminous with "civil society". And "civil society" was not composed of fictional individual and equal property owners, but rather populated by classes with unequal access to property and potentially diverging collective class interests. Ultimately, Smith's macro-dynamic theory of economic development, premised on a growing division of labour driven by self-regarding individuals, arrived at by the deployment of the deductive method, stood un-reconciled with his micro-theoretical insights into the class divisions between capitalists, landowners and wage workers as collective actors in a specific type of society, arrived at by the deployment of the historical-inductive method.

This multi-dimensional understanding also reached beyond the role of classes and included considerations of the political as an integral part of CPE. The market as an institution and as a "spontaneous" mechanism was premised on certain political preconditions, which could not be rendered external or contingent to the conception of PE as a holistic social science. Smith reflected not on "the economy" in the abstract as a discrete, self-regulating and autonomous sphere of the market, but on public guarantees for private property rights, civil law and public jurisdiction to enforce contracts, legislation to maintain competitive markets against monopolies and privileges, and the development of moral sentiments through public education. Smith theorised a specific empirical referent society, even if he naturalised and de-historicised its origins and constitution. Smith's view of PE remained suffused with an unresolved tension between a transhistorical concept of the market, premised on a quantitatively ever-widening division of labour, and a historically more circumspect conception of capitalist social relations, anchored in a qualitatively distinct class configuration. However, the question of the historical origins of this novel set of social relations that constituted the economy – the transition to capitalism – and the role of power and politics in this transition, disappeared from view.

The historicisation and theorisation of the empirical and seemingly natural categories in the works of Smith and particularly of David Ricardo – value, money, capital, profit, etc. – formed the entry point for Marx to locate the existence, analysis and critique of capitalism in the historically specific conditions of its emergence, development and potential transformation.[2] However, a new problem appeared: the tension between a logical concept of capitalism as a system, and a more historicist understanding of capitalism as a social relation. Marx acknowledged that CPE "indeed analysed value and its magnitude ... and uncovered the content concealed within these forms [that is: human labour; BT/FW]" (Marx 1990: 173f.). Yet, it failed to understand the specific *social form* in which labour was expressed in value, quantifiable by labour time. Marx argued that while all goods (natural goods excepted) embody a certain amount of labour time, it is only when social reproduction depends on the exchange of products of separate private labours that these products are exchanged as proportions of the respective individual labours in all socially expended labour – expressed in their exchange value. In other words, it is not simply labour time that determines the value of a commodity, but a specific organisation of social labour: qualitatively different and in their productivity variable, privately expended labours are equalised through the act of exchange – universally expressed in the form of money – as embodiments of *abstract labour*, measured as "socially necessary labour time".

That an exchange of equivalent values allows for the accumulation of a surplus (value) posed major theoretical difficulties for Ricardo. Marx explained surplus by differentiating between labour (the actual labour expended in production) and labour power (the capacity to work). A surplus arises because specific social property relations force workers to exchange labour power against a wage lower than the value added by their labour to the product appropriated by the capitalist: exploitation. This is premised on the dispossession of direct producers from their means of reproduction, transforming the latter into private capital and producing two market-dependent classes: propertyless wage labourers needing to sell their labour power, and the new owners of the means of production, capitalists. In standard Marxist discourse, this is referred to as the transition to capitalism:

> The process, therefore, which creates the capital-relation can be nothing other than the process which divorces the worker from the ownership of the conditions of his own labour; it is a process which operates two transformations, whereby the social means of subsistence and production are turned into capital, and the immediate producers are turned into wage-labourers. So-called primitive accumulation, therefore, is nothing else than the historical process of divorcing the producer from the means of production. (Marx 1990: 874f.)

Marx's analysis of capitalism is thus grounded in *class relations* – in theory, through the value form of social labour; and in history, through the socio-political conditions that generate the separation of direct producers from the means of subsistence. This also implies, contra Smith, that human nature is nothing innately pre-given and amenable to a generic conception of individuality and rationality, but shaped by historically specific social relations. This reinforces the ambiguities in Smith's double reading of the market as flowing naturally from anthropological essences and its

[2] Marx uses the term *capitalism* rarely and relatively late (for the first time in 1863 in *Theories of Surplus Value*, Ch. 17). Until the 1850s, he usually speaks of "bourgeois society" before beginning to analyse the "capitalist mode of production" as the dominant characteristic of modern societies in distinction from preceding modes of production.

specific class composition, and foregrounds the historicist side of Marx. Inversely, Marx never resolved the divide between an abstract logic of capital as a system and this historicism – tracking the history of capitalism as a social relation. For *Capital* analyses primarily "the internal organization of the capitalist mode of production, its ideal average, as it were" (Marx 1991: 970), devoting only one chapter to an explanation of its origins. Marx' general thesis that the logic of capital applies to "societies in which the capitalist mode of production prevails" (1990: 125) renders an explanation of the historical emergence of, and ongoing history of, capitalism external to the logical/dialectical conceptual argument presented. This ambivalence has been phrased as a dominance of economic-technical ("scientific") over practical-political concepts ("class struggle") as a driving factor in the analysis of history (Korsch 1981: 86).

Still, even though CPE also conceived of society in class-divided terms, Marx was able to solve the mystery of capitalist profit generation by revealing its source in the exploitation of the working class. This insight, obscured by the liberal argument that free workers enter freely into a legal contract that exchanges equivalences (wages for labour), led Marx to claim that capitalism is not only rooted in exploitative class relations, but is ultimately an unsustainable condition of human relations. Consequently, rather than writing a better political economy, Marx's interest revolved around the *critique* of CPE as an explanatory register to understand *history*. Simultaneously, this provided a theoretical foundation and analytical *tool* for the struggles of the labour movement. It was explicitly meant to function as a theoretically informed political-normative intervention into ongoing social conflicts. However, the "scientific" and "class struggle" readings of capitalism engendered long-lasting controversies within the socialist tradition.

The Methodenstreit and the struggle over "economics"

While CPE identified a proto-conception of the economic largely revolving around the market, but still circumscribed by moral and social philosophy, and while Marx oscillated between logical and historical conceptions of capitalism, an altogether different tradition of PE, the German Historical School (GHS) (Knies, Schmoller, Sombart), emerged during the 1840s. In critical engagement with CPE and against the idea of a tendentially cosmopolitan and abstract market, this School directed research towards the concrete, spatio-temporally diverse, and "real" phenomena of "economic" activity in the actual course of history. This implied the acceptance of inductivism (reasoning from observation to generalities), the rejection of nomothetic laws, and the replacement of the abstract individual profit-maximiser (methodological individualism) with a subjectivist conception of human beings embedded in "moral communities" and institutions (family, Church, associations, nation, state). Historically grown institutions set the context-dependent parameters for culturally, socially and politically constituted motivations for economic conduct. Society remained an organic concept, composed of collectivities, rather than a mechanistic concept, understood as the aggregate of individual actions. The nation-state, rather than a politically disembodied market populated by rational market participants, constitutes the adequate unit of analysis.

The GHS was centrally concerned with the question of the origins and historical specificity of capitalism as a concrete phenomenon, but this raised the question of how to reconcile the "abstract-theoretical" with the "empirical-historical" method. Any general definition of capitalism as an economic phenomenon was immediately confronted with its manifold and specific "realities" that could only be captured by re-admitting history and sociology into the concerns of PE. So while some representatives were not shy to advance their definitions of capitalism, these were not meant to form the substantive core for further theoretical deductions, but were conceived as "ideal-types". "Capitalism", Sombart suggested,

> is a particular economic system, an organisation based on market exchange, in which two different parts of the population – the owners of the means of production, who simultaneously manage production, the economic subjects, and propertyless workers, the economic objects – regularly interact via the medium of the market. This organisation is governed by the profit-principle and economic rationalism. (Sombart, 1987 [1916]: 319)

This economic system, and economic theory more generally, was not discussed as an abstraction but recharged with historical, social and institutional content. Rejecting the articulation of general economic laws as abstract idealism, the GHS advanced an understanding of economic history in terms of the evolution of institutions that frame "economic" activity. History was conceived in terms of evolutionary laws of historical change, expressed in a sequence of political communities from the tribe, mark, village and town to the territory, the state and even larger confederations. While the mechanisms for these evolutionary laws remained unspecified and contingent, this historicisation reformulated economic theory as economic history.

The decisive break with historicity came with the arrival of marginalism. This group of scholars (with significant differences: Jevons, Walras, Menger) sought to move from a holistic study of capitalism to a "pure theory of economics" (Walras 1954: 71), recasting PE into "a theory of exchange based on the proportionality of prices *to intensities of the last wants satisfied*" (Walras, cited in Milonakis and Fine 2009: 95). With marginal utility becoming the axiomatic underpinning of pure economics, methodological individualism and the centrality of static equilibrium provided a new foundation for abstract deduction and algebraic modelling of the dynamics of economic activity. Economics was henceforth conceived as a positivist science, modelled on the conception of "value-free" theory in the natural sciences, revolving around price formation in subjective acts of exchange in a hypothetical situation of perfect competition (rather than around production grounded in the labour theory of value). Thus, marginalism broke not only decisively with Marxism and GHS, but also with CPE.

These differences came to a head in the *Methodenstreit* (Milonakis and Fine 2009), conducted primarily between GHS's leader, Gustav Schmoller, and the Austrian economist Carl Menger, in the 1880s. While Menger built on marginalism – accepting the concept of marginal utility, the view of the economy as composed of atomised individuals, and the deductive method – he dramatised the antinomies between a "clunky" and descriptive historicism and economics as an "exact science". The former, he charged, remained confined to the investigation of "full empirical reality", expressed in ideographic narratives, the spatio-temporal context-boundedness of economic phenomena, and the inductive method, yielding limited generalisations and abstractions. Economics as a science proceeded inversely to bridge the gap between description and explanation through the method of abstraction and isolation (from non-economic disturbances). This would yield theoretical rather than just empirical knowledge, leading to exact laws amenable to scientific generalisation. In the process, the emphasis on the "subjective" was effectively re-objectified, as the concern for understanding subjective economic motivation (choice) was reduced to an anthropological and essentialised axiomatic identification of individual self-interest, grounded in the satisfaction and maximisation of well-being. Preferences were posited and naturalised as pre-given. Only this move, according to Menger, could anchor economics as an exact science, generating nomothetic knowledge, removed from non-economic obfuscations. With classes as collective economic agents being replaced by individuals, historical specificity was sacrificed for simple transhistorical assumptions, and the social and political purged from the analysis. Ultimately, a holistic perspective was foregone and the term capitalism axed.

The controversy engendered remarkable and far-reaching consequences for the social sciences. With the triumph of marginalism, PE re-constituted itself as de-socialised, de-historicised and de-politicised "economics", independent from the cognate social sciences and subject to growing and increasingly professionalised standards of thematic, methodical and theoretical disciplinary self-identity, expert knowledge and boundary maintenance. The non-economic aspects of PE were rendered external and travelled towards the fields of sociology, history and politics. The multi-disciplinary and tendentially holistic thematic horizon of these disciplines shrank to strictly delimited and separate objects of investigation. The elision of the historical and socio-political from pure economics, evicting Marxism and historicism from the theoretical canon, left economics as a set of abstract deductions about the market and rational economic behaviour by individuals. This move from semi-institutionalised pre-disciplinarity to a fully institutionalised pluri-disciplinarity towards the end of the 19th century laid the tracks for the development of neoclassical economics.

Max Weber's social economics can be read as a final recovery act to bridge the gap between an a-historical science of economics and an a-theoretical field of economic history. Insisting on the non-separability of economic and non-economic phenomena and the essential historicity of both, Weber sought to re-convene a fragmenting field of knowledge in a multi-disciplinary understanding of sociology as a historical science. "The boundary lines of 'economic' phenomena are vague and not clearly defined ... as the economy does not exist in a social vacuum, but rather is part of society at large" (Milonakis and Fine 2009: 195). For Weber, culture – or, more widely, ideas – expressed in his sociology of the economic ethics of world religions, became the primary collective pre-condition (even if not mono-causally so) for a wider process of Western rationalisation, "laying the tracks" for the peculiarly Western form of instrumental rationality. This was expressed across all spheres of life, though not, critically for Weber, in politics, which he reserved as the sphere of charismatic leadership. While the economic ethos of non-Western world religions had blocked a breakthrough towards a rational form of capitalism outside Europe, Protestantism had inculcated a methodical spirit of inner-worldly aestheticism oriented towards salvation revealed in successful work. This stretched to the methodical-rational conduct of life across all social spheres, including the rational organisation of the enterprise. The *Protestant Ethic and the Spirit of Capitalism* (Weber 2011) provided a collectivist-culturalist explanation for the prevalence of individual rational value orientations, which had become, over time, sedimented in institutions that survived as "iron cages of obedience", even after the spirit of the Protestant Ethic had escaped in successive rounds of post-Reformation secularisation. Essentially, according to Weber, it was not capitalism as a specific set of social relations which generated methodical conduct (calculability, efficiency, profit maximisation, work discipline), but rather a religiously inspired spirit of rationality that came to suffuse all spheres and institutions, solidifying a capitalist economic order.

While Weber's Protestantism thesis is today widely refuted on empirical and logical grounds, his types of social action, including the rational type of economic action, offered a second lifeline for keeping a distinctly Weberian conception of capitalist economic action alive. Switching from ideational collectivism to methodological individualism, his types of social action were not conceived as culturally and space-time specific to post-Reformation Europe, but could, as universal ideal-types, in principle hold transhistorically for a variety of specific historical instances. In this sense, Weber's subjectivist conceptualisation of capitalist action as rational conduct oriented towards profit maximisation could hold for Antiquity, the Middle Ages, the Renaissance city-states and modernity at large. However, as capitalism was not defined as a set of spatio-temporally specific social relations, but as a value orientation somehow linked up with a wider Western notion of rationality, it tended to render the conception of capitalist action indiscriminate and arbitrary. For the concept of capitalism, in the pages of *Economy & Society* (Weber 1978), was now subjected to sub-types and further sub-sub-types, on a spectrum from peaceful exchange and commerce, i.e. purely economic profit maximisation, to political capitalism, i.e. politically secured profit maximisation, ranging from public monopolies to simple banditry and plunder visible across time and space. Ultimately, capitalism as a set of historically distinct social relations was dissolved into a transhistorical human disposition, unevenly present in very diverse historical settings.

How 'capitalism' disappeared from economics

After the end of the Second World War, challenges to Lionel Robbins' famous reduction of economics to the study of "human behaviour as a relationship between ends and scarce means which have alternative uses" (Robbins 1932: 15) withered away: Weber was confined to sociology, the GHS silently disappeared and historically oriented economists were sidelined at major universities in the US and the UK (Hodgson 2001, Pt III). Externally, economics became a parent science, modelling other disciplines after its de-historicised and universal image (e.g. Parsonian sociology). Internally, it was preoccupied with an extrapolation of its micro-foundations to explanations of macro-phenomena – first through general equilibrium theory, and later through game theory.

Thus, the economics mainstream today – neoclassical economics – can be understood as a formalisation, systematisation and extension of early marginalist principles. Larger economic phenomena are presented as an aggregation of rational, utility-maximising acts of individual behaviour. Value derives not from production costs – especially not from living labour – but from scarcity; and price is a judgement of value in exchange: an effect of individual choices. Under assumptions of perfect competition, symmetric information, no increasing returns to scale, and no barriers to market entry, the sum total of these choices will lead to an equilibrium between demand and supply.

Combined, partial equilibria for separate markets are supposed to add up to a general equilibrium, describing national economic dynamics and allowing for mathematical modelling. This equilibrium is, as a rule, Pareto-optimal, respectively allocatively efficient. If rigidly applied, economic phenomena not only can, but *must*, be explained as deductions of these basic principles.

With the axioms of economics defined without reference to socio-historical context and for all eternity, there was no explanatory value to be sought in historically specific concepts – such as *capitalism*. There was, however, a political one. During the Cold War, the concept of capitalism resurfaced as an "anti-collectivist" *Kampfbegriff* launched by the late Austrian School of Ludwig von Mises and Friedrich von Hayek – and by Chicago School figurehead Milton Friedman – against both real-existing Keynesianism and state socialism. To mobilise moral support, the liberal tradition was rewritten and equated with the advocacy of an abstract and idealised capitalism:

> A society in which liberal principles are put into effect is usually called a capitalist society, and the condition of that society, capitalism. Since the economic policy of liberalism has everywhere been only more or less closely approximated in practice, conditions as they are in the world today provide us with but an imperfect idea of the meaning and possible accomplishments of capitalism in full flower. (Mises 2002: 10)

Consequently, with real-existing capitalism being "imperfect", its true meaning had to be fathomed through a priori theorising. In a mind-boggling inversion of standard social-scientific protocol, aprioristically defined (and thus tautologically reaffirmed) principles of human action became the unquestionable maxim against which real-existing economies would have to be evaluated. Contested political processes were presented as problems of methodological (non-)adherence. To Mises, an economic system based on private property was preferable to any other, because it allowed the rationality of human action to be expressed in monetary terms, allowing for exact calculation and efficient allocation. Hayek went even further in insisting that private property and markets are the *only* necessary solution to humanity's "basic economic problems" of choice and scarcity (Hayek 1963: 12). This received its most explicit extension to contemporary politics across the Atlantic through Friedman's equation of capitalism with political freedom:

> The kind of economic organization that provides economic freedom directly, namely competitive capitalism, also promotes political freedom because it separates economic power from political power and in this way enables the one to offset the other. (Friedman 2002: 9)

In short, a radicalised abstract individualism forms the methodological, philosophical and political common denominator, allowing for a synthetic conceptual chain of "economics-liberalism-capitalism", with profound implications for political advocacy and practice. The works of Mises, Hayek and Friedman not only became a prominent template for attacks on socialism, but also for economic policy design in Pinochet's Chile, Thatcher's UK and Reagan's US.

Despite their differences, neoclassical and Austrian-style economics purge the social, political and historical from the theoretical apparatus, reduce rationality to utility maximisation, and define market processes as the optimal form of resource allocation and needs satisfaction. Other forms of human activity become irrational, extra-theoretical and render suboptimal outcomes. What, then, happens to history? By generalising individual choice and market exchange across all historical periods, the role of the historian is downgraded in a demoted sub-discipline of economic history to analyse history through the lens of economic theory. This approach is prominently represented by Douglass North and the tradition of New Institutional Economics (NIE), arguably the most sophisticated weapon currently launched against a concept of capitalism as a historical social relation. It upholds the core assumptions of neoclassical economics, most importantly its methodological individualism and the ontological starting point of "scarcity and, hence, competition for resources" (North 2005: 1), but allows for institutions to modify the interest-maximising behaviour of individual actors. Here, institutions are "the humanly devised constraints that structure political, economic and social interaction" (North 1991: 97): informal (moral) norms and formal (legal) rules. Effective institutions hence constitute the operative "rules of the game (with enforcement)", respectively the "incentive structure of a society" (1991: 98; 2005: 1). The core claim is that institutions affect economic performance by reducing or increasing *transaction costs* (costs of market exchanges or of estimating prices) and the stability of *property relations*.

Like the early American institutionalists (Veblen, Commons), NIE and its socio-political offspring (North 2005; North et al. 2009) are interested in how economic performance varies in the evolution of changing belief systems and habits across space and time, and leads to political agency that alters reality, triggering new rounds of habitual adaptation. But NIE limits the explanatory factors of these changes to the actions of utility-maximising individuals[3] – and, more importantly, to economic rationality itself: "Institutions change, and fundamental changes in relative prices are the most important source of that change" (North 1990: 84). Thus, NIE reduces the relevance of institutions to that of a mere modulator by virtue of their effects on costs. Institutions that foster capitalist development – usually a conceptual clarification of capitalism is circumvented altogether – are tautologically specified as those that allow for the unfolding of neoclassical core assumptions (North 1990). Getting these core institutions "right" (primarily markets, entrepreneurship, property rights and rule of law) becomes the benchmark against which past economic history and future policies are evaluated in a teleological and profoundly functionalist manner (North 2005; North et al. 2009). Ultimately, institutional variation is reduced to a more or less successful functional adaptation to the requirements of an essentially invariant economic logic.

The Capitalism/Market Divide and its Legacies in IR/IPE

The discussion thus far suggests that debates around the conceptualisation of "the economy" cleaved broadly into a wider historical understanding of capitalism as a

[3] "The agent of change is the individual entrepreneur responding to the incentives embodied in the institutional framework" (North 1990: 83).

social relation and into a more technical and abstract conceptualisation of "the market". The former, where it survived, was banished to and then marginalised in the disciplines of history and sociology; the latter reigned supreme in the new master discipline of economics and rose to the rank of a model science for other social sciences. Against this background, this section seeks to demonstrate how the adoption of specific understandings of capitalism/market in IR and IPE yields specific implications for the conceptualisation of international relations.

Neo realism and neo mercantilist IPE

Neo-realist thinking, as advanced by Kenneth Waltz, explicitly models its theory of international politics on the conception of the market in liberal economic theory. This procedure is purely analogical, as Waltz categorically excludes any interaction or co-production between the economic and the political to guard against "reductionism". Domestic social forces and, a fortiori, PE are bracketed as black boxes, and the effects of markets on state behaviour are externalised from the remit of theory (Waltz 1979). Theory construction proceeds from "micro-economic theory": the behaviour of states as self-regarding units focused on survival under structural constraints of international anarchy is modelled after the image of the behaviour of individual, self-regarding firms, whose rationality is structured through processes of socialisation and selection in competitive markets. The underlying conception of social science, theory, law and abstraction is directly borrowed from mainstream economics, positing a general law that is itself outside history. The result of Waltz's systematisation of "classical realism" through prevailing American positivistic conceptions of market behaviour is a "pure theory" undisturbed by PE and history, which does not integrate the concept of capitalism in any shape or form.

In the 1970s, some realist IR scholars re-cast their research in terms of IPE in a neo-mercantilist direction (Guzzini 1998). While the axiomatic entry-point posits that "national security is and always will be the principal concern of states" (Gilpin 2001: 18; see also Krasner 2009a: 5), realist IPE transcends the constricted security focus by supplementing the "pursuit of power" with the "pursuit of wealth", analysing their "reciprocal and dynamic interaction" (Gilpin 1975: 40): security depends on power, but power is affected by wealth, meaning that states intervene to channel "economic forces in ways favourable to their own economic interests" (Gilpin 2001: 21). This translates – normatively – into policy advice: international co-operation, in contrast to liberal IPE theory, should be subject to a calculation on achieving "relative" gains, accruing to one party, over "absolute gains" (Grieco 1990). The category of wealth – where it is not simply understood as a quantitative pool of available resources, rather than as a social power – is then contradictorily and eclectically linked to two conceptions of the economy: one grounded in neoclassical economics, the other in a re-definition of capitalism.

Capitalism, to Robert Gilpin, is characterised by a dynamic of creative destruction – the creation of "wealth through advancing continuously to ever higher levels of productivity and technological sophistication ... Technological progress [is] the ultimate driving force of capitalism" (Gilpin 2000: 3). The particularity of capitalism resides not in the emergence of a new constitution of the economic, but in its sustainable expansion – *continuous* wealth creation – through *industrial* production. This is combined with the security prerogative of (international) politics: to Gilpin, modern nation-states were a response to international security pressures that compelled feudal pre-state communities to rationalise their tax bases, in order to generate necessary revenues for military-technological innovations that guaranteed state survival. Territorial expansion and trade regulation as primary means of mercantilist wealth creation were increasingly replaced by productivity increases and trade between consolidated nation-states when the Industrial Revolution remodelled the incentive structure of the international system (Gilpin 1981, Chaps 2, 3). By the 19th century, we could therefore speak of an "international capitalist system" (Gilpin 2000: 3).

Gilpin's turn to history narrows down to a juxtaposition of two a-historical autonomous logics of the economic and the political: accepting "most, or at least much, of the corpus of conventional neoclassical economics", he asserts that "the market has its own logic, and its dictates must be heeded" (Gilpin 2001: 24, 74). But this acceptance of the autonomy of the market remains un-reconciled with the opening premise of security-driven economic policy. Realist IPE suggests that states and other actors modulate an essentially invariant economic logic by virtue of particular power constellations or "regimes" (e.g. Krasner 2009b, 2009c). But, in the end, irrespective of how "the economic" is conceived – either as wealth creation through capitalist technological innovations (productivity growth) or as the self-regulating market – this has no relevant effect on the primacy of security-driven state interests. For both conceptions of "the economic" remain socially disembodied, ruling out how variable domestic social interests may inform varying state interests. Ultimately, the concept of capitalism as a contested social relation drops out.[4]

Classical liberalism and neo-liberal institutionalism

Liberal IPE built originally on CPE and conceived of the expansion of markets as an essentially transnational and mutually beneficial affair, constituting a world market through a growing international division of labour and open markets. After the First World War, this assumption was supplemented with prescriptions for international political institution-building – cooperative security, democracy promotion, the rule of law, collective problem solving. This liberal internationalism faced a critique during the inter-war period that returned realism to the position of theoretical dominance, and this extended well into the 1970s. Yet, liberal models returned to prominence to explain the phenomena of institutionalised collaboration in international relations "after hegemony" (Keohane 1984).

Whereas realists argued that international regimes and institutions are derivative, reflecting the power and interests of dominant states, remaining on the whole confined to areas of "low politics" (Krasner 2009a, 2009b; Mearsheimer 1994), neo-liberal institutionalists argued that institutions arise from a plurality of self-interested actors, constituting mutually beneficial arrangements, which themselves influence co-operative state behaviour as they bind states into "rules of the game". Based on the works of Douglass North, institutions function to reduce uncertainty,

[4] This is perhaps best illustrated in hegemonic stability theory, which derives the establishment of liberal international economic orders from the material preponderance of a hegemonic state without inquiring into its social constitution and purpose.

lower transaction costs and solve collective action problems. Both perspectives, realist regime theory and neo-liberal institutionalism, relied on a common notion of egotistical state rationality to explain institution formation. While the former emphasised that co-operation was difficult to achieve given that states preferred "relative gains" from co-operation, liberals emphasised the likelihood of sustained co-operation across diverse sets of policy areas, due to the collective welfare-maximising effects accruing from co-operation, even if these effects were unevenly distributed ("absolute gains"). Ultimately, both approaches conceive of institutions as utilitarian and functional solutions to problems encountered by rational actors to advance "common interests".

Both approaches proceed by positing states as unitary actors with set preferences defined a priori. Realist regime theory highlights asymmetric inter-state power relations as the precondition for international institution-building that fix a given distribution of power within an international order to the advantage of the preponderant state. Neo-liberal institutionalism technically formalises the possibility of institutional co-operation, given greater inter-state power symmetries. Both approaches theorise institutions as a function of state rationality in terms of a calculus on mutual gains in abstraction from questions of national interest formation: power, interest and rationality become reified as political phenomena, decoupled from the domestic socio-economic interests and struggles that inform regime design and participation.

With neo-liberal institutionalism restricted to a state calculus, the "liberal moment" shrinks to perceived state-mediated mutual gains from political co-operation, mitigating anarchy. And if liberal international institution-building is conceived of as an outcome of states devising institutions to lower transaction costs, then a neoclassical conception of the world market needs to be imputed to which inter-state behaviour optimally adapts. Institution-building amongst states is either explained in analogy to market rationality, or it is explained as a function of the perceived mutual gains derived from the logic of the world market. Yet, for the model to work, liberal institutionalists have to either restrict the analysis to states whose markets are already more or less organised according to liberal precepts (Keohane 1984) or move towards a historical analysis of how victorious states, after major wars and multilateral peace settlements, engaged in successive rounds of liberal world order constructions, imposing institutions (Ikenberry 2001). The "liberal moment" shrinks here to the notion of "strategic restraint", apparently wielded by Western powers after world wars, and the creation of legitimacy in newly liberalised states. This, in turn, re-privileges coercive Western state power as the key agency for liberal world-ordering, including the promotion of the reading of capitalism as freedom.

Marxism and IR

To recall, Marx's work left two competing modes of thinking about capitalism: one pursued a logical-deductive register that derived further categories from the core concept of capital outside history; the other pursued a more historical mode that tracked the origins and development of capitalism as a historical phenomenon. Within the latter mode, Marx bequeathed two competing definitions of capitalism – one revolving around commerce and a growing division of labour; the other revolving around capitalism as a historically specific social relation, resulting from class conflicts. Yet, Marx never systematically addressed the question of the historical relation between capitalism and international relations (Teschke 2008). This section exemplifies the implications of adopting either of the two competing concepts of capitalism for IR, by contrasting world systems theory and Marxist international historical sociology.[5]

World systems theory

World systems theory (WST) sought to integrate the role of states in the trade-mediated deepening, rather than levelling, of the international division of labour composing the capitalist world market. Extending the insights of dependency theory (Frank 1967) of a systemic inequality in trade relations between developing and developed countries, WST claims that states differentiate functionally due to their position in international commerce – the latter being characterised as "capitalism" – forming a "capitalist world system".

According to WST, this system emerged in the "long 16th century" when, under the impact of colonial conquest, an international division of labour between sovereign but interdependent states emerged, which was not characterised by comparative advantages, but by inherent inequality. Areas concentrating on high-value activities – the *core* – used their economic advantage to maintain and strengthen their international position by contracting out lower-value activities to politically weaker and less developed areas – the *semi-periphery* and *periphery*. Regions within the latter two categories were thus "exploited" through resource transfers to the core, reinforcing their subordinate position in the hierarchy of states (Wallerstein 1974, 2004). Exploitation proceeds in the sphere of circulation rather than in the sphere of production. The world system is generically referred to as capitalist, since different regions, in spite of the presence of pre-capitalist modes of production in the periphery and semi-periphery, produce for sale on the world market. The state system is therefore a precondition for the rise and continuing reproduction of capitalism, since plural sovereignties are needed for the transfer of surplus from peripheries to cores through state-organised competition. A recurring cycle of successive hegemonic states (Genoa/Venice, Holland, the UK and the US) – invariably characterised as capitalist – periodically alters intra-core hierarchies, rearranging and realigning geo-commercial core–(semi-)periphery relations (Arrighi 1994). In contrast to realist hegemonic stability theory that anchors hegemony in military-political capacity alone, hegemony is here grounded in innovations in capital-intensive "labour regimes" (which spill over into commercial and then financial superiority), allowing hegemonic states to position themselves at the summit of the international division of labour. Hegemonic transitions are decided by hegemonic intra-core wars between rising challengers and declining status quo powers.

Building on the work of Fernand Braudel, capitalism in WST refers to "the top layer of the hierarchy of the world of trade" (Arrighi 1994: 24), and capitalists are "those participants in trade who systematically appropriate the largest profits, regardless of the particular nature of the activities" (Arrighi et al. 2003: 263). This conception of the capitalist world system raises a series of problems. First, since the nature of economic

[5] This choice comes at the expense of other neo-Marxist approaches – for a wider overview, see Teschke 2008.

activity is analytically irrelevant, the emergence of capitalism is dated to a point in time when *commerce* develops to a certain complexity – a procedure that invites the charge of arbitrariness and transhistoricity. Second, while state strength is functionally derived from a position in the international division of labour, WST neither addresses nor answers the question of whether the state system itself is causally created by – and not simply encountered by and functional to – capitalism. Third, like neoclassical economics, WST has no theory of value and profit generation except for "buying cheap and selling dear". It thus remains unable, despite attempts to disaggregate where and when profits are generated and "value" added to a product or service across "global value chains", to explain *why* this is the case. Class relations are expunged from an explanation of the emergence, reproduction and transformation of capitalism and replaced by quantitative inequalities in the sphere of circulation. WST is therefore unable to capture the regionally variegated class conflicts that generated differential outcomes in the encounter between core and peripheral states – for example, the reinforcement of pre-existing labour regimes (East-Elbian "second serfdom"), the imposition of completely new pre-capitalist labour regimes (slave-based plantation systems or *encomiendas* in the Americas), or their transformation in a (Marxian) capitalist direction (the creation of abstract wage labour). Finally, a state's strength and position in the world system are directly inferred from its dominant labour regime and ascribed interest of its trade-dependent ruling class. The "strength" of core states is premised on a high-skill/high-capitalisation regime that simultaneously generates the resources to state-organised surplus transfer from the periphery, thus reinforcing inter-regional hierarchies. This purely quantitative conceptualisation of power differentials fails to understand the specific qualitative character of state forms in their relation to class politics across all zones. It also operates with a profoundly un-historical, in fact neo-Smithian, conception of capitalism as commercial exchange grounded in a regional division of labour (Brenner 1977; Skocpol 1977).

Marxist international historical sociology

In contrast to WST, Marxist international historical sociology (IHS) retrieves Marx's second notion of capitalism as a historical social relation to rethink Marxist IR. In a renewed bifurcation within this sub-field, defenders of the law of Uneven and Combined Development (UCD) re-absorb this notion into a higher set of general conceptual abstractions that develop UCD as a universal and nomothetic law of IR. This contrasts with a historicist approach that critically builds on the tradition of Political Marxism (PM).[6] The division between general theory building (abstraction), which reads history as an expression of an overarching logic, and historicity (concretion), which tracks the agential making of history, which we encountered throughout the controversies in PE and the social sciences in this chapter, thus re-surfaces again in altered form in contemporary Marxist IHS.

Whereas proponents of UCD aim at general theory building in which capitalism becomes subsumed under the trans-historical covering law of UCD, PM conceives of

[6] Justin Rosenberg formalised the notion of UCD as a general Marxist theory of IR (Rosenberg 2006). For a critical discussion, see Teschke (2014) and Rioux (2015).

capitalism as a dynamic and historically contested social relation and invites a more radical historicism. This opens up a less deterministic, non-economistic, anti-structuralist and open-ended mode of inquiry, which seeks to track the historical specificities of the relational-agential construction of diverse capitalist international relations and political geographies. Instead of identifying unchanging structural imperatives underlying "capitalist geopolitics", a linear evolutionary developmental trajectory – such as the alleged contemporary shift from the "international" to the "global" – or a realm of "the international" spanning the period from 1648 to today based on inter-territorial security competition, PM rejects the idea of general laws and logics, and moves human construction to the center of analysis.

Drawing on the *Transition Debate* (Brenner 1985) on the rise of agrarian capitalism in late medieval England, one PM intervention into IR revolves around the co-development of the socially contested dynamics of capitalism, differential state formation, geopolitical strategies of spatialisation and the construction of specific political geographies (Teschke 2003; Lacher 2006). The account is theoretically premised on transformations in politically constituted and class-contested social property relations grounded in different balances of social forces. These inform the construction of different polities, modes of territoriality and geopolitical relations. It starts with a clarification of the *sui generis* character of feudal geopolitics, reconstructs the emergence of a late medieval geopolitical pluriverse and retraces the diverging, yet interconnected, trajectories of class and state formation in late medieval and early modern France and England.

Since French and continental "absolutisms" remained mired in pre-capitalist social property and authority relations, dynastic sovereignty and the persistence of "geopolitical accumulation" (territorial aggrandisement) among European powers imparted specific pre-modern practices of international relations (inter-dynastic marriages, personal unions, wars of succession, mercantilist trade wars, predatory equilibrium and empire formation) on the "Westphalian system". Although these practices constituted a system of multiple territories, it remained composed predominantly of the social relations of dynastic-absolutist sovereignty. The Westphalian Settlement as IR's "foundational moment" of the modern state system is thus revised. By rejecting "1648" as a system-wide turning point towards modern inter-state relations, the account retrieves the centrality of the 16th-century rise of agrarian capitalism in England and a new form of capitalist sovereignty in post-revolutionary Britain for an alternative perspective on the relation between capitalism and inter-state politics. Regulating continental inter-dynastic relations through the active management of the balance of power, Britain inadvertently exerted economic and geopolitical pressures that forced continental polities to design diverse counter-strategies of class and state formation through "revolutions from above" in a process of spatio-temporally differentiated and geopolitically combined development (Teschke 2005).

As a result, the state system is not conceived as "the obverse side" of capitalism, but as the cumulative consequence of century-long medieval and early modern class conflicts over rights of domination and exploitation over land and people, which finally crystallised in a plurality of militarily competing dynastic territories. Accordingly, the inter-state system is neither conceived as invariantly functional to the structural imperatives of capitalism, nor do capitalist international relations follow *one* logic. Rather, the relationship between capitalism and the state system is conceived in a processual perspective that tracks the socially and geopolitically contested management of the expansion, transformation and sometimes negation of capitalist relations within a territorially prefigured geopolitical pluriverse that itself underwent manifold alterations. Capitalist social relations, where implemented, became differentially institutionalised and territorialised in diverse polities. This suggests not only that a political geography of multiple sovereign-territorial polities preceded the rise of capitalism, but also that a singular and over-arching logic of capitalist international relations cannot be assumed. As a consequence, the focus of research switches back to the historically specific construction of conflicting grand strategies of spatialisation by multiple polities set within wider international contexts. These diverse strategies (national, regional, imperial, informal, hegemonic, global) require an agency-centred perspective that emphasises the variable geopolitics in the construction of spaces of capital accumulation, rather than an invariant Marxist law of international relations, a deterministic neo-realist logic of security, or a neo-liberal logic of transaction costs reducing institution-building amongst rational states.

Conclusion

This chapter has explored the conceptual history of capitalism that examined in the first part how the concept disappeared from mainstream economics in a century-long war over words, leading to its substitution by the abstract and apparently neutral counter-concept of the market. In the second part, we showed how this vanishing act affected the very constitution of the mainstream paradigms, largely of American provenance, of IR and IPE that are conceptually and theoretically reliant on the derivative import of technical – and profoundly unrealistic – conceptions of the market from mainstream neoclassical economics. These controversies were as much intellectual as political. This suggests that a conceptual history of capitalism cannot be constructed outside of these political battles and wider socio-historical conditions.

This history demonstrates not only a much richer spectrum of alternative conceptualisations of the economic, but also reveals the immense conceptual impoverishment of mainstream IR and IPE traditions. Where present at all, "capitalism" is essentially reduced to an "industrial" form of production, or forms a rhetorical device of no particular conceptual standing, designed to politically identify and denounce non-capitalist orders across space and time. The more widespread conversion of a broader notion of capitalism as a social relation, grounded in class relations, into a socially disembodied, a-historical and neutral sphere of the market populated by individual rational actors, had a decisive impact on the theoretical modelling of international relations, whose profoundness has rarely been acknowledged. For while mainstream IR/IPE deleted the economic from its explanatory purview, it paradoxically transposed assumptions about the operation of markets from "economics" for modelling international relations, functioning separately from but in theoretical analogy to competitive markets. Many non-Marxist approaches are confronted with similar analytical shortcomings, due to their adoption of mainstream economics as a direct template for a nomothetic theory of the international – neoclassical micro-economics for neo-realism; NIE for neo-liberal institutionalism.

The most immediate of these problems is the question of intellectual permissibility to simply equate the logic of international relations with that of market operations. In both neo-realist and neo-liberal institutionalist approaches, we are presented with mere analogies and normative expectations, not explanations, of why states in the international arena should behave like utility-maximising agents on abstract, respectively institutionally governed, markets. This is particularly problematic given the axiom that the operative logic of the economic is void of socio-political power relations and thus amenable to a singular and universal logic. By divesting the economic of socio-political conflicts, the market is essentially conceived as a politically neutral realm, working according to a handful of abstract principles, which themselves do not require any investigation into their adequacy to their subject matter or inherent political normativity. Even where institutions come into play, they are ultimately not privileged as constitutive of diverse economic "rules of the game", but as functional or dysfunctional adaptations to marginalist/neoclassical hard-core assumptions. The respective differences between neo-liberal and neo-realist approaches therefore unfold on the basis of shared and very narrow methodological assumptions.

The historicisation of "capitalism" as a historically dynamic social relation between classes, on the other hand, implies that the economic is neither a black box best left unconsidered and reduced to its wealth-creating function, nor following certain eternal principles, nor an effect of its location in the trade-mediated international division of labour. Instead, it is a particular historical and continuously contested, and therefore potentially transient, product of socio-political and geopolitical conflicts over the process of instituting and maintaining particular sets of social property relations within diverse political geographies. This emphasis on specific agential conflicts that differentially configure social relations is conceived as a world-historical process of active construction and counter-construction, which does not lend itself to a conception of theory that can be abstractly modelled and derived from pure, essentialised and ideal-typical notions of either capitalism or states as static or logical categories. It does, however, hold out the prospect of recovering the lost international history of capitalism – not as a testing ground for abstract theories, but as an active social relation between socio-politically and geographically differentially situated real-life people. But for this project to succeed, we need to be clear about the conceptual history of the capitalism–market split and the analytical choices it offers.

Suggested Readings

Aston, T.H. and Philpin, C.H.E., eds, 1985. *The Brenner Debate: Agrarian Class Structure and Economic Development in Pre-Industrial Europe*, Cambridge: Cambridge University Press.

A collection of articles on the debate on the transition to capitalism, including the two seminal statements by Robert Brenner on the origins of agrarian capitalism in late medieval England.

Lacher, H., 2006. *Beyond Globalization: Capitalism, Territoriality, and the International Relations of Modernity*, London: Routledge.

This volume provides a critique of globalisation theory, anchored in a historical analysis of the changing relations between territoriality and capitalism.

Marx, K., 1990. *Capital: A Critique of Political Economy, Vol. 1*, London: Penguin.

The classic text on Marx's concept of capital, including an account in part 8 on the historical origins of capitalism.

Meiksins Wood, E., 1995. *Democracy against Capitalism: Renewing Historical Materialism*, Cambridge: Cambridge University Press.
A collection of articles elaborating on the political-Marxist understanding of capitalism in discussion with non-Marxist and Marxist positions.

Teschke, B., 2003. *The Myth of 1648: Class, Geopolitics and the Making of Modern International Relations*, London: Verso.
Provides a critical intervention into the mainstream body of IR theories and a theoretically informed and empirically controlled reconstruction of the historical co-development of capitalism, war and the European system of states.

Bibliography

Adelman, J., 2015. What caused capitalism? *Foreign Affairs*, 94(3), pp. 136–44.
Arrighi, G., 1994. *The Long Twentieth Century: Money, Power, and the Origins of Our Times*, London, New York: Verso.
Arrighi, G., Hamashita, T. and Selden, M., eds, 2003. *The Resurgence of East Asia: 500, 150 and 50 Year Perspectives*, London: Routledge.
Clarke, S., 1991. *Marx, Marginalism & Modern Sociology: From Adam Smith to Max Weber*, 2nd edn, London: Macmillan.
Frank, A.G., 1967. *Capitalism and Underdevelopment in Latin America*, New York: Monthly Review Press.
Friedman, M., 2002. *Capitalism and Freedom*, Chicago: University of Chicago Press.
Gilpin, R., 1975. *US Power and the Multinational Corporation: The Political Economy of Foreign Direct Investment*, New York: Basic Books.
Gilpin, R., 1981. *War and Change in World Politics*, Cambridge: Cambridge University Press.
Gilpin, R., 2000. *The Challenge of Global Capitalism: The World Economy in the 21st Century*, Princeton, NJ: Princeton University Press.
Gilpin, R., 2001. *Global Political Economy: Understanding the International Economic Order*, Princeton, NJ: Princeton University Press.
Grieco, J., 1990. *Cooperation among Nations*, Cornell, NY: Cornell University Press.
Guzzini, S., 1998. *Realism in International Relations and International Political Economy: The Continuing Story of a Death Foretold*, London: Routledge.
Hayek, F.A. von, 1958. *Individualism and Economic Order*, Chicago: University of Chicago Press.
Hayek, F.A. von, 1963. *Collectivist Economic Planning: Critical Studies on the Possibility of Socialism*, London: Routledge.
Hodgson, G.M., 2001. *How Economics Forgot History: The Problem of Historical Specificity in Social Science*, London: Routledge.
Ikenberry, J., 2001. *After Victory: Institutions, Strategic Restraint, and the Rebuilding of Order after Major Wars*. Princeton, NJ: Princeton University Press.
Keohane, R.O., 1984. *After Hegemony: Cooperation and Discord in the World Political Economy*, Princeton, NJ: Princeton University Press.
Kocka, J., 2010, Writing the history of capitalism, *Bulletin of the German Historical Institute*, Washington, 47, pp. 7–24.
Korsch, K., 1981. *Karl Marx: Marxistische Theorie und Klassenbewegung*, Reinbek: Rowohlt.
Koselleck, R. 2002, Social history and conceptual history, in Koselleck, *The Practice of Conceptual History: Timing Space, Spacing Concepts*, Stanford, CA.: Stanford University Press, pp. 20–37.
Koselleck, R. 2006, Stichwort: Begriffsgeschichte, in Koselleck, *Begriffsgeschichten*, Frankfurt: Suhrkamp, pp. 99–102.

Krasner, S.D., 2009a. *Power, the State, and Sovereignty: Essays on International Relations*, London: Routledge.

Krasner, S.D., 2009b. State power and the structure of international trade. In *Power, the State, and Sovereignty: Essays on International Relations*, London: Routledge, pp. 129–150.

Krasner, S.D., 2009c. Structural causes and regime consequences: regimes as intervening variables. In *Power, the State, and Sovereignty: Essays on International Relations*, London: Routledge, pp. 113–128.

Lacher, H. 2006. *Beyond Globalization: Capitalism, Territoriality and the International Relations of Modernity*, London: Routledge.

Lacher, H. and Germann, J., 2012. Before hegemony: Britain, free trade, and 19th century world order revisited, *International Studies Review*, 14(1), pp. 99–124.

Marx, K., 1863. *Theories of Surplus Value*, Moscow: Progress Publishers.

Marx, K., 1953. *Grundrisse der Kritik der Politischen Ökonomie*, Berlin: Dietz.

Marx, K., 1990. *Capital: A Critique of Political Economy, Vol. 1*, London: Penguin.

Marx, K., 1991. *Capital: A Critique of Political Economy, Vol. 3*, London: Penguin.

Mearsheimer, J., 1994. The false promise of international institutions, *International Security*, 19, pp. 5–56.

Milonakis, D., and Fine, B. 2009. *From Political Economy to Economics: Method, the Social and the Historical in the Evolution of Economic Theory*, London: Routledge.

Mises, L. von, 2002. *Liberalism: In the Classical Tradition*, New York: Foundation for Economic Education.

Mises, L. von, 2003. *Epistemological Problems of Economics*, Auburn, AL: Ludwig von Mises Institute.

Mises, L. von, 2008. *The Anti-capitalistic Mentality*, Auburn, AL: Ludwig von Mises Institute.

Neal, L. and Williamson, J., eds., 2014a. *The Cambridge History Of Capitalism. Vol. I: The Rise of Capitalism: From Ancient Origins to 1848*, Cambridge: Cambridge University Press.

Neal, L. and Williamson, J., eds., 2014b. *The Cambridge History of Capitalism. Vol. II: The Spread of Capitalism: From 1848 to the Present*, Cambridge: Cambridge University Press.

North, D.C., 1989. Institutions and economic growth: An historical introduction. *World Development*, 17(9), pp. 1319–1332.

North, D.C., 1990. *Institutions, Institutional Change and Economic Performance*, Cambridge: Cambridge University Press.

North, D.C., 1991. Institutions. *The Journal of Economic Perspectives*, 5(1), pp. 97–112.

North, D.C., 2005. *Understanding the Process of Economic Change*, Princeton, NJ: Princeton University Press.

North, D.C., Wallis, J.J. and Weingast, B.R., 2009. *Violence and Social Orders: A Conceptual Framework for Interpreting Recorded Human History*, Cambridge: Cambridge University Press.

Piketty, T., 2014. *Capital in the Twenty-first Century: The Dynamics of Inequality, Wealth, and Growth*, Cambridge, MA: Harvard University Press.

Rioux, S. 2015. The collapse of "the international imagination": a critique of the transhistorical approach to uneven and combined development, in Radhika Desai (ed.) *Theoretical Engagements in Geopolitical Economy*, vol. 30A, *Research in Political Economy*. Bingley, UK: Emerald Group Publishing Limited, pp. 85–112.

Robbins, L., 1932. *An Essay on the Nature and Significance of Economic Science*, London: Macmillan.

Rosenberg, Justin (2006) Why is there no International Historical Sociology?, *European Journal of International Relations*, 12(3): 307–40.

Skinner, Q. 1969, Meaning and understanding in the history of ideas, *History and Theory*, 8(1), pp. 3–53.

Skocpol, T. 1997. Wallerstein's world capitalist system: a theoretical and historical critique, *American Journal of Sociology*, 82(5), pp. 1075–1090.

Sombart, W., 1987 [1916]. *Der Moderne Kapitalismus, Vol. 1*, Munich: DTV.

Steinmetz, W., 2008. Vierzig Jahre Begriffsgeschichte: The state of the art. In H. Kaemper and L. Eichinger, eds. *Sprache – Kognition – Kultur*, Berlin: de Gruyter, pp. 174–197.

Streeck, W., 2009. *Re-forming Capitalism: Institutional Change in the German Political Economy*, Oxford: Oxford University Press.

Teschke, B., 2003. *The Myth of 1648: Class, Geopolitics and the Making of Modern International Relations*, London: Verso.

Teschke, B., 2005. Bourgeois revolution, state-formation and the absence of the international. *Historical Materialism*, 13(2), pp. 3–26.

Teschke, B., 2008. Marxism. In C. Reus-Smit and D. Snidal, eds. *The Oxford Handbook of International Relations*, Oxford: Oxford University Press, pp. 163–187.

Teschke, B. 2014. IR theory, historical materialism, and the false promise of international historical sociology. *Spectrum: Journal of Global Studies*, 6(1), pp. 1–66.

Wallerstein, I., 1974. *The Modern World-System, 1: Capitalist Agriculture and the Origins of the European World-economy in the Sixteenth Century*, New York: Academic Press.

Wallerstein, I., 2004. *World-Systems Analysis: An Introduction*, Durham, NC: Duke University Press.

Walras, L., 1954 (1874). *Elements of Pure Economics*, London: Augustus M. Kelley.

Waltz, K. 1979. *Theory of International Politics*, Reading, MA: Addison-Wesley.

Waltz, K. 1986. Political structures. In R.O. Keohane, ed., *Neorealism and its Critics*, New York: Columbia University Press, pp. 70–97.

Weber, M., 1978. *Economy and Society: An Outline of Interpretive Sociology*, Berkeley, CA: University of California Press.

Weber, M., 2011. *The Protestant Ethic and the Spirit of Capitalism*, Oxford: Oxford University Press.

Wood, E., 1981. The Separation of the "Economic" and the "Political" in Capitalism. *New Left Review*, I, 127, pp. 66–93.

Wood, N. 2002. *Reflections on Political Theory: A Voice of Reason from the Past*, London: Palgrave Macmillan.

Systems of Governance

11

Sovereignty

Tanja Aalberts

As a basic concept of international relations, sovereignty is both essentially contested and essentially uncontested (Bartelson 1995). It is a fundamental concept, yet apparently not given. It is often treated as a natural category and matter of fact, but at the same time subject to continuous conceptual quarrels. It is both absolute and relative or relational. It connotes supreme authority, as well as its lack. It is said to be indivisible and unitary, yet increasingly presented as shared, unbundled and fragmented too. It is both a powerful force and a mythical abstraction. It is a formal status, yet under constant attack. It both has an appearance of permanency and is equally claimed to be obsolete. It is both common sense and elusive. Against this background, it is hardly surprising that there have been calls to dispel this protean and erratic concept (Henkin 1999). Indeed, as Hans Morgenthau noticed some 50 years ago: "Denunciations of the principle of sovereignty ... are much more frequent than a serious endeavor to comprehend its nature and the function it performs for the modern state system" (Morgenthau 1948: 243).

Apart from its conceptual elusiveness, sovereignty seems to have been outrun by empirical reality. Within the debate on globalization and global governance, sovereign states seem to have lost much of their authoritative and exclusive power. Within Europe, this is even formalized and institutionalized, with a far-reaching delegation of decision-making power to European institutions, whose regulations have direct effect in the member states and are as such beyond the control of national governments. Within Schengen, they have even lost control over who is allowed to enter their country. Within the broader globalization debate, a lot of interest goes to the increasing role of international institutions (like the United Nations or the World Trade Organization), multinational corporations (like Apple, Shell, General Motors), and non-governmental organizations (like Amnesty International, the International Committee of the Red Cross, the Catholic Church) to influence world politics. Moreover, in light of the atrocities in Rwanda, Somalia and more recently Lybia and Syria, sovereignty is argued to be normatively bankrupt when it is used as a shield for abuses of power by state governments. As the former UN Secretariat General Kofi Annan (1999) declared at the turn of the millennium: "[T]he world cannot stand aside when gross and systematic violations of human rights are taking place." And yet, these empirical and normative developments notwithstanding, neither practitioners nor scholars have given up on sovereignty. Sovereignty is a powerful trope that seems to remain central to contemporary discourse and practice. As one of its most ardent critics has lamented: despite its death often and long foretold, it seems impossible to give up on the S-word (Henkin 1999).

This chapter investigates the function and recalcitrance of sovereignty as a foundational concept of international politics and the discipline of international relations (IR). It starts from the view that concepts, in general, are tools that help us to focus and structure the complexity of the world around us, and as such also enable action. Yet, behind this functionality lies a more complicated issue of how concepts relate to that reality, also known as the "word/world" relationship. Generally speaking, there are two strands. The first conception conceives of language as the neutral transmitter of facts; words are mere labels that objectively describe the "world out there", as an independent reality. Following Ludwig Wittgenstein, this is the so-called correspondence notion: words correspond to the facts they describe (Wittgenstein 1922: 2.1–2.2). As outlined in the introductory chapter to this volume, conceptual analysis from such a positivist-scientific perspective seeks to develop precise concepts that aim to describe reality as accurately as possible. In his later work, Wittgenstein criticizes such reduction of the meaning of a word to "the object for which the word stands". Rather than searching for the truthfulness of words (i.e. how well they correspond to reality), he argued that their meaning comes about in their use in particular situations and by particular agents (Wittgenstein 1958: paras 1, 23, 43). This second conception, reflected in both the "historical" and the "critical" approaches discussed in the introductory chapter, holds that language is performative: words do not merely describe but *bring about* a particular reality. In highlighting the constitutive power of language, a critical perspective also points to the political function of language by showing how certain interpretations shape our knowledge of the world and render particular actions (im)possible and (il)legitimate.

This second conception of the word/world relationship and meaning in use seems particularly relevant when we look at the concept of sovereignty. Although it tends to be seen as the founding principle of the modern state, there is no comprehensive account of sovereignty that universally applies to all cases of statehood. In fact, the concept of sovereignty lacks a clear referent object. While we can list many things that are closely related to, symbols or manifestations of sovereign statehood – such as armies, citizens, embassies or monarchical rituals – none of these capture sovereignty completely. Similarly, sovereignty relates to many intangible elements – for example, supremacy, territoriality, jurisdiction, autonomy – yet none of them is equivalent to sovereignty in its entirety. Rather, like any concept, sovereignty relates multiple elements, aspects and experiences to each other. Moreover, these elements can only be identified as territory (rather than mere soil) and citizens (rather than random human beings) by virtue of sovereign statehood as an institution of international society. And, crucially, sovereignty itself is the product of this configuration. In other words, sovereignty forms part of a web of concepts, each of which provides elements that together constitute its meaning within a particular historical or theoretical frame (Bartelson 1995). This also means that practices of conceptualizing sovereignty are neither historically, politically nor theoretically innocent.

With this in mind, the next section outlines the story of origin of sovereignty as the foundation of modern international relations. The discussion proceeds by examining multiple understandings of sovereignty within contemporary approaches in IR theory: sovereignty as state property; as an institution of international society; as a language game or discursive fact. These conceptualizations reveal very different understandings of the relationship between concepts and reality, between politics and law, and between sovereignty and the international society in which states are embedded. The chapter concludes with a discussion on the ambiguity of sovereignty in contemporary political discourse.

Historical Context and Origin

For all its ambiguity as a concept, the most popular definition of sovereignty in IR theory identifies sovereignty as "express[ing] the idea that there is a final and absolute authority in the political community [and] that no final and absolute authority exists elsewhere than in the community" (Hinsley 1986: 26). The repetition in the definition highlights independence as the logical corollary of supreme authority, which allegedly also renders sovereignty an indivisible quality that cannot be shared (Onuf 1991). By the same token, Hinsley's definition identifies sovereignty as simultaneously facing inwards and outwards, based on a territorial logic of exclusive jurisdiction (Ruggie 1993). As flipsides of the sovereignty coin, internal sovereignty connotes supreme authority over the community, and hence a hierarchical order; whereas external sovereignty connotes the lack of such an overarching authority in the international realm, also referred to as anarchy, independence and/or equality. It is the concomitant distinction and linking together of inside and outside that (i) makes sovereignty a defining term of modern international politics; (ii) reveals its territorial logic that ties sovereignty to the state; and that (iii) has made the sovereign state the default unit of analysis in IR. Indeed, when IR scholars speak about the state, they always assume "sovereignty" as its constituting principle: "It is [an] unavoidable redundancy to speak of the modern 'state', for there is no other kind of state properly understood. No less is it redundant to speak of the 'sovereign state,' and no less avoidable. Sovereignty unproblematically defines the state as unique to modernity" (Onuf 1991: 426).

This disciplinary practice notwithstanding, the notion of sovereignty as "supreme authority" is not necessarily tied to the state as bearer of that authority. As the Oxford English Dictionary reminds us, sovereignty used to be linked to relations of supremacy more generally, e.g. between God and His creation, between husband and wife, or between the King and his people. Moreover, in modern democratic discourse it is the people who have supreme authority ("popular sovereignty"), which they in turn delegate to their government. However, in both IR and diplomacy, sovereignty is wedded to the state, which also still counts as a key actor in world affairs. This link between statehood, sovereignty and agency is reconfirmed in international law. The 1933 Montevideo Convention defines "the state as a person of international law" based on: (a) permanent population; (b) defined territory; (c) government; and (d) the capacity to enter into relations with other states. While other entities have limited international personality (e.g. the UN and the Holy See), to date only states qualify as legal subjects with sovereignty rights and duties, based on mutually exclusive territorial jurisdictions. This territorial identification of sovereignty, based on a separation of inside and outside, is also reflected in the UN Charter in the principles of sovereign equality (article 2(1)), territorial integrity (article 2(4)) and non-intervention (article 2(7)).

The territorial grounding of sovereignty goes back to Jean Bodin (1530–1596), who allegedly invented the term *souverainité* to describe the shifting configuration of rule and authority from medieval to modern society. In the Middle Ages, authority was divided between the Pope and the Holy Roman Emperor, and *Respublica Christiana* operated on the basis of overlapping feudal power structures based on how far one's power could reach. Modern society, on the other hand, is organized on the basis of exclusive, state-based authority defined by sacrosanct borders: there is only one sovereign in each territory. In traditional IR historiography, the Peace of Westphalia 1648, counts as the mythical birthday of the modern state system. The Westphalian system is typically and casually identified by several Latin axioms: "*cuius regio, eius religio*" (he whose region, his religion), "*rex in regno sui est imperator regni sui*" (the king in his kingdom is emperor of his realm) and "*per in parem imperium non habet*" (among equals nobody rules). Together, these mottos highlight the territorial logic of sovereignty, which links supremacy and hierarchy inside to independence and equality outside. This basic ordering principle sought to end the continuous fights over power and authority in the *Respublica Christiana*, and to create a peaceful and stable international order based on exclusive authority and jurisdictions. However, in practice, sovereignty seems to be seen as a solution to, as much as a source of, intra- and inter-state conflict.

While still a popular benchmark date, the Westphalian "myth of origin" of the modern state system has been forcefully debunked in the run-up to its 350th birthday. The most prominent reasons for this revision of the disciplinary chronicles are semantic and historical. For one, the Westphalian Treaties themselves do not refer to sovereignty as a modern concept. Moreover, the fundamental shift to modern international society did not happen overnight, but was a process that dates back to the 14th century, and was only consolidated in 1814–15 (e.g. Krasner 1993; Osiander 2001; Teschke 2003). Westphalia 1648 as a myth of origin nevertheless is helpful in reminding us that "[o]nce upon a time ... the world was not as it is now" (Walker 1993: 88). For all its apparent naturalness as the foundation for international politics, the sovereign state is not a fact of nature but the product of human activity. At the same time, and somewhat paradoxically, as a foundational legend Westphalia still has "a powerful hold over categories of analysis and methodological strategies" (Walker 1993: 89). Even if IR scholars now generally accept that sovereignty is a complex construct that has evolved over time, this is not always reflected in their theories.

Practices of conceptualizing sovereignty

A useful starting point for discussing conceptualizations of sovereignty in IR is to look at the distinction between internal and external sovereignty, which makes it both an exclusive and an exclusionary concept. For one, the exclusive authority gets to decide who is included and who is excluded from the community. Sovereignty is also exclusionary in the spatial sense: where the one sovereignty begins, the other ends. Yet, the fact that this is an exclusive authority in turn links it to the wider system in which sovereign states are embedded. In this context, the Westphalian system can be characterized as a "living-apart-together" of sovereign states. As sovereign entities, states rely on the reciprocal acceptance of their exclusive jurisdictions by their fellow states. To *be* sovereign requires recognition *as* sovereign, as the supreme authority within a particular territory, both internally and externally:

> [T]he modern concept of sovereignty designates the collectively recognized competence of entities subject to international law and superior to municipal law. It thus involves not only the possession of self and the exclusion of other but also the limitation of self in the respect of others, for its authority presupposes the recognition of others who, per force of their recognition, agree to be so excluded. (Ashley 1984: 272, fn. 101)

While sovereignty is often addressed as a notion of power and control, the Westphalian narrative reveals that it is foremost a social capacity or legal status. As the definitions by Hinsley and Ashley emphasize, it is about authority – not just a material capacity to exercise power, but a recognition of one's right to exercise that power. While effective control does play a (contingent) role in practices of recognition, as will be elaborated on below, sovereignty foremost is a matter of convention and pertains to a form of legitimation and social empowerment (Ashley 1984; Osiander 2001). In the shift from the medieval order to the state system, the issue "was not who had how much power, but who could be designated *as* a power" (Ruggie 1993: 162). As a form of socio-legal empowerment, sovereignty plays a double role: it both defines the distinction between inside and outside, and it offers the parameters for interaction and rules of conduct between formally independent states. Principles like territorial integrity, sovereign equality and non-intervention at once define and limit the spaces of authority. This ties sovereignty not only to the state, but also to both politics and law (Aalberts 2012).

Sovereignty as State Property

As aforementioned, concepts are embedded in theories. In the discipline of IR, the sovereignty concept is particularly important for realism, given its focus on the state as the key "unit" in international relations. The notion of sovereignty is thus crucial for realist ontology and, indeed, explanations. As a founding father of American IR and a classical realist, Hans Morgenthau offers a careful discussion of sovereignty as a "political fact, defined and circumscribed in legal terms". Morgenthau, who originated as a German lawyer, views legal principles like territorial jurisdiction, independence and equality as the "logical precondition[s] for the existence of a multiple state system" (Morgenthau 1948: 252, 244). He addresses formal independence, equality and unanimity – by which he means that legal status and legislative power are independent of size, population and power – as synonyms of sovereignty. Moreover, Morgenthau notes that divisible sovereignty is both "logically absurd" and "politically unfeasible", as supreme authority cannot be shared. Yet he also holds that sovereignty stands above international law – it is not the quantity of legal commitments but their quality that determines if they undermine sovereignty (Morgenthau 1948: 247).

However, Morgenthau's discussion of sovereignty as a politico-legal practice got lost in his legacy as the scholar of "power politics". In realist thinking, it was overshadowed by Kenneth Waltz's prominent identification of states as being "like units" in a system of international anarchy: "a state = a state = a state" as a political autonomous unit. Sovereignty refers to a state's capacity "to decide for itself how it will cope with its internal and external problems" (Waltz 1979: 96). Hence, he reduces sovereignty to a given property of state actors. While his research does not focus on the concept of sovereignty as such, Waltz' short-cut description significantly influenced IR thinking on the state as sovereign actor. Sovereign statehood in this perspective is presented as a matter of fact, having a permanent essence as a unitary category across time and place.

Waltz relates the striking sameness of states throughout the ages to the anarchical structure of the international system, which for him means a lack or even impossibility of a substantive order and society within the international realm. Waltz hence adds a normative qualifier to the distinction between internal and external sovereignty, insofar as it is linked to hierarchy, order and society internally, and anarchy and "laws of the jungle" externally. It seems that Waltz collapses international and external sovereignty into one and the same thing – a capability or power to decide for oneself, which is an individual capacity. There is no room for international law as a meaningful force in international affairs, let alone as a guide for understanding what sovereignty is all about. In Waltz' framework, the sovereign state is absolute, fundamental, indivisible, unitary and uncontested as a key actor in world politics.

Waltz' postulation of an abstract, straightforward and universal concept of sovereign statehood caters to the widespread desire to place IR scholarship on a more "scientific" footing. One important aspect of this agenda is a positivist search for universal laws and objective knowledge. In this perspective, concepts need to be simple, parsimonious and universal (both geographically and historically), and hence Waltz' conception of sovereignty is high up Sartori's ladder of abstraction, deliberately ignoring the different meanings concepts can have depending on their cultural or geographical context. For Waltz, this abstraction is necessary to develop a theory of the international system. To understand the big picture of international politics, we do not need to know domestic politics and hence the state can be treated as a black box. Nor do we need to know much of the historical and social context in which states emerge and operate. All we need to know is the anarchical structure of the international system in which states function as autonomous units across time and space and the particular logic of this system that drives international politics.

Waltz' reading of sovereignty as autonomy, independence and decision-making power no doubt identifies important elements of sovereignty. However, it has also been criticized for reducing sovereignty to little more than self-interested policy-making; a variant of "possessive individualism", where states exist independently of each other and only join the international realm if it is in their national interest (Ruggie 1983; Ashley 1988). This is rooted in Waltz' depiction of states as given, natural-like entities that are ontologically prior to and exist independent of a social collective in which they are embedded. In other words, sovereign power originates from and resides with the state itself. Both the state and its sovereignty are treated as metaphysical conditions of modern life. The crucial phrase here is "are treated as", for Waltz (1979: 91) indeed explicitly states that his reductionist conception of the state is a pragmatic, analytical choice, rather than a claim about the reality of sovereign statehood. Thus, Waltz accepts that the quest for parsimonious theorizing leads him to adopt an abstract conception of sovereignty that cannot claim empirical accuracy.

Sovereignty as "Organized Hypocrisy"

Waltz' approach contrasts with the empiricist ambition that concepts should (aim to) provide a truthful picture of reality. One of the most prominent realist attempts to rectify this weakness comes from Stephen Krasner (1999), who criticizes the unitary conception of sovereign statehood. He was also one of the first IR scholars to problematize Westphalian sovereignty as a myth (Krasner 1993), but, rather than historical or semantic fallacies, his critique focused on its empirical inaccuracy. Krasner notes that as a foundational template for international politics the Westphalian model has never matched reality. To develop more accurate descriptions, Krasner subdivides sovereignty into four different usages: Westphalian sovereignty, international legal sovereignty, domestic sovereignty, and interdependence sovereignty. Each of these usages highlights one or more related concepts – such as authority, control, autonomy, territory – that together compose the meaning of sovereignty in different practices. The latter two notions focus on sovereignty as material capacity: domestic sovereignty addresses the effective exercise of authority within a polity, while interdependence sovereignty focuses on a state's capacity to control its own borders. The other two usages highlight the central role of authority, as a rule-governed form of power: Westphalian sovereignty refers to exclusive authority within a territory (internal sovereignty), while international legal sovereignty links authority to formal independence and mutual recognition (external sovereignty). As such, Krasner separates the duality of sovereignty into different exercises of power and authority, which, he emphasizes, are neither logically coupled nor covariant in practice (Krasner 1999: 9). Statehood and sovereignty hence are partially decoupled, insofar as not all states share the same amount or dimension(s) of sovereignty, because they differ in their ability to exercise it.

At face value, these different kinds of sovereignty establish a more precise conceptualization of sovereignty practices in different spatial and temporal contexts. The rejection of a unitary universal concept seems to fit with conceptual history as discussed in this volume, as does the identification of sovereignty as composed of different situated practices. Nevertheless, Krasner joins Waltz in the scientific strand of conceptual analysis. Within this strand, however, they take opposite positions on Sartori's ladder of abstraction. Whereas Waltz works with concepts as universal and parsimonious abstractions, Krasner seeks to develop universal concepts through empirical fine-tuning and by tracing the lowest common denominators as their core essence. In such a perspective, concepts have to descriptively approximate their empirical referent to function as research tools. This is based on the positivist model of knowledge production, which assumes that there is an independent reality "out there", about which we can obtain objective knowledge through theoretical models, precise concepts and empirical analysis.

Overall, in Krasner's framework the functioning of sovereignty is assessed against behavioural patterns of states as the given and core actors of the international system. This assessment turns out negatively for sovereignty, which Krasner provocatively identifies as "organized hypocrisy" – while widely recognized in public discourse, in practice sovereignty rules are constantly violated as states behave according to their national self-interest. Hence, while states in Krasner's framework are not "like units" as sovereign entities, ultimately they function like Waltz' possessive individualists.

While the collectivity of the international system figures as a constitutive element of both Westphalian sovereignty and international legal sovereignty, in reality international norms only exist as a thin normative disguise to political business-as-usual. In the end, Krasner argues, sovereignty is dependent on power – it is a property only the powerful can claim and ignore as they like.

Sovereignty as an Institution of International Society

As opposed to realism, other approaches put the collective or social character of sovereignty (more) upfront and link the units (states) more explicitly to the international society in which they are embedded. Conceptualizing sovereignty as an institution links its quality as a state characteristic to the wider social context in which this capacity emerges. As elaborated by Hedley Bull, one of the founding fathers of the English School, sovereignty indeed is considered "an attribute of all states" but, crucially, this attribute derives from "recognition as a basic rule of coexistence within the states system" (Bull 1995 [1977]: 35). Bull refers to the internal and external assertion of sovereignty, identified as supremacy inside and independence outside. In comparison to Waltz' conception, there is an important shift from autonomy and independence per se, to sovereignty as a *right* to supreme authority inside and independence outside, and the manifestation of these rights through effective control. As transpired from the Westphalian (hi)story, autonomy and territorial integrity as the basis for sovereignty are derived from mutual recognition, and thus sovereignty concerns a status rather than a power concept. Hence, external sovereignty is not just the lack of an overarching authority structure and residual to sovereignty's internal dimension, but first of all connotes the recognition of each other's sovereign status as independent states. Consequently, sovereignty is both a norm and a fact: "An independent political community which merely claims a right to sovereignty (or is judged by others to have such a right), but cannot assert this right in practice, is not a state properly so-called" (Bull 1995 [1977]: 8). While identifying sovereignty as an attribute of states, it is not conceived of as individualist state property existing apart from social context. Sovereignty is a right that has to be claimed, recognized and exercised – in that particular order.[1]

What transpires here is a "thicker" or more social understanding of the international realm, in which international politics is not just driven by the laws of the jungle, but where an anarchical structure can go together with the development of a society where states "conceive themselves to be bound by a common set of rules in their relations with one another, and share in the working of common institutions" (Bull 1995 [1977]: 13). These institutions are the gluon that lifts the collection of individual states to a social collectivity. Sovereignty in this context functions as a foundational institution, which not only regulates the interaction between states (via procedural rules such

[1] Contrary to Krasner, Bull does not consider norm violation proof of the irrelevance of international law. Quite the contrary: without misbehavior, rules would be redundant in the first place. Moreover, the justifications for violations often reconfirm the significance of the norm, i.e. norms have counterfactual validity (Bull 1995 [1977]: 53, 131–2).

as non-intervention, diplomatic immunity, prohibition of aggression), but also is a constitutional principle that identifies the kind of international order by means of key actors and their codes of conduct. Hence, sovereignty connotes both a status conferred to states as the legitimate members of that society, and regulative rules for their co-existence and interaction. Crucially, these membership rules are informed by the normative development of international society itself; they change in time, in tandem with changing ideas about political authority (Reus-Smit 1999; Philpott 2001).

In this context, Bull not only relates sovereignty to international law but also values a historical approach over abstract scientific concepts (Bull 1966). The historical expansion of the international state system is an important research strand within the English School. Originally, sovereignty was limited to an exclusive club of European, Christian states in the 17th century. This was turned into a legal doctrine in the 19th century, which claimed that only entities that met the so-called Standard of Civilization would qualify as sovereign states within contemporary international society (Gong 1984). This also legitimized colonialism as a civilizing mission, in which it was the "White man's burden" to turn barbarian tribes into civilized nations worthy of sovereignty. During the post-1945 decolonization process, sovereignty instead was linked to the emerging universal right to self-determination, expanding the international society to encompass all landmass of the globe as sovereign territories (Bull and Watson 1984).[2] This was facilitated by annulling not only normative criteria like the Standard of Civilization, but also the apparently empirical criterion of a capacity to govern. As explicitly stated in the UN Declaration on the Granting of Independence to Colonial Countries and Peoples: "Inadequacy of political, economic, social or educational preparedness should never serve as a pretext for delaying independence" (General Assembly Resolution 1514 (XV), 1960, art. 3). In other words, the right to self-determination tilted the balance toward sovereignty as a juridical status as opposed to an empirical fact, which led to the emergence of so-called "quasi-states": "What has basically changed ... are the international rules of the game concerning the obligation to be a colony and the right to be a sovereignty state" (Jackson 1990: 21).

In the English School, sovereignty is conceptualized as a foundational, enduring *and* changing institution of international society. It draws attention to its characteristic as a political-legal concept that is historically conditioned. As elaborated by Alexander Wendt in the development of a constructivist agenda for IR theory, sovereignty norms are "both presupposed by and an ongoing artefact of practice ... If states stopped acting on those norms, their identity as 'sovereigns' (if not necessarily as 'states') would disappear" (Wendt 1992: 413). The constructivist emphasis on practice leads to a less parsimonious, less abstract and more contingent reading of sovereignty – to see what sovereignty means, what rules apply, you need to study it in its historical context. Yet, there is a universal, more abstract notion of sovereignty underlying such a conceptualization, namely its feature as a recognized status of independence (connoting internal supremacy with formal external equality) within international society. This suggests that statehood is a territorial container in which state authority governs a population; and sovereignty refers to the external dimension of its recognition (Biersteker and Weber 1996: 2). Sovereignty then is conceptualized

[2] With the notorious exception of Antarctica and the continuous controversies over the Arctic.

as a normative layer of status or identity – based on historically variant rules of recognition and co-existence – added on to states as empirical entities.

A popular metaphor to identify sovereignty as a fundamental but changing institution is to conceive of it as a game, as a political-legal order constituted and regulated by rules, including both criteria for membership and rules of conduct. A historical approach to sovereignty draws further attention to the fact that not only are the membership criteria (who may join the international community) historically contingent, but also the scope of sovereignty itself (what rights and duties a sovereign state has). For instance, whereas the prohibition of force now counts as a fundamental rule of the international legal order, until the 1920s the external use of force was a prerogative of sovereign states. The contemporary rules of co-existence, which apply for all members of the club (193 states to date), are formulated in the UN Charter. The most basic rules are those of sovereign equality (art. 2(1)), territorial integrity and the non-use of force (art. 2(4)), and non-intervention (art. 2(7)).

Yet, even the scope of these principles is evolving in international practice as, for instance, the debate on humanitarian intervention and "Responsibility to Protect" (R2P) reveals. While the link between sovereignty and responsibility is not as novel as is often suggested (Aalberts and Werner 2008; Glanville 2010), R2P does illuminate changing conceptions of what it means to be a sovereign state in contemporary world politics. Whereas throughout most of the 20th century sovereignty duties were limited to respecting the territorial integrity of other states, today the international responsibilities in the exercise of sovereignty stretch much further, and include obligations towards one's own citizens, humans everywhere and even non-personal entities, such as the environment (Aalberts and Werner 2008, 2016). Moreover, while not yet a codified legal norm, R2P does show that sovereignty is no longer sacrosanct as an absolute ordering principle; indeed, interventions can be justified in the name of sovereignty, rather than criticized as its transgression (see also Chapter 16, this volume).

Sovereignty as a Discursive Practice

While the popular metaphor of the sovereignty game is usually invoked to identify sovereignty as a rule-governed activity, as originally applied by Wittgenstein it was meant to highlight the performative aspect of language and to make sense of the use of language when clear referent objects were missing. Searle (1995) has elaborated on this in terms of speech acts, to emphasize the action that is inherent to language. He distinguishes between regulative rules and constitutive rules. Regulative rules are everyday rules, which regulate activities that exist prior to these rules. A clear example is the introduction of traffic lights to regulate the expanding traffic in the 20th century. This regulative conception is central to the common usage of the sovereignty game metaphor: it exists to order relations of states, to prevent war, and to regulate conflicts and restore peace between states, who themselves exist independent of and prior to the game (Jackson 1990: 36, 38). It is highlighted by Bull in his discussion of sovereignty rules and is also implied by the brackets in Wendt's quote above: if states stopped adhering to sovereignty norms, they would still exist as states.

However, such a reading has been criticized for presenting the territorial state as a natural fact, and for ignoring that statehood itself, too, is a human arrangement and dependent on social practice and norms that define soil as territory and create agency for state actors (Weber 1998: fn. 27). In other words, it is through the practice of international relations that entities can emerge as states, and be sovereign too.[3] This points to sovereignty as (a set of) constitutive rules, which "do not merely regulate, they also create the very possibility of certain activities" (Searle 1995: 27). Whereas traffic can exist as an activity without rules to regulate it, this is different in the case of a marital ceremony, to mention an often used example of constitutive rules: it is the speech act of "I do" and the rule-bound context in which the act is performed that defines and enables the activity of marriage and creates the new status and identity of the two persons involved. Here, the rules do not regulate a pre-existing condition, but actually bring about the marriage that they seem to describe.

The reading of "sovereignty" as a performative language game has been elaborated on by post-structuralist approaches. As critical approaches to concept analysis, they address the politics of sovereignty by focusing not on what sovereignty *is* – indeed rejecting the possibility of universal definitions as neutral descriptions of an independent reality – but on how its meaning is produced through discursive practices. As suggested by Ashley and Walker (1990: 381): "To speak of sovereignty ... is never to name something that already is. It can never be to refer to some source of truth and power that is self-identical, that simply exists on its own, that goes without saying." Crucially, a critical approach focuses on what this "saying" *does*, i.e. its "world-making" effects – what realities it creates, how it informs thinking, how it makes particular actions rational or legitimate, how sovereignty divides the "inside" from the "outside" and "us" (European citizens) from "them" (irregular boat migrants).

From a critical perspective, internal and external sovereignty are not neutral dimensions of what sovereignty is, but analyzed in terms of their performativity. Rather than describing a reality "out there", these dimensions project a particular understanding of political ordering, by separating the domestic as an orderly society based on the rule of law and hierarchical government, from the international as the negation of these orderly structures, legitimizing that it is driven foremost by military and economic power (Ashley 1988). Moreover, these two dimensions can be distinguished as separate realms only by virtue of their interdependence: the notion of the "inside" determines what is "outside" and vice versa (Walker 1993). Similarly, poststructuralist approaches analyze how seemingly opposed concepts, such as sovereignty and intervention, in fact are mutually constitutive practices: it is only through transgressions (i.e. intervention) that we can know what is contemporarily considered the normal state of affairs (i.e. what state sovereignty is supposed to look like) (Weber 1998).

An important critical approach consists of genealogies of sovereignty to deconstruct the contingent relationship between sovereignty, politics and knowledge – in other words, to uncover how the concept of sovereignty has been used differently in different ages (Bartelson 1995; Skinner 2010). One way of doing so is in tracing the (hi) story of the expansion of sovereignty by exploring how it neither was a given fact for the European international community, but was indeed (re)produced in relation to the

[3] To apply Searle's formula for speech acts "X counts as Y in context C": "a political collective (X) counts as a state (Y) in the context of a sovereignty discourse (C)" (Werner and De Wilde 2001: 292).

practice of colonialism itself. It is only through its encounter with the barbarian non-sovereigns (Others) that European states could identify themselves (their Selves) as civilized sovereigns (Grovogui 1996; Anghie 2005). Moreover, while the expansion thesis tells a progressive narrative from an exclusive European club to an inclusive community of sovereign states based on the universal right to self-determination and equality, a critical approach highlights how this legal innovation is immersed in practices of domination. For one, the newly emerged principle of self-determination at once limited the kind of "selves" that were deemed legitimate authorities to exercise this right. It was based on a European conception of what this "self" is, namely a replica of the colonial, territorial state as the only possible successor to colonial powers, thus naturalizing the European concept of political order and foreclosing the option of pre-colonial forms of tribal communities. And while the quasi-statehood thesis discusses a loosening of sovereignty norms based on self-determination, critical approaches have highlighted how it at once reified (Western) sovereignty as a fixed category or standard that the quasi-states as proto-sovereigns need to approach to become "real" sovereigns one day (Doty 1996).

As Weber (1998) argues, sovereignty pertains to a continuous performativity based on apparently natural and universal, but ultimately contingent "standards of normality", i.e. what it means to be a proper or real sovereign state. Illustrative in this regard is that while ineffective government was formally dismissed as irrelevant during the process of decolonization, it has re-emerged in the debate on state failure and rogue states. It has gained a particular meaning in contemporary neo-liberal governance, which links sovereignty to liberal statehood based on good governance, human rights, market economy and democracy (Zanotti 2005). It has furthermore gained critical urgency in the context of the Global War on Terror, which turned state failure from a developmental problem into a security issue (Bilgin and Morton 2002). This shows the productive and legitimating force of discourse. Deviance from the prevailing and allegedly universal standard of what a proper sovereign looks like in turn legitimizes far-reaching measures that go against the basic ordering principles of sovereignty, non-intervention and autonomy itself.

Sovereignty in Political Practice

If we look at the importance of sovereignty in political practice, there seem to be two opposing trends. On the one hand, state sovereignty is often said to be in decline as a result of processes of globalization and regional integration. Both the expansion of trans-border flows, non-state actors and supranational governance are difficult to square with supreme authority, autonomy, territoriality and control as the commonplaces of sovereignty. While these processes led to some revolutionary predictions in the 1970s and 1980s about the end of both sovereignty and the state, both concepts have turned out to be recalcitrant. Nevertheless, it is suggested that the "state" and "sovereignty" are no longer wedded in contemporary political discourse. Whereas states have not disappeared, they are no longer automatically or singularly sovereign but increasingly conceived as "disaggregated", and sovereignty as "pooled", "shared" or "delegated" (Keohane 2002). Thus, attention is drawn to different "sites" of sovereignty both below and above the state, i.e. to individuals as bearers of sovereignty, and to regions and supranational organizations, which do not qualify as states themselves, but do transform and take over some sovereignty practices and sovereign qualities. These changes inform the popular distinction between different types of sovereign statehood in contemporary international society: the modern Westphalian state, postcolonial or quasi-states and the postmodern member states of the EU (Sørensen 2001). They also raise questions about sovereignty being a matter of degree and how to reconcile this with its indivisibility as a legal status.[4] How much sovereignty can be compromised, or how many of its norms can be violated, before one ceases to be sovereign? This question will be more puzzling for approaches that see sovereignty as a descriptive term that can be measured on the basis of empirical characteristics, than for approaches that address sovereignty as a changing institution and discursive practice.

A second trend is that, while it has been dismissed as outmoded and ambiguous, sovereignty nevertheless remains a useful abstraction and popular claim in a globalized world. Even if it is unclear what it exactly "is", sovereignty is a powerful trope. Something happens when states (still more than other entities) pull their sovereignty card, and scholars need to explore what this "something" is by analyzing the contexts in which claims to sovereignty occur (Werner and De Wilde 2001: 286). State sovereignty may be compromised by integration, yet discussions about opt-outs or even exits from the European Union illustrate that even this allegedly most far-reaching and institutionalized project beyond Westphalian statehood is not immune to the sovereignty game (Adler-Nissen 2014). Similarly, the continuing struggle by Palestinians for the recognition of their sovereign status, and the resistance to this by powerful actors like the US and Israel, illustrate the continuous popular aspiration of sovereignty in allegedly postmodern times, as well as the high stakes of inclusion and exclusion from the sovereignty game. The incorporation of Responsibility to Protect in political discourse shows that inclusion in turn is not just a wild card for freedom and autonomy, but can also be used against a state that does not live up to the standards of appropriate sovereignty.

What these two trends highlight is that our reading of "sovereignty" and how it is manifested and challenged in the world determines where we (want to) see the locus of authority, responsibility, and thus agency. And it shapes how we understand and characterize the contemporary international political legal order – as a modern state system, based on internal and external sovereignty as dual sides of the same coin, or as a "post-modern" system which is no longer characterized by sovereignty as its constituting principle.

Conclusion

The concept of sovereignty remains a crucial and powerful tool both in academia and in political practice. Like any other concept, it helps to reduce complexity and enables action, but its function as a lens to distinguish key issues from secondary matters also means it inevitably comes with blinders. One of the aims of this book is to confront

[4] The legal discourse provides an important clue by identifying both sovereignty as a status and sovereignty rights and duties as the contingent substance of that status (Koskenniemi 1991). Moreover, as was famously stated in the *Wimbledon* case (1923), it is a prerogative of states to limit their exercise of sovereignty by entering into international arrangements.

these blinders – not to solve them, or to come to a synthesis definition by combining different conceptualizations to fill each other's gaps, but to reflect on what key concepts, and the different meanings they contain, *do*. In this context, the heterogeneity, variety and contestation of a concept like sovereignty – though sometimes dazzling – is in itself insightful to scrutinize the work that concepts do. In this spirit, the aim of this chapter was not to take away the complexity of the concept of sovereignty by finding a universally acceptable definition, but to show how it is neither historically, nor theoretically, nor politically innocent. It showed that there is not only a debate about what the concept of sovereignty means, but also that there is disagreement about whether it is, or can be, used as a neutral description of empirical reality or whether we should see it primarily as a performative speech act and a tool of politics.

At the same time, the concept remains uncontested in the sense that it still functions as a basis for international discourse and IR as a discipline. In the search for some kind of essence or grounding, it is constantly filled with either empirical components or other abstract concepts that stand in close relationship to sovereignty, yet do not cover it in all its dispositions: supremacy, territoriality, authority, recognition, autonomy, to recall a few that have passed in review. As such, sovereignty is part of a "discursive formation within which we organize particular forms of life" (Huysmans 1998: 228). Analyzing such a concept cannot proceed as a matter of abstraction or definition, or by conceiving it as a "thing" that can be discovered through empirical fine-tuning, as a scientific approach to conceptual analysis would have it. Rather than addressing conceptual ambiguity as a problem that needs to be solved, we should explore its historical depth. And, rather than asking why sovereignty endures as a central concept despite its ambiguity and controversy, we need to come to terms with Jens Bartelson's (1995: 237) point that sovereignty's very centrality as a key concept in IR is conditioned by its ambiguity and vice versa.

Suggested Readings

Bartelson, Jens (1995) *A Genealogy of Sovereignty*, Cambridge: Cambridge University Press.
A critical deconstruction of sovereignty discourses through a conceptual history of sovereignty. The text engages in a sophisticated re-reading of philosophical and political texts of the Renaissance, classical age, and modern era to show that the meaning of sovereignty is contingent on the history of political science as a discipline.

Biersteker, Thomas J. and Cynthia Weber (eds) (1996) *State Sovereignty as Social Construct*, Cambridge: Cambridge University Press.
An important contribution to the debate on sovereignty as a norm of international society. The introduction on the meaning of the constructivist turn for our understanding of sovereignty is followed by informative chapters examining its transformation in light of, inter alia, colonialism, quasi-statehood, and nationalism.

Hinsley, F.H. (1986) *Sovereignty*, 2nd edition, Cambridge: Cambridge University Press.
While not as theoretically oriented as more recent analyses, this still counts as a classic volume on sovereignty, famous for its definition of internal and external sovereignty as two complementary assertions of sovereignty. The main focus is on the historical development of sovereignty within the national context.

Krasner, Stephen D. (1999) *Sovereignty: Organized Hypocrisy*, Princeton, NJ: Princeton University Press.

Writing from a realist perspective, Krasner argues that sovereignty is nothing but organized hypocrisy. He differentiates between different kinds of sovereignty (Westphalian, international legal, domestic, and interdependence sovereignty) to analyze the continuous compromises of the sovereignty norm.

Walker, R.B.J. (1993) *Inside/Outside: International Relations as Political Theory*, Cambridge: Cambridge University Press.

A groundbreaking contribution that problematizes essentialist understandings of sovereign states underpinning contemporary IR theory. The author argues that reification of the distinction between the domestic and the international realm limits our conception and ethics of world politics.

Bibliography

Aalberts, Tanja E. (2012) *Constructing Sovereignty between Politics and Law*, London/New York: Routledge.

Aalberts, Tanja E. and Wouter G. Werner (2008) 'Sovereignty Beyond Borders: Sovereignty, Self-Defense and the Disciplining of States', in Rebecca Adler-Nissen and Thomas Gammeltoft-Hansen (eds), *Sovereignty Games: Instrumentalising State Sovereignty in Europe and Beyond*, Houndmills: Palgrave.

Aalberts, Tanja E. and Wouter G. Werner (2016) 'Mastering the Globe: Law, Sovereignty and the Commons of Mankind', in Rens van Munster and Casper Sylvest (eds), *Assembling the Planet: Post-War Politics of Globality*, London: Routledge.

Adler-Nissen, Rebecca (2014) *Opting Out of the European Union: Diplomacy, Sovereignty and European Integration*, Cambridge: Cambridge University Press.

Anghie, Antony (2005) *Imperialism, Sovereignty and the Making of International Law*, Cambridge: Cambridge University Press.

Annan, Kofi A. (1999) 'Two Concepts of Sovereignty', *The Economist*, 18 September.

Ashley, Richard K. (1984) 'The Poverty of Neo-Realism', *International Organization*, 38(2): 225–286.

Ashley, Richard K. (1988) 'Untying the Sovereign State: A Double Reading of the Anarchy Problematique', *Millennium*, 17(2): 227–262.

Ashley, Richard K. and R.B.J. Walker (1990) 'Conclusion: Reading Dissidence/Writing the Discipline – Crisis and the Question of Sovereignty in International Studies', *International Studies Quarterly*, 34(3): 367–416.

Bartelson, Jens (1995) *A Genealogy of Sovereignty*, Cambridge: Cambridge University Press.

Biersteker, Thomas J. and Cynthia Weber (1996) 'The Social Construction of State Sovereignty', in Thomas J. Biersteker and Cynthia Weber (eds), *State Sovereignty as Social Construct*, Cambridge: Cambridge University Press.

Bilgin, Pinar and Adam David Morton (2002) 'Historicising Representations of "Failed States": Beyond the Cold-War Annexation of the Social Sciences?', *Third World Quarterly*, 23(1): 55–80.

Bull, Hedley (1966) 'International Theory: The Case for a Classical Approach', *World Politics*, 18(3): 361–377.

Bull, Hedley (1995 [1977]) *The Anarchical Society: A Study of Order in World Politics*, 2nd edn, London: Macmillan.

Bull, Hedley and Adam Watson (eds) (1984) *The Expansion of International Society*, Oxford: Oxford University Press.

Doty, Roxanne Lynn (1996) *Imperial Encounters: The Politics of Representation in North–South Relations*, London: University of Minnesota Press.
Glanville, Luke (2011) 'The Antecedents of "Sovereignty as Responsibility"', *European Journal of International Relations*, 17(2): 233–55.
Gong, Gerrit W. (1984) *The Standard of 'Civilization' in International Society*, Oxford: Clarendon Press.
Grovogui, Siba N'Zatioula (1996) *Sovereigns, Quasi Sovereigns, and Africans: Race and Self-Determination in International Law*, Minneapolis, MN: University of Minnesota Press.
Henkin, Louis (1999) 'That "S" Word: Sovereignty, and Globalization, and Human Rights, Etcetera', *Fordham Law Review*, 68(1): 1–14.
Hinsley, F.H. (1986) *Sovereignty*, 2nd edn, Cambridge: Cambridge University Press.
Huysmans, Jef (1998) 'Security! What Do You Mean? From Concept to Thick Signifier', *European Journal of International Relations*, 16(2): 223–246.
Jackson, Robert H. (1990) *Quasi-States: Sovereignty, International Relations and the Third World*, Cambridge: Cambridge University Press.
Keohane, Robert O. (2002) 'Ironies of Sovereignty: The European Union and the United States', *Journal of Common Market Studies*, 40(4): 743–765.
Koskenniemi, Martti (1991) 'The Future of Statehood', *Harvard International Law Journal*, 32(2): 397–410.
Krasner, Stephen D. (1993) 'Westphalia and All That', in Judith Goldstein and Robert O. Keohane (eds), *Ideas and Foreign Policy: Beliefs, Institutions, and Political Change*, Ithaca, NY/London: Cornell University Press.
Krasner, Stephen D. (1999) *Sovereignty: Organized Hypocrisy*, Princeton, NJ: Princeton University Press.
Morgenthau, Hans J. (1948) *Politics among Nations: The Struggle for Power and Peace*, New York: Alfred A. Knopf.
Onuf, Nicholas G. (1991) 'Sovereignty: Outline of a Conceptual History', *Alternatives*, 16: 425–446.
Osiander, Andreas (2001) 'Sovereignty, International Relations and the Westphalian Myth', *International Organization*, 55(2): 251–287.
Philpott, Daniel (2001) *Revolutions in Sovereignty: How Ideas Shaped Modern International Relations*, Princeton, NJ: Princeton University Press.
Reus-Smit, Christian (1999) *The Moral Purpose of the State: Culture, Social Identity, and Institutional Rationality in International Relations*, Princeton, NJ: Princeton University Press.
Ruggie, John Gerard (1983) 'Continuity and Transformation in the World Polity: Towards a Neorealist Synthesis', *World Politics*, 35(2): 261–285.
Ruggie, John Gerard (1993) 'Territoriality and Beyond: Problematizing Modernity in International Relations', *International Organization*, 47(1): 139–174.
Searle, John R. (1995) *The Construction of Social Reality*, New York: Free Press.
Skinner, Quentin (2010) 'The Sovereign State: A Genealogy', in Hent Kalmo and Quentin Skinner (eds), *Sovereignty in Fragments: The Past, Present and Future of a Contested Concept*, Cambridge: Cambridge University Press.
Sørensen, Georg (2001) *Changes in Statehood: The Transformation of International Relations*, Houndmills: Palgrave.
Teschke, Benno (2003) *The Myth of 1648: Class, Geopolitics and the Making of Modern International Relations*, London: Verso.
Walker, R.B.J. (1993) *Inside/Outside: International Relations as Political Theory*, Cambridge: Cambridge University Press.
Waltz, Kenneth N. (1979) *Theory of International Politics*, Reading, MA: Addison-Wesley.
Weber, Cynthia (1998) 'Performative States', *Millennium*, 27(1): 77–95.

Wendt, Alexander (1992) 'Anarchy is What States Make of It: The Social Construction of Power Politics', *International Organization*, 46(2): 391–425.

Werner, Wouter G. and Jaap H. De Wilde (2001) 'The Endurance of Sovereignty', *European Journal of International Relations*, 7(3): 283–313.

Wittgenstein, Ludwig J.J. (1922) *Tractatus Logico-Philosophicus*, London: Routledge.

Wittgenstein, Ludwig J.J. (1958) *Philosophical Investigations*, 3rd edn, trans. G.E.M. Anscombe, London: Prentice-Hall.

Zanotti, Laura (2005) 'Governmentalizing the Post-Cold War International Regime: The UN Debate on Democratization and Good Governance', *Alternatives*, 30: 461–487.

12
Hegemony

Alejandro Colás

The hierarchy of power in global politics has always stalked the foundational premise of international relations (IR) that ours is a world structured by sovereign anarchy. While it may be true that there is no higher political authority than the sovereign territorial state in the international system, clearly some states and social forces are more powerful than others. This is where the concept of hegemony – broadly "leadership" – has played a signal role in IR by way of explaining the structural power inequalities in international relations. More specifically, the US-led invasions and occupations of Afghanistan and Iraq following the 9/11 attacks put the question of imperialism and hegemony firmly back on the political and academic agenda, as have the more recent Russian incursions and annexations into its own "near abroad". Explaining the return of a territorialized, military interventionism abroad by the Great Powers has become one of the most pressing issues for students of IR. These are some of the reasons why we should be especially concerned about the meaning and mobilization of hegemony today. Yet this contribution, in line with the rest of the volume, also poses the further query: what are the political stakes at play in defining this concept?

Inspired by Koselleck's programme for "conceptual history" (*Begriffsgeschichte*), this chapter addresses both questions by exploring the diverse and contested meanings of "hegemony" as it has been deployed in both the history of international relations and the academic discipline of IR. Indeed, one of the immediate attractions of an approach informed by conceptual history is the focus on the conflictual and dynamic interrelationship between social relations and intellectual history; between the lived experience of world politics and the body of scholarship that aims to explain it. While I cannot present here a comprehensive semantic reconstruction of the term "hegemony", this chapter nonetheless tries to offer a survey of the multiple meanings and trajectories of hegemony, as well as its role in IR theories and political practice, guided by a contextual analysis of concept formation. In doing so, I hope to illustrate the conceptual power of hegemony in world politics, as well as demonstrate its groundedness in historical developments, particularly since 1945.

A first section of the contribution elaborates on the methodological assumptions of a conceptual history, broadly understood. Perhaps inevitably, given the chapter's focus on hegemony, Antonio Grasmci's own historicist understanding of culture and ideology will be brought to bear in this discussion. In the subsequent section, I consider in greater detail the uses of hegemony in world politics – both as an explanatory concept in the discipline of IR (itself a product of a hegemonic world order) and as a category used in political action and debate, particularly during the Cold War. Examples taken from reconstruction efforts in postwar Europe and the more recent histories of military intervention in the greater Middle East illustrate the uses of hegemony in international relations. Two important paradoxes emerge from this account, guiding much of what follows in the chapter. On the one hand, the concept of hegemony was first deployed in the twentieth century by Marxists focusing on Bolshevik Russia, yet it was subsequently adopted by IR theorists, mainly with reference to American external relations. On the other hand, the use of hegemony by IR theorists only really took flight in the 1970s – *after* American postwar global leadership had reached its zenith, and as it experienced relative decline post-Vietnam. There is no straightforward explanation for these paradoxes, although I posit in this chapter that the political contestation over the usage of a category like hegemony means it cannot be aligned mechanically or instrumentally with this or the other foreign policy: states and social classes may exercise hegemony incoherently or without achieving their aims. At the same time, however, I subscribe in what follows to a broadly Gramscian understanding of "hegemony" as a form of leadership mediated through the structures of the capitalist market and generally exercised by ruling classes and their guiding ideas. Hegemony on this reading is not a purely academic description of international "stability" or "equilibrium", but quite the opposite: a very political conception of power in international relations, as exercised by leading states and social classes in support of their privileges. A final part of the chapter considers the difference between hegemony and other cognate categories such as empire, imperialism or primacy, thus returning discussion to the original starting point of this book, namely the continuing political dispute over, and theoretical ambivalence of, key concepts in IR.

For a Conceptual Historicism

In his introduction to the monumental dictionary on "Basic Concepts in History" (*Geschichtliche Grundbegriffe*), Reinhart Koselleck identified the genesis or transformation of certain modern keywords in what he labelled the European "saddle time" or "threshold period" (*Sattelzeit*) of 1750–1850. Spurred on by the French Revolution and the Enlightenment (both these concepts themselves products of the *Sattelzeit*), the semantic field of socio-political action during this period became, according to Koselleck, characterized by four processes: temporalization, democratization, ideological incorporation and politicization (Brunner, Conze and Koselleck, 1972). Terms like "democracy", "nation", "civil society" and "culture", which had long histories and complex genealogies traceable to Antiquity, were during this revolutionary *Sattelzeit* re-appropriated and recharged with new, often radical and politically contested meanings. For Koselleck and his dictionary co-editors, this conceptual transformation went far beyond the mere (re)definition of language, and instead involved a self-consciously modern mobilization of political categories by various antagonistic social classes and organizations in the pursuit of conflicting ideological aims (Richter in Lehmann and Richter, 1996). Such was the socio-political power and influence of certain words during this period that they merited promotion to the status of "basic concepts": terms that are indispensible when understanding the socio-economic and political structures and processes of a given historical conjuncture, but also – and crucially – without which the historical agents of that period could not themselves have made sense of their time.

Viewed in international comparison, the study of socio-political concepts has witnessed the development of remarkable methodological parallelisms, if not necessarily consensus, since the 1960s. The pioneering research of Koselleck and his colleagues found resonance with the *Annales*' histories of mentalities, which in turn bear a family resemblance to the more recent Anglophone work of scholars like J.G.A. Pocock, Quentin Skinner, John Tully and John Tuck – all linked to the so-called "Cambridge School" of the history of ideas. "Language", "grammar", "rhetoric", "discourse", "concepts", "mentality" or "attitude" all appear in these writings as variations on the theme that politics always relies on certain linguistic conventions and hermeneutics which in turn shape and inform conceptual meanings. There are, to be sure, important differences in emphasis. John Pocock, for instance, suggests that the study of discourse or language sets "a premium upon the synchronic" (Pocock in Lehmann and Richter, 1996: 49). This contrasts with the more diachronic approach of conceptual history or indeed the history of mentalities, which emphasizes the shift in meaning across longer periods of time.

Yet, it would be fair to say that in both approaches, there is a strong recognition that the interpretation of political debate and contestation cannot be detached from its immediate socio-economic and political setting. As Koselleck himself avers: "Without common concepts there is no society, and above all, no political field of action ... A 'society' and its 'concepts' exist in a relation of tension which is also characteristic of its academic historical disciplines" (Koselleck [1974] 1985: 74). Consider this "relation of tension" between concepts and societies in the following statement:

> The philosophy of an age is not the philosophy of this or that philosopher, of this or that group of intellectuals, of this or that broad section of the popular masses. It is a process of combination of all these elements, which culminates in an overall trend, in which the culmination becomes a norm of collective action and becomes concrete and complete (integral) "history". (Gramsci, 1971: 345)

Despite being written in markedly different contexts, and notwithstanding their contrasting ideological provenance, both these understandings of concept formation emphasize the attachment of ideas to specific historical epochs and the determination of their meaning through complex socio-political contestation by conflicting social groups. For Gramsci, as for Koselleck, concepts are always *historical* in the deep sense that they cannot be interpreted or indeed applied outside determinate temporal parameters. They are also necessarily *political* insofar as their meaning and usage are disputed by antagonistic social forces.

These interpretative axioms arguably run contrary to the prevailing conceptual understanding in IR where settled, descriptive typologies are the norm. A notable example is Robert O. Keohane's classic *After Hegemony* – a text which initially adopts a mainstream definition of the term as "a preponderance of [four] material resources ... control over raw materials, control over sources of capital, control over markets, and competitive advantages in the production of highly valued goods" (1984: 32) and subsequently modifies this to argue that hegemony "is less a concept that helps to explain outcomes in terms of power than as a way of describing an international system in which leadership is exercised by a single state" (1984: 39). On this reading, certain key features of hegemony (power, leadership, coercion, consent, cooperation and rule-making) are distilled into a core definition which is then deployed in the empirical differentiation between, say, the postwar *Pax Americana* and the preceding *Pax Britannica*, or between hegemonic and non-hegemonic cooperation.

The weight which mainstream IR places on the explanation of international *order* in large measure accounts for the dominant typological approach to concepts like hegemony. A focus on stability and equilibrium in the international system militates against a more historicist method that underlines the contestation of hegemony and the consequent disruption of its meaning and practice through time. In contrast to a static taxonomy of different hegemonic regimes, a "conceptual historicism" proposes a dynamic account of the *changes* in both the social understanding and political operation of hegemony; that is, both in the shifting, unstable meaning of the term across historical time, and its changing nature as a tool of foreign policy. Here, the challenge lies in identifying patterns of rupture and continuity, charting both moments of conceptual genesis and turning points in the structural transformation of hegemony.

The approach adopted in this chapter draws on Antonio Gramsci's "philosophy of praxis" in emphasizing what he labelled "absolute 'historicism', the absolute secularisation and earthliness of thought, an absolute humanism of history" (Gramsci, 1971: 465). This is a materialist application of historicism which, in contrast to its idealist counterparts that identify the Idea of "Spirit" (Hegel) or "Liberty" (Croce) as driving History progressively towards a *telos*, instead emphasizes the role of conflict – particularly class antagonisms – in determining the emergence and staying power of a given concept. In the specific case of "hegemony", Gramsci's perspective is doubly significant as it simultaneously grants this concept a semantic and a political force: "hegemony", as we shall see, acquires fresh meaning in the modern period but also acts as a self-conscious instrument of ideological mobilization and contestation. A good illustration of this eminently modern, self-reflexive understanding of concepts as products of their own time is Gramsci's reworking of "hegemony" as a category acquiring a distinctive meaning only after the triumph of the Bolshevik revolution in Russia and its failure in western Europe. For Gramsci, the divergent trajectories of revolutionary politics in the East and West after 1917 offered very specific insights into the operation of socio-political and economic power in the twentieth century. The "historicity" of this concept, then, rested not only on the novel historical conjuncture in which it re-emerged, but also on the political possibilities for a socialist future it adumbrated.

"Hegemony", Raymond Williams indicates in his *Keywords*, "was probably taken directly into English fw *egemonia*, re *egemon*, Gk – leader, ruler, often in the sense of a state other than his own. Its sense of a political predominance, usually of one state over another, is not common before C19 but has since persisted and is now fairly common, together with hegemonic, to describe a policy expressing or aimed at political predominance" (Williams, 1976: 117). Lebow and Kelly draw on Thucydides to distinguish between *hegemonia* (legitimated leadership) and *arkhe* (control), suggesting that a third quality – *time*, or the "gift of honour" retained by consent not force – is what differentiates the former from the latter as an expression of power (2001). Thus, we already have some of the complex and contradictory elements that characterize hegemony as a "basic concept in history" – a pedigree that stretches back to Antiquity, yet is reinvigorated during the twentieth century; a combination of coercion and consent as sources of power; and an international, or more precisely, inter-societal exercise of that power which nonetheless operates at numerous geographical scales – national, regional, global. According to John Agnew, hegemony signifies "domination or leadership" by a state or group of states combining coercion and consent, in ways that "can be diffuse and widespread or concentrated geographically" (2005: 20; see also Chapter 2, this volume).

In the sections that follow, I explore these various dimensions of hegemony as it unfolded particularly during the Cold War. The Russian revolution occasioned not just the reconsideration of "hegemony" as a concept of socialist strategy and analysis, but also as a category that helps to explain the antagonism between the American and Soviet blocs which characterized the international "order" of the short twentieth century. The "long interregnum" since the end of the Cold War has now raised fresh challenges to our understanding of global hegemony, with some arguing that it is best replaced by the more muscular notions of "empire" and "imperialism", and others suggesting that we are witnessing the secular decline of American hegemony and its gradual replacement by a leaderless multi-polar order.

Hegemony in the Short Twentieth Century

Crudely put, IR conceptions of global hegemony come in three forms: realist, liberal and Marxist-inspired. For the first, global hegemony involves peerless worldwide domination – a situation which, in the realists' view, has never existed in world history. In an anarchical system, there is always competition for power, and the most Great Powers can aspire to on this view is regional domination over a specific geographical area, like the US does over the western hemisphere (Mearsheimer, 2002: 40).

From the liberal-internationalist perspective, global hegemony is about international leadership coordinated through multilateral rules, norms and institutions. Direct military-diplomatic coercion can, on this understanding, be deployed by a hegemonic power, but it is the exception rather than the rule. A liberal hegemonic order like that sustained from Washington, in particular, relies on the cooperative and diplomatic resolution of conflict through rule-governed institutions and international regimes. With the end of the Cold War, the notion of "global governance" came to embody this liberal-internationalist understanding of "benevolent hegemony" coordinated by the major powers with the assistance of both supranational organizations and transnational civil society. In John Ikenberry's apt summary: "Americans are less interested in ruling the world, than in creating a world of rules" (Ikenberry, 2014: no pagination).

In contrast to the two mainstream approaches above, a Marxist, or more broadly critical-radical tradition in IR, emphasizes the dialectics of coercion and consent, suggesting that rule-governed institutions contribute significantly to the reproduction of existing hierarchies in any given world order. Thus, far from representing opposites, on this reading cooperation and domination, law and violence simply reflect two sides of the same proverbial coin that is global hegemony. The "global commons" of international cooperation – from the Nuclear Non-Proliferation Treaty to the role of the US dollar as the global reserve currency – are stacked in favour of America and its closest allies, and in fact shore up their structural power. Moreover, when the hidden hand of the market and its accompanying legal infrastructure fails to incentivize cooperation, the clenched fist of US military might and its attendant alliances (most notably NATO) are mobilized to enforce global governance. It is far easier, as the saying goes, to work *for* the Americans than to work *with* them.

For all their methodological and ideological differences, these three broad schools of thought on global hegemony share the assumption that it is principally American hegemony after the Second World War that requires explanation and analysis. There is certainly a recognition that other modern hegemonic orders (most obviously, the British) informed the postwar *Pax Americana*. There are also instances of direct comparisons with the ancient Hellenic world, where the US is deemed to lead a democratic mercantile league in the style of ancient Athens, in contrast to the imperialist militarism of the Spartans, imitated by the USSR. Yet what these stylized juxtapositions overlook is the unique historical conjuncture that facilitated the emergence and crystallization of American hegemony. Whilst there were plainly discernible continuities between nineteenth-century American expansionism and its postwar emergence as an aspiring global leader (the famed "Manifest Destiny"), the discussion below emphasizes the historical specificity and the contested nature of US hegemony (and that of its Soviet rival). Indeed, the focus on the Cold War as a distinctive historical epoch that witnessed an inter-systemic contest between two hegemonic blocs, led respectively from Washington, DC and Moscow, brings to light the temporalization and politicization of a keyword like "hegemony". For the purposes of exposition, I consider first the operationalization of hegemony as foreign policy strategy, and then explore its conceptual articulation in the field of IR, though clearly these two were and continue to be closely interlinked.

Exercising hegemony

"Hegemony" entered twentieth-century vernacular through the Bolshevik revolution. The concept's principal theorist, Antonio Gramsci, explicitly discussed this term in his *Prison Notebooks* as part of a wider debate within the international communist movement regarding revolutionary leadership in a hostile international environment characterized by retrenchment and defeat: in the wake of the First World War communism had prevailed in Russia, but failed in Europe. The new Soviet state, moreover, was born in a context of counter-revolutionary intervention, civil war and deep ideological fissures within the international working-class movement itself. Gramsci's formulation of hegemony as "the supremacy of a social group" that manifests itself "in two ways, as 'domination' and as 'intellectual and moral' leadership" (Gramsci, 1971: 57) was applied to both the experience of ruling "historical blocs" like those which crystallized around the Italian *Risorgimento*, and potential communist counter-hegemonic blocs. The latter found concrete expression in the Communist International (Comintern), which, during the "Second Period" of 1922–28, promoted the "United Front" tactic agreed at its Fourth Congress in December 1922.

By the end of that decade, the Comintern had established outposts across Asia, the Middle East and Africa and was starting to exercise considerable influence, even leadership among the anti-colonial movements in those regions. The new world order forged at Versailles had – by promising eventual self-government for some colonial peoples, developing collective security through the League of Nations and encouraging global cooperation via international organizations – in large measure been designed with the aim of thwarting the export of the Bolshevik revolution to the rest of the world. Thus, as Rick Saull (2007) and Odd Arne Westad (2005) have in different ways suggested, it is helpful to think of the Cold War as a conflict that originated in 1917 rather than 1945; and one which during the "short" twentieth century divided the globe into two competing ways of realizing a universal modernity – a Soviet model focused on justice and an American formula based around liberty (Westad, 2005). Viewed in this way, "hegemony" emerges not simply as a project of world domination designed by state functionaries in Washington, DC or Moscow, nor as the latest expansionist phase of two historic empires. It is conceived instead as a product of real class antagonisms mediated through the international system in the context of world-wide general crisis during the decades either side of the Second World War. Hegemony exemplifies, through its deployment in a global Cold War, what we saw earlier Gramsci understood as the "absolute secularisation of thought, an absolute humanism of history"; that is, a notion of concept formation rooted in concrete (geo)political struggles, not merely issuing from the minds of men. From this more materialist standpoint, the different conceptions and articulations of hegemony in international relations can thus be seen as *emerging* from specific socio-historical circumstances rather than representing static definitions of the term and its practice.

For the Soviet Union and the Comintern (increasingly synonymous after 1928), hegemony became a matter of defending the sovereignty of the Russian "proletarian fatherland" and of building support for the Comintern's national affiliates, chiefly though not exclusively through institutional mechanisms of trade union activity, electoral campaigns and parliamentary representation. After 1945, with the Comintern officially dissolved, Soviet hegemony was pursued mainly through direct alliances with sympathetic movements and states or, in the case of eastern Europe, through military occupation. The effective disappearance of a "civil society" in Stalinist Russia was replicated in its foreign relations, as hegemony was exercised almost exclusively through direct political and military domination until the period of de-Stalinization after 1956. Under Khrushchev's strategy of "peaceful co-existence", the USSR significantly expanded its diplomatic relations with newly independent states of "socialist orientation", conducting a more conventional Great Power leadership through the use of military-technical assistance, cultural-educational programmes and economic aid.

In contrast to this, postwar the US emerged as the world's most powerful economy with a significantly expanded and reconstituted state apparatus – the so-called National Security State. This economic and institutional capability was certainly translated externally into military-diplomatic might: Washington, DC – like Moscow did with east-central Europe – reshaped occupied West Germany and Japan in its own image as capitalist, liberal-democratic states. Yet here, the role of civil society in the unfolding of American hegemony was far more pronounced. This is chiefly because, as the world's leading capitalist state, the US was best placed to exercise hegemony in the Gramscian sense: reproducing its power through the seemingly consensual, rule-driven mechanisms of civil society, rather than relying exclusively on coercive imposition through the naked power of the state. The Soviets, in direct contrast, had no civil society to speak of, and certainly no capitalist *Bürgerliche Gesellschaft*, so their attempts at extending hegemony almost always took one of two expressly state-led, political forms: military occupation or (particularly after de-Stalinization) diplomatic support for sympathetic social movements, be they communist parties and trade unions, national liberation movements or pacifist organizations.

Gramsci himself had presciently identified in the early 1930s a specifically American combination of a productive "base" and an ideological "superstructure" during the period he labelled "Americanism and Fordism". The acceleration and rationalization (Taylorization) of the labour process that took hold of the American economy after the First World War had, according to the Sardinian, generated a series of tensions and contradictions between the public and private lives of workers, and between the realms of work and leisure more broadly, which elicited the regulation of morality both within and outside the workplace. Thus, seemingly "cultural" issues surrounding sexual behaviour, alcohol consumption or what today might be called "lifestyle choices" came under the purview of "economics" by virtue of their effect on labour productivity. These "new methods of work", Gramsci reflected, "are inseparable from a specific mode of living and of thinking and feeling life ... In America rationalisation of work and prohibition are undoubtedly connected. The enquiries conducted by the industrialists into the workers' private lives and the inspection services created by some firms to control the 'morality' of their workers are necessities of the new methods of work" (1971: 302).

This expression of hegemony as "moral and intellectual leadership" became a central plank of the US-led postwar reconstruction of western Europe and Japan. American hegemony was here not simply exercised through military-diplomatic domination over other states. It was also, and fundamentally, reproduced at the inter-societal level through the import of American management techniques, labour relations and forms of recreation (think of Japanese baseball or European jazz). The European Recovery Programme or "Marshall Plan" is perhaps the most notable example of this combination of coercion and consent at both inter-state and inter-societal levels.

Kees van der Pijl's (1984) detailed analysis of how the "Marshall Offensive" after 1947 re-ordered class relations in western Europe in Washington's favour by mobilizing all sorts of transnational social forces – from the international trade union movement to the Catholic Church – underlines once more how a purely institutionalist (liberal) or inter-statist (realist) conception of liberal order as "interdependent cooperation" and "coordination" misses the crucial dynamics of class antagonism mediated through the dull compulsion of the capitalist market (van der Pijl, 1984). Americans may have integrated Europeans into the Transatlantic Empire "by invitation" (Lundestad, 1986), but they did so by securing capitalist social relations imbued with a specific form of private coercion which is central to the exercise of hegemony – namely, the unequal social dependence on the market.

American state managers were fully aware during and immediately after the Second World War that generalizing this market dependence across its spheres of influence required a complex exercise in social engineering, carefully combining state-building, socio-economic reconstruction and military-diplomatic power (Smith, 2003). In western Europe, labour productivity acted as the engine of post-war stabilization and the Marshall Plan as its chief catalyst. The desired outcome of the European Recovery Programme (ERP) was certainly to integrate that continent into an open, rule-governed global market in goods, services, money and capital. But in order to secure this objective, the first task was to discipline European labour into a distinctively American regime of accumulation, labelled by Michael J. Hogan as the "New Deal synthesis" (Hogan, 1987). The core of this synthesis, Hogan has argued, "was an emphasis on co-operating links between private economic groups and between these groups and government authorities", aimed at "equipping particular countries with American production skills, fashion[ing] American patterns of labor-management teamwork, and, in this and other ways, maximiz[ing] the chances for economic integration and social peace on the Continent" (Hogan, 1987: 136).

Across postwar Europe, agencies of the US state and civil society (including secret services) mobilized ethnic diasporas, engaged in covert operations, forged transnational links between political movements, funded anti-communist cultural and religious organizations (Filipelli, 1989), and even established the secret pan-European counter-revolutionary militia GLADIO (Glaser, 2005) – all in the service of inducing the new liberal international order. American agents and funds were directly targeted at splintering the labour movement, steering social democrats towards Atlanticism and reinvigorating liberal and Christian-Democratic forces in Europe. European social forces were active participants in this process, and while many in northwest Europe benefited from their incorporation into the American Empire for several decades after 1947, other social sectors within and beyond the north Atlantic resisted the wholesale imposition of the New Deal synthesis with varying degrees of success.

Explaining hegemony

These historical experiences of postwar national reconstruction and global re-ordering are the most emblematic of expressions of American hegemony. The "embedded liberalism" which characterized this new world order delivered what in retrospect was a "long boom" of the "Golden Years" between roughly 1950 and 1973 (Hobsbawm, 1997). In the Soviet bloc too, and among many of the newly independent Third World states, the period bookended by de-Stalinization and the Bandung Conference of 1955 on the one side, and the advent of the neo-liberal counter-revolution and the rise of the "Second Cold War" in the early 1980s on the other, witnessed a period of socio-economic development and political optimism. Having rigidly adhered to a view of hegemony as Soviet military domination and vanguard leadership over satellite states and progressive social forces under Stalinism, Moscow adopted a more flexible framework in its external relations after 1956, supporting national liberation movements and newly independent "national democracies" in "strengthening the state sector of the economy and land reform … to prepare them for a gradual transition to a non-capitalist path of development" (Light, 1988).

Paradoxically, however, it was only with the perceived decline of American hegemony after 1973 (signalled by the collapse of the Bretton Woods regime and defeat in Vietnam) and, to a lesser extent, the first signs of terminal crisis in the Soviet bloc during the late 1970s that the study of hegemony took centre stage in IR. The "Discipline of Western Supremacy", as van der Pijl (2014) labels IR, had certainly flourished under the shadow of the Cold War, and indeed acted as a fertile nursery for organic intellectuals and state operatives of national security. Yet, "hegemony" was until the 1970s rarely presented as a social-scientific problematic requiring analysis and explanation by IR scholars. As a profoundly north Atlantic discipline, postwar IR *assumed* American leadership of the free world and invested most of its theoretical energies in concepts like "security", "balance of power", "national interest" or "strategy" that might contribute to the reproduction of that very hegemony (Anderson, 2013). Hegemony, then, only became a core IR concept retrospectively.

It is also noteworthy that the first wave of IR studies explicitly concerned with hegemony was written in the register of the sub-discipline of International Political Economy (IPE). Thus, the conception of hegemony deployed in IR after the 1970s was detached from its deeply political moorings and drifted toward the realm of international economics where the separation between states and markets, politics and economics was naturalized as a static interrelationship. It was only with the re-introduction of Gramsci into IPE through the critical work of Robert Cox and others from the late 1980s onwards that the concept of hegemony recovered its social and political content. Following the conventional methodological division used earlier, we can identify three – roughly chronological – approaches to postwar American hegemony in IR.

The first of these is represented in the works of Robert Gilpin (1972) and Charles P. Kindleberger (1973). In their own ways, both these authors posited what was soon to become known as the "hegemonic stability theory" (HST) – the idea that the international public or collective goods underwritten by the US after 1945 (the US dollar or multilateral Bretton Woods institutions, for instance) sustained a global political and economic order that required leadership by a dominant state. In the absence of such a hegemon, the anarchical international system would soon collapse into zero-sum mercantilist rivalry between capitalist powers, as was the case during the interwar crisis. In Kindleberger's famous formulation, "[p]art of the reason for the length and most of the explanation for the depth of the world depression was the inability of the British to continue taking on the role of underwriter to the system, and the reluctance of the US to take it on until 1936" (1973: 11). On this account, hegemony reflects the distribution of power among states, and the willingness of the most powerful state to take on the burden of guaranteeing the institutional reproduction of an open, rule-governed global capitalist economy. The naturalization of such a global economy and its co-existence with an anarchical system of states are both axiomatic to this realist viewpoint – their chief concern is whether any given state has sufficient coercive capabilities to enforce the "rules of the game" on potential shirkers or, in game-theoretical language, "cheats".

A decade on after this initial salvo in the study of hegemonic stability, another doyen of American IR, Robert O. Keohane, posed a question that only made sense in the aftermath of the Bretton Woods crisis: "how can cooperation take place in world politics in the absence of hegemony?" (1984: 14). The answer for Keohane lay in international regimes: "Regimes provide information and reduce the costs of transactions that are consistent with their injunctions, thus facilitating interstate agreements and their decentralized enforcement" (1984: 246). In what he insisted was an "institutionalist modification" of the realist HST, Keohane made an empirical case for the resilience of international regimes which, though forged through American power, could and did outlive US hegemony after 1971. Thus, Keohane removed the concept of hegemony from its realist association with stability or order, and instead suggested that it was one of several foreign policy strategies of cooperation: "Hegemony and international regimes may be complementary, or even to some extent substitute for each other: both serve to make agreements possible and to facilitate compliance with rules" (1984: 15).

Keohane's emphasis on institutional durability and the power of rule-governed multi-lateralism, together with his interest in post-hegemonic orders, resonates strongly with a second broad approach to the idea of hegemony in IR, namely the liberal internationalist conception which has been most eloquently developed by the American IR scholar G. John Ikenberry. As Rick Saull has rightly highlighted, Ikenberry's institutionalism is distinctive in its emphasis on the liberal and constitutional nature of American hegemony (Saull, 2012). For Ikenberry, US postwar order is characterized by strategic constraint ("reassure[ing] weaker states that it would not abandon or dominate them"), an institutional "stickiness" that reduces the "returns to power" and increases the "returns to institutions", and finally a specifically liberal property of being an "open and accessible institution" (Ikenberry, 1998: 45–46). Like Keohane, Ikenberry argues for an institutional "path dependency" that can outlive both Great Power balancing and hegemonic orders, but he also goes beyond the focus on international regimes by underscoring the domestic sources of American hegemony: "Because of its distinctively open domestic political system, and because of the array of power-dampening institutions it has created to manage political conflict, the United States has been able to remain at the center of a large and expanding institutionalized and legitimate political order" (Ikenberry, 1998: 47).

This attention toward the internal make-up of states and societies is a welcome move into what are otherwise highly reified inter-state conceptions of global hegemony. As we have already seen, such statist reductionism implies a crude narrowing of the concept of hegemony, which, from its origins, and certainly in its twentieth-century incarnation, has always conceived of power as a deeply social, indeed inter-societal phenomenon (a point throughly discussed in Ives and Short, 2013). The third broad approach to hegemony in IR – that represented by so-called "neo-Gramscian" IR scholars like Robert W. Cox, Mark Rupert or Stephen Gill, among others – is the only tradition to take seriously the earlier plea for a "conceptual historicism" insofar as it critically and reflexively recognizes the temporalization, democratization and politicization of its own conceptual categories: "In the process of constructing [a] critique of capitalist social reality, ontology itself is radicalized; no longer viewed *a priori* i.e. as prior to and constitutive of the reality which we can know, it becomes instead an ongoing social product, historically concrete and contestable" (Rupert, 1995: 16).

In the early 1980s, the Canadian IR theorist Robert W. Cox mobilized Gramsci's concepts of hegemony and historical blocs to explain the production and transformation of successive world orders. According to Cox, a hegemonic world order is a universal aspiration that cannot rely exclusively on the domination or exploitation by a single state of other subaltern societies. It is, rather, premised on the convergence of interests with the dominant social classes of subordinate states (Cox, 1993). Cox modified and geographically up-scaled Gramsci's conception of hegemony to encompass the historical triangulation between social relations of production, forms of state and world orders. These in turn combine ideas, material capabilities and institutions to forge durable social structures we can call world orders. Cox identified the *Pax Britannica* of 1845–75 and the *Pax Americana* of 1945–65 as two periods of world hegemony where a leading state provided collective social, ideational and institutional infrastructure that satisfied the interests both of elites in dominant states and their counterparts in allied states. The key marker of a hegemonic order for Cox (and which I applied earlier to the brief Cold War illustration) lies in the stable alignment of sympathetic social forces with the prevailing modes of social reproduction (e.g. capitalism) and their institutional coordination through international organizations or multilateral regimes.

Since the 1980s, successive waves of IR scholars have adopted this neo-Gramscian framework to explore the concrete manifestation of hegemonic order in different parts of the world. An early sample of this "transnational historical materialism" (Gill, 1993) considered the detail of how different societies in East Asia, Latin America, southern Europe and Russia were transformed internally – productively, institutionally and socially – through their subordinate (re)integration into the capitalist world economy. Later studies by Bill Robinson, Henk Overbeek, Bastiaan van Apeldoorn and Stuart Shields, among others, have documented the self-conscious organization by transnational elites of regional hegemonic orders in Europe and Latin America. The upshot of this rich and diverse academic inquiry has been a radical re-working of hegemony as a term that mobilizes societies as well as states (or, more appropriately, "state–society complexes") and which operates transnationally on both regional and global scales.

Hegemony, Empire or Primacy?

We have seen how a concept that re-emerged at the start of the twentieth century as a revolutionary call to arms was transformed by the end of that century into a category designating a particular international order. This semantic shift has not erased the multiple usages and meanings of hegemony, but it cannot escape our attention that its conceptual value has increased in IR relative to the perceived waning of American global power. Like the famed owl of Minerva, "hegemony" is a concept in IR that started its flight in the 1970s as dusk fell on postwar American leadership. This is partly a result of IR's tendency as a late developer to adopt trends and concepts in the social sciences long after they first appear. But from the perspective of conceptual history, it can also be seen as a reflection of the certainty among Western elites and many of their subaltern supporters that US hegemony over the capitalist world was assured during the long boom: you only miss something when it's gone. Susan Strange did argue persuasively in the late 1980s that the "declinism" expounded by Keohane and Nye (1977) or Gilpin (1983) was grossly exaggerated, and that it in fact masked the "structural power" she claimed Washington continued to exercise over global finance, security, knowledge and production (Strange, 1988: 28). Yet this empirical assessment does not contradict the growing awareness among IR scholars after 1973 that US leadership was being challenged, if not surpassed – hence their preoccupation with the concept of hegemony.

The collapse of the Soviet Union and the end of the Cold War have thrown up a fresh conundrum for IR scholars: why does American hegemony appear to have outlived the demise of its Cold War rival? Given the emphasis placed (in this chapter as elsewhere) on the conjunctural emergence of the US as the leader of the capitalist world during the Cold War, surely the term "hegemony" ceases to have purchase with the end of that global conflict? There are two broad responses to these kinds of questions. The first turns our attention to the notions of empire and imperialism, arguing that the US has from its inception been an imperial republic whose quest for global supremacy took the form of an overseas "informal" empire once the domestic frontier of this settler-colonial society was "closed" at the turn of the twentieth century (Appleman Williams, 1972). On this account, emphasis should be placed on the *American* character of global hegemony. A contrasting view underlines the *capitalist* nature of recent hegemonic world orders, suggesting that, while certain dominant states – Britain in the late nineteenth century, the US in the twentieth – have plainly acted as *primus inter pares* on the world stage, it is possible to conceive of a post-American capitalist hegemonic order. These debates are in turn conditioned by disputes over the empirical evidence for American decline (Cox, 2007) as well as conceptual variations on which term – hegemony, empire, primacy – might best explain the international dispensation of power in the twenty-first century.

The US-led invasion and occupation of Afghanistan and Iraq in the aftermath of the 9/11 attacks is the inevitable starting point for these considerations. On all the definitions considered above, coercion is a mere – generally secondary – complement to consent in the exercise of hegemony. Yet the new millennium was inaugurated with an outright conquest and pacification of extra-European peoples in a manner reminiscent of nineteenth-century colonial domination. For many, we had returned to a "colonial present" (Gregory, 2004) where the exogenous and forcible re-organization of entire societies was being conducted not through the benign influence of culture, law and diplomacy (so-called "soft" power) but through the very hard power of shock-and-awe and proconsular administration. Authors across the political spectrum, from Andrew Bacevich (2002) and Michael Mann (2003) to Chalmers Johnson (2000) and David Harvey (2003), recognized this as imperialism – the expansion of US power through war and territorial conquest. Their conception of imperialism was, to be sure, diverse: some, like Bacevich, understand American imperialism as a policy which has been intermittently adopted by US administrations since the nineteenth century as part of an expansionist "Grand Strategy". Others, like Harvey, conceive of the "new" imperialism as a complex dialectic between the "capitalist logic" of markets and the "territorial logic" of inter-state diplomacy and geopolitics which unfolds in moments of global crisis. Hegemony, on this reading, appears to refer to a historical era (the long postwar boom) rather than a strategy of rule or a structure of global power. Thus, a distinction is insinuated between "empire" and "imperialism", on the one hand, as directly coercive, territorial domination by a powerful state over another, weaker state, and "hegemony", on the other hand, as indirect rule through the largely consensual mechanisms of the global market.

In the work of John Agnew, this contrast between empire and hegemony becomes spatially codified in the conceptual distinction between a globalizing, market-led hegemony and a coercive, territorially-bound empire. Indeed, Agnew is an eloquent advocate of the view that globalization reflects what he calls the "new geography of power", delivered through US hegemony, yet since the 1990s characterized by an increasingly de-centralized, fragmented and uneven global system where no single state can dominate. American hegemony, Agnew insists, needs to be qualitatively and quantitatively distinguished from preceding world orders because "US hegemony has been based on a rejection of territorial limits to its influence, as would necessarily come with empire. In this sense it has been a nonterritorial enterprise, notwithstanding periods when territorial strategies have been pursued" (Agnew, 2005: 52).

We have in these various interpretations of Washington's post-Cold War place in the world a rehearsal of some of the intra-Marxist debates about imperialism either side of the Second World War. Then, as in recent years, intellectuals of both radical and Marxist orientation have tended to either emphasize the inherently expansionist and conflictual nature of capitalism (Lenin-Bukharin's inter-imperialist rivalry) or the potential for capitalist powers to cooperate in their shared domination of subordinate states and societies (Kautsky's ultra-imperialism). What gets lost in such formulations is both the distinctively strategic conception of power inherent in the idea of hegemony (the question of leadership) and the consideration of what, if anything, is unique about the postwar international order (the question of American exceptionalism). Somewhat paradoxically, it has been mainstream IR discussions that have addressed these issues most consistently, under the rubric of "American decline".

There were several waves of "declinist" literature: initially, after the fall of Saigon and the collapse of Bretton Woods, this took the form of hegemonic stability theory. In the 1980s, it was reflected in the concern over a "Pacific Century" through the rise of Japanese and other East Asian economies, as well as fears over US "imperial overstretch" (Kennedy, 1987). The latest round follows the perceived challenge to American hegemony from emerging powers, most notably China, and the accompanying concerns over Washington's various fiscal and current account deficits (Quinn, 2011). The empirical disputes over data and permutations of what is covered by the term "decline" cannot detain us here. Suffice it to say that, though few doubt the US absolute military, economic and diplomatic leadership of the world in the foreseeable future, much of the debate surrounds America's relative decline in relation to China's "peaceful rise" and the accompanying trend toward a much more multi-polar world order.

The question occupying American analysts and policymakers today, then, is: (how long) can American hegemony survive the "unipolar moment" (Krauthammer, 1990/91) that followed the end of the Cold War? For advocates of American primacy like Brooks and Wohlforth (2008), US hegemony is here to stay on account of its overwhelming preponderance in all key indicators of both "hard" and "soft" power. Emerging powers like China, India and Brazil benefit from the global commons provided by US primacy and are too distracted by regional rivals to seek a global challenge to American hegemony. From this perspective, there has been no counter-hegemonic balancing since the end of the Cold War because Washington has seized the opportunity proferred by the "unipolar moment" to redefine the post-Cold War order in ways that make it far too costly for hegemonic contenders to threaten America, or to radically transform the rules that sustain the current world order.

In contrast to this, proponents of a nascent multipolarity focus attention not on the existing power dispensation, but on the discernible socio-economic and diplomatic tendencies which indicate a wider distribution of future capabilities. Fareed Zakaria (2008) is one mainstream exponent of the view that emerging economies will eventually translate their growing market share into military and diplomatic clout which, while perhaps not debunking US hegemony, will certainly erode and modify it in ways that will require Washington to share power in a multilateral framework. Underlying this argument is the possibility not just of a post-American world, but also of a post-hegemonic order in the style originally formulated by Keohane (1984) and recast by Ikenberry (1998). Here, the liberal institutions that underpinned the American-led capitalist order after 1945 are deemed to be "locked in" in ways that can serve a twenty-first-century multipolar order made up of market states. Yet, as prominent neo-realist Christopher Layne has warned, "[b]ecause of the perception that the United States' hard power is declining, and because of the hit its soft power has taken as a result of the [2008 financial] meltdown, there is a real question about whether the US hegemon retains the credibility and legitimacy to take the lead in institutional reform" (2009: 166).

My aim is not to enter this mainstream debate and try to establish which position is correct. Rather, in lieu of a conclusion, I want to note that the framing of hegemony in these debates as a question of leadership and balance of power betrays the stubborn persistence of state-centrism in our discipline. A fluid concept like "hegemony" becomes, in these renditions, a static, transhistorical cipher for capabilities, power and stability. In all this, "hegemony" is contrasted with "empire" and "imperialism" in a semantic ruse aimed at establishing American exceptionalism: unlike previous empires, it is claimed, the US is an anti-colonial republic that leads an alliance of free-market states through cooperation and consent.

This chapter has offered an alternative route to understanding hegemony in IR, through a historicist conception of our political vocabulary that underlines its temporality and partisanship. From this perspective, each of these concepts carries with it an historical and ideological baggage which needs to be unpacked and examined before rushing into typological classifications. Once this is done, it becomes clear that the specificity of American empire should not be confused with its exceptionalism; nor should Washington's postwar leadership of the capitalist West be conflated with the realist requirement for hegemonic stability. Instead, I have argued, it is worthwhile understanding a concept like hegemony as a product of specific historical conjunctures shaped by concrete social antagonisms: if during the interwar period these were defined by the Bolshevik revolution and the subsequent twenty years' crisis, after 1945 it was the Cold War as a global inter-systemic conflict that characterized the period. With the defeat of a world-historical challenge to capitalism after 1989, the struggle for hegemony seems to have been "domesticated" and regionalized as contending social forces in East and South Asia, as well as Latin America, fight out politically radically different models of state and society for their own countries and respective regions.

Suggested Readings

Cox, R. 1987. *Production, Power, and World Order: Social Forces in the Making of History* (New York: Columbia University Press).

The original statement on the neo-Gramscian conception of international relations, with particular attention to hegemony and world orders.

Ikenberry, J.G. 2000. *After Victory: Institutions, Strategic Restraint, and the Rebuilding of Order after Major Wars* (Princeton, NJ: Princeton University Press).

A theoretically sophisticated, historically detailed liberal account of hegemony and world order in the modern era.

Mearsheimer, J. 2002. *The Tragedy of Great Power Politics* (New York: W. W. Norton).
A classic statement for the 21st century of realist conceptions of power in international relations.

Rupert, M. 1995. *Producing Hegemony: The Politics of Mass Production and American Global Power* (Cambridge: Cambridge University Press).
A Marxist analysis of hegemomy in the postwar American-led world order.

Worth, O. 2015. *Rethinking Hegemony* (London and New York: Palgrave Macmillan).
The most up-to-date, accessible and informed English-language overview of the concept of hegemony.

Bibliography

Agnew, J. 2005. *Hegemony: The New Shape of Global Power* (Philadelphia, PA: Temple University Press).

Anderson, P. 2013. 'Consilium', *New Left Review*, 83, Sept.–Oct.

Appleman Williams, William. 1972. *The Tragedy of American Diplomacy*, 2nd edition (New York: Dell Publishing).

Bacevich, A.J. 2002. *American Empire: the Realities and Consequences of US Diplomacy* (Cambridge, MA: Harvard University Press).

Brooks, S.G and W.C. Wohlforth. 2008. *World Out of Balance: International Relations and the Challenge of American Primacy* (Princeton, NJ: Princeton University Press).

Brunner, O., W. Conze and R. Koselleck (eds).1972. *Geschichtliche Grundbegriffe: Historisches Lexikon zur politisch-sozialen Sprache in Deutschland* (Stuttgart: Klett-Cotta).

Cox, M. 2007. 'Is the United States In Decline – Again?' *International Affairs* 83(4), 643–653.

Cox, R. 1987. *Production, Power, and World Order: Social Forces in the Making of History* (New York: Columbia University Press).

Cox, R.W. 1993. 'Gramsci, hegemony and international relations: an essay in method', in Stephen Gill (ed) *Gramsci, Historical Materialism and International Relations* (Cambridge University Press), pp. 49–66.

Filippelli, R.L. 1989. *American Labor and Postwar Italy, 1943–1953* (Stanford, CA: Stanford University Press).

Gill, S. (ed.). 1993. *Gramsci, Historical Materialism and International Relations* (Cambridge: Cambridge University Press).

Gilpin, R. 1972. 'The Politics of Transnational Economic Relations', in Joseph S. Nye Jr and Robert O. Keohane (eds). *Transnational Relations and Word Politics* (Cambridge, MA: Harvard University Press), pp. 48–69.

Gilpin, R. 1983. *War and change in World Politics* (Cambridge: Cambridge University Press).

Glaser, D. 2005. *Nato's Secret Armies: Operation Gladio and Terrorism in Western Europe* (London and New York: Cass).

Gramsci, A. 1971. *Selections from the Prison Notebooks*, ed. and trans. Q. Hoare and G. Nowell Smith (London: Lawrence and Wishart).

Gregory, D. 2004. *The Colonial Present: Palestine, Iraq, Afghanistan* (Oxford: Blackwell).

Harvey, D. 2003. *The New Imperialism* (Oxford: Oxford University Press).

Hobsbawm, E.J. 1997. *The Age of Extremes: the Short Twentieth Century* (London: Abacus).

Hogan, M.J. 1987. *The Marshall Plan, America, Britain and the Reconstruction of Western Europe* (Cambridge: Cambridge University Press).

Ikenberry, G.J. 1998. 'Institutions, Strategic Restraint, and the Persistence of American Postwar Order', *International Security* 23(1), 43–78.

Ikenberry, G.J. 2014. 'Illusions of Empire: Defining the New American Order', *Foreign Affairs*, March/April. www.foreignaffairs.com/articles/59727/g-john-ikenberry/illusions-of-empire-defining-the-new-american-order (accessed 25 February 2015).

Ives, P. and N. Short. 2013. 'On Gramsci and the International: a Textual Analysis', *Review of International Studies* 39(3), 621–642.

Johnson, C. 2000. *Blowback: The Costs and Consequences of American Empire* (New York: Little Brown).

Kennedy, P. 1987. *The Rise and Fall of the Great Powers: Economic Change and Military Conflict from 1500–2000* (London: Fontana).

Keohane, R. and J.S. Nye. 1977. *Power and Interdependence: World Politics in Transition* (New York: Little and Brown).

Keohane, R.O. 1984. *After Hegemony: Cooperation and Discord in the World Political Economy* (Princeton, NJ: Princeton University Press).

Kindleberger, C.P. (1973) *The World in Depression*, 1929–1939 (Berkeley, CA: University of California Press).

Koselleck, R. 1985 (trans. K. Tribe) *Futures Past: On the Semantics of Historical Time* (New York: Columbia University Press).

Krauthammer, C. 1990/91. 'The Unipolar Moment', *Foreign Affairs* 70(1), 23–33.

Layne, C. 2009. 'The Waning of US Hegemony: Myth or Reality? A Review Essay', *International Security* 34(1), 147–173.

Lebow, R.N. and R. Kelly. 2001. 'Thucydides and Hegemony: The United States and Athens', *Review of International Studies* 27(4), 593–609.

Lehmann, H. and Richter, M. 1996. (eds), *The Meaning of Historical Terms and Concepts: New Studies on Begriffsgeschichte*, Occasional Paper 15 (Washington, DC: German Historical Institute.)

Light, M. (1988) *The Soviet Theory of International Relations* (London: Palgrave Macmillan).

Lundestad, G. 1986. 'Empire by Invitation? The United States and Western Europe, 1945–1952', *Journal of Peace Research* 23(3), 263–277.

Mann, M. 2003. *Incoherent Empire* (London and New York: Verso).

Mearsheimer, J. 2002. *The Tragedy of Great Power Politics* (New York: W.W. Norton).

Morera, E. 1990. *Gramsci's Historicism: A Realist Interpretation* (London and New York: Routledge).

Quinn, A. 2011. 'The Art of Declining Politely: Obama's Prudent Presidency and the Waning of American Power', *International Affairs* 87(4), 803–824.

Richter, M. 1996. 'Appreciating a Contemporary Classic: The *Geschichtliche Grundbegriffe* and Future Scholarship', in H. Lehmann and M. Richter (eds), *The Meaning of Historical Terms and Concepts: New Studies on Begriffsgeschichte*, Occasional Paper 15 (Washington, DC: German Historical Institute).

Rupert, M. 1995. *Producing Hegemony: The Politics of Mass Production and American Global Power* (Cambridge: Cambridge University Press).

Saull, R. 2007. *The Cold War and After: Capitalism, Revolution and Superpower Politics* (London: Pluto Press).

Saull, R. 2012. 'Hegemony and International Political Economy', in R. Denemark (ed.), *The International Studies Encyclopaedia* (Oxford: Wiley).

Smith, N. 2003. *American Empire: Roosevelt's Geographer and the Prelude to Globalization* (Berkeley, CA and London: University of California Press).

Strange, S. 1988. *States and Markets* (London: Pinter).

Van der Pijl, K. 1984. *The Making of an Atlantic Ruling Class* (London: Verso).

Van der Pijl, K. 2014. *The Discipline of Western Supremacy: Modes of Foreign Relations and Political Economy, III* (London and New York: Pluto Press).

Westad, O.A. 2005. *The Global Cold War: Third World Interventions and the Making of Our Times* (Cambridge: Cambridge University Press).

Williams, R. 1976. *Keywords: A Vocabulary of Culture and Society* (Glasgow: Fontana, Croom Helm).

Zakaria, F. 2008. *The Post-American World* (New York: W.W. Norton).

13

Democracy

Piki Ish-Shalom

What is democracy? Think of Gaddafi's Libya, North Korea, Congo, or the former East Germany. They all share at least two common features. The first is that they are not known for being particularly democratic. The second is that their official name declares them to be democratic. Thus, Libya's official name during the Gaddafi era was the "Great Socialist People's Libyan Arab Jamahiriya", "Jamahiriya" meaning "the masses", in other words "republic" in Arabic. The hereditary dictatorship of North Korea refers to itself as "The Democratic People's Republic of Korea". Congo, where human rights are violated on a massive scale and elections are reportedly fraudulent, proudly boasts of being the "Democratic Republic of the Congo". And in the five decades of its dictatorial existence, the former East Germany dubbed itself the "German Democratic Republic". And the list goes on and on. While in these four cases we might say that the official name is misleading and does not adequately describe the character of the system, it is not always clear which countries are democracies. In fact, the category can be quite blurry. How about Venezuela, Turkey, and Mexico? Freedom House defines all three as partly free (2013) – but weren't the heads of their executive branches elected freely and, at least in Venezuela and Turkey, hugely popular? What is the link between freedom and democracy? And then consider the controversial 2000 presidential election in the US, where the candidate with the majority of the popular vote lost. Does that mean the US is not a democracy?

Looking for a measure for judging these cases, we might go back to the "original", the polis of Athens, widely celebrated as the birthplace of democracy. As historians tell us, Athens brought political activities into the agora and engaged in many public acts of self-rule and direct democracy. All Athenian citizens had the right to participate in public life and the self-rule of the city state. No wonder we consider Athens the birthplace of democracy. But let us take a closer look at who those citizens were; at the tiny fraction of the population that enjoyed the right and authority to participate in public life. We know that the only people who were considered citizens were property-owning males. Women, slaves, alien residents, and people without property were denied such rights and authority. We can only estimate the numbers, of course, but somewhere around 20% of the total population of 250,000–300,000 (in the 4th century BC) were right-holding citizens. This was a very limited and exclusionary system of suffrage, too exclusionary to be considered today a true democracy. But it was considered that some 2500 years ago, and in many eras since.

These examples raise a number of issues. First, that democracy is a concept with rhetorical capital (Ish-Shalom, 2008). When a country is identified as a democracy, it can lead to political advantages. That is because democracy bears a whiff of legitimacy, internally and internationally. Second, the meaning of democracy has changed throughout human history, following normative and cultural changes (Hobson, 2009). Third, although elastic and changing, the concept of democracy does have its limits, even if there are debates about what those limits are. Everything does not go, and despite what Gaddafi thought or wanted others to think, his Libya was neither a republic nor democratic. Fourth, the discussion of democracy covers many issues, including freedom, political domination, representation, minority rights, legitimacy, elections, etc. Do they all have to exist for a state to be called a democracy? What happens if some of them clash? Consider, for example, Arend Lijphart's call for consensual as opposed to majoritarian democracy, at least in divided societies (1999). In a sense, Lijphart is sacrificing the democratic principle of majority rule (which stems from a concern for political equality) for another democratic principle – that of rule by consent. In Lijphart's case, as well as in other cases when different aspects of democracy clash, how do we evaluate where a society or state "ranks" in the table of democracies?

Etymologically, democracy is a relatively simple word. It comes from the Greek and means "rule by the people"; hence its closeness with the word republic, that comes from the Latin and means "of the people". But the definition of democracy as "rule by the people" does not go far enough. It leaves the concept shrouded in mystery and fuzziness, because ultimately, what is meant by "the people rule", what domains do the people rule, which mechanisms can and should the people rule by, what is the normative foundation and justification for the people to rule, what are the conditions of rule by the people, and what are the limitations of that rule? And despite all the rhetorical potency of Abraham Lincoln's addenda "of the people", "by the people" and "for the people", we are still left facing definitional questions.

Hence, it should come as no surprise that when W.B. Gallie penned his seminal article on essentially contested concepts, democracy was one of the paradigmatic examples he employed. Gallie (1956) noted that democracy fulfils the conditions for a concept being essentially contested: (1) it is an appraisive or evaluative concept; (2) it is internally complex because it contains different principles and values, such as majority rule, equality, and active participation; (3) its internal complexity allows for a differentiation of ranking, namely its complexity creates a hierarchy of principles and values with greater or lesser importance for defining an entity as a democracy; (4) the concept is also open, in that it enables the bar used when judging and ruling a polity as democracy to be lowered or raised; (5) the concept can be used to defend one's own state as democratic or attack other states as undemocratic; (6) democracy can be attributed to a host of historical exemplars, such as Athens and the French Revolution; and (7) it is possible that debates about the nature of democracy do not help to disperse the fuzziness of the concept, but to increase its vagueness, i.e. its contestedness (Gallie, 1956, 183–7; in IR, see Kurki, 2010).

Simply put, defining democracy is not just a methodological act but an act that is shrouded in normative commitments and political struggle. Democracy's essential contestedness also sheds new light on the Freedom House measures used above. Though oft-quoted and used in research, the Freedom House project which measures democracy with a set of universal quantitative indicators, ignores democracy's definitional questions and therefore has evaluation difficulties and inbuilt biases.

The discussion in this chapter roughly follows the political and critical approach outlined in the introductory chapter to this volume and, using Gallie's framework, tries to explain democracy's essential contestedness and demonstrate it in three key contexts. Two of these contexts are theoretical: political ideologies and philosophies, displaying the different normative backgrounds of conceptualizing democracy, and international relations (IR) theory, specifically how the different conceptions of democracy play out in the "democratic peace" literature. The third context is political and relates to the various manifestations of the concept in policy proposals that present democracy as their principal organizing principle for international relations.

The Essential Contestedness of Democracy

Academic writing is generally expected to provide definitions in order to create a common language with the readership. And, it is true, definitions help to clarify standpoints and understand the source of disagreements. However, for a chapter that wishes to show the essential contestedness of a concept, it does not make much sense to offer a single authoritative definition. The aim here is, rather, to present and analyze a spectrum of available definitions in an effort to reveal their essential contestedness and analyze their political function; in other words, how the definitions function in certain fields, including the political one.

There are several broad understandings of democracy, two of which dominate contemporary discourses. Each stems from a different normative worldview; and each understanding is based on a specific conception or definition of democracy and is distinct from other bordering concepts, such as dictatorship, liberalism, popular sovereignty, etc. Each conception informs a different theory of democracy; theory that explains, analyzes, and/or justifies the workings of democracy. I will start with the two dominant understandings and then proceed to analyze some of the other representative ones.

The first understanding, which could be called the "liberal" reading, combines several distinct conceptions and theories of democracy, including the normative and cultural and the deliberative and participatory theories. It is easy to overlook the commonalities between deliberation and participation. When democracy is seen merely as a political mechanism, one can even argue that these theories conflict. Diana Mutz (2006), for example, sees the demands for participation and deliberation as two opposing and conflicting expectations. Wider participation may result in undermining the conditions for deliberation and impair its quality. Mutz argues that waiting for valued, meaningful, and useful deliberations may mean limiting participation and only holding discussions within narrow circles of educated and politically motivated citizens, namely elite deliberations. However, when we analyze the normative foundations of the two theories, certain fundamental similarities do emerge.

First, they emphasize individual citizens and their society rather than the political system and the regime. Second, they do not settle for procedures and structures but expect democratic norms and democratic culture. Among other things, these expectations imply a consolidation of tolerance, openness, political participation, civil and political rights like protection from arbitrary discrimination, freedom of speech, conscience, and expression, as well as the internalization of a sense of civic responsibility (see, for example, Mansbridge, 1970; Pateman, 1970; Barber, 1984; Elster, 1998; Habermas, 1998; Dryzek, 2002).

The normative and cultural conception of democracy is thus far-reaching and arises out of an optimistic, liberal view of human rationality (see also Chapter 4, this volume). It sees human beings as rationally driven creatures; they do not lack emotions, desires, instincts, or communal bonds, but these are largely controlled by rationality and rational calculations. In the tradition of the Enlightenment, the rational individual is also the locus of indivisible civic rights and the best judge of her/his own interests and preferences. Democracy is understood normatively and culturally and therefore centers on citizenship and rights, while seeking to widen the scope and political efficacy of participation and deliberation, thus extending the meaning of democracy.

The second dominant understanding of democracy, which might be called the "conservative" reading, is both narrower in the expectations of the citizenry and in its conception of democracy. It combines the formal and procedural conceptions of democracy with its elitist and structural theories. It tends to understand democracy in a relatively minimalist way (see, for example, Lippmann, 1955; Schumpeter, 1962; Przeworski, 1999). A regime is democratic if it passes a certain structural threshold, and has free, fair, open elections, autonomous branches of government, division of power, and checks and balances. This precludes the tyrannical concentration of power in the hands of a small, unresponsive elite.

The minimalist structural conception of democracy stems from a conservative skepticism regarding human faculties. Joseph Schumpeter targeted what he called the classical theory of democracy which he criticized for being overly optimistic and having an unrealistic utopist faith in human nature (1962: 270). Schumpeter saw democracy as simply a competition among members of the elite over government, where the public's role is limited to casting a vote for this or that elite. This minimalist view is based, among other things, on a distrustful and conservative understanding of human capabilities where the main driver of human action is not rationality but a mixture of perennial desires, instincts, and communal traditions. That mixture is extra-rational and drives humans to compete for power. Human beings are what the great realist theoretician, Hans Morgenthau, called Homo Dominandi. And indeed, along with conservatism and the elitist theory of democracy, realism shares some fundamental and grounding ontological, anthropological, and normative assumptions (Ish-Shalom, 2006).

There are two major consequences of the conservative understanding of humans as power-seekers; the first is that social and political organizations are under constant threat of destabilization because everyone wants power. Among other things, this was the grounds for Aristotle's disdain for democracy which he considered a deviant version of the good polity (2009, III: 8). It was also why the great nineteenth-century British conservative Edmund Burke feared the French Revolution (1987). He believed that the only natural outcome of the disposal of the old regime by a horde of revolutionaries was political chaos and a reign of terror. There is a second and obverse consequence of the conservative view of humans as irrational and that is a constant fear of a dictatorial concentration of power accumulating in the hands of whoever seizes power. That elite would look to its own sectarian interests without considering the citizenry and with no accountability – in other words, a dictatorship would ensue, and not necessarily a benign one. The conservative solution to these two dangers is minimal and structural democracy. On the one hand, by holding regular elections democracy guarantees no power will last forever and prevents the concentration of power in a dictatorship. On the other hand, by confining political participation to elections (and in combination with a commitment to the rule of law and a separation of powers), democracy precludes political and social destabilization.

As mentioned, the normative/substantive liberal and procedural/minimalist conservative understandings of democracy are most accepted nowadays, at least in the West. Furthermore, their contenders see them as the benchmarks for developing alternatives. Thus, the alternatives are mostly seen as challengers that try to chip away at the more popular conceptions of democracy.

Whereas the liberal understanding of democracy focuses on values, human rights, and the individual, and the conservative understanding focuses on elites, procedures, and structures, the socialist understanding expands democracy to classes and the economic field (Luxemburg, 1961). It argues that political equality will not suffice. Political equality demands that all citizens should have equal voting rights and (some) access to the policy-making process. Being economically minded, socialist conceptions of democracy argue that without true economic equality the liberal insistence on political equality is but a mirage. Consider American democracy, where vast sums are needed to run a successful political campaign. This is an advantage to wealthy politicians and heavy donors whose support is rewarded by free access to the ears of decision-makers and their inner circles. The same holds for mass media proprietors who have the opportunities and resources to advance their own preferences and interests. Economic inequality also gives organized interest groups greater opportunities to employ lobbyists in decision-making circles and tilt policies in their favor. Those lacking in material wherewithal are left by the democratic wayside and their preferences and interests have less political representation.

Noam Chomsky gave an anarchical twist to this critique (see below) in arguing that "democracy is largely a sham when the industrial system is controlled by any form of autocratic elite, whether of owners, managers, and technocrats, a 'vanguard' party, or a state bureaucracy" (1970). With the more radical notions of socialism, there is a demand to democratize other socio-economic domains besides the political. Thus, for example, revolutionary syndicalism demands democratization in workplaces and equal say for workers. Only economic equality and the democratization of the economy (including in workplaces) can provide real and effective democracy where everyone's preferences and interests will enjoy equal representation and political efficacy. This socialist worldview challenges the liberal separation of politics and economics, resulting in a welfare or social democracy (Cohen and Rogers, 1983; Meyer with Hinchman, 2007). Its radical undercurrents also challenge the fear of destabilization. Destabilization creates opportunities for social struggle and change. It opens up a social space for insurgent democracy that can achieve "social democracy, justice, and equality" (Holston, 2008: 35).

But whatever the democratic model advocated by socialism, government and hierarchy play a vital role in it, in particular as devices and instruments for changing the existing socio-economic order. The goal of social democracy is to achieve genuine freedom, resolve social conflicts, and achieve harmony. However, as a hierarchical structure, it is very likely based on domination and occasionally force and violence. Hence, anarchism parts ways with socialism and Marxism. Anarchists insist that aim and method must match and if the aim is equality and freedom the path must not involve force and domination. Moreover, anarchists fear that even a benign elite will be corrupted by power and work to secure its own power. Where there is rule, anarchism argues, we will also find domination and self-interested abuses of power. In other words, where government exists, so by definition does dictatorship. This is so in socialist and Marxist democracies and no less in capitalist representative democracy. For anarchists, electoral and representative democracy is nothing but a masked mechanism that grants popular legitimacy to a regime that serves the power and interests of people with property and power (Chomsky, 1970). Furthermore, electoral and representative democracy keeps society adversarial. True democracy, the anarchists argue, is an anarchist democracy that rejects representation and advocates direct and participatory democracy in which sincere deliberations rule and consensual decisions are reached and inspired by communal voluntarism (Graeber, 2002; see also Chapter 8, this volume).

Other understandings challenge other aspects of the two dominant understandings of democracy. Note that these understandings are not only based on different normative worldviews, they also strive to implement specific and contrasting normative visions regarding the nature and function of democracy. Challenging these understandings and conceptions is, therefore, ipso facto, a head-on normative and political challenge to the visions they encapsulate. For example, the individualistic vision of liberalism is challenged by the communitarian vision. Not surprisingly, some communitarian understandings of democracy originate in non-Western communitarian traditions. For example, Bhikhu Parekh, the Indian-born British political theorist, who is a member of the British House of Lords, criticizes the individualist assumption of liberalism for being culture-specific, a product of the West, and so to some extent lacking in universal moral appeal (1992). He argues that a culturally adjusted democracy should take multiculturalism more seriously and enable other models of democracy that are more culturally sensitive. For Parekh, democracy should not be based on representing individual interests. He believes that the antagonistic individual is an idée fixe in this Western model. In non-Western polities, which are based on communitarian cultures, democracy can be less adversarial and more harmonious and represents communities' preferences and local cultural sensitivities. There is a word for this in the Nguni African language – ubuntu (Comaroff and Comaroff, 2009: 44). These non-Western democracies will have a multicultural thrust in which representation and popular sovereignty are based on collectives and communities.

Since the end of the Cold War, another understanding has gained some prominence: cosmopolitan democracy. This understanding fundamentally challenges the state and state system as we know it, because it questions the assumption, which is almost taken for granted, that democracy is a political system that should be confined to the modern state. The communitarian and structural (conservative) understandings normatively accept the state as the political embodiment of the national community. The liberal and many variants of the socialist understandings accept the state as a necessary political tool for realizing, maintaining, and distributing the common goods.[1]

Cosmopolitan democracy attempts to escape the confines of the state. The normative gist of democracy, shared generally by most conceptions and theories, is that everyone has the right (and responsibility) to be involved in shaping decisions and policies that can affect their lives. This is commonly translated into the all-affected principle. Those who are affected by a decision should have the right to be involved (directly or through representation) in making that decision. The traditional assumption is that our lives are affected primarily by the political unit of the state (along with some sub-state units such as the city) and therefore voting rights belong to citizens, not foreigners; or, in other words, the borders of suffrage lie at the borders of the state. For cosmopolitans like David Held (2010) and Daniele Archibugi (2008), this assumption is deeply problematic. Consider environmental and law-enforcement policies. In our deeply globalized world, environmental hazards and unchecked criminal organizations know no borders and mercilessly attack citizens regardless of any borders. The transnational effects of national policies are even more dramatic in the case of the great powers, including economic powers. When the US or European economies falter, it is not a ripple but an economic tsunami that sends the economies of other countries reeling. When the US decides its national security policy, the results are felt around the world.[2] So, how can the all-affected principle justify state borders as the borders of suffrage and confine democracy to the state? For scholars like Held, a legitimate and true democracy, a democracy that upholds the all-affected-principle, can only exist at the global level.

The cosmopolitan view is not necessarily that the state should be rejected for a cosmopolitan polity. That polity might be a monstrous bureaucracy, remote and detached from its citizens, which in the absence of states to impose checks and balances would emerge as an unrestrained and frightful global Leviathan. Held (2010) argues therefore that the global world should be organized on multiple levels where different polities crosscut each other – borders and cities, regions, states, and the world as a whole form a multilayered decentralized democracy in which we all enjoy "multilevel citizenship".

The theories and conceptions of democracy surveyed in this section have normative foundations. Definitions are the interpretative meeting point of empirical observation, experience, and moral commitment, and hence are essentially contested. They are heuristic devices that help in delineating empirical phenomena and categories from each other, and the delineation achieved is morally no less than empirically based. The same is true for many of the concepts we use and define in the social sciences, including democracy. And as we shall see below, these conceptions are not just the concern of political theorists, nor are they merely a futile scholastic splitting of hairs. They have real-world ramifications as well. However, before we examine these

[1] John Rawls presents the paradigmatic argument regarding the importance of the democratic state within the liberal theory of justice (1999a), and maintains his statist perspective even in his *The Law of Peoples* (1999b).

[2] Other cosmopolitan concerns are global poverty and distributive justice issues, and hence some cosmopolitans emphasize the moral obligation for a global overall redistribution of resources (see, for example, Peter Singer, 1972).

and the way that particular conceptions of democracy influence foreign policy/political practice in international relations, first let us examine another theoretical context, namely the way in which different conceptions of democracy affect how we theorize international relations.

Democratic Peace

We can demonstrate the inherent relation between conceptualizing democracy and theorizing international relations by focusing on a major family of IR theories: the theories of democratic peace. This section will discuss how the various conceptions of democracy play out in the democratic peace literature and how different theories of democratic peace are each grounded in a different conception of democracy.

Democratic peace theorization took off in the early 1990s and it was no accident that it surged in these years. The end of the Cold War and the emergence of a new international system characterized by more peaceful cooperation between powers was seen as the victory of the free world and proof in general of the superiority of democracy and liberal conceptions of order (Fukuyama, 1992). Optimism was on the rise and the peacefulness of the new international system and the victory of the democratic world seemed to have discredited realist theories of IR. It was believed that the end of the Cold War proved that war was not unavoidable and that the domestic features of the state were important in explaining international behavior (in terms of both intentions and outcomes). Thus, the path was clear for the rise of the liberal theories of international relations, including the democratic peace theories, which not only seemed to explain international "zones of peace" but also provided policy blueprints in support of democracy (see also Chapter 7, this volume).

In 1993, Zeev Maoz and Bruce Russett persuasively argued that two distinct theories exist – the normative and the structural – which rival each other in explaining the democratic peace phenomenon. These two theories are conceptually grounded in the two dominant understandings of democracy discussed above. That being so, we need to understand the differences between the two democratic peace theories, not just in terms of their various methodologies or the empirical evidence they mobilize, but by grasping their moral and ideational groundwork and differing conceptions of democracies (and peace). Over the years, these two theories have become more sophisticated and have probed deeper into the nature of democracy and the mechanisms that account for peaceful relations between democratic dyads. Two seminal examples demonstrate how the essential contestedness of democracy also plays out in theorizing international relations.

William Dixon's article "Democracy and the Peaceful Settlement of International Conflict" (1994) is a paradigmatic example of the normative theories of democratic peace. Dixon opens his account of the phenomenon of democratic peace by saying that we need "a clear conception of democracy" (1994: 15). And to Dixon, the essential feature of democracy, the characteristic that defines it conclusively, is the norm of bounded competition (1994: 15). Bounded competition regulates conflicts of interests, thus curbing their escalation into forceful struggles, bringing peaceful settlement. Moreover, in an act that links him to the normative and participatory understanding of democracy, Dixon ascribes fairly extensive roles to the citizens of democracies

(1994: 15). For Dixon, political processes are not, and should not be, confined to elites. Elites must be involved and indeed have an important political function, but likewise the lay citizens who must participate routinely in politics. These ideas all point to Dixon's endorsement of a normative understanding and participatory theory of democracy for theorizing democratic peace. Without these democratic norms and practices, we cannot expect peace nor would we be able to theorize democratic peace. Dixon's normative commitment to a specific conception of democracy is manifested in his theory of democratic peace.

Structural explanations of democratic peace focus on the division of power, checks and balances, and the accountability of the leadership to the public. Simply put, the structural view argues that these structural attributes slow the decision-making process, making it complex and allowing decision-makers in democratic states to settle their conflicts peacefully. This argument has developed into a very sophisticated body of literature, which analyzes how the structure of democracy generates mechanisms that reduce the chances of war between democracies.

One example of this view is the article by Bueno de Mesquita and colleagues (Bueno de Mesquita, Morrow, Siverson and Smith, 1999), which offers a behavioralist perspective that treats norms, including democratic norms, as a byproduct of structurally induced behavioral incentive. In other words, this view does not regard norms and democratic norms as independent explanatory variables but as a derivative of structure. Structure interacts with the universal incentive and a desire to achieve and retain office. This is the nexus around which the analysis is built, using selectorates and winning coalitions as explaining variables. "Selectorate" refers to all those with a right to participate in choosing a government; "winning coalitions" is a subset of the selectorate whose support is necessary to form and maintain government (1999: 793). According to this reading of politics, politicians do all they can to hold on to power. They will treat national resources as a private good for buying the support of the winning coalition. The problem for the democratic politician is not a moral but a structural one: the winning coalition is too big to be bought off with private goods (1999: 797). Thus, driven by the structural necessity, the democratic politician uses the public good allocation tactic, which means s/he will be concerned with policy failure, especially in the context of winning and losing wars, and hence will engage in fighting only when winning is predicted (1999: 794). This is very much an elitist Schumpeterian perception of democracy as just a competition within the elite over governance in which the public's only role is to walk to the ballot box every few years and decide which contestant wins.

The essential contestedness of democracy thus also affects theorizing about international relations. The normative infiltrates the explanatory through the essential contestedness of democracy, weaving them together. Normative commitments spill over into definitions and then into the act of theorizing. Thus, the normative understanding of democracy constitutes what is seen, described, and theorized in domestic and international politics. Selectorates and winning coalitions are seen kicking into action, or, alternatively, we see norms and values acting to shape and bound political behavior. The normative turns our theoretical gaze towards this or that phenomenon and where we look is what we see. And that does not just refer to what we see in and about democracy. When we define democracy, we also define its mirror image, non-democracy, and ask ourselves whether non-democracies are polities without a separation of powers, or where individual autonomy is not consolidated. The basic theoretical act of comparing and distinguishing is thus also shaped by the essential contestedness of democracy and by the normative worldview. And as we shall see in a moment, the essential contestedness of democracy also crosses from the abstract and the theoretical to the political and the realm of international politics, with some important implications for political debates and real-life actions.

From Theory to the World of International Politics

Academia discusses the correct conceptions of democracy, effective ways of promoting democracy at home and abroad, and an understanding of how democracy affects the behavior of states internationally. But ideas about democracy are not confined to the halls of academia. They are debated and used elsewhere, including in the political world. Indeed, quite often policy pundits and politicians center their political agendas and strategic designs on democracy, envisioning it as an organizing principle to be applied internationally, designing policies for promoting it abroad and mobilizing democratic norms to empower their countries. Let us now take a closer look at how conceptualizing democracy interacts with the political world.

One would be hard pressed to find examples of politicians adopting cosmopolitan conceptions of democracy as their visionary organizing principle. This is because cosmopolitan democracy would undermine the sovereignty of their states and create a dynamic for global integration. This is very obvious in the context of the UN, the most global institution of governance. The cosmopolitan orientation of the UN is checked and undermined by the sovereignty of states. Consider the General Assembly's "one state one voice" principle. This democratic principle clashes fundamentally with cosmopolitan democracy on two fronts: first, it ignores population size. Why does Mauritius with its population of one million have the same voice as India with 1.2 billion? Each Mauritian is represented more powerfully than any Indian, which is hardly consistent with notions of cosmopolitan democracy. The same is true for the membership of non-democracies in the UN. How can a state like North Korea "represent its citizens"? So sovereignty is enshrined over democracy in the UN General Assembly. And things are no better in the Security Council where the veto powers of the five permanent members belie democracy.

Perhaps the closest approximation to cosmopolitan democracy in international politics is Robert Schuman's vision for Europe following the Second World War. That vision, although far from fully implemented, did guide the European Union in its policies of integration and enlargement. But although democracy is a cornerstone of EU identity and institutional design, Schuman's vision and the institutional reality built on it have remained only regional in scope. Other plans for internationalizing democracy are more global in reach, but limited in their functioning logic. They opt to divide the world into "us" and "them", "us" being the democracies, "them" being the autocracies (Kupchan, 2008: 97). Hence, democracy as an organizing principle works to divide the world, not to integrate it into one cosmopolis. Some of those plans emerged in the US and were fashioned to serve American interests (Alessandri,

2008: 83; Carothers, 2008: 46; Geis, 2013: 263). One such plan, the Community of Democracies, was conceived at the end of the Cold War by President Bill Clinton and his advisors, together with Polish Foreign Minister, Bronisław Geremek. It was intended as a framework for bringing together the world's democracies into a single functioning community. The plan sought to use the end of the Cold War as a window of opportunity to promote democracy in countries that renounced communism and dictatorship. As its name implies, the idea was to establish a wide cooperative community with democracy as its organizing principle both within and between states. However, notwithstanding its good intentions, the Community remains little more than a debating club (Kupchan, 2008: 97) and though it still exists, few expect much of it.

A decade and a half later, an academic initiative sparked a wave of similar schemes. In 2006, following two years of intensive work, a Princeton team published the "Princeton Project on National Security". Described as bipartisan and directed by two Princeton professors, Anne-Marie Slaughter and John Ikenberry, the project hoped to develop a new American national strategy. Focusing on national security and believing that security is best served by a balance of order (read law and liberal democracy) and liberty, one of its highly publicized and contested proposals was the establishment of a Concert of Democracies. This concert would act as a new international organization aimed at "forging a world of liberty under law" (Princeton Project on National Security, 2006: 20). The report states that the system of international organizations orchestrated by the US after the Second World War no longer worked and that the world lacks an organizing principle. Among other measures and principles, the remedy was democracy. Other proposals came (and went) in its wake. One was by Ivo Daalder and James Lindsay (2007) and another was by Senator McCain in his 2008 presidential campaign (2007). Despite their liberal optimism, the different schemes worked not so much as a universal organizing principle but as a dividing principle, where democracies belonged on one side united by a community or concert, and non-democracies were cast into the other camp. This was a major source of criticism leveled at those schemes; they were seen as splitting rather than uniting, contributing further to global schisms. Another problem associated with those schemes, which rendered them futile, was that they were considered American-centered, serving American interests, and attempting to prevent America's decline. No wonder few Europeans embraced those schemes, which could not succeed without their support (Geis, 2013: 273). Moreover, the idea of a concert of democracies was promoted in the context of the so-called Global War on Terror and, within it, the declared American attempt to coerce Afghanistan and Iraq into democratizing.

Exporting democracy has long been a tradition of US foreign policy, at least since Woodrow Wilson (Smith, 1994; Cox, Lynch, and Bouchet, 2013). However, and this is a fundamental change, the strategic merits of democracy established by the democratic peace thesis have reversed the link between democracy and security. By insisting on the scientific validity of the claim that democracies do not fight each other, the Bush administration could argue the strategic merits of exporting democracy and hence try to legitimize war aimed at regime change in Iraq as a war aimed at positive regional transformation and, ultimately, peace. Unlike Wilson, for Bush, it was not a question of making the world safe for democracy but of making democracy safe for the world:

> We know from history that free nations are peaceful nations. We know that democracies do not attack each other, and that young people growing up in a free and hopeful society are less likely to fall under the sway of radicalism. And so we're taking the side of democratic leaders and reformers across the Middle East ... We will replace violent dictatorships with peaceful democracies. We'll make America, the Middle East, and the world more secure. (Bush, 2006: n.p.)

Democracy promotion became the new creed. This was evident not only in the Afghanistan and Iraq wars but also in the Greater Middle East and North Africa project of building a democratic alliance, and in the 2002 US National Security Strategy which institutionalized democracy promotion as the main strategy for fighting global terrorism (White House, 2002: Foreword). There was an added urgency to the agenda of exporting democracy in the form of security reasoning, or securitization (see Chapter 3, this volume).

The liberal and conservative conceptions of democracy not only shape the grand visions of exporting democracy but also the tactical and concrete policies of democratization. If democracy is understood as structure and as an elite project, then promoting democracy will be understood as a top-down building of the structural attributes of democracy, a relatively easy and swift political act. Alternatively, if democracy is conceptualized as a moral and cultural political phenomenon, then democracy promotion will focus on disseminating democratic norms and values in an intricate, slow, daunting process, mainly on the level of civil society, that both necessitates and enables broad participation and effective deliberation. As conservatives and neoconservatives, Bush and his top advisers conceived democracy mainly in structural terms and assumed that these structures could be grafted onto any set of norms and values since structure is almost bereft of normative content. For them, the democratic structure – the separation of powers, checks and balances, and periodic elections – could rather easily be exported to, promoted and installed in any society and religion.

Moreover, democratization could be achieved by military means. If democratizing other countries pacifies them and secures regional stability, then democratization is a vital US interest. And if democratizing is a top-down business, then that interest can and should be attained militarily, even in the face of massive resistance (see Boot, 2003; Donnelly and Kristol, 2004). Hence, the Bush administration expected to succeed in democratizing Afghanistan and Iraq at gunpoint. They believed that regime change would unleash the universal aspiration to freedom among the local populations who would seize the opportunity to lock up their former oppressors and realize their yearnings. They would cooperate with the Western liberators/occupiers in building the structure of democracy and the occupying army would create the conditions for these reforms. Thus, the occupying army would be able to graft a democratic structure onto a nation which, while readily welcoming it (or doing so with the help of a tamed elite), would also maintain what could not be changed: namely its civilizational identity, norms, and culture. However, as we know, the project ended in bitter failure. Iraq slipped into civil war and endless and bloody insurgency, dragging the US into evermore questionable and illegitimate counterinsurgency practices. Promoting democracy failed dismally and with it went the whole agenda of promoting democracy. Furthermore, the legitimacy of the US as a promoter of democracy was damaged, together with its global standing.

This process of delegitimizing the US as a global leader has strengthened an ongoing process that involves another aspect of democracy as a debated and contested ordering principle in international politics: it is not only statist actors and mainstream intellectuals who participate in this debate, but also more radical groups. Many of these groups came under the loose association of an anti-globalization movement that formed in the early 1990s, criticizing the neo-liberal world order, the dominant economic and political role of corporations, environmental degradation, etc. During George W. Bush's presidency, this movement targeted American global hegemony more than ever before. Among the contentious issues raised by the activists was the mainstream and statist understanding of democracy and its importance as an ordering principle of world politics. As Naomi Klein's rhetorical question exemplified so eloquently, are American-led globalization and representative democracy tied together, "Or is globalization, at its core, a crisis of representative democracy in which power and decision-making are delegated to points further and further away from the places where the effects of those decisions are felt – until representative democracy means voting for politicians every few years who use that mandate to transfer national powers to the WTO and the IMF" (2002: 9). Klein's scorn leads to a political agenda in which democracy indeed plays a crucial role, but it is a different sort of democracy: a true participatory democracy "seeking to increase popular control of political and economic life in the face of increasingly powerful corporations, unaccountable global financial institutions, and US hegemony" (Engler, 2007: 150–1; see also Ross, 2003: 281). Thus, the anti-globalization movement's vision is the mirror image of the neoconservative one. It is not an elitist-led hierarchal structure but "an activist model that mirrors the organic, decentralized, interlinked pathways of the Internet – the Internet come to life" (Klein, 2002: 5). And this anarchical network of a democracy attempts to eschew further the global standing of the US that, for the activists, is the harbinger of the autocratic corporate sham otherwise known as democracy.

Conclusion

This chapter has examined different aspects of democracy and its functioning in theory and practice. In the real world of politics, democracy serves as an organizing principle, a normative guide and motivator to action. The ways in which democracy functions politically can be traced to how it is conceptualized and defined. As an essentially contested concept, defining democracy is not merely a methodological hurdle but an interpretative meeting between empirical observations, experience, and moral commitment. The definitions are political and normative projects no less than scientific necessities. Defining and conceptualizing democracy demands a specific normative foundation and assumptions about human nature. It also involves challenging the moral and political visions of alternative definitions. As Gallie perceptively argued, defining and using an essentially contested concept is always both a defensive and an aggressive move (1956: 172, 187).

Thus, we cannot expect the various conceptions of democracy to be somehow incrementally fine-tuned and cohered into a single scientific definition accepted across the board. We see the impossibility of this not only from the various political projects surveyed in the chapter's last section and the political theories in the first section, but also from the second section where we saw that each of the two main theories of democratic peace, the normative and the structural, are based on different conceptions of democracy: the former on the normative, participatory conception and the latter on the minimalist, structural conception. It seems that international relations is also nourished by conceptual and normative discussions about the essentially contested concept of democracy as well as by other concepts. Hence, when studying international politics, there is no avoiding the elastic, fuzzy, historicist, and essential contestedness character of concepts.

Suggested Readings

Bridoux, J. and M. Kurki (2014). *Democracy Promotion: A Critical Introduction*, London: Routledge.

Employing critical theory, the authors examine the policy agenda of democracy promotion with an eye to the political dynamics and power relations involved in shaping and performing it.

Crick, B. (2002). *Democracy: A Very Short Introduction*, Oxford: Oxford University Press.

A very concise and vivid account, by a leading political theorist who was also involved in politics, of the idea, history, and practice of democracy; an account which is sensitive to the plurality of democracy's understandings and conceptions.

Cunningham, F. (2002). *Theories of Democracy: A Critical Introduction*, London: Routledge.

A clear overview and analysis of the main contemporary theories of democracy and the keystone theorists behind them.

Dickson, D. (2014). *The People's Government: An Introduction to Democracy*, Cambridge: Cambridge University Press.

Through analyzing the values of freedom and liberty, the author offers a multi-dimensional study of democracies and their life-cycle, with an emphasis on the US.

Held, D. (2006). *Models of Democracy*, 3rd edn, Stanford, CA: Stanford University Press.

The third edition of a contemporary classic that surveys theories of democracy from Athens to our day, with a special chapter on cosmopolitan democracy in the current global system.

Bibliography

Alessandri, Emiliano (2008). World Order Re-founded: The Idea of a Concert of Democracies. *The International Spectator: Italian Journal of International Affairs*, 43(1), 73–90.

Archibugi, Daniele (2008). *The Global Commonwealth of Citizens: Toward Cosmopolitan Democracy*, Princeton, NJ: Princeton University Press.

Aristotle (2009). *Politics*, new edn, trans. Ernest Barker, Oxford: Oxford University Press.

Barber, Benjamin (1984). *Strong Participatory Politics for a New Age*, Berkeley, CA: University of California Press.

Boot, Max (2003). What Next? The Bush Foreign Policy Agenda beyond Iraq. *The Weekly Standard*, May 5: 27–33.

Bueno de Mesquita, Bruce, James D. Morrow, Randolph M. Siverson, and Alastair Smith (1999). An Institutional Explanation of the Democratic Peace. *American Political Science Review*, 93(4), 791–807.

Burke, Edmund (1987). *Reflections on the Revolution in France*, ed. J.G.A. Pocock, Indianapolis, IN: Hackett Pub. Co.

Bush, George W. (2006). President Bush Discusses Progress in the Global War on Terror. Cobb Galleria Centre, Atlanta, Georgia, 7 September. Accessed at http://georgewbush-whitehouse.archives.gov/news/releases/2006/09/20060907-2.html (9 July 2014).

Carothers, Thomas (2008). A League of their Own. *Foreign Policy*, 167, Jul.–Aug.: 44–49.

Chomsky, Noam (1970). Notes on Anarchism. *New York Review of Books*, 14(10), May 21: 31–5.

Cohen, Joshua and Joel Rogers (1983). *On Democracy: Toward a Transformation of American Society*, London: Penguin Books.

Comaroff, John L. and Jean Comaroff (2009). *Ethnicity, Inc.* Chicago and London: University of Chicago Press.

Cox, Michael, Timothy J. Lynch, and Nicolas Bouchet, eds (2013). *US Foreign Policy and Democracy Promotion: From Theodore Roosevelt to Barack Obama*. London: Routledge.

Daalder, Ivo and James Lindsay (2007). Democracies of the World Unite. *Public Policy Research*, 14(1), 47–58.

Dixon, William J. (1994). Democracy and the Peaceful Settlement of International Conflict. *American Political Science Review*, 88(1), 14–32.

Donnelly, Tom and William Kristol (2004). More Caissons Rolling Along. *Weekly Standard*, 9 February: 7–8.

Dryzek, John S. (2002). *Deliberative Democracy and Beyond: Liberals, Critics, Contestations*, Oxford: Oxford University Press.

Elster, Jon (1998). *Deliberative Democracy*, Cambridge: Cambridge University Press.

Engler, Mark (2007). Defining the Anti-Globalization Movement. In Gary L. Anderson and Kathryn G. Her, eds, *The Encyclopedia of Activism and Social Justice*, Thousand Oaks, CA: Sage, pp. 150–155.

Freedom House (2013). *Freedom in the World 2013*, Available at: www.freedomhouse.org/report/freedom-world/freedom-world-2013#.Uxyzqj9mPTp

Fukuyama, Francis (1992). *The End of History and the Last Man*, New York: Free Press.

Gallie, Walter Bryce. (1956). Essentially Contested Concepts. *Proceedings of the Aristotelian Society*, 56: 167–198.

Geis, Anna (2013). The 'Concert of Democracies': Why Some States are more Equal than Others. *International Politics*, 50(2), 257–277.

Graeber, David (2002). The New Anarchists. *New Left Review*, 13: 61–73.

Habermas, Jürgen (1998). *Between Facts and Norms: Contributions to a Discourse Theory of Law and Democracy*, trans. William Rehg, Cambridge, MA: MIT Press.

Held, David (2010). *Cosmopolitanism: Ideals and Realities*, Cambridge: Polity Press.

Hobson, Christopher (2009). Beyond the End of History: The Need for a 'Radical Historicisation' of Democracy in International Relations. *Millennium: Journal of International Studies*, 37(3), 627–653.

Holston, James (2008). *Insurgent Citizenship: Disjunctions of Democracy and Modernity in Brazil*. Princeton, NJ and Oxford: Princeton University Press.

Ish-Shalom, Piki (2006). The Triptych of Realism, Elitism, and Conservatism. *International Studies Review*, 8(3), 463–464.

Ish-Shalom, Piki (2008). The Rhetorical Capital of Theories: The Democratic Peace and the Road to the Roadmap. *International Political Science Review*, 29(3), 281–301.

Klein, Naomi (2002). Farewell to 'The End of History': Organization and Vision in Anti-Corporate Movements. *Socialist Register*, 38: 1–14.

Kupchan, Charles A. (2008). Minor League, Major Problems: The Case against a League of Democracies. *Foreign Affairs*, 87(6), 96–109.

Kurki, Milja. (2010). Democracy and Conceptual Contestability: Reconsidering Conceptions of Democracy in Democracy Promotion. *International Studies Review*, 12(3), 362–386.

Lijphart, Arend. 1999. *Patterns of Democracy*, New Haven, CT: Yale University Press.
Lippmann, Walter (1955). *Essays in the Public Philosophy*, Boston, MA and Toronto: Little, Brown and Co.
Luxemburg, Rosa (1961). *The Russian Revolution, and Leninism Or Marxism?* Ann Arbor, MI: University of Michigan Press.
Mansbridge, Jane J. (1970). *Beyond Adversary Democracy*, Chicago and London: University of Chicago Press.
Maoz, Zeev and Bruce Russett (1993). Normative and Structural Causes of Democratic Peace, 1946–1986. *American Political Science Review*, 87(3), 624–638.
McCain, John (2007). An Enduring Peace Built on Freedom Securing America's Future. *Foreign Affairs*, Nov.–Dec.: 19–34.
Meyer, Thomas with Lewis Hinchman (2007). *The Theory of Social Democracy*, Cambridge: Polity.
Mutz, Diana Carole (2006). *Hearing the Other Side: Deliberative Versus Participatory Democracy*, Cambridge: Cambridge University Press.
Parekh, Bhikhu (1992). The Cultural Particularity of Liberal Democracy, *Political Studies*, 40(Suppl.), 160–175.
Pateman, Carole (1970). *Participation and Democratic Theory*, Cambridge: Cambridge University Press.
Princeton Project on National Security (2006). *Forging a World of Liberty under Law: US National Security in the 21st Century*, Princeton, NJ: The Woodrow Wilson School of Public and International Affairs, Princeton University.
Przeworski, Adam (1999). Minimalist Conception of Democracy: A Defense. In Ian Shapiro and Cassiano Hacker-Cordon, eds, *Democracy's Value*, Cambridge: Cambridge University Press, pp. 23–55.
Rawls, John (1999a). *A Theory of Justice*, revised edn, Cambridge, MA: Belknap Press of Harvard University Press.
Rawls, John (1999b). *The Law of Peoples*. Cambridge, MA and London: Harvard University Press.
Ross, Stephanie (2003). Is this what Democracy Looks Like? The Politics of the Anti-Globalization Movement in North America. *Socialist Register*, 39: 281–304.
Russett, Bruce (1993). *Grasping the Democratic Peace: Principles for a Post-Cold War World*, Princeton, NJ: Princeton University Press.
Singer, Peter (1972). Famine, Affluence, and Morality. *Philosophy & Public Affairs*, 1(3), 229–243.
Schumpeter, Joseph A. (1962). *Capitalism, Socialism and Democracy*, 3rd edn, New York: Harper Torchbooks.
Smith, Tony (1994). *America's Mission: The United States and the Worldwide Struggle for Democracy in the Twentieth Century*, Princeton, NJ: Princeton University Press.
White House (2002). *The National Security of the United States*, 17 September.

14

Religion

Maria Birnbaum

> I have portrayed matters of religion as the focal point of enlightenment, i.e. of man's emergence from his self-incurred immaturity ... because religious immaturity is the most pernicious and dishonorable variety of all. (Immanuel Kant 1991 [1784]: 59)

Until recently, scholars of international relations (IR) paid limited attention to the question of religion. As a discipline developed and dominated by Western scholarship, IR and political science more generally had approached its objects of study through a framework of the modern and the rational, both of which explicitly refrained from engaging with the religious. Indeed, with the secular seen both as a normative necessity of the modern state and its historical evolution characteristic of modernity, the relevance of religion was expected to decline as modern society developed (Berger 1999: 2ff; Casanova 1994; Kippenberg 2003; Weber 1988 [1920]). In addition, the current international order was considered to have emerged at a point in time when religion had been separated from politics, at the Peace of Westphalia in 1648. Religion was considered best kept private and not allowed to interfere with public politics and certainly not politics of international concern. Finally, the community of IR scholars and the discipline they constituted were increasingly rooted in a positivist method and rationalist ontology that were unable to provide a quantitative measurement of the "intangible" or accommodate the "non-rational" or "irrational". In short, religion did not belong in international relations or the study of it.

Yet, with the start of the century, voices have been growing to include religion in both the practice and study of international affairs. The strong presence of religious references in global conflicts has triggered a wave of international scholarship on religion across theoretical divides (Kratochwil 2005; Petito/Hatzopoulos 2003; Snyder 2011). Religion is seen both "at the root of modern international relations" and the present Westphalian international order (Philpott 2000: 206) and as an integral part of the institutions of war and diplomacy that "should be recognised as part of any post-Westphalian international order" (Thomas 2000: 816). Further, efforts to involve religion in international peacebuilding missions, global health initiatives, or democracy development has allowed large international organizations and institutions to ask their state members and consulting experts for more "religious competence" (Hurd 2015).

Of course, religion had not disappeared from the international realm but, in fact, had structured and been structured by it long before IR emerged as a discipline. In imperial Britain and Spain, for example, questions regarding the treatment of colonial subjects were often answered with reference to religious scripture to authorize – but also to challenge – racial hierarchies and discrimination (Todorov 1999). International affairs also structured the way in which scholars and practitioners think about religion and what is perceived to be religious. A recent example is the right to religious freedom, which grants the right of individuals to practise and live according to their religious tenets (Sullivan et al. 2015). In order to gain protection under this right, one must be recognizably religious in the eyes of those who extend the protection. According to the "International Religious Freedom Act" (IRFA), a foreign policy instrument of the US set to protect and promote the religious freedom of individuals and groups, "religious" individuals belong to discrete faith communities with identifiable leaders and bounded orthodoxies (Hurd 2015). Individuals and groups who do not fit this conception cannot claim protection under the IRFA, unless they adjust to the understanding of religion used by the institution and, thereby, become recognizable to it.[1] This points to the power of conventions and even the foreign policies of particular states to shape the scope and meaning of religion in international affairs and, as such, constitute "religion".

In this chapter, I will not argue that religion is to be excluded or included in IR. Rather, I ask what the concept of religion in IR refers to and will attend to some of the processes that have shaped and are shaping the meaning of the concept. In starting to disentangle this web of meanings, it is useful to see religion as a basic concept that works on three levels: on the one hand, it is a first-order concept used by actors to describe, make sense of and justify their versions of the good, of community and of international political orders. It can be traced through the ways people talk and write (discourses), act (practices) and usually deal with religion (institutions), all of which have consequences that can be analyzed. But religion is also a second-order or generic concept used by scholars to explain, and by policymakers to make sense of and control, a world that exceeds in complexity (Smith 1998). Finally, the first and second levels of the use of religion can be analyzed from a third level, a so-called meta level of analysis. Here, students and scholars can analyze the assumptions made about religion and the consequences of different ways of using it. This is the perspective taken here.

The etymological roots of the term are a matter of debate. One major point of reference is the writings of Roman consul Marcus Tullius Cicero who treated it in its contrast to *superstitio* as the correct performance of the cultic practices in the general worship of gods. Not directed towards a true or correct inner "faith", Cicero derived *religio* from *relegere* – to "treat again" or "reread" that which belongs to the venation of the gods (Feil 1986: 39–49, 60–64; Kehrer 1998). *Religio* as the notion of a "correct cult" never completely disappeared from the language of Christian culture (Feil 1986: 78). In the 4th century AD, the Latin Rhetoric Lactantius, seeking to integrate the concept with the biblical Creator, derived religion from

[1] The international politics of religion is visible in the fates of the Chinese Falun Gong, the Egyptian Bahá'í, and the Burmese Rohingya, to name a few.

religare or *religari*, which implied a binding to a transcendent God and the praise of the one true Deity (Flood 1999: 47, 60–64). Into the 19th century, and partly further still, the connotation of "religion" was the Christian one of a "bond" between a transcendent Deity and man (Kippenberg/von Stuckrad 2003: 63). By the 16th century, the term had come to have a more general connotation as the source of truth, and with the Deists and the Enlightenment it became the abstract category which we have inherited (Feil 1986: 273–281; Flood 1999). This European notion of religion, however, seldom had equivalents in other cultures, or even in other European epochs. The Greek tradition had concepts like *eusébeia* (reverence), *sebos* (awe) and *threskéia* (service), which all connect to our understanding of religion but which were applied far beyond any religious arena (Fowden 1999). The concept of "dîn" in Islamic traditions, with its denotations of "custom", "tradition", "justice", or "law", indicates a much broader meaning than religion, as does "dharma" in the Vedic traditions describing the rules controlling social and religious life and order (Emon 2012; Hock 2008). The fact that IR scholarship seems to uncritically adopt a concept defined by the relation between the biblical Creator and man should at least make us ask how this plays out in a discipline that, by definition, stretches far beyond this particular Christian context. This is what this chapter tries to do.

Specifically, the chapter follows the concept of religion through different contexts and outlines (a) what religion meant, (b) how these meanings were shaped, and (c) their political and social consequences. In other words, I will trace the concept through international history and try to drive home the point that it is contested, political and necessarily vague, but nevertheless a powerful concept for an analysis of the international. The discussion is structured in four parts. The first section, "Religion and Westphalia", will look at accounts of the Westphalian Peace and find a broad palette of meanings of religion connected to a variety of institutions, ideas and identities. The second section, "Religion and the Colony", will read colonial history as part of the emergence of religion as a relevant political category in international affairs and trace the governing practices enabled thereby. The third section, "Religion and the Secular", enters the recent debate on secularism in international political theory and shows how different understandings of the secular have been productive of the meaning of religion. I will end with an argument for an approach to religion that goes beyond debating its inclusion and exclusion in the IR discipline.

Religion and Westphalia

The Peace of Westphalia has become an "icon" in international relations and is regarded as the beginning of the current international system (Krasner 1993: 235; Osiander 2001: 251).[2] It refers to the settlement of conflicts throughout Europe in the 16th and 17th centuries in which the authority of the Catholic Church was questioned

[2] This account of Westphalia has been under critique by scholars who either question its historical accuracy (Krasner 1993; Osiander 2001; Spruyt 1994; Werner/de Wilde 2001) or the way in which it stabilizes a particular status quo of international politics, ordering and limiting the thinking of IR scholars (Bartelson 2009; Campbell 1992; Kratochwil 1986). In the eyes of these critics, Westphalia is a "myth" (Osiander 2001).

by "Protestant" alliances following the Christian Reformation, and the power of the Holy Roman Empire and its Habsburg-held crown was challenged by princes of the surrounding estates. As a consequence of the conflicts and their settlement, so the story goes, the modern international order of sovereign, equal and territorially bound states started taking shape. Apart from lending its name to the international system of sovereign states, Westphalia is also seen to mark the move from a religious to a modern, secular world, from the idea of Europe as unified by Christendom to a system – or society – of independent states (see also Chapter 11, this volume).

Westphalia is not only seen as the emancipation of the political realm from the religious but also as the birth of the principle of – religious – toleration by establishing the equality between Protestant and Catholic states and by providing safeguards for religious minorities (Gross 1948: 5; Krasner 1993: 242ff.). After almost a century of wars that had largely been fought within a religious framework, it seemed necessary to bracket religious issues from the international domain to secure peace and order. The European "Wars of Religion" of 1550–1650 had shown that, when religion was brought into public life, it caused political upheaval, intolerance and war, destabilizing the international order (Connolly 1999). With the Diet of Augsburg in 1555, religious toleration was settled on as an international norm – "Cujus Regio ejus Religio" (no interference with the religious of other territories). The Treaty of Osnabrück in 1648 further limited the ruler's power over the religious within his own territory and called on him to tolerate recognized – Catholic, Lutheran and Calvinist – confessions (Asch 1997; von Druffel 1896: 722ff.). Thus, in a succession of treaties religion was being "privatized" to keep the international order peaceful. According to the conventional story, Westphalia thereby also separated religion from politics (Krasner 1993; Skinner 1978). As Stephen Krasner puts it, the Westphalian Peace "delegitimized the already waning transnational role of the Catholic Church and validated the idea that international relations should be driven by balance-of-power considerations rather than the ideals of Christendom" (2001: 21). The "secularizing spirit" of this settlement then expanded through the globalization of the Westphalian state system "to a global dominion that still endures" (Philpott 2002: 71). In this sense, Westphalia secularized the international system.

Another reading of the Westphalian Peace highlights that religion did not disappear from the world stage but, rather, shaped the settlement itself and therefore lies at the heart of the international order that emerged from it. Religion, in other words, is at the very center of Westphalia. The idea here is that Westphalia brought peace to a conflict that had emerged as a consequence of the Protestant Reformation's challenge to the authority of the Catholic Church and its allied empire. The new ideas of Martin Luther in 1517 – challenging the authority of the Pope, the source of divine knowledge, and arguing for a separation of the political and the religious realm – were made increasingly available through developments in the printing press. These ideas influenced the political setting, on the one hand, through the transformation of identities of the individuals who adopted them. On the other hand, the ideas had a political impact through the social position of those who adopted these new identities. This way, the Protestant ideas became materially embodied and allied with the princes in their struggle against the Catholic Roman Empire. The polities that "experienced a Reformation crisis [the Protestant challenge to Catholic authority] were the same ones that adopted an interest in Westphalia" (Philpott 2000: 207). "No Reformation, no

Westphalia", as Daniel Philpott puts it. Accordingly, the Westphalian order would never have emerged, were it not for the way in which the Reformation and Protestant ideas of political authority shaped the polities' interests in sovereign statehood (Philpott 2000: 244; 2002: 66f., 93).

Yet another account highlights the centrality of religion to Westphalia. Here, religion was, indeed, separated from the realms of the political but done so by a change in the meaning of the concept itself. According to Scott Thomas, 16th-century Europe was still deeply infused with religious authority. It drew the lines between communities, shaped the form and content of its practices and gave legitimacy to social and political hierarchies. As the sovereign state emerged, it needed to transfer the ultimate loyalty of its population from religion to the state in order to consolidate the state's power. The "previous [intellectual and social] discipline of religion was taken over by the state, which was given the legitimate monopoly on the use of power and coercion in society" (Thomas 2000: 822).

The only way, however, of separating religion – and its previous disciplinary power – from the realms of the state was to reject the way in which this very state power and international society depended on it. A new version of religion was needed, a "modern" version which could be much more easily accessed and controlled. The new religion – as an abstract, privately held belief – was to remain in the private sphere and not interfere with public matters of the state or the international system (Thomas 2000, 2003, 2005). After Westphalia, Thomas writes, religion lost its attachment to community and practices and became privatized in the abstract form of belief and conscience. This, Thomas continues, not only furnishes a false picture of Westphalia as the secularization of international relations, but also skews an understanding of the international "resurgence of religion" today. This seems especially problematic in the global South, or other regions that never experienced the Westphalian "privatization" of religion but where it retained its social and political power. Leaving the "Westphalian presumption" at work, the global resurgence of religion seems like the internationalization of a private matter, the reemergence of something that should have long since retreated into the inner life of individual people. From this perspective, the increased international importance of religion lurks as a threat to the Westphalian "secular" settlement and its international order and stability (Thomas 2003: 24).

Concept and consequences

These different stories about the Westphalian Peace carry with them different understandings of the concept of religion and its role in international politics. The first version of Westphalia saw religion retreating in light of the emerging sovereign state. The new Westphalian system recognized the state as the dominant actor "replacing the transnational authority of the Catholic Church" (Thomas 2000: 54). The following "secularization" of Europe, the separation of religion and politics, mainly refers to the Catholic Church's loss of authority and influence. Religion, in this sense, was the institution of the Catholic Church. But religion did not simply retreat in the form of a weakening Church. This "secularization" was joined with the view that the destructive violence of the "Wars of Religion" could only be contained if the meaning of life, the divine source of morality and the proper conduct for life after death were detached from the public realm and located in the private sphere (Connolly 1999: 19–25). In this sense, religion was a collection of ideas, norms, doctrine and the beliefs therein.

Similarly, the story about religion at the heart of Westphalia is a story about the power of ideas. Here, Protestant ideas transgressed individual communities and shaped the identities and actions of those who embodied them. Religion was not necessarily tied to the religious institution or practices of the Roman Catholic Church, but rather referred to the ideas that came to affect individuals regardless of social, political or religious belonging. Religion, in this sense, referred to ideas which shaped identities and spurred action. Our last account, however, stated that precisely this understanding of religion – as abstract ideas detached from community – was an invention that the emerging sovereign state needed in order to consolidate its power. Religion had to become private in order not to interfere with matters of the state. Here, religion emerged as a two-headed creature, once carrying a social meaning referring to the practices of a particular community and, later, in its "modern" version, as the abstract set of principles and ideas that has come to manifest itself most dominantly among scholarly accounts of the Westphalian Peace.

What are the consequences in the analysis of world politics today if we use a "modern" concept of religion, that is, if we use an abstract concept detached from the social context from which it emerged? What does it mean for international politics to use the European Westphalian state as a model for all political communities and to view religion as an abstract and privately held set of ideas and the beliefs therein, located outside the public realm? This account may allow conventional IR literature to comfortably assume the secular nature of international relations, but how does it structure an understanding of world politics when religion is brought into the picture? Most obviously, it will make societies where religion is part of public and political everyday life, appear deviant at best and dangerous at worst. Assuming the presence of religion in international politics to be the internationalization of a private matter will risk misunderstanding societies where religion is an integral part of a struggle for independence or a source of public authority. Further, assuming religion to be an abstract body of doctrines or ideas that structures people's behavior and actions ignores the notion that ideas are not independent of practice. While ideas influence what people do, they can themselves also be the rationalization of the actions and practices conducted in their name. Practices not only flow from ideas but also constitute them (Asad 1993, 2003).

It is important to see that the assumption of an international system filled with secular Westphalian states carries with it the concept of religion as a privatized set of ideas that has no place in international politics. It reaffirms and globalizes a very particular understanding of what religion is, empowers those who can claim this version of religion, naturalizing it, and sidelines the debates and struggles on how this present state of affairs came to be. Moreover, it sidelines the fact that the Peace of Westphalia was a European and, thus, a provincial settlement, one of numerous possibilities of structuring the relation between the religious and the political. And yet, this arrangement is assumed to be necessary for the sovereign state in general.[3] Against this backdrop, we need to treat the agenda of (re)turning attention to the

[3] For a critique of the globalization of the local settlement of Westphalia, see Hurd (2008).

concept of religion with some caution. Indeed, while the main story about the Westphalian settlement is problematic as it construes religion as an inherent threat to international order, simply "including religion" in the study and practice of international relations is not the solution. Like all basic concepts, religion is political and bound to the setting and history in which it features. And so to include *a particular understanding* of religion risks stabilizing and reinforcing the meaning of the concept as defined and enforced by powerful actors and those who benefit from it, while sidelining those who do not. I will return to this argument in the conclusion.

Religion and the Colony

Westphalia did not expel religion from international affairs. Rather, religion featured in different shapes and forms throughout the centuries. Most of the time, it was synonymous with European Christianity but this began to change during the 19th century when other so-called "world religions" emerged in the salons of Europe's intellectuals, challenging Christianity's monopoly. Whereas Islam and Muslims came to feature prominently on the map of international relations, today Indian Hindus and Sinhalese Buddhists, evangelical Christians and orthodox Jews also receive attention from IR scholars. Yet any acknowledgment that world affairs are permeated by different "world religions" must be mindful, once again, that this concept grows out of a very specific European tradition interwoven with theories of racial and linguistic hierarchies.

As Tomoko Masuzawa shows, 19th-century European intellectuals structured the debate on "world religions" through an evolutionary lens that regarded certain languages, peoples and religions as superior and as evolving without any external influence. This ability to develop by themselves carried the term inflection. Whereas "Indo-Germanic" or "Aryan" languages, peoples and religions, such as Buddhism and Christianity, were seen to have a great ability to progress by themselves – containing a high level of inflection – this ability was seen as very limited in Semitic languages, peoples and religions, making them hard and rigid. This taxonomy generated and endorsed the strongly hierarchical ordering of religions and nations by "attributing authenticity, creativity, freedom, and therefore the capacity for indefinite growth and expansion to some nations, while relegating other languages and nations to various branches of developmental dead-ends" (Masuzawa 2005: 209). While the interest in categorizing religions dissipated at the end of the 19th century, the specific representations for the major religions seem to have endured. Buddhism is still largely perceived as an originally humanistic and humanitarian religion, while Islam as a Semitic religion is widely considered rigid and unable to evolve and adapt to modern forms of political government, binding it to violence and intolerance. (For work on Buddhism and IR, see Fierke 2013; Patomäki 2002.) The naturalization, rationalization and legitimization of these categories – Buddhism, Aryan, Semitic, or the idea of "world religion" – disguises the fact that they were built on a speculative logic within a racial and linguistic hierarchical worldview. This is a problem since these terms are used today as neutral descriptions by scholars and politicians and in everyday language.

Embedded in hierarchical worldviews, it is not surprising that the concept of religion features prominently in colonial history. Yet it was not only an instrument of imperial governance, used to legitimize violence and to divide and rule colonial subjects. Religion was also an instrument of emancipation that was mobilized to unite a divided population and legitimize its struggle for postcolonial independence. As such, it was central to the development of international relations during the last major transformation of the international order, namely the process of decolonialization after the Second World War, when political borders and boundaries were drawn along acclaimed "religious" lines.

A good example to illustrate this is the international recognition of Pakistan in 1947. The state of Pakistan was claimed, enacted and subsequently recognized along the lines of religious difference between Muslim and non-Muslim British India.[4] This difference was said to be constitutive of the state and by being recognized by other states in the international system it gained international relevance. However, international actors assumed this "religious difference" to already exist and paid little or no attention to the way in which these differences had taken shape and become politically relevant, or the way in which the process of international recognition itself had contributed to their stabilization. Rather than depicting religious difference as a stable category parting people and land, let me outline some of the processes by which these differences were manifested and became internationally salient.

The first and probably most obvious way in which religion emerged on the political radar in British India was through the Indian census. The British colonial government conducted a census in India every ten years, beginning at the end of the 19th century. This census was intended to serve as a "scientific" basis for knowledge about Indian local society, mapping the population according to professions, language, caste, religion, etc. The Indian Hindus, Muslims, Sikhs and Christians therefore became "countable" as communal entities (Talbot/Singh 2009). According to the strength in numbers, these groups were to be politically represented in the local parliaments. The census therefore linked religion to political representation, power and patronage and contributed to homogenizing the heterogeneous group of Indian Muslims into a politically representative entity. Although the close connection between the census, political representation and power was highly charged and widely challenged, it remained influential until the very end of British rule.[5] The census thus played an important role in differentiating Muslims from non-Muslims and separating the new Pakistani state from the Indian Union (Cmd. 7136).

In British India, the All-India Muslim League became the main representative body for Indian Muslims, and came to voice the claim to an "independent sovereign" Pakistani state (Burke 2000: 25). In his presidential address to the Muslim League, Muhammad Ali Jinnah made his position clear on the relationship between the Indian Muslim and non-Muslim populations and presented the "two-nation theory"

[4] Note the fact that this was one feature and that the leader of the Pakistani independence movement, Muhammad Ali Jinnah, himself did not seek a homogenous Muslim state.

[5] The counsel of the Indian National Congress loudly contested the reliability of the 1941 census figures (Ahmed 1999: 124), which were said to have been particularly problematic due to an unprecedented increase in the Muslim population between 1931 and 1941. While its contestability was not questioned by the other members, the representative of the Muslim League, Muhammad Zafrullah Khan, argued that the Commission had no choice but to rely on the figures (1999: 142).

as a justification for a separate Muslim "Homeland". Hindus and Muslims, he stated, were two nations, two irreconcilably "different civilizations", a difference that went through every grain of human life down to marriage and food. Due to this fundamental difference, no settlement between the nations was to be expected nor should it be imposed (Saiyd 1940: 13). The real struggle in which the Muslim League and Jinnah took part, however, was not only one for a territorial homeland for India's Muslims, but rather to conduct this struggle in the face of their cultural, linguistic, demographic, religious and political plurality (Devji 2007; Gilmartin 1998: 1071; Jalal 1994 [1985]). The "two-nation theory" contributed to create a unified image of the Indian Muslims, as did the fact that Jinnah became their "sole spokesperson" (Jalal 1994 [1985]). As the Second World War came to an end, the Muslim League had sidelined other Muslim representatives – including the Indian National Congress (INC) which had claimed to represent all Indians, Muslims and non-Muslims alike. Subsequently, Jinnah was invited by the British on an equal footing with the Congress leaders to discuss the future of Indian government after the end of British rule, thereby implicitly accepting the Muslim League's claim to speak for all Indian Muslims, a claim that contained an independent state.

Against this backdrop, "Muslim" became a salient and politically relevant category during the actual drawing of borders between India and Pakistan. Commissions led by British lawyer Cyril Radcliffe were to "demarcate the boundaries of the two parts of [the Punjabi and Bengali Provinces] on the basis of ascertaining contiguous majority areas of Muslims and non-Muslims", using the 1941 census figures as the authoritative source (Jalal 1994 [1985]). In addition to the census, Radcliffe primarily relied on colonial maps, which had been commissioned for two principal reasons (Chatterji 1999: 224f.). The first had been colonial administration, such as tax collection, and logistics, like transportation, roads and railways. The second main function of the maps of British India had been military, especially in the northeast, where the advancement of the Japanese forces in 1942 had highlighted the need for precise cartographical knowledge (Chester 2009; Khan 2007). Lines of communication, roads, railways, canals and military bases thus came to trump questions of trade patterns, kinship and the cultural significance of cities and regions in Radcliffe's drawing of the Indian–Pakistani border (Chester 2009: 21). While the census had shaped the perception that the Partition territories were made up of clearly distinguishable religious communities, the colonial maps, dependent on administrative and military knowledge, superimposed these religious communities onto visible territory. The census and the map came together to create the image of natural fault lines between the communities of Muslims and non-Muslims, which were to give shape to the new international border. Thus, through the process of partition the meaning and scope of Muslim identity and a "Muslim homeland" were (trans)formed and different "religious communities" and the states formed around them inscribed into the international system.

Concept and consequences

Using religions as descriptive terms and assuming the concept of religion itself to be neutral hides the manifold processes behind the formation and construction of "religious differences". It blends out how religion(s) become politically relevant and how entire populations were placed into abstract concepts such as the Pakistani

"Muslim homeland". In this and other cases, rather than reading religion as a historically unchanged and transnationally recognizable entity, we need to understand "world religions" as context dependent and deeply rooted in colonial history (Bosco 2009). It is also important to be sensitive to the normative content of the concept, especially when used in popular discourse. As noted earlier, the characterization of certain "world religions" such as Buddhism and Islam, as either tolerant and humanistic or rigid and violent, does not simply stem from empirical facts but is deeply rooted in European intellectual history of the development of language and race. If the normative roots of these categories are left intact and assumed to be an adept description of the "way things are", chances are high that they will impact policy decisions concerning the role of religion in international affairs and the people embodying them.

The early 21st century has seen a particular international interest in the "world religion" of Islam, regularly characterizing "it" as inherently backwards and violent. While it is relatively easy to dismiss essentialist arguments about a stereotypically "violent" Islam – exemplified perhaps most famously in Samuel Huntington's depiction of Islam's "bloody borders" – the assumption of a "stalemate" Islam seems harder to get rid of. Accordingly, Islam's proclaimed problem with democracy is not assumed to be a problem of the essence of Islam but a problem of Islam's integration of political and religious institutions (Toft/Philpott/Shah 2011). The view that "real world" Islam lacks an equivalent to the Protestant Reformation separating the political from the religious sphere is common not only in public discourse but also in the IR literature: "(U)nlike Christianity, Islam has not gained an incentive to interpret its texts in ways that permit or encourage the separation of religion and state. On the contrary, religion and state are fused" (Toft 2006: 23). According to Monica Toft, Daniel Philpott and Timothy Shah, this explains the Freedom House statistics that only three out of 47 Muslim majority countries are ranked fully "free". "Behind the deficit", they continue, "is the wide prevalence within Islam of integrated institutions and of a political theology that advocates such institutions" (Toft et al. 2011: 116f.). Along the same lines, *The Routledge Handbook of Religion and Politics* maintains that "it is clear that Islam makes no distinction between religion and politics" and that these "remain elements within 'actually existing Islam' ... that are problematic for democratic development" (Anderson 2009: 205; Fox 2009: 284). In other words, if only the "real-world religion" of Islam would (or, indeed, could) evolve and separate religion from politics, it would be better suited to liberal democracy.

These accounts almost seamlessly pick up where the 19th-century discussion on world religions left off. Back then, the "rigid" Semitic religion of Islam was assumed to be unable to adapt and evolve through its own resources and to be stuck in its premodern rigid form. Today, the "stalemate" Islam depicted in much of IR seems unable to adapt to modernity's separation of religion and politics and to the idea of democracy, at least if left to itself. This normative content in accounts of the character of "world religions" is highly problematic as it presents a hierarchical view of race and religion as a neutral description of reality. And so, again, while many IR scholars today argue for including religion, taking it seriously or recognizing its importance in international affairs, simply adding "it" to our analytical vocabulary will not make this vocabulary richer. Instead, it risks stabilizing the normative historical construction of the concept – or particular manifestations thereof – and reaffirming the power structures relying on it. Addressing religion in IR can, and should, be done differently.

Religion and the Secular

Rather than treating religion as a distinct category independent of time and place, it is necessary to investigate how it became a stand-alone concept and what the consequences are of thinking of it as such. In particular, as Elizabeth Shakman Hurd notes, we need to ask how "processes, institutions, and states come to be understood as religious versus political, or religious versus secular, and how might we ascertain the political effects of such demarcation" (Hurd 2011: 72; see also 2008: 16). In this vein, this last section turns to a debate that takes the contrasting concept of the "secular" as its starting point and argues that this "secular" is productive of religion rather than being its antidote.

Like the concept of religion, the concept of the secular carries multiple meanings depending on the time in which it features and which political and social authorities it refers to. It emerged during the Middle Ages as a reference to members of the Christian clergy who were part of religious orders but who served worldly, local parishes. Today, "the secular" often features as a description of a social or political context freed from the influence of religion. The secularization of society is seen to go hand in hand with its modernization and secularism – the ideological underpinning of secular society and politics – seen as intimately connected to modern progress and providing the moral and theoretical basis for an equal, just and tolerant social order. Secularity is seen as the negative space left when religion has been removed and as the neutral ground on which society's many conceptions of the good and real can coexist, also reflected in rhetoric emphasizing "value-freedom" and "objectivity" (see Asad 2003; Bowen 2010; Cady/Hurd 2010). As noted earlier, the secularity of international affairs is by and large taken for granted in Western IR scholarship, seen as the outcome of a process that began with the Peace of Westphalia, sedimented by the Enlightenment and the development of liberal political thought. Accordingly, the secular represents a neutral public space where rationality reigns and religion is a private issue.

This assumption is now put in question, not least by those who see religion manifesting itself widely in world affairs. Following the attacks of 11 September 2001, even liberal IR theorists like Robert Keohane wondered whether the discipline was not missing out on important parts of international life by turning away from religion. For Keohane, the attacks "reveal that all mainstream theories of world politics are relentlessly secular with respect to motivation. They ignore the impact of religion, despite the fact that world-shaking political movements have so often been fueled by religious fervor" (2002: 72; see also Calhoun et al. 2011). But more than merely questioning the secular assumptions underlying international research, arguments emerged that this very secularism in itself was ideologically invested (Asad 2003; Calhoun et al. 2011; Hurd 2008). In this sense, the secular was not an empty, neutral space but a mode of thought built on particular assumptions regarding private and public, the individual and the self, authority and sovereignty. It was built on a very particular understanding of what religion was and what role it played – or was supposed to play – in society. Secularism was a mode of thought and governance structuring ideas and practices concerning religion; a regime of knowledge that placed religion outside the realm of the political and emphasized the importance of a "secular" public sphere. By making sure that the public was free from religion, however, secularism also defined what the public needs to be freed from and thereby defined the scope of religion itself.

By drawing the boundaries of what is understood to be religious and what not, secularism exercises productive power that constitutes religion as something distinct from the public, political and liberal secular sphere of international relations and, generally, designates it as something private, apolitical and illiberal (Cady/Hurd 2010; Connolly 1999; Hallward 2008). Consequently, it is not only that religion appears to be missing from IR because most scholars adopt a view of the world based on a secular reality. IR scholars also miss out on "secularism's role in the production of the subjects that it presupposes", that is, both religion *and* the secular (Hurd 2004: 254ff.). A secular public sphere is a particular form of government producing a particular understanding of the concept of religion and its legitimate space and place. Ignoring the fact that this is a unique and non-universal arrangement, we can, according to Hurd, expect those negatively affected by secularist politics, namely those defining their identity in religious terms, to raise their voices and even their arms (2004).

Concept and consequences

Considering this debate on secularism – the same way we did with the two examples above – what does religion amount to? What "is" religion in these accounts of secularism critique? It is certainly not a fixed set of ideas or norms, as some of the accounts of Westphalia would have it. It is also not the source of a political identity, as participants of the Pakistani independence movement would argue. In light of the "secular" nature of international relations and the critique thereof, religion emerges as a construct, as a product of a wide variety of practices and ideas, institutions and discourses. By arguing that secularism has a productive power over religion, religion becomes an ever-moving target temporarily and selectively fixed in attempts to order and control international society.

What are the consequences of treating religion as a product and not a thing in its own right? If we accept the deconstruction of religion according to the critical voices in the debate on secularism, is religion still helpful as an analytical concept or does the continued use of it hide the working of particular actors and structures?[6] One consequence of viewing religion as a product of secularism and this secularism being problematic is a search for alternatives to it. Critical readings of the secular in world affairs thus give way to *post*-secular accounts, articulating alternatives that go beyond contemporary secular arrangements (Mavelli/Petito 2012). While some have tried to come to terms with – and to a certain extent also cater to – a "return" or "resilience" of religion in modern life (Habermas 2005; for a critical account, see Birnbaum 2015), others have suggested different forms of arrangements (Asad et al. 2013; Calhoun et al. 2011; Taylor 2007). Searching beyond the limits of the secular, William Connolly is looking to find an arrangement that transcends the absolutist mode of secularist

[6] The role of different versions of secularism have been analyzed in various settings, for example as tools of power of the modern state, as a Eurocentric framework of thought with powerful workings in the postcolonial world and in the (re)production of an Islamic "other"; see Barbato 2010; Bilgin 2008; Byrnes/Katzenstein 2006; Hallward 2008; Luoma-Aho 2009; Mavelli 2012a, 2012b; Wilson 2011.

thinking and strict boundaries of a secular inside and a religious outside. For Connolly, these boundaries and the gatekeepers of them punish those transgressing and seeking other alliances and new forms of being and thereby hinder a true plural society from developing. In order to foster a "deep plurality", Connolly does not seek to eliminate secularism but rather to decenter it and convert it into one perspective alongside many others. In his efforts to rethink common ideas of plurality, Connolly has proposed an "ethos of generous engagement", which aims to rework and cultivate the reactions of individuals and societies to that which it considers alien or that which calls the naturalness of its own identity into question (Connolly 1999, 2005). To Connolly, this is true for politics, religion and sexuality alike: "The negotiation of such an ethos, in turn, depends on reciprocal acknowledgement by a significant set of partisans on the uncertainty and profound contestability of the metaphysical suppositions and moral sources they honor the most" (1999: 185).

Conclusion

The concept of religion was long excluded from the study of international relations. This is in itself a problem. But is the inclusion of religion the best way to address this neglect? Building on points made in this chapter, I want to conclude by arguing that the critique of the exclusion of religion from IR does not need to amount to an argument for the inclusion of it. In including religion in our analytical vocabulary – "recognizing" its central role in the discipline and practice of IR – religion needs to be recognizable as such (Birnbaum 2015). Yet, having neglected the concept for such a long period of time, IR scholars may be prone to recognize only that which fits a conventional understanding of what religion is, what it looks like and what it does. This would, for example, occlude the historical processes through which the British Indian colonial regime crafted categories for its census and fitted the culturally, linguistically, socially diverse population into them. It would take only the final product of a religious difference between the British Indian Muslims and non-Muslims as constitutive of the future Muslim Homeland of Pakistan.

Bringing religion "back" into the analysis of the current "secular" international order ignores the fact that the secularity of this order emerged from a 17th-century settlement between European Christian communities in the wake of the Reformation and the fact that both the secular and religious carry with them the meaning(s) bound to those circumstances. It risks "bringing in" a particular understanding of religion(s), ignoring the fact that the very distinction between secular and religious is deeply political. If a government in a Westphalian world order needs to be secular and if religion is seen as the opposite of the secular, then the definition of who or what is religious becomes politically relevant. It is tied to conceptions of legitimate political power and participation: if rationality is an expected attribute of international actors and if rational actors are necessarily assumed to be secular – in the sense that Kant argued at the beginning of the chapter – then the question of who is secular and who is not becomes a question of rational and accountable international agency.

From this, it does not follow that we should leave the concept of religion out of IR's vocabulary. Rather, it means that "religion" cannot simply be treated as a fixed unit that can be added to the set. The question remaining, then, is how are we – as students and scholars of international affairs – to investigate religion without fitting it into recognizable concepts or pre-construed categories? How to analyze a world where religion plays a part without forcing it into pre-determined epistemological straight-jackets? This chapter does not offer a simple answer, because there is none. My approach has been to highlight the different contexts in which the concept has formed international affairs and in return has been formed by it. I sought to demonstrate the diversity of the concept and the political consequences of these different meanings. Above all, I hope to have shown the importance of analyzing how a particular meaning of religion has come about, what it enabled, what it deemed relevant and irrelevant and who stood to gain and lose thereby.

Suggested Readings

Bosco, Robert (2009) Persistent Orientalisms: The Concept of Religion in International Relations, in: *Journal of International Relations and Development*, 12: 90–111.
A useful article on the orientalist baggage in many assumptions guiding IR accounts on religion.

Calhoun, Craig/Juergensmeyer, Mark/Van Antwerpen, Jonathan (eds) (2011) *Rethinking Secularism*, Oxford: Oxford University Press.
This collection of essays is a great introduction to secularism by different political theorists.

Hurd, Elizabeth Shakman (2004) The Political Authority of Secularism in International Relations, in: *European Journal of International Relations*, 10(2): 235–262.
An important article on the problems concerning the religion–secular dichotomy and the productive power and politics of secularism in IR.

McCutcheon, Russell T. (1997) *Manufacturing Religion: The Discourse on Sui Generis Religion and the Politics of Nostalgia*, New York: Oxford University Press.
An indispensable book on the critical approach to religion from the perspective of religious studies.

Snyder, Jack (2011) *International Relations and Religion*, New York: Columbia University Press.
A good overview of different approaches to and aspects of religion in international relations.

Bibliography

Ahmed, Ishtiaq (1999) The 1947 Partition of Punjab, in: Talbot, Ian/Singh, Gurharpal (eds) *Region and Partition: Bengal, Punjab and the Partition of the Subcontinent*, Oxford: Oxford University Press.

Anderson, John (2009) Does God Matter, and if so Whose God? in: Haynes, Jeffrey (ed.) *Routledge Handbook of Religion and Politics*, London: Routledge, 192–210.

Asad, Talal (1993) *Genealogies of Religion*, Baltimore, MD: John Hopkins University Press.

Asad, Talal (2003) *Formations of the Secular*, Stanford, CA: Stanford University Press.

Asad, Talal/Brown, Wendy/Butler, Judith/Mahmood, Saba (2009) *Is Critique Secular? Blasphemy, Injury, and Free Speech*, Berkeley, CA: University of California Press.

Asch, Ronald G. (1997) *The Thirty Years War: The Holy Roman Empire and Europe, 1618–1648*, Basingstoke: Palgrave Macmillan.

Barbato, Mariano (2010) Conceptions of the Self for Post-Secular Emancipation: Towards a Pilgrim‘s Guide to Global Justice, in: *Millennium*, 39(2): 547–564.

Bartelson, Jens (2009) *Visions of World Community*, Cambridge: Cambridge University Press.

Berger, Peter (1999) *The Desecularization of the World*, Washington, DC: Ethics and Public Policy Centre.
Bilgin, Pinar (2008) The Securityness of Secularism? The Case of Turkey, in: *Security Dialogue* 39(6): 593–614.
Birnbaum, Maria (2015) Exclusive Pluralism, in: Stack, Trevor/Goldenberg, Naomi/ Fitzgerald, Timothy (eds) *Religion as a Category of Governance and Sovereignty*, Leiden: Brill, 182–196.
Bosco, Robert M. (2009) Persistent Orientalism, in: *Journal of International Relations and Development*, 12(1): 90–111.
Bowen, John R. (2010) Secularism, in: *Comparative Studies in Society and History*, 52(3): 680–694.
Burke, S.M. (2000) *Jinnah: Speeches and Statements 1947–1948*, Karachi: Oxford University Press.
Byrnes, Timothy A./Katzenstein, Peter. J. (2006) (eds) *Religion in an Expanding Europe*, Cambridge: Cambridge University Press.
Cady, Linell E./Hurd, Elizabeth Shakman (2010) *Comparative Secularisms in a Global Age*, New York: Palgrave Macmillan.
Calhoun, Craig/Juergensmeyer, Mark/VanAntwerpen, Jonathan (2011) *Rethinking Secularism*, New York: Oxford University Press.
Campbell, David (1992) *Writing Security*, Minneapolis, MN: University of Minnesota Press.
Casanova, José (1994) *Public Religions in the Modern World*, Chicago, IL: University of Chicago Press.
Chatterji, Joya (1999) The Fashioning of a Frontier: The Radcliffe Line and Bengal's Border Landscape, in: *Modern Asian Studies*, 33(1): 185–242.
Chester, Lucy (2008) Factors Impeding the Effectiveness of Partition in South Asia and the Palestine Mandate, in: Kalyvas, Stathis N./Shapio, Ian/Masoud, Tarek (eds) *Order, Conflict, and Violence*, Cambridge: Cambridge University Press, 75–96.
Chester, Lucy (2009) *Border and Conflict in South Asia*, Manchester and New York: Manchester University Press.
Connolly, William E. (1999) *Why I am Not a Secularist*, Minneapolis, MN: University of Minnesota Press.
Connolly, William E. (2005) *Pluralism*, Durham NC: Duke University Press.
Devji, Faisal (2007) The Minority as Political Form, in: Chakrabarty, Dipesh/Majumdar, Rochona Sartori, Andrew (eds) *From the Colonial to the Postcolonial: India and Pakistan in Transition*, Oxford: Oxford University Press.
von Druffel, August (1896) Beiträge zur Reichsgeschichte, vol. 4, in: *Briefe und Akten zur Geschichte des sechzehnten Jahrhunderts mit besonderer Rücksicht auf Bayerns Fürstenhaus*, Munich: Gustav Himmer: 722–724.
Emon, Anver (2012) *Religious Pluralism and Islamic Law*, Oxford: Oxford University Press.
Feil, Ernst (1986) *Religio*, Göttingen: Vandenhoeck & Ruprecht.
Fierke, Karin (2013) *Political Self-Sacrifice*, Cambridge: Cambridge University Press.
Flood, Garvin (1999) *Beyond Phenomenology*, London; New York: Cassell.
Fowden, Garth (1999) Religious Communities, in: Bowersock, Glen Warren/Brown, Peter/ Grabar, Oleg (eds) *Late Antiquity*, Cambridge, MA: Harvard University Press, 82–106.
Fox, Jonathan/Sandler, Shmuel (2004) *Bringing Religion into International Relations*, Houndmills: Palgrave Macmillan.
Fox, Jonathan (2009) Integrating Religion into International Relations Theory, in: Haynes, Jeffrey (ed.) *Routledge Handbook of Religion and Politics*, London: Routledge, 273–292.
Gedicks, Frederick, Mark/Annicchino, Pasquale (forthcoming) Cross, Crucifix, Culture, in: *13 First Amendment Law Review*.
Gilmartin, David (1979) Religious Leadership and the Pakistan Movement in the Punjab, in: *Modern Asian Studies*, 13(3): 485–517.

Gilmartin, David (1998) Partition, Pakistan, and South Asian History, in: *The Journal of Asian Studies*, 57(4): 1068–1095.
Gross, Leo (1948) The Peace of Westphalia, 1648–1948, in: *American Journal of International Law*, 42(1): 20–41.
Habermas, Jürgen (2005) *Zwischen Naturalismus und Religion: Philosophische Aufsätze*, Frankfurt a.M.: Suhrkamp.
Hallward, M. C. (2008) Situating the "Secular": Negotiating the Boundary between Religion and Politics, in: *International Political Sociology*, 2(1): 1–16.
Hock, Klaus (2008) *Einführung in die Religionswissenschaft*, Darmstadt: Wissenschaftliche Buchgesellschaft.
Hunter, Ian (2005) Kant's Religion and Prussian Religious Policy, in: *Modern Intellectual History*, 2(1): 1–27.
Hurd, Elizabeth Shakman (2004) Political Authority of Secularism in International Relations, in: *European Journal of International Relations*, 10(2): 235–262.
Hurd, Elizabeth Shakman (2008) *The Politics of Secularism in International Relations*, Princeton, NJ: Princeton University Press.
Hurd, Elizabeth Shakman (2011) Secularism and International Relations Theory, in: Snyder, Jack (ed.) *Religion and International Relations Theory*, New York: Columbia University Press: 60–90.
Hurd, Elizabeth Shakman (2012) International Politics after Secularism, in: *Review of International Studies*, 38(5): 943–961.
Hurd, Elizabeth Shakman (2015) *Beyond Religious Freedom*, Princeton, NJ: Princeton University Press.
Jalal, Ayesha (1994 [1985]) *The Sole Spokesman*, Cambridge: Cambridge University Press.
Kant, Immanuel (1991 [1784]) What is Enlightenment? (Was ist Aufklärung?), in: Reiss, Hans (ed.) *Political Writings*, Cambridge: Cambridge University Press.
Kehrer, Günter (1998) Religion, in: Cancik, Hubert/Gladigow, Burkhard/Kohl, Karl-Heinz (eds) *Handbuch religionswissenschaftlicher Grundbegriffe*, Stuttgart: Kohlhammer, IV: 418–425.
Keohane, Robert (2002) The Globalization of Informal Violence, Theories of World Politics and 'The Liberalism of Fear', in: Calhoun, Craig/Price, P./Timmer, A. (eds) *Understanding September 11*, New York: New York Press.
Khan, Yasmin (2007) *The Great Partition*, London: Yale University Press.
Kippenberg, Hans (2003) Religiöse Gemeinschaften, in: Albert, Gert/Bienfait, Agathe/Sigmund, Steffen/Wendt, Claus (eds) *Das Weber-Paradigma*, Tübingen: Mohr Siebeck, 211–233.
Kippenberg, Hans G./von Stuckrad, Kocku (2003) *Einführung in die Religionswissenschaft*, München: C.H. Beck.
Krasner, Stephen (1993) Westphalia and All That, in: Goldstein, Judith/Keohane, Robert (eds) *Ideas and Foreign Policy*, Ithaca, NY: Cornell University Press, 235–264.
Krasner, Stephen (1999) *Sovereignty: Organized Hypocrisy*, Princeton, NJ: Princeton University Press.
Krasner, Stephen (2001) Sovereignty, in: *Foreign Policy* (Jan.–Feb.), 122: 20–29.
Kratochwil, Friedrich (1986) Of Systems, Boundaries, and Territoriality: An Inquiry into the Formation of the State System, in: *World Politics*, 39(1): 27–52.
Kratochwil, Friedrich (2005) Religion and (Inter-)National Politics, in: *Alternative*, 30(2): 113–140.
Luoma-Aho, Mika (2009) Political Theology, Anthropomorphism, and Person-Hood of the State: The Religion of IR, in: *International Political Sociology*, 3(3): 293–309.
Masuzawa, Tomoko (2005) *The Invention of World Religions: Or, How European Universalism was Preserved in the Language of Pluralism*, Chicago IL: Chicago University Press.
Mavelli, Luca/Petito, Fabio (2012) The Postsecular in International Relations, in: *Review of International Studies*, 38(5): 931–942.

Mavelli, Luca (2012a) *Europe's Encounter with Islam: The Secular and the Postsecular*, New York: Routledge.
Mavelli, Luca (2012b) Security and Secularization in International Relations, in: *European Journal of International Relations*, 18 (1): 177–199.
Norris, P./Inglehart, R. (2004) *Sacred and Secular*, Cambridge: Cambridge University Press.
Osiander, Andreas (1994) *The States System of Europe, 1640–1990*, Oxford: Clarendon Press.
Osiander, Andreas (2000) Religion and Politics in Western Civilization, in: *Millennium*, 29(3): 761–790.
Osiander, Andreas (2001) Sovereignty, International Relations and the Westphalian Myth, in: *International Organization*, 55(2): 251–287.
Pagden, Anthony (1987) *The Language of Political Theory in Early-Modern Europe*, Cambridge: Cambridge University Press.
Parker, Geoffrey (1980) *Europe in Crisis, 1598–1648*, Brighton: The Harvester Press.
Patomäki, Heikki (2002) From East to West, in: *Theory, Culture & Society*, 19(3): 89–111.
Petito, Fabio/Hatzopoulos, Pavlos (eds) (2003) *Religion in IR*, New York: Palgrave Macmillan.
Philpott, Daniel (2000) The Religious Roots of Modern International Relations, in: *World Politics*, 52(2): 206–245.
Philpott, Daniel (2002) The Challenge of September 11 to Secularism in International Relations, in: *World Politics* 55(1): 66–95.
Philpott, Daniel (2009) Has the Study of Global Politics Found Religion? in: *Annual Review of Political Science*, 12: 183–202.
Sadullah, Mian Muhammd/al Mujahid, Sharif/Wasti, S. Razi/Ahmed, Ashfaq/Zaman, S.M. (eds) (1983) *The Partition of the Punjab 1947*, Lahore: Sajjad Zaheer Publishers.
Saiyd, M.H. (1940) *India's Problem of her Future Constitution: All-India Muslim League's Lahore Resolution*, Bombay: Saxon Press.
Schmidt, Sebastian (2011) To Order the Minds of Scholars, in: *International Studies Quarterly*, 55(3): 601–623.
Skinner, Quentin (1978) *The Foundations of Modern Political Thought*, I & II, Cambridge: Cambridge University Press.
Smith, Jonathan Z. (1998): Religion, Religions, Religious, in: Taylor, Mark C. (ed.) *Critical Terms for Religious Studies*, Chicago: Chicago University Press.
Snyder, Jack (2011) *International Relations and Religion*, New York: Columbia University Press.
Spruyt, Hendrik (1994) *The Sovereign State and Its Competitors*, Princeton, NJ: Princeton University Press.
Stolz, Fritz (2001) *Grundzüge der Religionswissenschaft*, Göttingen: Vandenhoeck & Ruprecht.
Sullivan, Winnifred Fallers/Hurd, Elizabeth Shakman/Mahmood, Saba/Danchin, Peter (eds) (2015) *Politics of Religious Freedom*, Chicago, IL: The University of Chicago Press.
Talbot, Ian/Singh, Gurharpal (2009) *The Partition of India*, Cambridge: Cambridge University Press.
Taylor, Charles (1994 [1992]) *Multiculturalism*, Princeton, NJ: Princeton University Press.
Taylor, Charles (1998) Modes of Secularism, in: Bhargava, Rajeev (ed.) *Secularism and its Critics*, Delhi: Oxford University Press.
Taylor, Charles (2007) *A Secular Age*, Cambridge, MA: Belknap Press of Harvard University Press.
Thomas, Scott (2000) Taking Religious and Cultural Pluralism Seriously, in: *Millennium*, 29(3): 815–841.
Thomas, Scott (2003) Taking Religious and Cultural Pluralism Seriously: The Global Resurgence of Religion and the Transformation of International Society, in: Hatzopolous, Pavlos/Petito, Fabio (eds) *Religion in IR*, New York: Palgrave Macmillan, 21–54.
Thomas, Scott (2005) *The Global Resurgence of Religion and the Transformation of International Relations*, New York: Palgrave Macmillan.

Todorov, Tzvetan (1999) *The Conquest of America: The Question of the Other*, Norman, OK: University of Oklahoma Press.

Toft, Monica Duffy (2006) *Religion, Civil War, and International Order* (Discussion Paper, 2006–03), Belfer Center for Science and International Affairs, John F. Kennedy School of Government, Harvard University, Cambridge, MA.

Toft, Monica Duffy/Philpott, Daniel/Shah, Timothy (2011) *God's Century*, New York: W.W. Norton & Co.

Weber, Max (1968 [1913]) Über einige Kategorien der Verstehenden Soziologie, in: Winckelmann, Johannes (ed.) *Gesammelt Aufsätze zur Wissenschaftslehre*, Tübingen: Mohr Siebeck, 427–474.

Weber, Max (1988 [1920]) *Gesammelte Aufsätze zur Religionssoziologie*, Tübingen: Mohr Siebeck.

Werner, Wouter G. and Jaap H. de Wilde (2001) The Endurance of Sovereignty, in: *European Journal of International Relations*, 7(3): 283–313.

Wilson, Erin K. (2011) *After Secularism: Rethinking Religion in Global Politics*, New York: Palgrave.

Zamidar, Vazira Fazila-Yacoobali (2007) *The Long Partition and the Making of Modern South Asia*, New York: Columbia University Press.

Modes of Transformation

15

Revolution

Rahul Rao

The concept of revolution has, until recently, been largely absent from the discipline of international relations (IR). At a theoretical level, revolutions have tended to be seen as processes unfolding within states and, hence, not of primary concern to a discipline studying conflict and cooperation between states. From a historical perspective, the rigid bipolarity of the international system in the Cold War years appeared unpropitious for the eruption of those grand upheavals that led Eric Hobsbawm (2000 [1962]) to characterise the period 1789–1848 as "the age of revolution", the reverberations of which continued to be felt till the middle of the twentieth century. In the lull that followed, the Iranian and Nicaraguan revolutions of 1979 appeared anachronistic and, indeed, as the last revolutions to generate ideologically driven radical regimes, they were (Goldstone 2014: 132). To contemporary observers, it seemed as if revolution was on its way out.

Few anticipated the waning of geopolitical tensions that culminated in the end of the Cold War or the wave of revolutions that would be triggered by its denouement, from the anti-apartheid movement in South Africa to the "velvet" and "colour" revolutions in Eastern Europe and the former Soviet Union. Yet, even in the face of these insurrections, IR scholars were slow to re-evaluate the place of revolution in the conceptual architecture of their discipline. Perhaps swayed by the rhetoric of the movements themselves and under the spell of liberal triumphalism, they tended to subsume these processes under the banner of democratisation, interpreting them as a "return" to a unified world order under Western hegemony (as indeed many of them were), rather than fundamental ruptures in the fabric of international society. For those more attentive to the significance of these movements, something about them seemed different. Goldstone (2014: 132) describes post-Cold War revolutions as being more likely to be nonviolent and to produce weak democracies or pragmatic semi-authoritarian regimes. Yet the term "revolution" endured in both popular and academic discourse as a description of diverse forms of protest culminating in an overthrow or change of government. This begs a number of interesting questions for conceptual analysis. Has "revolution" become something of an empty signifier, denoting simply a different way of doing *anything* (the industrial revolution, the green revolution, the revolution in military affairs)? Does it have a thicker set of connotations when applied specifically to *political* change? And if so, have those connotations remained consistent through the changing historical contexts in which "revolutions" take place?

In his introduction to this book, Felix Berenskoetter outlines three ideal-typical approaches to conceptual analysis. Historical approaches, associated particularly with the work of Reinhart Koselleck, seek to demonstrate how concepts have evolved over time to arrive at their contemporary meanings. They are interested in drawing out the ways in which changing historical conditions shape conceptual evolution. "Scientific" approaches, beholden to the work of Giovanni Sartori, seek to identify the core characteristics and basic structure of concepts. Recognising that concepts travel, such approaches aim to produce minimal definitions that might enable conceptual adaptation without a loss of coherence. Political/critical approaches, perhaps most indebted to the work of Michel Foucault, begin from the premise that all knowledge is a form of power and that concepts, as the basic building blocks of knowledge, are deeply implicated in power relations. In common with historical approaches, political approaches seek to demonstrate how concepts are assembled and reified, but with the further aim of revealing the power structures that are upheld by particular stabilisations of meaning within concepts, as well as rival, subjugated understandings that might destabilise such meaning.

This chapter pursues a combined historical and political approach to the conceptual analysis of revolution. My wariness of the "scientific" approach stems from a number of concerns. First, attempts to arrive at a minimal definition that captures core characteristics have typically foundered on recognition of the essentially contested character of the concept. This is illustrated in one recent work where the author tries to identify common elements in the most influential studies of revolution to arrive at a definition of revolution as "a phenomenon marked by the coincidence of violence, popular involvement, and a change in the governing body" (Kotowski 2009: 218). Yet, he immediately problematises this putative consensus by noting that the authors whom he has analysed might disagree amongst themselves over this definition because of the very different semantic fields – "forms of collective violence", "forms of historical transformation", and "forms of political change" – in which they quite legitimately locate "revolution" (2009: 230). Furthermore, assumptions about the normative connotations of "revolution" – as something associated either with progress or with chaos and violence – invariably skew the ambit of the concept to produce different definitions between which it is impossible to adjudicate without reference to these normative preferences.

Second, a scientific approach fails to alert us to the historical contingency of any definition. As George Lawson (2015*a*: 17–18) notes, "requiring that revolutions fulfil a set of inalienable characteristics ... distorts understanding of how revolutions change according to historically produced circumstances". Taking issue with Theda Skocpol's influential definition of revolutions as "rapid, basic transformations of a society's state and class structures [that] are accompanied and in part carried through by class-based revolts from below" (Skocpol 1979: 4), Lawson argues that such a definition predisposes the analyst to studying cases of "total change", of which there are probably not more than ten – all of which date before 1979, which is also incidentally the year in which Skocpol's work appeared. One could of course adopt such a definition and view social revolutions as anachronistic phenomena unlikely to be reproduced in the contemporary world. But this would render inexplicable the continued use of the term "revolution" to describe later political upheavals in both academic and popular discourse: a faithful adherent of Skocpol's definition would have to condemn such usage as inappropriate. In contrast, a historical approach to conceptual analysis is curious about the elements of continuity and change in understandings of revolution, and in the ways in which these relate to shifts in the historical conditions under which revolutions take place.

Third, in its attempt to identify a common denominator in varying approaches to revolution that might give the concept some stability, "scientific" approaches effectively reinforce the common sense of the time. As Gramscian understandings of hegemony have taught us, this common sense typically reflects the interests of the powerful masquerading as the common interest. Purportedly neutral understandings of revolution can obscure rival, subjugated knowledges that might transform our understanding of what enables revolutions and how we should evaluate them morally and politically. The politics of knowledge about revolutions is reflected, for example, in the relative absence of Haiti in conceptual analyses of even the small universe of "total" revolutions in which France, Russia and China are typically more prominent. This absence is, at one level, puzzling because of the self-evident world-historical importance of the Haitian revolution as the first ever victorious slave revolt leading to the establishment of the first black republic and indeed the first non-European postcolonial state in the modern world.

Yet, as Michel-Rolph Truillot (1995: 82) explains, "The events that shook up Saint-Domingue from 1791 to 1804 constituted a sequence for which not even the extreme political left in France or in England had a conceptual frame of reference. They were 'unthinkable' facts in the framework of Western thought". So unthinkable was the possibility that black slaves had planned and executed a rebellion on their own, that Western observers reacted with disbelief, "shoving the facts into the proper order of discourse" (Truillot 1995: 91). Attributions of the rebellion to white planter miscalculations, mulattoes, or the geopolitical machinations of foreign states – everything, that is, except the political agency of the slaves themselves – later gave way to pessimism that an independent state run by former slaves would survive diplomatic rejection, and eventually grudging accommodation. Historians played their part in silencing the revolution through what Truillot describes as formulas of erasure and banalisation that trivialised and evacuated events of their revolutionary content. It was only in the 20th century with the decisive weakening of scientific racism and colonialism and in the context of the re-issue in 1962 of C. L. R. James' (2001 [1938]) magisterial account of the Haitian revolution against the backdrop of the civil rights movement in the US, that the revolution acquired a new centrality in genealogies of black resistance (Truillot 1995: 104). Which revolutions matter, why and for whom therefore ought to raise deeply political questions for the conceptual analysis of revolutions.

This chapter is divided into two parts. Drawing on a historical approach to conceptual analysis, the first part offers a roughly chronological account of how revolutions have been studied over time. As befits a textbook on international relations, the second part of the chapter focuses more specifically on the relationship between revolutions and the international system. Here, we will examine how revolutions invariably have international dimensions insofar as their causes and effects are concerned. We will also consider why IR as a discipline has, with notable exceptions, neglected or downplayed the significance of revolution as a fundamental institution of international society. Doing so will also require engaging in a more explicitly political approach to conceptual analysis.

Trends in the Study of Revolution: A Brief History

The word "revolution" was originally an astronomical term used to describe the movements of heavenly bodies. In its suggestion of recurring, cyclical movement beyond human control, the connotations of the term were very distant from contemporary understandings of revolution as a political phenomenon involving mass mobilization, often violent, which results in the forcible overthrow of government and the transformation of ruling institutions and ideologies. As Hannah Arendt (1990 [1963]: 40–2) reminds us, although the notion of legitimate rebellion was known in the medieval period, its aim was not the challenge of authority per se but simply an exchange of persons in authority. Indeed, the term revolution first came to be used in a political sense to describe the frequent rotations of power between different elites in the Italian city-states of the Renaissance period (Goldstone 2014: 54). The use of the Latin "revolvere", meaning to cycle or revolve, to describe these transfers of power seems to have hewed quite closely to the astronomical connotations of the term. This was also the case in the English-speaking world of the time. It is salutary to recall that the term revolution was used in England, not to describe the Parliamentary overthrow of Charles I, but rather the *restoration* of monarchy in 1660 (Arendt 1990 [1963]: 42). For political observers at the time, a revolution was something that returned or restored the order of things to a prior state of being.

The idea that revolution might constitute a fundamental break or rupture in political order was an invention of the late 18th century. In part, this was a function of Enlightenment ideas of linear time and specifically Hegelian notions of progress: as if to justify the cataclysmic upheavals through which they forced their societies, revolutionaries began to depict such moments as necessary steps in a teleology of moral and political improvement. But here too, it is important to distinguish between contemporary and retrospective understandings of the meaning of the revolutionary upheavals of the time. Participants in the American and French revolutions often spoke and acted as if they were restoring "ancient liberties", invoking classical Greek and Roman notions of government and citizenship to legitimate their actions. Yet, compelled by the sheer force of events, they soon found themselves struggling to make the world anew, conceiving of revolution in ever more total terms as encompassing the transformation of the political, economic, social, cultural, religious and all other aspects of life and civilisation. Still, one element of the astronomical understanding of revolutions survived in the new political usage, namely the connotation of irresistibility. Few anecdotes better capture the sense of doom and foreboding that the tide of popular insurrection aroused in elites than the brief exchange that is said to have taken place between Louis XVI of France and the Duc de la Rochefoucauld-Liancourt. Told of the storming of the Bastille, Louis is said to have asked "C'est une révolte?", only to be corrected by the duke with the sobering rejoinder: "Non, sire, c'est une révolution" (Schama 2004: 353).

Within this broad understanding of revolution as fundamental socio-political change, the evolution of the modern academic study of revolutions is often narrated in a sequence of four generations of scholarship (Stone 1966; Halliday 1999: 165–71; Lawson 2005: 46–76). The generational metaphor is potentially misleading, because while each "generation" chronologically succeeded the one before it, it also drew on the ideas of classical theorists of revolution such as Marx, Tocqueville, Weber and Durkheim. Still, it is useful to sketch how discussion of the concept shifted over time, focusing mostly on the question of causation but with implications for the understanding of the trajectories and outcomes of revolutions. As much of the contemporary literature on revolutions is situated in a conversation between third- and fourth-generation theorists, the following devotes relatively greater attention to these phases of scholarship.

The first generation, dominated by historians such as George Pettee and Crane Brinton, engaged in the comparative study of revolutions with the aim of extracting recognisable patterns from such analyses. Many in this generation appear to have held a clear normative bias against revolutions, viewing them as regrettable disruptions of order and likening them, through a range of evocative biological metaphors, to physical illness and disease. As Fred Halliday (1999: 167) pointedly remarked of these writers, their "focus on the violence of the oppressed ignores the violence of the dominators".

A second generation, constituted by the work of political sociologists like Chalmers Johnson, James Davies, Ted Gurr and Charles Tilly, resorted to a range of psychological, sociological and political explanations to account for breakdowns in social order. Contra Marx, who saw revolution as the product of increasing misery, the work of this generation bears the imprint of Tocqueville who regarded revolution as the consequence of increasing prosperity (Stone 1966: 169). Central to the accounts offered by these theorists were the tensions of modernisation, which were seen to create dissatisfaction at the individual and group level, and "dysfunction" or disequilibrium at the societal level. As Davies saw it, successful revolution was neither the work of the destitute nor of the satisfied, but of those whose situation was improving less rapidly than they expected. On this account, societies in which expectations were heightened by economic improvement and social and political reforms, and then dashed by economic downturns, governmental reaction and/or aristocratic resurgence, were ripe for revolution (ibid: 170–1). Critics have pointed out that gaps between social expectations and outcomes are a virtually universal feature of modern life that does not always provoke revolutionary eruptions. Second-generation explanations therefore shed light on why people revolt, but tell us little about how, where and under what circumstances this is likely to take place (Lawson 2005: 48–9).

Structuralism and the study of revolution

Third-generation scholars, coming largely out of the field of historical sociology, emphasised macro-level structural factors in their accounts of the conditions under which revolutions are likely to take place. They acknowledged – for the first time, albeit in a limited way – the influence of international factors on the modernisation processes that second-generation theorists were interested in; and they also refocused attention on the state. In Skocpol's (1979) account, perhaps the most widely cited work of this generation, social revolutions are triggered by political crises. These are most likely to occur in states where the state apparatus is vulnerable to administrative and military collapse because of intensified pressure from more developed states abroad, which the state is unable to respond to because of constraints imposed by existing political institutions and class structures. Social revolutions become likely when such political crises occur in states with particular kinds of agrarian socio-political structures – specifically, where the peasantry enjoy pre-existing solidarities, some autonomy from the state, and political opportunities for contention (Skocpol 1979: 154).

Skocpol deploys this framework to explain the outbreaks of the French, Russian and Chinese revolutions. It may be useful to look at the first of these by way of illustration, not least because many have seen in the French Revolution the trajectory of subsequent, especially "bourgeois", revolutions (Hobsbawm 2000: 83). By the late 18th century, the French state had been involved in near constant warfare in the decades preceding the outbreak of the revolution. These military ventures drained the royal treasury, leaving the Bourbon monarchy in a state of considerable debt. Successive royal proposals for raising money were opposed by the French *parlements*, the provincial appellate courts administered by aristocrats who, in addition to exercising judicial functions, also had powers of taxation. Refusing to pay without an extension of their privileges, the nobility demanded the summoning of the long-defunct Estates-General, a tripartite assembly comprising the clergy, nobility, and the bourgeoisie and common people. Convened by a reluctant Louis XVI, the Estates-General was almost immediately paralysed by disagreements over voting procedures. This quarrel within the ruling class opened the doors for the expression of popular discontent. Leaders of the Third Estate, seizing the initiative and co-opting urban unrest, reconstituted themselves as a National Assembly and went on to form new municipal governments in the summer of 1789, displacing royalist officials in the process. Meanwhile, in the countryside, the failure of the grain harvest had triggered bread riots the previous year. While not unprecedented in themselves, the coincidence of these riots with intra-elite quarrels proved to be highly combustible. Skocpol (1979: 123) argues that peasant solidarity and collective action were enabled by the very process set in motion by the king's decision to convene the Estates-General: deputies to the Third Estate had been elected by urban and rural communities in a process that brought peasants together, enabling deliberation on their collective grievances and a strengthening of collective consciousness and organisation, better equipping them to act for insurrectionary ends in 1789.

Skocpol's (1979: 14–31) approach departs from a traditional Marxist view of revolutions in at least two ways. First, in contrast to Marxists from Lenin (1902) onwards, who place great emphasis on the role of revolutionary vanguards, Skocpol offers a structural, non-voluntarist approach, insisting that vanguards have historically tended to exploit structurally induced revolutionary crises rather than create them. Second, in contrast to both liberals and Marxists who tend to see the state as an arena that is captured by particular interests, Skocpol views states as administrative and coercive organisations that are potentially autonomous from society. Without such a conceptual separation of state from society, she argues, it is impossible to explain how and why conflicts of interest open up between states and elite groups in society.

These elements apart, Skocpol's account is indebted to a Marxist class analysis, given its attention to class structures and interests, and its international dimension – characteristics not shared by all third-generation scholars. In a resolutely domestic state-centred argument, Jeff Goodwin (2001: 26–30) has suggested that strong revolutionary movements emerge in opposition to only certain kinds of states. These tend to be militarised but infrastructurally weak states that are consistently exclusionary, anti-reformist and indiscriminately repressive of their political opponents. Policies of exclusion and repression push the oppressed into revolutionary movements, while those of accommodation obviate the need for such movements. Goodwin (2001: 143) uses this thesis to explain the outbreak of revolutions in Nicaragua, Guatemala and El Salvador but not in Honduras, where the military regime was more tolerant of politically moderate labour and peasant unions. He further claims that revolutions are likely to succeed where they confront personalistic or "sultanistic", neopatrimonial dictatorships that alienate large sections of the population. Such regimes rest on the distribution of patronage to clients in exchange for political loyalty, typically to an individual leader or family. This dynamic was exemplified in Nicaragua, where the Somoza family's virtual monopoly over the economy and polity pushed even capitalist elites into a broad coalition of oppositional forces led by the Frente Sandinista de Liberación Nacional (FSLN), which spearheaded the only successful revolution in the region. Goodwin (2001: 144) does not deny the relevance of internal class relations and external pressures that play such a crucial role in Skocpol's theory. Yet, he insists that because the institutions and practices of *states* mediate the effects of such variables, focusing on the nature of the state offers the most powerful and parsimonious explanation for the outbreak and success of revolutions.

Critics of structuralist approaches argue that while their explanations shed considerable light on the factors that predispose states and societies towards revolution, they cannot account for why revolutions break out in unpromising circumstances or, conversely, why revolutions do not occur despite propitious structural conditions. The focus on structure elides the role of ideologies, belief systems and values, as well as the organisational work of political agents who mobilise people to respond to "structural" crises in revolutionary ways – a response, the critics emphasise, that is by no means inevitable. We can see the force of this objection by looking more closely at another of Skocpol's case studies, namely the Chinese Revolution.

Skocpol's (1979: 67–81, 147–60) theory accounts well for the onset of political crisis in late 19th-century China that culminated in the toppling of the Manchu dynasty and the establishment of a constitutional republic in 1912, but less well for the eventual triumph of the Communists in 1949. In line with Skocpol's account, the Qing dynasty was indeed weakened by external military and political challenges, first from Britain in the Opium War of 1839–42, then from France, Russia and Japan, which conquered former tributary areas and imposed the notorious unequal treaties. The Imperial state had difficulty adapting to these challenges thanks to administrative and financial weakness, a burgeoning population and its over-reliance on a restive and relatively autonomous gentry class of landowners and bureaucrats whose coercive power it relied on for the suppression of numerous peasant rebellions. Wide-ranging as its reforms of 1901–11 were, the Manchu state appeared insufficiently dynamic in the eyes of the gentry who, enamoured of the idea of constitutionalism now associated with the power of more advanced states, launched a revolution that ended the nearly three-century rule of the Qing. Nonetheless, between 1912 and 1949, no new national system emerged, with power devolving to regional warlords, while the bourgeois nationalist Guomindang and the Chinese Communist Party (CCP) struggled against one another and against Japanese invasion and occupation in rival state-unification projects.

Crucially, Chinese peasants lacked the kind of pre-existing solidarity and autonomy that Skocpol considers necessary for the class-based revolts from below that combine with elite political crisis to produce a social revolution in her account. Such solidarity was slowly and painstakingly forged during the interregnum by the efforts of the CCP which, pushed into the rural interior by both the Japanese and the Guomindang, had found it necessary to attempt to fuse its efforts with those of peasant-based social banditry to build a Red Army capable of taking and holding territory. Through its military, administrative and propaganda activities and under the leadership of Mao, it was able to organise the peasants collectively to the point where they began to revolt in the 1940s against the remnants of the gentry. This process culminated in the unification of the country under communist rule in 1949. The prolonged nature of the Chinese Revolution calls into question Skocpol's understanding of social revolutions as "rapid". But, more profoundly, it is impossible to fully account for the success of the revolution without reference to the leading role of a revolutionary vanguard committed to the production and dissemination of a new ideological and political culture.

Agency and the study of revolution

Fourth-generation scholars like John Foran (2007: 18) supplement structural accounts of revolution with the claim that successful revolution requires the elaboration of effective and powerful cultures of resistance. Such cultures may draw on formal ideologies, folk traditions and popular idioms of protest, and may be animated by a range of political claims including nationalism (or, more loosely, resentment of control by outsiders), socialism (desires for equality and social justice), democracy (demands for representation and participation) and religious belief (resistance to evil and suffering and a belief in the coming of a better world). Eric Selbin seems to go further when he elevates narrative and storytelling to the status of a causal factor in the making of revolutions. As he puts it,

> Revolutions seem possible when people articulate compelling stories that provide those anxious to change the material and ideological conditions of their everyday lives with the belief that such change is achievable, with the energy to do so, and in some cases even with the strategies and tactics that can be utilized. (Selbin 2010: 75)

For Selbin, revolutions have historically been narrated as four kinds of stories. First is the "civilizing and democratizing story", whose central tropes have been the checking of absolutist power, the claim that governments derive their power from the consent of the governed, and the insistence on accountability. This is the story of the English, American, 1905 Russian and 1989 East European revolutions, amongst others. Second is the "social revolution story" that has dreamed of making the world anew in the most comprehensive fashion imaginable. This has been the driving narrative of revolutions in France, Mexico, Russia (1917), China (1949), Cuba, Nicaragua and Iran. Third, the "freedom and liberation story" calls for a people's emancipation from foreign control, most evident in slave revolts (Haiti), anticolonial movements, and wars of national liberation (Vietnam, Algeria, Angola and Mozambique, to mention only a few). Fourth, the "lost and forgotten stories" of everyday resistance, rebellion and revolution accompany all revolutions, perhaps especially those that are unsuccessful, and are contained in myth, poetry, song and allusion.

In paying attention to the sorts of stories that animate revolution, questions of identity have invariably become more prominent. Scholars have drawn attention to the relatively marginal place of race and gender (as compared with class) in the theorisation of revolution (Foran 2001). Consider, by way of example, Robbie Shilliam's reading of the Haitian revolution as being driven "far less by the dialectic of capital and labor – that is, the modern politics of class – and far more by what might be described as the dialectic of master and slave – the politics of race" (Shilliam 2008: 781). Focusing not on the moment of rebellion but on its aftermath, Shilliam describes how, despite the abolition of slavery, successive Haitian leaders felt compelled to consolidate and expand the militarised plantation system within which slaves had laboured before the revolution. A straightforwardly historical materialist view would regard this as the development of a new black elite beginning to form around a new exploitative mode of plantation production. Shilliam argues that leaders from Toussaint L'Ouverture through Jean-Pierre Boyer were, in the different policies that they pursued, animated less by the capitalist imperative of instituting private property relations and more by the geopolitical imperative of defending emancipated slaves against slave-holding powers. The military, diplomatic and economic hostility that these powers brought to bear on the Haitian state with a view to denying its sovereign independence threatened not only a loss of political power, but a loss of the very political being enabled by the existence of the world's first independent black republic (Shilliam 2008: 799). At a conceptual level, we might see Shilliam's reading as an explicitly political intervention in the analysis of revolutions because of the way in which it seeks to reveal the racial hierarchies that drove revolutionary developments that are missed by class-oriented analyses. This is political because the "forgetting" of race in social theory is not so much an oversight as a demotion of certain categories of oppression in the agenda of both the scholarship *and* practice of revolutions.

Gendered readings of revolution are likewise political in the way they challenge both the analytical lenses of scholars and the programmatic priorities of revolutionaries themselves. Such readings offer a variety of insights into the puzzle of why, when virtually all revolutions have sought to mobilise women, none has succeeded in destroying patriarchy. Indeed, revolutions informed by a variety of ideologies have frequently deferred the "Woman Question" till putatively more pressing objectives – national liberation, socialist utopia, racial emancipation and so forth – have been achieved. In some cases, the promised engagement with women's issues has never come, with women being pushed back into their accustomed place once they have served their purpose of contributing to the "larger" cause. In other cases, the engagement has been more ambivalent. As Kumari Jayawardena explains in her landmark study of feminism and Third World nationalism, male bourgeois nationalists sought to fashion a "new woman" who exemplified modernity through attainment of the education and employment that would enable her to contribute to capitalist development without undermining her traditional subordination within the family and other patriarchal institutions (Jayawardena 1986: 15).

While the disavowal, deferral or demotion of women's emancipation might be thought of as a straightforward consequence of the greater power wielded by men in revolutionary as much as other situations, it also follows from ontological assumptions about social change that are themselves gendered. Orthodox Marxists, for example, might argue that the transformation of class relations in the economic base of society is a precondition for the overthrow of oppressive relations (racism, sexism, homophobia) in the socio-political superstructure (Andrijasevic et al. 2014: 2). Besides calling into question such hierarchies of value, race and gender, analyses of revolution also offer rich theorisations of power and resistance. Indebted to the insights of leading theorists and practitioners of anti-colonial revolution, many of whom regarded the violence of colonialism as both material and epistemic (Gandhi 1938 [1909]; Fanon 1967 [1961]), such analyses have extended our understanding of revolution as encompassing the transformation of not only external material structures, but internal psychic ones as well.

Revolutions and the International

Without the benefit of hindsight, it can be difficult to discern the distinctively unifying characteristic of contemporary scholarship on revolution. Yet, if there is an overarching theme, it is probably the emphasis on agency. In its anxiety not to lose the insights of prior waves of scholarship, some of this work can appear naively additive, grafting agency onto older structural models of revolution while reinforcing the separation between the two (see, for example, Foran 2007: 18). Lawson (2015*a*) has underscored the inadequacy of such an approach, reminding us that if agentic accounts mythologise persons as existing prior to society, structural accounts suffer from the reverse fallacy of mythologising society as a pre-existing entity. Both positions are unsatisfactory insofar as they assume their basic units of analysis to be static. Reflecting on methodological dilemmas of this sort, David Harvey has recommended a move away from an Aristotelian conception of the world as composed of distinct and autonomous things, towards more dialectical and process-oriented philosophies organised around the view that things have no unchanging essence and "do not exist outside the processes, flows, and relations that create, sustain, or undermine them" (Harvey 2009: 232). Applied to the study of revolutions, this would lead us to think of revolutionary dynamics as being constituted not by "structures" or "agents" understood as discrete and static entities, but by relations between social sites. One would expect a discipline like international *relations* to be particularly well placed to enable such inquiry.

And yet, the question of how and why revolutions might be thought of as international phenomena has not, until recently, received considerable attention. Indeed, the tendency to view revolutions as domestic or unit-level phenomena seems embedded in the very practice of naming revolutions after the states in which they take place, as "French", "Haitian", "Russian", "Chinese", etc. While third- and fourth-generation scholarship took some note of the implication of the international in the causes of revolutions, as critics (Halliday 1999: 170–1; Lawson 2015: 305) have pointed out, such attempts have been inadequate in a number of ways. First, attention to the international has been inconsistent: recall and contrast Skocpol's interest in how international pressures help to induce revolutionary political crisis with Goodwin's domestic state-centred perspective. Second, where analysts have been interested in the international, they have tended to take a reductive and rationalist view of it: Skocpol's international factors are limited to "hard power" challenges emanating from the international state system (principally military defeat) and the world capitalist economy, neglecting the international as a source and conveyor of revolutionary ideas. Third, where they are acknowledged at all, international actors and processes tend to be seen as irruptions into otherwise endogenously constituted states rather than as constitutive of the state undergoing revolutionary transformation.

As noted at the outset, for much of its existence IR has done little to remedy this neglect of the international in the scholarship on revolutions. Writing in the immediate aftermath of the Cold War, Stephen Walt confidently pronounced that "a revolution is first and foremost a *national* phenomenon" (Walt 1992: 358, emphasis in original). In a revealing footnote, he cites the Polish communist Karl Radek explaining the failure of the Bolshevik revolution to spread with the comment that "revolutions never originate in foreign affairs but are made at home" (1992: 358). Unsurprisingly for a realist, in addition to bracketing revolutions as unit-level phenomena, Walt sees them as remarkably alike. Discussing widely disparate cases, he nonetheless characterises all revolutionary ideologies as sharing certain essential features given that they are rational responses to a common dilemma that all revolutionaries face, namely the imperative of extracting maximum sacrifice from as many people as possible with no guaranteed prospect of success (1992: 336–41). Reconstructed in this essentially rationalist fashion, it becomes impossible to understand on their own terms, for example, millenarian revolutionary ideologies that exhort their followers to embrace martyrdom and to reap the fruits of their efforts in the afterlife (for a remarkably different treatment of such ideologies, see Devji 2005). Contrasted with the richness and variety of the stories that Selbin (2010) has shown revolutions to be informed by, we can appreciate in hindsight just how impoverished early IR treatments of revolution were.

International causes

Perhaps the first IR theorist to take the international dimensions of revolution seriously was Fred Halliday (1999). Halliday saw revolutions as being produced and enabled by international factors, but also as being challenged by, and transforming, international society. He identifies four ways in which revolutions might be said to have international causes (1999: 161–91). First, the international system can play a significant role in weakening states, thereby setting off the political crises that snowball into Skocpol's "social revolutions". Most obviously, international military defeat can provide windows of opportunity for domestic revolutionary constituencies, not only because these are moments of state weakness, but also because critics of the state acquire enhanced legitimacy in these moments to present ideological alternatives to the prevailing dispensation. Trotsky's (1932) theory of uneven and combined development, first articulated as an explanation for the Russian Revolution, offers another example of state weakness induced by international competition: attempts by less developed states to catch up with more advanced rivals can stretch their resources so considerably that states are forced to extract greater resources from their populations, thereby coming into conflict with those class segments that are expected to bear the brunt of these costs.

Second, "conjunctural crises", or what Foran (2007: 18) calls "world systemic openings", can enable revolutionary outbreaks, often in several places at the same time, giving the appearance of a wave. This typically happens when great powers lose the ability or willingness to maintain the balance of power by intervening in client states where governments face serious challenges to their authority. This is a particularly important enabler of revolution in dependent states. One such systemic opening may be said to have occurred following the US retreat from Vietnam in 1973 and its subsequent reluctance to commit troops to Third World proxy wars till the advent of the Reagan administration in 1980, which found new ways of fighting such wars. This interval witnessed some of the most significant revolutions of the postwar era, many of which took place in US client states such as Iran and Nicaragua. An analogous systemic opening occurred after the Soviet Union withdrew from Afghanistan in 1988 and declined to continue to support authoritarian communist governments in Eastern Europe, enabling the "velvet" revolutions that swept the region the following year.

Third, the international system has always been a source and conveyor of ideas, many of which (Protestantism, nationalism, socialism, anarchism, Islam) have provided the ideological basis for revolutionary upheaval. Such ideologies have furnished both revolutionary ends – general principles and aspirations such as equality, social justice, and universal community imagined in a variety of ways – and means – organisational methods such as vanguard parties and guerrilla war (Mao 1937; Guevara 2013 [1961]). Revolutionaries frequently articulate their ideologies in universalist terms, partly to give their claims the widest possible legitimacy, and partly also from a recognition that because their opponents are international (or have international allies) they must respond in equivalent spatial terms. The *Communist Manifesto* is a good illustration of this kind of internationalism: Marx and Engels' (2004 [1848]) theorisation of the bourgeoisie as cosmopolitan directly underpins their call for "workers of the world" to unite. Fourth, the international can be a source of material aid to revolutionaries. As we shall see in subsequent sections, such external sponsors are often other revolutionary states or movements. But this need not be the case: the French monarchical state was perfectly happy to aid American republican revolutionaries against arch-rival Britain.

International effects: revolutionary export

If revolutions have international causes, they may also be thought of as having international effects. These effects are the result both of what revolutionary regimes attempt to do through their foreign policies and of what is done to them by the international society in which they find themselves. In an exploration of this dynamic, David Armstrong (1993) suggests that the imperative of survival as a state enjoying the recognition of other members of international society can temper the initial hostility of revolutionary regimes towards the fundamental institutions of that society. Despite its recognition of the two-way relationship between revolutionary states and international society, the promise of this early work is attenuated by Armstrong's categorical conclusion that "on balance, the Westphalian conception of international society has proved more durable than revolutionary internationalism, so the impact of international society on revolutionary states through the socialization process may be judged to have been stronger than the reverse interaction" (1993: 307). In contrast,

Halliday's dialectical account of the relationship between revolutionary foreign policy and international counterrevolution circumvents the question of which of these is stronger by demonstrating that even "successful" counterrevolution bears the imprint of its antagonist. To appreciate this, it is helpful to look at revolutionary foreign policy and international counterrevolutionary activity in turn.

At the core of revolutionary foreign policies is a reconceptualisation of international relations as relations between peoples rather than states (Halliday 1999: 95). This conviction generates an impatience with conventional diplomacy, which can manifest itself in a commitment to open rather than secret diplomacy, or in attempts to bypass state authorities to establish direct relationships with like-minded popular and oppositional movements in other states. At their most ambitious, revolutionary foreign policies profess a commitment to exporting the revolution itself. This may be done through a variety of means including propaganda, the creation of international organisations formally committed to supporting revolution, as well as the delivery of diplomatic, monetary, material and military support to other revolutionary states or movements.

A plethora of historical examples illustrate this dynamic (Halliday 1999: 99–128). Surrounded by hostile neighbours and at the urging of radical internationalists at home, the French revolutionary state shifted from a declaration of peace with the outside world in 1790 to the promotion of revolution abroad between 1792–4. The Soviet Union was similarly committed to revolutionary export, experimenting with a variety of methods of doing so, including (failed) attempts to foment revolution in Mongolia, Iran and Poland before 1920, the creation of international organisations for the coordination of revolution such as the Comintern (1919–43) and the Cominform (1947–57), the use of the Red Army to impose communist governments in Eastern Europe, and the giving of massive military aid to communist insurgencies in China, Vietnam, Cuba, Angola, Mozambique and Afghanistan, among other places, at crucial junctures of the Cold War. Tiny Cuba was a major exporter of revolution, supporting guerrilla movements in virtually every Latin American country, particularly Nicaragua, Guatemala and El Salvador, contributing regular troops to support allies in Algeria, Angola and Ethiopia, and pioneering a novel medical internationalism by sending thousands of doctors and nurses to the aid of revolutionary regimes elsewhere. The Iranian regime committed itself to *sudur-i-inqilab* or the export of its revolution, providing military assistance to Shia forces in Afghanistan, Iraq, Lebanon and Bahrain, as well as rhetorical solidarity with the struggles of fellow Muslims further afield.

The tendency to export revolution, where evident, is typically an outgrowth of two dynamics. First, revolutionary export can be the expression of an ideological belief in the universality of one's claims and the moral necessity of their propagation. Second, export can be a strategic response to external hostility or internal factionalism. Successful revolutions tend to arouse hostile international reactions because they threaten to disrupt the normal conduct of international relations. In such circumstances, international counterrevolution may call into being revolutionary internationalism as an inescapable strategic necessity. Conversely, where revolutionary regimes are internally divided, factions within the regime may precipitate a confrontation with the international system with a view to unifying the domestic public and/or discrediting more moderate rivals as less committed to the cause.

International effects: counterrevolution

The concept of revolution is inextricably entangled with that of counterrevolution, which we may understand as the attempt to prevent or contain a revolution, or to weaken or overthrow a revolutionary regime that has captured power. Halliday (1999: 208) reminds us that counterrevolution has itself generated other political concepts such as "conservatism", formulated in the writings of Edmund Burke and Josèphe de Maistre as a response to 1789, and has given the terms "reaction" and "reactionary" their contemporary connotations. Counterrevolution can involve both domestic and international actors working in alliance with one another. If revolutionary export antagonises international society as a result of its tendency to violate norms of sovereignty and non-intervention, one of the more striking ironies of counterrevolution is that it finds itself doing very much the same in the attempt to contain or roll back revolution. During the Cold War, both superpowers challenged core values of international society as a result of their frequent and flagrant interventions in the affairs of client states. The broader point here is that counterrevolution, like revolution, is an inescapably international affair.

Counterrevolution can take a number of forms (Halliday 1999: 210). Domestic opponents may attempt to overthrow the revolution with international assistance, as in the case of the Nicaraguan contras supported by the Reagan administration against the Sandinista regime. Counterrevolution may occur through the seizure of power by a counterrevolutionary faction within the revolutionary regime: while the Egyptian military played an ambiguous even if helpful role in the overthrow of Hosni Mubarak in 2011, its suppression of the democratically elected Muslim Brotherhood and subsequent assumption of power would seem to be an example of this variety of counterrevolution. Counterrevolutionary forces may seize power pre-emptively, in anticipation of a revolution: the military coups by Franco (1936) and Pinochet (1973) are good examples. Most interestingly, counterrevolutionary regimes may undertake pre-emptive reforms in an attempt to stave off the possibility of revolution. The creation of welfare states in western Europe was motivated, in large part, by a desire to prevent the spread of communism. The Kennedy administration's "Alliance for Progress" aid programme to Latin America in areas such as education, health and land reform, was also intended to weaken the appeal of communism. We can see, in these examples, the tendency of counterrevolution to attempt to obviate the need for revolution by co-opting significant elements of its agenda. These are precisely the sorts of revolutionary effects that Armstrong's rather blunt "socialization" thesis cannot make sense of.

If counterrevolution sometimes "steals" revolutionary ends, albeit in watered-down form, it also employs a number of its means: propaganda, diplomatic, monetary, material and military support. Crucially, counterrevolution has frequently been institutionalised in international agreements and alliances (Halliday 1999: 212–21). The 1815 Congress of Vienna must be understood as a counter-revolutionary pact: having defeated revolutionary France in war, its enemies – Britain, Austria, Prussia and Russia – committed themselves to suppressing the recurrence of revolution in France and elsewhere. The 1919 Treaty of Versailles was another great counterrevolutionary moment, this time directed against the Bolsheviks who were formally excluded from the peace talks. Following the Second World War, the architecture of the UN Security Council and, in particular, the institution of permanent membership with veto power, gave both superpowers the ability to suppress challenges to and within their respective blocs: in effect, UN institutional design was powerfully informed by counterrevolutionary imperatives. Thus, revolutions do not need to be successful on their own terms in order to have international effects. The very threat of revolution has radically reshaped international society at a number of historical junctures.

Halliday's exhaustive and systematic attention to the international dimensions of revolutions has had a transformative impact on IR's engagement with revolutions. Nonetheless, his effort to foreground "the international" should be seen as no more than a heuristic device. In practice, international and domestic factors cannot, and perhaps should not, be easily bifurcated. Arguing that the ostensibly domestic factors in Foran's five-fold causal account of revolutions (authoritarian states, cultures of resistance, economic downturns) are themselves thoroughly permeated by international influences and processes, Lawson (2015: 305–6) prefers what he calls an "intersocietal" approach that attempts to capture the full extent of the relationship between the "internal" and "external" of the nation-state, throughout the course of the revolutionary process. Such an approach would be attentive to the ways in which differently located but interactively engaged social sites affect the development of revolutions, without making prior assumptions about what these sites are and which ones are most significant (ibid: 309).

Conclusion

If we are not to think of revolutions as static entities but as historically contingent phenomena, we must be open to the possibility that the very character of revolutions might be changing. Timothy Garton Ash has suggested that from the 1960s onwards, "civil resistance has assisted at the birth of a new genre of revolution, qualitatively different from the Jacobin-Bolshevik model of 1789 and 1917" (Ash 2009: 377). Similarly, Sharon Nepstad's work on nonviolent revolutions departs from the observation that of the 67 authoritarian regimes that were dismantled between 1972 and 2002, more than 70% of these were the result of nonviolent civilian uprisings (Nepstad 2011: 4–5). Such uprisings resemble earlier revolutions in their reliance on mass mobilisation, but differ in the tactics that they deploy and the cross-class coalitions that they forge. The reasons for these shifts in the nature of revolution are complex and multifaceted, particularly given their association with two other elements that have accompanied such movements – elections and negotiation. They have to do with the deepening of democracy in established democratic states as well as with its extension to formerly authoritarian states. This latter development is itself a function of the end of the Cold War, which has reduced (but not eliminated) the willingness of great powers to support authoritarian client regimes, thereby weakening the coercive power of such states. Moreover, the attenuation of the ideological warfare that marked the Cold War seemed to bring in its wake a series of revolutions, particularly in Eastern Europe and the former Soviet Union, characterised less by strong and novel ideological worldviews than by a desire to (re)gain freedoms that these societies had once possessed or watched others enjoy.

These shifts in the nature of revolution might have two possible consequences for the conceptual study of revolution. First, they might generate new cognate concepts. Observing that the outcome of nonviolent revolutions effected through negotiation and election can often disappoint radical expectations, sometimes even calling into question the very applicability of the label "revolution", Ash has elsewhere suggested the term "refolution" to capture the elements of reform (continuity) and revolution (change) that such upheavals typically combine (Ash 1989; see also Bayat 2013). Alternatively, the increasing tendency towards nonviolent change may decentre violence as an integral element in our understanding of revolution itself. Nonetheless, we should be cautious to embrace this latter, more drastic, conceptual possibility. For one thing, the systemic shifts that heralded changes in the nature of revolution in 1989 already seem overtaken by the conjuncture in the early 21st century, which features a different balance of power and newly prominent ideological currents. Even if nonviolent movements are the new norm, the bloodiness of the Libyan and Syrian revolutions and the puritanical zeal of the so-called Islamic State, evident at the time of this writing, remind us that neither violence nor radical ideology have become obsolete features of revolutions.

In this chapter, I have offered a conceptual analysis of revolutions that combines elements of historical and political approaches. I justified my eschewal of the "scientific" approach on the ground that such an approach provides a temporally static understanding of revolution that is inattentive to the ways in which "revolution" – as a concept – is a product of its historical context and changes over time. Rather than offering a single authoritative definition of revolution, I have been more interested in the ways in which understandings of revolution have shifted and in the different kinds of questions that scholars have asked about revolutions over time. I have also addressed the question of why revolutions matter to international relations by drawing out the ways in which revolutions might be thought of as international, insofar as both their causes and effects are concerned. Along the way, I have tried to illuminate what is at stake politically in the conceptual analysis of revolutions.

Suggested Readings

Arendt, H. (1990 [1963]) *On Revolution*, London: Penguin.

A classic liberal account of revolution, with a particular focus on the American and French revolutions.

Foran, J. (2007) *Taking Power: On the Origins of Third World Revolutions*, Cambridge: Cambridge University Press.

An exemplar of fourth-generation scholarship on revolution, with a particular emphasis on revolutions in the Third World.

Halliday, F. (1999) *Revolution and World Politics: The Rise and Fall of the Sixth Great Power*, London: Macmillan.

An early, still influential, and comprehensive treatment of revolution in international relations.

Skocpol, T. (1979) *States and Social Revolutions: A Comparative Analysis of France, Russia, and China*, Cambridge: Cambridge University Press.

An exemplar of third-generation structuralist accounts of revolution, with exhaustive analyses of three major social revolutions.

Truillot, M.-R. (1995) *Silencing the Past: Power and the Production of History*, Boston, MA: Beacon Press.
A masterful account of the silencing and "forgetting" of the Haitian Revolution; will also appeal to those with an interest in memory and the writing of history.

Bibliography

Andrijasevic, R., Hamilton, C. and Hemmings, C. (2014) 'Re-imagining Revolutions', *Feminist Review* 106: 1–8.

Arendt, H. (1990 [1963]) *On Revolution*, London: Penguin.

Armstrong, D. (1993) *Revolution and World Order*, Oxford: Clarendon Press.

Ash, T. G. (1989) 'Revolution: The Springtime of Two Nations', *The New York Review of Books*, 15 June.

Ash, T. G. (2009) 'A Century of Civil Resistance: Some Lessons and Questions', in *Civil Resistance and Power Politics: The Experience of Non-violent Action from Gandhi to the Present*, Roberts, A. and Ash, T. G. (eds), Oxford: Oxford University Press.

Bayat, A. (2013) 'Revolution in Bad Times', *New Left Review* 80: 47–60.

Devji, F. (2005) *Landscapes of the Jihad: Militancy, Morality, Modernity*, London: Hurst.

Fanon, F. (1967 [1961]) *The Wretched of the Earth*, London: Penguin.

Foran, J. (2001) 'Studying Revolutions through the Prism of Race, Gender, and Class: Notes toward a Framework', *Race, Gender & Class* 8(2): 117–41.

Foran, J. (2007) *Taking Power: On the Origins of Third World Revolutions*, Cambridge: Cambridge University Press.

Gandhi, M. K. (1938 [1909]) *Indian Home Rule or Hind Swaraj*, Ahmedabad: Navajivan Publishing House.

Goldstone, J. A. (2014) *Revolutions: A Very Short Introduction*, Oxford: Oxford University Press.

Goodwin, J. (2001) *No Other Way Out: States and Revolutionary Movements, 1945–1991*, Cambridge: Cambridge University Press.

Guevara, E. C. (2013) [1961] *Guerrilla Warfare*, North Charleston, SC: CreateSpace.

Halliday, F. (1999) *Revolution and World Politics: The Rise and Fall of the Sixth Great Power*, London: Macmillan.

Harvey, D. (2009) *Cosmopolitanism and the Geographies of Freedom*, New York: Columbia University Press.

Hobsbawm, E. (2000 [1962]) *The Age of Revolution, 1789–1848*, London: Abacus.

James, C. L. R. (2001 [1938]) *The Black Jacobins: Toussaint L'Ouverture and the San Domingo Revolution*, London: Penguin.

Jayawardena, K. (1986) *Feminism and Nationalism in the Third World*, London: Zed Books.

Kotowski, C. (2009) 'Revolution: Untangling Alternative Meanings', in *Concepts and Method in Social Science: The Tradition of Giovanni Sartori*, Collier, D. and Gerring, J. (eds), London: Routledge.

Lawson, G. (2005) *Negotiated Revolutions: The Czech Republic, South Africa and Chile*, Aldershot: Ashgate.

Lawson, G. (2015) 'Revolutions and the International', *Theory and Society* 44: 299–319.

Lawson, G. (2015*a*) 'Within and Beyond the "Fourth Generation" of Revolutionary Theory', *Sociological Theory* (forthcoming).

Lenin, V. I. (1902) *What is to be Done?* www.marxists.org/archive/lenin/works/1901/witbd/

Mao Tse-Tung (1937) *On Guerrilla Warfare*, www.marxists.org/reference/archive/mao/works/1937/guerrilla-warfare/

Marx, K. and Engels, F. (2004 [1848]) *The Communist Manifesto*, London: Penguin.
Nepstad, S. E. (2011) *Nonviolent Revolutions: Civil Resistance in the Late 20th Century*, Oxford: Oxford University Press.
Schama, S. (2004) *Citizens: A Chronicle of the French Revolution*, London: Penguin.
Selbin, E. (2010) *Revolution, Rebellion, Resistance: The Power of Story*, London: Zed Books.
Shilliam, R. (2008) 'What the Haitian Revolution Might Tell Us about Development, Security, and the Politics of Race', *Comparative Studies in Society and History* 50(3): 778–808.
Skocpol, T. (1979) *States and Social Revolutions: A Comparative Analysis of France, Russia, and China*, Cambridge: Cambridge University Press.
Stone, L. (1966) 'Theories of Revolution', *World Politics* 18(2): 159–76.
Trotsky, L. (1932) *History of the Russian Revolution*, Chicago, IL: Haymarket Books.
Truillot, M.-R. (1995) *Silencing the Past: Power and the Production of History*, Boston, MA: Beacon Press.
Walt, S. (1992) 'Revolution and War', *World Politics* 44(3): 321–68.

16

Intervention

David Chandler

This chapter seeks to analyse fundamental shifts in the concept of intervention since the end of the Cold War by tracing the political and ideational context through which the normative perception, function and performance of intervention has been transformed. It does this with the view, highlighted in the introductory chapter to this volume, that concept analysis is not so much concerned with changes in formal definitions as with the semantic fields within which a concept operates. Indeed, concepts can maintain their broad definitional "meaning" while being understood very differently in different socio-historical contexts. Complementing broader historical overviews, such as that by Reus-Smit (2013), this chapter shines light on shifts in Western understandings of the concept of intervention since the end of the Cold War in relation to both traditional disciplinary understandings of sovereignty in IR and to Western, liberal or modernist forms of knowledge. It thus adopts elements from both the historical and the political (critical) approach, highlighting changes in meaning over time and how these changes are embedded in Western foreign policies seeking to order the world, including understandings of conflict and effective forms of governance.

In international law, intervention is a legal term for the use of force by one country in the internal or external affairs of another. In most cases, intervention is considered to be an unlawful act but some interventions may be considered lawful, as acts of self-defence or when supported by the UN Security Council to uphold international security. This chapter is not concerned with the legal debates surrounding this issue, not least because it holds that the traditional focus on military intervention must be complemented by an understanding of intervention through practices falling under the broad label of development. At a deeper level, this chapter shows how debates over international intervention have seen a shift from political concerns of sovereign rights under international law to concerns of knowledge claims of cause and effect highlighted through the problematisation of interventions' unintended consequences. This can be illustrated by contrasting the difference between the confidence – today, critics would say "hubris" (Mayall and Soares de Oliviera, 2011) – of 1990s' understandings of the transformative nature of external intervention and current, much more pessimistic, approaches.

In the 1990s, leading advocates understood international intervention as a clear exercise of Western power in terms of a "solutionist" approach to problems which could otherwise have increasingly problematic knock-on effects in a global and interconnected world (see, for example, Blair, 1999). They aspired to address problems at the level either of universalisable or generalisable solutions, exported from the West ("top-down" interventions), or through ambitious projects of social and political engineering (attempting to transform society from the "bottom up") (see, for example, Ramalingam, 2013). Today, analysts are much more likely to highlight that the complexity of global interactions and processes, in fact, mitigate against ambitious schemas for intervention. They argue that causal relations cannot be grasped in the frameworks which constituted Western intervention in terms of either "top-down" or "bottom-up" understandings of the mechanisms of socio-political transformation, which both involved challenges to, or redefinitions of, the conception of sovereignty and self-governance. In a more complex world, such linear or reductionist explanations of policy efficacy appear discredited, with growing awareness that any forms of external intervention or social engineering will have unintended side-effects (Rist et al., 2014). In the attempt to minimise these unintended consequences, the focus of policy-makers has shifted to the governance of effects rather than seeking to address ostensible root causes. For example, rather than seeking to solve conflict or to end it, international intervention is increasingly articulated as "managing" conflict, developing societal strategies to cope better and thereby limit its effects (DfID et al., 2011). Focusing on managing effects rather than engaging with causative chains provides a very different context in which the concept of intervention acquires meaning.

The chapter thus highlights how the epistemic challenge to linear causal understandings affects the conceptualisation of intervention: from an emphasis on the asymmetrical and potentially oppressive discourse of the "right of intervention" (based on the superior knowledge and resources of the policy-intervener and the clash of rights of intervention and sovereignty) to an increasing emphasis on the problem of the linear and reductive understandings of policy intervention itself (and the unintended consequences of such mechanistic approaches in the international sphere). The shifting understanding first negated disciplinary conceptions of intervention as undermining rights of autonomy (Chandler, 2010) and then displaced concepts of autonomy with more organicist understandings of emerging order, immune to traditional mechanisms of intervention. The shift to conceptualisations of intervention as the governance of effects thus shifted understandings of intervention away from the paradigmatic normative power and knowledge assumptions at the heart of the discipline of international relations.

The discussion proceeds in the following steps: first, the limits of traditional disciplinary attempts to analyse intervention are drawn out; second, the chapter analyses the radical shifts in the formal disciplinary understanding of the concept of intervention, from the 1990s to the 2010s, through the heuristic use of three frameworks or models. These can be demarcated both in their conceptualisation of the formal political categories of sovereignty and intervention and in their approach to causal knowledge claims. It is then argued that it is these discursive linkages that enable evolving forms of intervention that tend to no longer engage at the level of formal political authority and thus no longer require legitimisation on the basis of hierarchical claims of power or knowledge superiority.

The Limits of the Conceptualisation of Intervention within International Relations

In the policy debates of the 1990s, international intervention was often conceived of as an exception to the norm of international politics, which was legally based on a sovereign order. Intervention was posed as necessary in the case of crises that threatened the peace and security of international society and the UN Security Council incrementally relaxed its restrictions, making intervention increasingly permissible (ICISS, 2001). The legal and political exception to accepted international norms assumed the problem-solving capabilities of external international actors: the undermining of sovereign rights was legitimised by the hierarchical assumption of the superior knowledge and resources of the policy-interveners, thus discourses of international intervention necessarily assumed that knowledge and power operated in, what are increasingly seen today as, linear and reductive ways.

International relations theory has traditionally been concerned with questions of power and international order: how power politics and conflict may be tamed by international institutions and norms. In the traditional concerns of the discipline, the institution of sovereignty was seen to be key and intervention was therefore problematised (and contained) as destabilising international order and potentially leading to the internationalisation of conflict (see, for example, Bull, 1995; Schmitt, 2003). For this reason, advocates of intervention were keen either to keep intervention covert or to legitimise intervention on the basis of redefining sovereignty to enable intervention without destabilising international legal norms (see, for example, Krasner, 1999). As Cynthia Weber noted, it was not possible to speak of intervention without speaking of sovereignty: without sovereignty, there could be no framework of understanding, enabling judgements to be made as to "who would be the target of intervention and what would be violated or transgressed" (1995: 11). Critical constructivist theorist Helle Malmvig noted the co-constitutive relationship of the two concepts, arguing:

> Whether any given event constitutes an intervention or a non-intervention, is hence dependent on what meaning sovereignty is attributed in advance. In order for something to be portrayed as an intervention, there must always already be an idea of what falls and what does not fall within the sovereign sphere of the state. (2006: 16)

In fact, Malmvig argued, the relationship worked both ways as the concept of state sovereignty was also dependent on intervention. In discourses of intervention, at stake was the boundary line to be drawn between the inside and the outside of states: what counted as a national and as an international concern. In other words, the content of state sovereignty was not given in advance – prior to intervention – but was temporally constituted in the process of intervention itself (Malmvig, 2006: 17; see also Chapter 11, this volume).

Constructivist approaches were undoubtedly insightful in understanding sovereignty and intervention as mutually constitutive concepts (see further, Biersteker and Weber, 1996) and in providing useful conceptual tools for the analysis of how the concepts of sovereignty and intervention had been discursively deployed in the field of international politics. However, these approaches have been unable to grasp the transformation and then the severing of the ties between sovereignty and intervention since the heated debates of the 1990s. Today, it increasingly seems that the intervention–sovereignty binary no longer operates as a paradigm or "research assemblage", able to stabilise the meaning of intervention (see further, Law, 2004).

In order to analyse the changing meaning of intervention, it is also important to link conceptual discussions of sovereignty with epistemic questions of knowledge. This link is highlighted here by the development of Giorgio Agamben's heuristic framing of a shift from a concern with causation to that of effects, which he understands as a depoliticising move (Agamben, 2014). Debates about addressing causation involve socio-political analysis and policy choices, putting decision-making and the question of sovereign power and political accountability at the forefront. Causal relations assume power operates "from the top down", with policy outcomes understood to be direct products of conscious choices, powers and capacities. Agamben argues that whilst the governing of causes is the essence of politics, the governance of effects reverses the political process:

> We should not neglect the philosophical implications of this reversal. It means an epoch-making transformation in the very idea of government, which overturns the traditional hierarchical relation between causes and effects. Since governing the causes is difficult and expensive, it is more safe and useful to try to govern the effects. (Agamben, 2014: n.p.)

The governance of effects can therefore be seen as a retreat from the commitments of earlier interventionist approaches of the 1990s, in terms of both resources and policy goals. However, the shift from causation to effects involves a shifting conceptualisation of intervention itself; it is this connection which is the central concern of this chapter. Intervention conceptualised as the governance of effects relocates the subject position of the intervener, both in relation to the problem under consideration – which is no longer amenable to external policy solutions – and in terms of the society or community being intervened in – which is no longer constructed as lacking knowledge or resources, but as being the key agency of transformation. Transformation comes not through external cause-and-effect policy interventions but through the facilitation or empowerment of local agential capacities. The regulation of effects shifts the focus away from the formal public, legal and political sphere to the more organic and generative sphere of everyday life. The management of effects involves ongoing facilitative engagement in social processes and evades the question of government as political decision-making (see further, Chandler, 2014). The shift in meaning of the concept of intervention is traced below using this heuristic, drawing out how its implications enable conceptual analysis to go beyond the sovereignty–intervention binary of constructivist approaches.

Solutionism: Intervention against Sovereignty

The view of intervention and sovereignty as conceptually opposite and as mutually constitutive was predominant in the 1990s. In this period, there were heated debates about the clash of rights of intervention and rights of sovereignty, demonstrating the hold of the traditional international relations and international law perspective of the co-constitution of these two concepts. Even the Responsibility to Protect report of 2001 sought to maintain this conceptual binary: arguing, in the constructivist vein, that sovereignty was conditional on the state's will and ability to maintain human rights and that therefore the increasing permissibility of intervention meant the definition of sovereignty was changing to make this a condition of sovereignty (ICISS, 2001). Sovereignty and intervention were still co-constitutive opposites, affirmed by the fact that states were understood to lose their sovereignty if they failed to uphold the human rights of their citizens.

The "solutionist" cause-and-effect model – the archetypal model of intervention in the policy debates in the 1990s and early 2000s (particularly around the legal and political concerns of the right of humanitarian intervention and regime change under the auspices of the War on Terror) – operated on the basis of the superior moral, political, governance and military capacities of intervening actors. In this framing, the policy response tended to be one of centralised direction, under United Nations or United States and NATO command, based on military power or bureaucratic organisation, which often assumed that policy interveners operated in a vacuum, where social and political norms had broken down, and little attention needed to be given to the particular policy context.

This hierarchical model was articulated in universal terms. Intervening states and international institutions were understood to have the power, resources and objective scientific knowledge necessary to solve the problems of conflict and human rights abuses. This framework of intervention reached its apogee in international statebuilding in the Balkans, with long-term protectorates established over Bosnia and Kosovo, and was reflected in the RAND Corporation's reduction in such interventions to simple cost and policy formulas that could be universally applied (Dobbins et al., 2007).

Debates in the early and mid-1990s assumed that Western states had the knowledge and power to act and therefore focused on the question of the political will of Western states (see, for example, Held, 1995; Wheeler, 2000). Of particular concern was the fear that the US might pursue national interests rather than global moral and ethical concerns (Kaldor, 2007: 150). In this framework, problems were seen in terms of a universal and linear understanding. For "solutionists", humanitarian and human rights interventions, even including regime change and post-conflict management, could be successful on the basis that a specific set of policy solutions could solve a specific set of policy problems. This set up a universal understanding of good policy-making – the idea that certain solutions were timeless and could be exported or imposed – like the rule of law, democracy and markets.

This policy framework was highly mechanistic. The problems of non-Western states were understood in simple terms of the need to restore the equilibrium of the status quo – which was understood as being disrupted by new forces or events. It was illustrated, for example, in the popular "New Wars" thesis, which argued that stability was disrupted by exploitative elites seeking to destabilise society in order to cling to resources and power (Kaldor, 1999) or that the lack of human rights could be resolved through constitutional reforms (Brandt et al., 2011). The assumption was that society was fundamentally healthy and that problematic individuals or groups could be removed or replaced through external policy intervention which would enable equilibrium to be restored. This was a mechanistic view of how societies operated – as if they were machines and a single part had broken down and needed to be fixed. There was no holistic engagement with society as a collective set of processes, interactions and inter-relations (see also Chapter 9, this volume). The assumption was that external policy interveners could come up with a "quick fix" – perhaps sending troops to quell conflict or legal experts to write constitutions – followed by an exit strategy.

The universalist framework legitimising policy intervention thereby established a hierarchical and paternalist conceptualisation of intervention. Western liberal democratic states were understood to have the knowledge and power necessary to solve the problems that other "failed" and "failing" states were alleged to lack. It was therefore little surprise that these interventions challenged the sovereign right to self-government, which had long been upheld after decolonisation in the 1950s and 1960s. Many commentators have therefore raised problems with the idealisation of liberal Western societies and the holding up of abstract and unrealistic goals which tend to exaggerate the incapacity or lack of legitimacy of non-Western regimes (see, for example, Heathershaw and Lambach, 2008; Lemay-Hébert, 2009). Beneath universalist claims promoting the interest of human rights, human security or human development, critical theorists suggested that new forms of international domination were emerging, institutionalising market inequalities or restoring traditional hierarchies of power reminiscent of the colonial era (see, for example, Bickerton et al., 2007; Pugh et al., 2008).

Endogenous Causality: Building Sovereignty

The "solutionist" perspective, with its clear hierarchies of power and knowledge, began to be transformed with less linear and universal and more plural and endogenous views of causation. This shift began to be articulated in ways which understood sovereignty and intervention to be compatible, becoming increasingly predominant in the 2000s. This second model took local context much more into account, understanding problems as the results of complex processes of social and historical path dependencies that needed to be carefully intervened in and adjusted. Thus, the relation between external intervening actors (as agents or causes of policy changes) and the subsequent policy outcomes becomes understood to be much more socially, politically and historically mediated and contingent. This model is exemplified by the work of Roland Paris in the early 2000s on the need for "Institutionalisation before Liberalisation", in which it was argued that external interventions need to work "bottom-up" on the social and historical preconditions for statebuilding rather than "top-down" with the wholesale export of Western models and assumptions (Paris, 2004).

This model was popularised in the discipline of international relations by Stephen Krasner, who argued that the concept of sovereignty could be "unbundled" into three types: international legal sovereignty – the right to formal legal recognition; domestic sovereignty – the capacity to maintain human rights and good governance; and "Westphalian sovereignty" – the medieval concept of autonomy and self-government, where whatever the prince declared right was accepted as law (2004). Krasner argued that fragile states, which lacked the full capacities of domestic sovereignty, required international intervention but that this intervention should not be viewed as undermining sovereignty. Instead, international legal sovereignty should be used to sign international agreements allowing external governing intervention in order to build sovereignty, understood as a set of functional capacities. In this way, the Westphalian sovereignty of political autonomy was weakened but in exchange for the strengthening of domestic sovereignty.

This position gained further traction as international statebuilding and the extension of peacekeeping interventions led international interveners to expand the remits of their policy interventions well beyond the initial problem-solving policy interventions with their short time spans and exit strategies. The response to the shock terrorist attacks of 9/11 appeared to intensify the trend for extended international policy interventionism. The 2002 US National Security Strategy expanded and securitized the interventionist remit, arguing that: "America is now threatened less by conquering states than we are by failing ones" (NSS, 2002: 1). The recognition that we live in a globalized and interconnected world seemed to bind the needs of national security with those of human rights, democracy and development, creating a powerful consensus around intervention as sovereignty-building (see Mazarr, 2014).

The "intervention-as-sovereignty-building" form of intervening shifted away from addressing causes in universal and linear ways and towards a focus on endogenous processes and new institutionalist framings, easing a transition to the governance of effects. Rather than going for quick problem-solving fixes, policy advocates increasingly argued that policy needed to be concerned more holistically with social processes and analysis of state–society relations in order to overcome the "sovereignty gap" (Ghani and Lockhart, 2008). However, this perspective can still be understood as having some legacies of universalist cause-and-effect understandings in that it aimed at establishing viable market-based democracies and still presupposed that external policy interveners had the necessary superior knowledge and resources to shape policy outcomes.

Governing Effects: Intervention without Sovereignty

The third form of intervention – that of governing effects without a concern for causation – increasingly prevalent today, is a framing that evades discussion of the relationship between intervention and sovereignty. Western policy interveners increasingly claim not to be taking over decision-making processes, to be setting external goals, or to be measuring progress using external yardsticks. Rather than the external provision of policy solutions or the use of "conditionality" to guide states in specific directions, international actors are more likely to understand intervention in terms of enabling organic systems and existing knowledges, practices and capacities. This model forwards more homeopathic forms of policy intervention designed to enhance autonomous processes rather than undermine or socially engineer them (see, for example, Drabek and McEntire, 2003; Kaufmann, 2013, on emergent responses to disasters).

These forms of intervention cannot be grasped within the paradigm of claims for political authority central to the discipline of international relations.

The shift from intervention at the level of causation to intervention at the level of effects has been predominantly discussed in relation to the need to take into account the "law of unintended consequences". The problem of "unintended consequences" has become a policy trope regularly used as a shorthand expression for a profound shift in the understanding of intervention, addressed in this chapter, and can be understood as a generalised extension of Ulrich Beck's view of "risk society", with the determinate causal role of "side-effects" or of Bruno Latour's similar analysis of today's world as modernity "plus all its externalities" (see further, Beck, 1992; Latour, 2003). It seems that there is no way to consider intervention in terms of intended outcomes without considering the possibility that the unintended outcomes will outweigh these.

While, in 2002, the US State Department was focusing on extensive policy interventions to address the crucial question of state failure, in 2012, a decade later, the US Defense Strategic Guidance policy was illustrative of a different set of assumptions: that US forces would pursue their objectives through "innovative, low-cost, and small-footprint approaches" rather than by the conduct of "large-scale, prolonged stability operations" (DSG, 2012: 3, 6). In 2013, discussion over potential coercive intervention in Syria was dominated by fears that the unintended outcomes would outweigh the good intentions of external actors (Ackerman, 2013). General Martin Dempsey, chairman of the US Joint Chiefs of Staff, warned that policy caution was necessary as: "We must anticipate and be prepared for the unintended consequences of our action" (Ackerman, 2013).

As Michael Mazarr argued in the influential US foreign policy journal *Foreign Affairs*, in 2014, securing US goals of peace, democracy and development in failing and conflict-ridden states could not, in fact, be done by instrumental cause-and-effect external policy interventions: "It is an organic, grass-roots process that must respect the unique social, cultural, economic, political, and religious contexts of each country … and cannot be imposed" (Mazarr, 2014). For Mazarr, policy would now follow a more "resilient mindset, one that treats perturbations as inevitable rather than calamitous and resists the urge to overreact", understanding that policy intervention must work with rather than against local institutions and "proceed more organically and authentically" (Mazarr, 2014). This shift is also reflected by high-level policy experts in the US State Department; according to Charles T. Call, senior adviser at the Bureau of Conflict and Stabilization Operations, current US approaches seek not to impose unrealistic external goals but instead to facilitate local transformative agency through engaging with local "organic processes and plussing them up" (cited in Chandler, 2015: 43).

Intervention, today, is increasingly understood to be problematic if it is based on the grand narratives of liberal internationalism, which informed and drove the debate on international intervention in the 1990s, when issues of intervention and non-intervention in Africa and the Balkans were at the centre of international political contestation. International policy intervention is not opposed per se or on principle, but on the basis of the discrediting of universal and hierarchical knowledge assumptions which informed policy interventions and produced the hubristic and reductionist promises of the imposition of external solutions.

"Organic" versus "Political" Understandings of Intervention

The critique of cause-and-effect understandings of intervention has a long scientific heritage in similar critiques of modern medical interventions based on antibiotics and other artificial chemical and technical remedies (see, for example, Thacker and Artlett, 2012; Krans, 2014). The reductionist understanding of intervention in the biomedical sciences has often been problematised for its lack of attention to unintended consequences, which can easily mean that the cure can be worse for individual and societal health care than the initial affliction. These critiques have operated as a readily available template for the rapid rethinking of the meaning of the concept of intervention in the discipline of international relations; relocating it in a "semantic field" that has little relation to traditional concerns of international stability, international law, sovereign rights of independence or to postcolonial sensibilities.

The critiques of linear and reductionist cause-and-effect approaches have tended to focus on the value of organic, natural or endogenous powers of resistance and resilience which have been understood to be unintentionally undermined through the mechanistic assumptions of intervention (at work in both Western natural and social sciences; see, for example, Capra, 1983: 118–165). In parallel arguments in discourses of international intervention, the organic processes of endogenous development tend to be prioritised over universalising, mechanistic or reductionist approaches to policy intervention, which seek to introduce policy solutions from the outside. For example, while markets, development, democracy, security and the rule of law might be good when they develop organically, it is often argued that when they are extracted from their context and applied in a "pure" form they can be dangerous as they lack the other ingredients connected to institutions and culture.

This perspective first began to be argued in relation to intervention in the Balkans in the late 1990s, when interventionist policy-making began to shift attention to the endogenous or internal capacities and capabilities of the local society, rather than seeking externally managed "military solutions, quick fixes [and] easy, early exits", associated with simple cause-and-effect understandings (Bildt, 2003). However, the critique of cause-and-effect assumptions, which focused on the knowledge and expertise of external policy interveners, rapidly extended beyond the critique of coercive or military interventions to cover a broad range of policy interventions, including "bottom-up" attempts at socio-political engineering, associated with liberal internationalist goals of promoting markets, democracy and the rule of law.

The governance of effects, increasingly taken up by international policy interveners, thereby insists that problems cannot be dealt with merely at the level of causation, by identifying and categorising a problem as if it could be understood in the reductionist terms of cause-and-effect. Intervention based on the governance of effects therefore has no need for ready-made international policy solutions that can simply be applied or implemented, and therefore implies little possibility of learning generic lessons from intervention that could be applied to all other cases of conflict or of underdevelopment, on the basis that if the symptoms appear similar the cause must be the same. Crucially, this non-linear and context-dependent framing takes intervention out of the context of "top-down" policy-making and policy understanding and out of the political sphere of democratic debate and decision-making.

The focus therefore shifts away from international policies (supply-driven policy-making) and towards engaging with the internal capacities and capabilities that are already held to exist. In other words, there is a shift from the agency, knowledge and practices of policy interveners to that of the society which is the object of policy concerns. As the 2013 updated UK Department for International Development Growth and Resilience Operational Plan states: "We will produce less 'supply-driven' development of product, guidelines and policy papers, and foster peer-to-peer, horizontal learning and knowledge exchange, exploiting new technologies such as wiki/huddles to promote the widest interaction between stakeholders" (DfID, 2013: 8).

"Supply-driven" policies – the stuff of politics and of democratic decision-making – are understood to operate in an artificial or non-organic way, and to lack an authentic connection to the effects that need to be addressed. The imposition of (accountable) external institutional and policy frameworks has become increasingly seen as artificial and thereby as having counterproductive or unintended outcomes. Effects-based approaches thereby seek to move away from "liberal peace" policy interventions – seeking to export constitutional frameworks, to train and equip military and police forces, to impose external conditionalities on the running of state budgets, to export managerial frameworks for civil servants and political representatives or to impose regulations to ensure administrative transparency and codes of conduct – which were at the heart of international policy prescriptions in the 1990s and early 2000s (ActionAid, 2006; Eurodad, 2006; World Bank, 2007).

It is argued that the "supply-driven" approach of external experts exporting or developing liberal institutions does not grasp the complex processes generative of instability or insecurity. Instead, the cause-and-effect model of intervention is seen to create problematic "hybrid" political systems and fragile states with little connection to their societies (MacGinty, 2010; Richmond and Mitchell, 2012). The imposition of institutional frameworks, which have little connection to society, is understood as failing, not only in not addressing causal processes but as making matters worse through undermining local capacities to manage the effects of problems, shifting problems elsewhere and leaving states and societies even more fragile or vulnerable than they were before. It is alleged to fail to hear the "message" of problematic manifestations or to enable societies' own organic and homeostatic processes to generate corrective mechanisms. In short, external intervention is said to shortcut the ability of societies to reflect on and take responsibility for their own affairs and is seen as a counterproductive "over-reaction" by external powers (see further, Desch, 2008; Maor, 2012). Instead, the argument is that effective and sustainable solutions can only be developed through practice by actors on the ground.

As noted above, following Agamben, the conceptualisation of policy interventions in terms of the governance of effects evades the traditional disciplinary understanding of intervention as an exercise of external political power and authority. It does this through denying intervention as an act of external decision-making and policy direction, as understood in the political paradigm of liberal modernist discourse. Indeed, it suggests there is no intervention. This can be illustrated through highlighting some examples of policy shifts in key areas of international concern: security and the rule of law; development; and democracy and rights.

Security and the rule of law

Policy interventions are shifting not only with regard to an understanding of sovereignty but in relation to the understanding of conflict. There is much less talk of conflict prevention or conflict resolution and more of conflict management. As the UK government argues, in a 2011 combined DfID, Foreign and Commonwealth Office and Ministry of Defence document, conflict per se is not the problem: "Conflict is a normal part of human interaction, the natural result when individuals and groups have incompatible needs, interests or beliefs" (DfID et al., 2011: 5). The problem which needs to be tackled is the state or society's ability to manage conflict: "In stable, resilient societies conflict is managed through numerous formal and informal institutions" (DfID et al., 2011: 5). Conflict management, as the UK government policy indicates, is increasingly understood as an organic set of societal processes and practices, which international policy intervention can influence, but it cannot import solutions from outside or impose them. This understanding very much follows the approach long advocated by influential peace theorist, Jean Paul Lederach, who argued that: "The greatest resource for sustaining peace in the long term is always rooted in the local people and their culture" (1997: 94). For Lederach, managing conflict means moving away from cause-and-effect forms of instrumental external intervention which see people as "recipients" of policy, and instead seeing people as "resources", integral to peace processes; it is therefore essential that:

> we in the international community adopt a new mind-set – that we move beyond a simple prescription of answers and modalities for dealing with conflict that come from outside the setting and focus at least as much attention on discovering and empowering the resources, modalities, and mechanisms for building peace that exist within the context. (1997: 95)

One of the central shifts in understanding conflict as something that needs to be "coped with" and "managed", rather than something that can be "solved" or "prevented", is the view that state-level interventions are of limited use. Peace treaties can be signed by state parties, but unless peace is seen as an ongoing and transformative, inclusive societal process these agreements will be merely superficial and non-sustainable (1997: 135; see also Chapter 7, this volume).

Just as peace and security are less understood as able to be secured through cause-and-effect forms of intervention, reliant on policy interveners imposing solutions in mechanical and reductive ways, there has also been a shift in understanding the counterproductive effects of attempts to export the rule of law. The governance of effects approach is driven by a realisation of the gap between the formal sphere of law and constitutionalism and the social "reality" of informal power relations and informal rules. This perspective has also been endorsed by Douglass North, the policy guru of new institutionalist economics, who has highlighted the difficulties in understanding how exported institutions will interact with "culturally derived norms of behavior" (1990: 140). The social reality of countries undergoing post-conflict "transition" is thereby less capable of being understood merely by an analysis of laws and statutes. In fact, there increasingly appears to be an unbridgeable gap between the artificial constructions of legal and constitutional frameworks and the realities of everyday life, revealed in dealings between individual members of the public and state authorities.

Development

A key policy area where the shift from addressing causes to the governance of effects has had an impact has been in the sphere of development – the policy sphere previously most concerned with transformative policy interventions. Coping with poverty and with disasters is clearly a very different problematic from seeking to use development policy to reduce or to end extreme poverty. However, discourses of disaster risk reduction have increasingly displaced those of sustainable forms of development because of the unintended side-effects of undermining the organic coping mechanisms of communities and therefore increasing vulnerabilities and weakening resilience (see, for example, IRDR, 2014; UNDP, 2014). Claudia Aradau has highlighted the importance of the UK Department for International Development (DfID) shift in priorities from poverty-reduction strategies to developing community resilience, which assumes the existence of poverty as the basis of policy-making (Aradau, 2014). As she states: "resilience responses entail a change in how poverty, development and security more broadly are envisaged"; this is clearly highlighted in DfID's 2011 report outlining the UK government's humanitarian policy:

> Humanitarian assistance should be delivered in a way that does not undermine existing coping mechanisms and helps a community build its own resilience for the future. National governments in at-risk countries can ensure that disaster risk management policies and strategies are linked to community-level action. (DfID, 2011: 10, cited in Aradau, 2014)

As George Nicholson, Director of Transport and Disaster Risk Reduction for the Association of Caribbean States, argues explicitly: "improving a person's ability to respond to and cope with a disaster event must be placed on equal footing with the process to encourage economic development", highlighting the importance of disaster risk as a strategy for managing effects versus the cause-and-effect approach associated with development policy interventions (Nicholson, 2014). Whereas development approaches put the emphasis on external policy assistance and expert knowledge, disaster risk reduction clearly counterposes an alternative framework of intervention, where it is local knowledge and local agency that count the most. Disaster risk reduction strategies stress the empowerment of the vulnerable and marginalised in order for them to cope with and manage the effects of the risks and contingencies that are concomitant with the maintenance of their precarious existence.

Democracy and rights

As emphasised above, the management of effects approach does not seek to assert sovereign power or Western hierarchies of power and knowledge; in fact the governance of effects operates as both an epistemological and ontological challenge to the cause-and-effect understandings of intervention, dominant until the last decade. These points are highlighted, for example, in Bruno Latour's critical engagement with modernist modes of understanding: arguing that Western societies have forgotten the lengthy processes which enabled them to build liberal institutions dependent on the lengthy process of the establishment of a political culture, which has to be steadily maintained, renewed and extended and cannot be exported or imposed (Latour, 2013: 343).

This shift away from formal universalist understandings of democracy and human rights is increasingly evidenced in the shifting understanding of human rights-based approaches to empowerment. Understanding empowerment in instrumental cause-and-effect terms based on the external provision of legal and political mechanisms for claims is increasingly seen to be ineffective. Rights-based NGOs now seek not to empower people to access formal institutional mechanisms but to enable them to empower themselves. The governance of effects approach places the emphasis on the agency and self-empowerment of local actors, not on the introduction of formal frameworks of law, supported by international human rights norms (Moe and Simojoki, 2013: 404).

The approach of "finding organic processes and plussing them up" (as articulated by the US State Department policy advisor, cited earlier in the chapter) is not limited to government policy interventions but has been increasingly taken up as a generic approach to overcome the limits of cause-and-effect understandings. A study of Finnish development NGOs highlights that rather than instrumentally selecting groups or civil society elites, new forms of intervention appear as anti-intervention, denying any external role in this process and stressing that there is no process of external management or selection as policy interveners work with whatever groups or associations already exist and "have just come together … it is not our NGO that brought them together but we just found them that way" (Kontinen, 2014: 12).

A similar study, in southeastern Senegal, notes that policy interveners are concerned to avoid both the "moral imperialism" of imposing Western human rights norms and a moral relativism which merely accepts local traditional practices (Gillespie and Melching, 2010: 481). The solution forwarded is that of being non-prescriptive and avoiding and "unlearning" views of Western teachers as "authorities" and students as passive recipients (2010: 481). Policy intervention is articulated as the facilitation of local people's attempts to uncover traditional practices and in "awakening" and "engaging" their already existing capacities: "By detecting their own inherent skills, they can more easily transfer them to personal and community problem solving" (2010: 490). These processes can perhaps be encouraged or assisted by external policy interveners but they cannot be transplanted from one society to another and, even less, can they be imposed by policy actors.

Conclusion

A shift in the meaning of the concept of intervention – from taking responsibility for external solutions to problems to the facilitation of endogenous capacities, focusing on the problem society's own capacities and needs and internal and organic processes – has left the basic definition of intervention unchanged. We might say that what shifted during the two decades since the end of the Cold War was an understanding of the practice of intervention, from a dramatic decision and show of physical force in a particular moment to intervention as an everyday practice which is less visible and much more time-consuming. Of course, the former has not disappeared and we might say that the two readings complement each other. Significantly, what has changed in both cases has been the discursive context in which intervention has been located, which has moved namely towards one marked by a growing scepticism of attempts to export or impose Western models. If this is a "lessons learned" approach, it is one that learns that knowledge cannot be readily extracted from the concrete context in order to be applied elsewhere.

The importance of this change should not be underestimated: understood as the governance of effects, intervention as a set of practices is transformed along with the political problematic within which it is located. The problematic of intervention is now less that of sovereign power and the denial of autonomy on the basis of hierarchical understandings of capacity. Intervention today appears to take the form of a much more distributed or "flatter" ontology of power and knowledge. In fact, in this paradigm, intervention requires little specialist knowledge and tends to problematise hierarchical claims; instead being understood to require more therapeutic capacities and sensitivities, attuned to open and unscripted forms of engagement, mutual processes of learning and unpredictable and spontaneous forms of knowledge exchange (see, for example, Duffield, 2007: 233–4).

In the illustrative examples of the conceptualisation of intervention, given above, it is clear that problems are no longer conceived of as amenable to political solutions in terms of instrumental governing interventions on the basis of cause-and-effect understandings. Those subject to new forms of empowerment and capacity-building are not understood as citizens of states – capable of negotiating, debating, deciding and implementing policy agendas – but instead are caught up in never-ending processes of governing effects at the local or community level. Politics disappears from the equation and with it the clash of the co-constitutive concepts of sovereignty and intervention and the legitimating claims of power and knowledge through which these claims were contested.

Suggested Readings

Chandler, David (2010) *International Statebuilding: The Rise of Post-Liberal Governance* (London: Routledge).

This book covers the theoretical frameworks and practices of international state-building, the debates they have triggered and the way that international state-building has developed in the post-Cold War era.

Ghani, Ashraf and Lockhart, Claire (2008) *Fixing Failed States: A Framework for Rebuilding a Fractured World* (Oxford: Oxford University Press).

Includes practical policy proposals to overcome the "sovereignty gap" from policy experts serving as World Bank officials, as advisers to the UN and as high-level participants in the new government of Afghanistan.

Paris, Roland (2004) *At War's End: Building Peace after Civil Conflict* (Cambridge: Cambridge University Press).

Based on a range of case studies of peacebuilding, Paris argues that peace-builders should establish the foundations of effective governmental institutions prior to launching wholesale liberalisation programs.

Reus-Smit, Christian (2013) 'The concept of intervention', *Review of International Studies*, 39(5): 1057–1076.

This article questions the "sovereignty frame" conception of intervention, arguing that it distorts our understanding of interventionary practices and forms of reasoning that occur in non-sovereign international orders.

Weber, Cynthia (1995) *Simulating Sovereignty: Intervention, the State and Symbolic Exchange* (Cambridge: Cambridge University Press).
Weber presents a critical analysis of the concept of sovereignty. Combining critical international relations theory and foreign policy discourses about intervention, she radically deconstructs sovereignty by questioning the historical foundations of sovereign authority.

Bibliography

Ackerman, Spencer (2013) 'US military intervention in Syria would create "unintended consequences"', *The Guardian*, 22 July. Available at: www.theguardian.com/world/2013/jul/22/us-military-intervention-syria

ActionAid (2006) *What Progress? A Shadow Review of World Bank Conditionality* (Johannesburg: ActionAid). Available at: www.actionaid.org.uk/sites/default/files/what_progress.pdf

Agamben, Giorgio (2014) 'For a theory of destituent power', *Chronos*, 10. Posted February. Available at: www.chronosmag.eu/index.php/g-agamben-for-a-theory-of-destituent-power.html

Aradau, Claudia (2014) 'The promise of security: resilience, surprise and epistemic politics', *Resilience: International Practices, Policies and Discourses*, 2(2): 73–87.

Beck, Ulrich (1992) *Risk Society: Towards a New Modernity* (London: Sage).

Bickerton, Christopher J., Cunliffe, Philip and Gourevitch, Alexander (eds) (2007) *Politics without Sovereignty: A Critique of Contemporary International Relations* (Abingdon: University College London Press).

Biersteker, Thomas J. and Weber, Cynthia (1996) *State Sovereignty as Social Construct* (Cambridge: Cambridge University Press).

Bildt, Carl (2003) 'Europe's future in the mirror of the Balkans', *openDemocracy*, 3 April. Available at: www.opendemocracy.net/democracy-open_politics/article_1123.jsp

Blair, Tony (1999) 'Doctrine of the international community', 24 April. Available at: http://webarchive.nationalarchives.gov.uk/+/www.number10.gov.uk/Page1297

Brandt, Michele, Cottrell, Jill, Ghai, Yash and Regan, Anthony (2011) *Constitution-making and Reform: Options for the Process* (Geneva: Interpeace). Available at: www.constitutionmakingforpeace.org/sites/default/files/Constitution-Making-Handbook.pdf

Bull, Hedley (1995) *The Anarchical Society: A Study of Order in World Politics* (2nd edn) (Basingstoke: Palgrave).

Capra, Fritjof (1983) *The Turning Point: Science, Society and the Rising Culture* (London: Flamingo).

Chandler, David (2010) *International Statebuilding: The Rise of Post-Liberal Governance* (London: Routledge).

Chandler, David (2014) 'Democracy unbound? Non-linear politics and the politicisation of everyday life', *European Journal of Social Theory*, 17(1): 42–59.

Chandler, David (2015) 'Resilience and the "everyday": beyond the paradox of "liberal peace"', *Review of International Studies*, 41(1): 27–48.

Collier, Paul (2010) *War, Guns and Votes: Democracy in Dangerous Places* (London: Vintage).

Defense Strategic Guidance (DSG) (2012) *Sustaining US Global Leadership: Priorities for 21st Century Defense* (Washington, DC: White House).

Department for International Development (DfID) (2011) *Saving Lives, Preventing Suffering and Building Resilience: The UK Government's Humanitarian Policy* (London: DfID).

Department for International Development (DfID) (2013) *Operational Plan 2011–2015: DFID Growth and Resilience Department* (London: DfID).
Department for International Development (DfID), Foreign and Commonwealth Office (FCO) and Ministry of Defence (MoD) (2011) *Building Stability Overseas Strategy* (London: DfID, FCO, MoD).
Desch, Michael C. (2008) 'America's liberal illiberalism: the ideological origins of overreaction in US foreign policy', *International Security*, 32(3): 7–43.
Dobbins, James, Jones, Seth G., Crane, Keith and DeGrasse, Beth Cole (2007) *The Beginner's Guide to Nation-Building* (Santa Monica, CA: RAND).
Drabek, Thomas E. and McEntire, David A. (2003) 'Emergent phenomena and the sociology of disaster: lessons, trends and opportunities from the research literature', *Disaster, Prevention and Management*, 12(2): 97–112.
Duffield, Mark (2007) *Development, Security and Unending War: Governing the World of Peoples* (Cambridge: Polity).
Eurodad (2006) *World Bank and IMF Conditionality: A Development Injustice* (Brussels: European Network on Debt and Development). Available at: www.eurodad.org/uploaded files/whats_new/reports/eurodad_world_bank_and_imf_conditionality_report.pdf
Ghani, Ashraf and Lockhart, Claire (2008) *Fixing Failed States: A Framework for Rebuilding a Fractured World* (Oxford: Oxford University Press).
Gillespie, Diane and Melching, Molly (2010) 'The transformative power of democracy and human rights in nonformal education: the case of Tostan', *Adult Education Quarterly*, 60(5): 477–498.
Heathershaw, John and Lambach, Daniel (2008) 'Introduction: post-conflict spaces and approaches to statebuilding', *Journal of Intervention and Statebuilding*, 2(3): 269–289.
Held, David (1995) *Democracy and the Global Order: From the Modern State to Cosmopolitan Governance* (Cambridge: Polity).
Integrated Research on Disaster Risk (IRDR) (2014) *Issue Brief: Disaster Risk Reduction and Sustainable Development*. Available at: www.preventionweb.net/english/professional/publications/v.php?id=35831
International Commission on Intervention and State Sovereignty (ICISS) (2001) *The Responsibility to Protect* (Ottawa: International Development Research Centre).
Kaldor, Mary (1999) *New and Old Wars: Organized Violence in a Global Era* (Cambridge: Polity).
Kaldor, Mary (2007) *Human Security: Reflections on Globalization and Intervention* (Cambridge: Polity).
Kaufmann, Mareile (2013) 'Emergent self-organisation in emergencies: resilience rationales in interconnected societies', *Resilience: International Policies, Practices and Discourses*, 1(1): 53–68.
Kontinen, Tiina (2014) 'Rights-based approach in practice? Dilemmas of empowerment in a development NGO', unpublished paper, presented at 'After Human Rights' workshop, University of Helsinki, 13–14 March.
Krans, Brian (2014) '5 frightening consequences of overusing antibiotics', *HealthlineNews*, 11 March. Available at: www.healthline.com/health-news/five-unintended-consequences-antibiotic-overuse-031114
Krasner, Stephen D. (1999) *Sovereignty: Organized Hypocrisy* (Princeton, NJ: Princeton University Press).
Krasner, Stephen D. (2004) 'Sharing sovereignty: new institutions for collapsed and failing states', *International Security*, 29(2): 85–120.
Latour, Bruno (2003) 'Is re-modernization occurring – and if so, how to prove it? A commentary on Ulrich Beck', *Theory, Culture & Society*, 20(2): 35–48.
Latour, Bruno (2013) *An Inquiry into Modes of Existence: An Anthropology of the Moderns* (Cambridge, MA: Harvard University Press).
Law, John (2004) *After Method: Mess in Social Science* (Abingdon: Routledge).

Lederach, Jean Paul (1997) *Building Peace: Sustainable Reconciliation in Divided Societies* (Washington, DC: United States Institute of Peace).
Lemay-Hébert, Nicolas (2009) 'Statebuilding without nation-building? Legitimacy, state failure and the limits of the institutionalist approach', *Journal of Intervention and Statebuilding*, 3(1): 21–45.
MacGinty, Roger (2010) 'Hybrid peace: the interaction between top-down and bottom-up peace', *Security Dialogue*, 41(4): 391–412.
Malmvig, Helle (2006) *State Sovereignty and Intervention: A Discourse Analysis of Interventionary and Non-Interventionary Practices in Kosovo and Algeria* (London: Routledge).
Maor, Moshe (2012) 'Policy overreaction', working paper, Hebrew University of Jerusalem. Available at: http://portal.idc.ac.il/he/schools/government/research/documents/maor.pdf
Mayall, James and Soares de Oliviera, Ricardo (eds) (2011) *The New Protectorates: International Tutelage and the Making of Liberal States* (London: Hurst & Co.).
Mazarr, Michael J. (2014) 'The rise and fall of the failed-state paradigm: requiem for a decade of distraction', *Foreign Affairs*, Jan.–Feb. Available at: www.foreignaffairs.com/articles/140347/michael-j-mazarr/the-rise-and-fall-of-the-failed-state-paradigm
Moe, Louise W. and Simojoki, Maria V. (2013) 'Custom, contestation and cooperation: peace and justice in Somaliland', *Conflict, Security & Development*, 13(4): 393–416.
National Security Strategy (NSS) (2002) *The National Security Strategy of the United States of America* (Washington, DC: White House). Available at: www.state.gov/documents/organization/63562.pdf
Nicholson, George (2014) 'Inequality and its impact on the resilience of societies', Association of Caribbean States, 22 July. Available at: www.eturbonews.com/48253/inequality-and-its-impact-resilience-societies
North, Douglass C. (1990) *Institutions, Institutional Change and Economic Performance* (Cambridge: Cambridge University Press).
Paris, Roland (2004) *At War's End: Building Peace after Civil Conflict* (Cambridge: Cambridge University Press).
Pugh, Michael, Cooper, Neil and Turner, Mandy (eds) (2008) *Whose Peace? Critical Perspectives on the Political Economy of Peacebuilding* (London: Palgrave Macmillan).
Ramalingam, Ben (2013) *Aid on the Edge of Chaos: Rethinking International Cooperation in a Complex World* (Oxford: Oxford University Press).
Reus-Smit, Christian (2013) 'The concept of intervention', *Review of International Studies*, 39(5): 1057–1076.
Richmond, Oliver P. and Mitchell, Audra (eds) (2012) *Hybrid Forms of Peace: From Everyday Agency to Post-Liberalism* (Basingstoke: Palgrave).
Rist, L., Felton, A., Nyström, M., Troell, M., Sponseller, R. A., Bengtsson, J., et al. (2014) 'Applying resilience thinking to production ecosystems', *Ecosphere*, 5(6): article 73.
Schmitt, Carl (2003) *The Nomos of the Earth: In the International Law of the Jus Publicum Europaeum* (New York: Telos Press).
Thacker, James D. and Artlett, Carol, M. (2012) 'The Law of Unintended Consequences and Antibiotics', *Open Journal of Immunology*, 2(2): 59–64.
United Nations Development Programme (UNDP) (2014) *Disaster Risk Reduction Makes Development Sustainable*. Available at: www.undp.org/content/dam/undp/library/crisis%20prevention/UNDP_CPR_CTA_20140901.pdf
Weber, Cynthia (1995) *Simulating Sovereignty: Intervention, the State and Symbolic Exchange* (Cambridge: Cambridge University Press).
Wheeler, Nicholas, J. (2000) *Saving Strangers: Humanitarian Intervention in International Society* (Oxford: Oxford University Press).
World Bank (2007) *Conditionality in Development Policy Lending* (Washington, DC: World Bank). Available at: http://siteresources.worldbank.org/PROJECTS/Resources/40940-1114615847489/Conditionalityfinalreport120407.pdf

17

Integration

Thomas Diez

Integration as a concept of international relations (IR) is closely tied to the territorial differentiation of the international system. In the broadest sense of the term, it designates a process of altering or overcoming the boundaries of states, thus it falls in the "modes of transformation category" outlined in the introductory chapter to this volume. This transformative process is often considered positive; indeed, for advocates of integration it is a recipe for peace. Viewing modern war as a result of the rise of the territorial state in an anarchical system, the argument is that once states are bound up in a network of rules and institutionalised transactions across borders, war becomes too costly or even unimaginable. As such, the concept comes with strong normative undertones and a close link to liberal thought. In fact, from Kant, as an advocate of an international republic of states, to Mitrany as the main proponent of functionalism as a "working peace system" (Mitrany 1966), the classical thinkers of integration would all be found in the chapters on liberalism in IR textbooks. Yet, they nonetheless had different visions of integration, sometimes advocating federalisation through treaties, sometimes emphasising linkages between societies arising from increased interaction. Part of the liberal legacy is that integration projects are often framed in a technical, expert-driven manner, even though their aim may be outright political (Hansen and Williams 1999). Yet, once we look beyond technical discussions, the nature and legitimacy of (international) integration is contested among both scholars and practitioners.

This chapter tries to establish the main lines of debate regarding the concept of integration, both in its political and in its academic use, which are intertwined in shared discourses. The underlying assumption is that integration is a contested concept that, following Laclau and Mouffe (1985), works as a "nodal point" in many debates about the future of political organisation in international society. As such, articulations of integration are always attempts to stabilise particular understandings about politics and society. They exercise power even if they seem to innocently advocate peace. In fact, it is precisely because scholars tend to be sympathetic to integration projects that we ought to scrutinise the underlying concept carefully – not with the aim of reinstating the nation-state, but in order to openly discuss the impact of what would replace it, and to shape that future. This chapter is thus largely written from a political-critical approach, to use the terminology from Chapter 1. In the Foucauldian tradition, I am interested in how the concept of integration is articulated to stabilise societies. Such fixations of meaning are always situated in particular historical contexts and they marginalise alternative discourses. Thus, a core characteristic of my approach is a focus on the power of interrelated discourses. However, I am not pursuing a genealogical approach proper. In drawing out the main lines of contention, my approach is closer to the earlier writings of Foucault and more interested in the order of discourses. That said, my discussion of the elements that bind articulations of integration together is in no way meant to reject an approach that would focus more on the internal contradictions and ruptures, which I will not ignore.

The chapter proceeds in three main steps. The next section lays out the main dimensions of the debates about integration (section 2). This provides me with an analytical frame with which it will then be possible to trace these debates. I will first do so by summarising some of the main historical integration projects (section 3). This will establish the European experience as the main reference point, but also point to alternative understandings and practices of integration elsewhere. The following section is dedicated to political and theoretical controversies about integration. As I will show, these are often linked and mutually sustain each other. My conclusions will reaffirm integration as a powerful political concept, coupled with a reminder that we need to take the articulations of integration more seriously than IR scholarship has done in the past.

Charting the Terrain: Dimensions of Integration

The debates on the concept of integration as a process of altering or overcoming the boundaries of states can be structured around two central dimensions – the sphere and the telos of integration. This provides us with a conceptual matrix that can serve as a heuristic device to analyse competing readings and practices of integration. All these readings deal with the transformation of boundaries, but to different degrees and focusing on different parts of society. Such a broad understanding of integration includes projects that emphasise "mere" co-operation between sovereign states, as even in such schemes, boundaries and sovereignty are being re-articulated and most of them involve some degree of supranationalism (the transfer of authoritative decision-making to the level "above states"). Likewise, while the development of what is now called the European Union (EU) plays a prominent role, we should not privilege integration efforts operating through the creation of a common market or take the experience of the EU as the only possible path to integration. And even if the EU serves as a model for most integration projects, sometimes in its explicit rejection, its nature is complex and there is no consensus over its purpose, which only serves to demonstrate the contestation in the articulation of the concept.

Another dimension concerns the geographical scope of integration. Classic integration conceptualisations have tended to be global in character, although they may have restricted participation in integration to states with particular political characteristics, such as some interpretations of Kant have done (but see MacMillan 2006).

Until today, a lively debate exists around whether Kant envisaged a world federal state or merely a voluntary association of states, which would have been much less supranational (see Kleingeld 2004). Mitrany's first rendering of functionalism was also global in scope, and he in fact despised the regional integration projects to come, including European integration, because they would ultimately lead to a replacement of nation-states with larger state-like units (Mitrany 1966). That said, most existing integration schemes have been regional in scope and this chapter will, therefore, focus on them. This is a practical choice, as the different historically and geographically confined integration schemes already reveal quite different conceptions of integration. It does not entail a judgement on whether these schemes are unique to – or indeed whether integration is only possible at – the regional level, or whether they may also be seen as operating at the global level. (On globalization, see Chapter 18, by Stetter, this volume.)

Integration sphere: economic, societal and political integration

The first dimension of integration discussed here concerns whether it is seen as economic, societal or political integration. Many integration projects of the post-Second World War world have been built around or even focused on some form of economic integration. To some extent, of course, increasing transnational trade may in itself be understood as a sort of integration (Phelps 1997). Yet most definitions of integration will be more demanding and include forms of economic governance that move beyond mere liberalisation, for instance through the implementation of a common customs area, a common currency (such as the Euro, the West African CFA franc) or shared production standards. Indeed, economic integration does not have to be part of a liberal agenda but can follow a socialist ideal. It is not that long ago that the EU was seen by some as a means to ensure the future of welfare policies under conditions of globalisation (see Ross 1995 on Jacques Delors' idea of a social Europe). The Venezuela-led Bolivarian Alliance for America (ALBA) even explicitly attempts to counter the neo-liberal economic hegemony (Petras and Veltmeyer 2011: 116).

The more integration is seen as providing positive forms of governance, for instance in the form of social policy, the more it takes on a political connotation. Again, there is no firm threshold between economic and political integration – the boundary is part of the contestations of the concept and depends on where and how we conceive of politics/the political. Some would therefore reserve the label political integration for the realm of so-called high politics, i.e. the integration of "core" interests and functions at the heart of the territorial state, such as those concerning security and defence (e.g. Hoffmann 1966: 867). Others see this as too narrow a conception of politics (Mols 1996: 54–55). Most obviously, political integration aims at or involves the merger of political units, for instance through the formation of a new federal state. Such integration can be seen as a later stage following from economic integration, or it may be seen as a necessary prerequisite of economic integration. Either way, it is quite popular to see integration in these two spheres as occurring in a sequence.

Finally, integration can be envisaged as a societal process. As such, integration takes place, for instance, through increased transnational interactions. Trade is such an interaction, but it is not the only one. Tourism (in particular, in cases of sustained practices such as regular and extended visits to holiday homes), city twinning, interaction between civil society groups, educational exchanges – all of these are examples of such a great density of transactions, in Karl Deutsch's terms. For Deutsch (1954), these would lead to a transnational sense of community, which in turn may lead to political integration in "amalgamated" (as opposed to "pluralistic") communities. Debates surrounding the concept of integration usually involve all three spheres. They are not easily separable – both because their definitions blur into each other and because they can be seen as interdependent. A good deal of the conceptual history of integration is therefore a debate over the mutual boundaries of economic, societal and political integration and how they relate to each other.

Integration telos: process and project

A second dimension concerns the question of whether integration has a finality and is therefore defined by a project target such as a federal state, or whether integration should be seen as an open-ended process. In the first case, there is an inherent telos to integration, and integration practices are instrumental in achieving this aim. Classically, in political integration, this is a federal state, but other final outcomes are possible. In economic integration, the aim could be the development of a Free Trade Area. In societal integration, one could see the development of a new supranational identity as an ultimate goal.

In the case of integration as a process, the ultimate shape of the integration outcome is left open. The focus is not on the realisation of a specific integration project, but on an ongoing practice. Politically, such a concept of integration is often more vague and therefore more difficult to "sell" than a clear vision of the final outcome. As we will see, this has led to the marginalisation of some integration concepts such as that of integral federalism within the European federalist movement. However, the EU as the most prominent regional integration organisation has been characterised as a system in constant flux through its continuous "deepening" as the supranationalisation of new policy areas and "widening" as the extension of membership (Schimmelfennig and Sedelmeier 2002). Indeed, Article 1 of the Treaty on European Union (TEU) uses the famous phrase of an "ever closer Union among the peoples of Europe", which does not proclaim a clear integration target and even implies that an endpoint of integration does not exist: it is an *ever* closer Union.

The absence of an explicitly defined target does not mean that there is no implicit telos. Some studies have looked into the often hidden integration aims in debates about European integration and neofunctionalism in particular (Jachtenfuchs et al. 1998; but see Mitrany 1966). Such an implicit telos shapes concrete integration steps, for instance the preference for state-like structures in neofunctionalism, as Mitrany (1966) claimed. At the same time, the explicit focus on process may hamper and undermine strong visions of organisational set-ups. Project and process may also be related to each other. Over time, a focus on process may be seen as insufficient and lead to the construction of concrete political structures. Vice versa, neofunctionalism as the main theory/ideology of European integration has been seen as fostering political institutions as a project in political integration, first in order to stimulate process

Table 17.1 A conceptual matrix of integration

Sphere **INTEGRATION** **Telos**	**Economic**	**Political**	**Societal**
Project			
Process			

in societal integration in the form of a "shift" of "loyalties, expectations and political activities towards a new centre" (Haas 1958: 61), which in turn would then feed back through spillover processes into the formulation of new integration projects.

The two dimensions of integration realm and method can be combined to form a conceptual matrix within which I suggest we can place articulations of integration (Table 17.1). It should be noted that this is not a matrix that can easily be filled as a result of "empirical" research, which would presuppose that the boundaries between the different categories are fixed. Instead, the matrix should be seen as a conceptual space within which ideas about integration are articulated and pursued, which includes the (re)negotiation of the boundaries between these categories.

Power and integration

Why does it matter whether integration is conceptualised as economic, political or societal integration, and as project or process? Ultimately, imbuing integration with meaning along these dimensions also fixes the meaning of other, related concepts that organise our societies. Integration is therefore not merely an instrument for cooperation and peace, as the (neo)liberal angle would have it; it is also an attempt to construct an alternative societal organisation and therefore needs to rearticulate the core features of society. Following Laclau and Mouffe (1985), integration in this context becomes the discursive nodal point around which the meanings of central societal concepts are to be fixed and put into relation with each other (see Diez 2001).

Advocating a Free Trade Area therefore not only situates integration within a programme of economic liberalism; it also draws a specific boundary between an economy such understood and the "political" and "societal" – very often, politics and society remain confined to the national level, so that "real" politics is only possible within the nation-state. Seeing integration as a process may emphasise the importance of societal practices over political projects, but there is no strict correlation between the two dimensions. Rather, a focus on process implies a different political ethos that is more open yet also more fragile, compared to the advocacy of a clear vision with its ontological security yet relative closure. The power of integration discourses, thus, is never only the power to legitimise integration policies or overcome territorial divisions. It is a discursive power that spills over into all fields of society, and which empowers particular actors and particular kinds of actions, and disempowers others.

Ironically, over time such disempowerment can lead to resistance, which in turn gives rise to alternative but also anti-integration movements. We have therefore seen a resurgence of nationalism and the rise of anti-integration parties from both left and right in most EU member states. The conditions for the emergence of such movements are complex and include broader global developments, as well as misgivings about specific EU policies, especially in the economic sector. Yet, to some extent, they are carried and supported by those who either stand to lose from or for other reasons fear further integration (e.g. Boomgaarden et al. 2011).

Historical Practices of Integration

The European experience as a central reference point

A discussion of integration, let alone regional integration, cannot take place without discussing the European experience in its temporal, material and socio-political context. In academic debates, European integration has been the main reference point for the development of integration theories, to the point where many have criticised the heavy bias and singular case ("N = 1") problem (Caporaso et al. 1997). Politically, European integration has served as a model for other integration schemes around the world – be it as a model to replicate or to distance oneself from. Indeed, the EU sees itself as a model for integration to be promoted internationally and thus has actively supported other regional integration processes both financially and ideologically (Farrell 2009).

The reason for this prominence of the European example is obvious. Nowhere is there a higher degree of supranationalism across such a wide spectrum of policies than in the European Union. Supranationalism in a formal sense refers to law-making on a level above the nation-state. In the EU, laws passed on the European level, following seminal court decisions in 1963–1964, have direct effect (they do not have to be transposed into national law in order to be effective), they are supreme (EU law beats existing national law in case of contradictions) and they pre-empt national policy makers from passing competing laws regulating the same policy area (de Witte 1999). Furthermore, the EU has been built among states who, until the mid-20th century, had been in "eternal" conflict with each other, and had just been at the heart of two world wars, which led to the EU receiving the 2012 Peace Nobel Prize. The EU has also been immensely successful in attracting new members, from the original six to now 28 member states, with more in the queue. Last but not least, while the EU has come under immense criticism for its legitimacy deficit since the 1990s (Follesdal 2006), it is often seen as unique in its development of a transnational parliamentary representation in the form of the European Parliament (Linklater 1996: 95–6; Moravcsik 2002).

This is not the place to provide a detailed history of European integration or discuss the complex web of EU institutions and policies.[1] However, because of the centrality of the EU to the integration debate, it is important to draw out its main features as

[1] For useful overviews, see Jørgensen et al. (2006) and Cini (2013).

they transport a specific underlying conception of integration, which feeds into the political and theoretical contestations reviewed in the following two sections. First of all, integration in the EU context covers all three spheres of integration identified above. A core integration project within the EU was the "Single Market"; the EU clearly has political institutions; and Art. 1 of the TEU refers to the integration of peoples, and thus a societal integration process. Yet there are different degrees of integration. A number of policy fields, in particular relating to the internal market, are entirely supranationally organised, to the point that it is the European Commission that negotiates on behalf of its member states in the WTO context, to give but one example. However, there are other policy fields such as foreign policy, which remain intergovernmental in nature; thus, the EU has a High Representative for its foreign policy with its own diplomatic organisation in the form of the European External Action Service, but the main foreign policy decisions ultimately need to be agreed by the member states' foreign ministers.

To complicate things further, the EU is a system of what has sometimes been called "variable geometry" (e.g. Stubb 1996) – not all member states participate in all policy integration, while some non-member states are part of some EU policy areas. Take the example of the common border area of Schengen: the UK and Ireland as EU members have opted out of this policy area, other EU members (Bulgaria, Croatia, Cyprus, Romania) have for various reasons not yet become part of Schengen, whereas Norway and Switzerland, while not EU members, are in Schengen. The reason for this complex set-up is partly to be found in the process character of European integration, the effects of which are compounded by path dependency. Although one may argue that political actors involved in the integration process had particular visions of where Europe was heading, there was never any explicit agreement on this telos. Indeed, integration remains a contested concept even within Europe. The pursuit of integration as a process is at least in part a result of the inter-war debates about the future of Europe and the applicability of federalist and functionalist ideas. When the Council of Europe was established in 1948 as a largely intergovernmentalist organisation (with the exception of the European human rights regime), the dream of a United States of Europe in the near future had gone. Instead, following a plan by the then French foreign minister Robert Schuman, largely drawn up by his aide and later Commission President Jean Monnet, integration was started off in the relatively technical but militarily and economically important area of coal and steel, leading to the foundation of the European Coal and Steel Community (ECSC) in 1952. Plans to move swiftly into integrating foreign policy and defence had failed by 1954, leaving military integration in particular to NATO. Instead, 1957 saw the addition of the European Economic Community (EEC) and the European Atomic Community (Euratom) to the ECSC. After various ups and downs, these three found their way into the 1992 Maastricht Treaty as the supranational first pillar of the newly founded European Union (EU), to which the Common Foreign and Security Policy (CFSP) and the cooperation in Justice and Home Affairs (JHA) were added.

The post-Cold War period saw an immense rise in the number of subsequent treaty revisions, including an attempt to establish a European Constitution, which failed in referendums in France and the Netherlands. The revisions led, among other things, to a further supranationalisation in JHA and to an extension of CFSP to cover defence issues and provide further institutional support for cooperation in the form of the High

Representative and the EEAS. At the same time, the institutional set-up was refined over time. At its heart remain a Commission with the right to initiate legislation, a Council as the representation of member states, and a Parliament which since 1978 has been directly elected. Over time, EU legislative processes have moved towards a system where both Council and Parliament need to approve laws, although there are still significant exceptions such as in the area of the Common Agricultural Policy, which is one of the main budget items within the EU. The European Court of Justice acts as a Supreme Court guarding the supremacy of EU law and can be called on by EU institutions, member states and national courts as much as by individual EU citizens.

Other regional integration projects

While the EU is the most prominent case of regional integration, it is by no means the only one. In fact, we see regional integration schemes in all regions of the globe. They vary in the concept of integration that they pursue, in the depth of integration they want to achieve, in geographical scope and of course also in their success rate. Instead of providing a comprehensive overview of such integration processes, let me focus on their conceptual differences and the extent to which they have taken the EU as a model to be imitated. First, there are some integration projects that have explicitly confined themselves to economic integration. Above all, this is the case in North America, where the North American Free Trade Area (NAFTA) is focused on the creation of a common market. In South America, too, economic integration dominates, for instance in MERCOSUR or UNASUR. Yet, most integration schemes nowadays, in what is sometimes called the "new" regionalism (Ethier 1998; Hettne and Söderbaum 1998; Hettne et al. 1999), include a security dimension, or set political standards for their member states in relation to democracy and human rights.

The setting of standards is an expression of a broader discourse on good governance, sometimes drawing on the republican reading of Kant's (con)federation, that has made such interventions in the internal organisation of states acceptable (Doornbos 2001; MacMillan 2006; Weiss 2000). After the end of the Cold War, this led to a re-establishing of regional integration with stronger ambitions in terms of political interference, most notably in the African Union (AU). This does not mean that such understandings of regional integration are uncontested. In fact, many would see the AU itself as a failure in this respect, evidenced, for instance, by the delays in setting up the agreed African Court of Justice. Some have therefore pointed out that the AU imitates the EU organisational structure, but that the political practices within the AU do not match EU-style supranationalism. Fioramonti (2013) has called this the "bumper sticker" approach to integration. Others have argued that there is a much greater variety of integration projects in Africa on a sub-regional level, such as ECOWAS or SADC, which include political, economic and societal integration sometimes pre-dating the EU experience (Matthews 2003).

The AU is unusual because in contrast to most other integration projects, it puts the integration of security issues at its centre from the start. This is all the more surprising given the emphasis on national sovereignty in many of the postcolonial states on the African continent, and it is largely due to the security context of the Cold War era, in which the EU has lent considerable financial support to the development of a security dimension within the AU. In South-East Asia, ASEAN has recently also started to deal with security measures, but in contrast to the EU and AU, does not see integration in political terms, referring to the "ASEAN way" of doing things and, thus, while acknowledging the EU model, also clearly marking the differences (Lee and Diez 2016).

Contestations: Five Readings of Integration

I have provided this brief overview of integration projects both to demonstrate the historical context in which the conceptual debates on integration have unfolded and to further demonstrate the contestations of integration. Differences in the scope of integration in both sphere and telos reflect attempts to order societies in different ways. These ordering practices can be grouped into five discourses of integration under the headings of state-centred federalism, integral federalism, neofunctionalism, state cooperation and economic community (see also Jachtenfuchs et al. 1998). As all five discourses carry within them an understanding of a desirable order and mode of governance, they have a strong normative dimension even if this is not always made explicit.

State-centred federalism

The classic understanding of integration is that it foresees a merger of states in a new federal state where sovereignty rests with the centre, but individual states retain autonomy in a number of defined policy fields. Existing federal states such as Germany, Switzerland and the US are often seen as models for, in the European case, a "United States of Europe". Such a conceptualisation of integration is clearly linked to a political project. There is a clear telos – the ultimate transferral of sovereignty to a bigger entity through a treaty. The focus is therefore on the construction of political institutions. Problems such as legitimacy are solved through the means of the modern territorial state, and diversity is guaranteed through the internal territorial division, as it is in existing federal states. Economic integration is part and parcel of this project, but it is not an aim in itself. Likewise, societal integration plays an important role in forming a new identity and demos that provide legitimacy to the new state.

While integration understood as a process towards a federal state has been central to European integration as well as visions of Arab unity, none of the existing integration projects has actually led to the founding of such a federal "super-state". This is not to say that regional entities such as the EU do not engage in "statecraft" (Borg 2013), in that they construct and patrol their new borders, for instance, or adopt key insignia of the nation-state such as passports and flags (Polat 2011). As such, territorial conceptions of the state continue to play a role even in regions that are sometimes seen as having moved "beyond territoriality" (Ruggie 1993). Yet articulations of integration as state-centred federalism have not managed to become hegemonic. In most regions, national identity and sovereignty provide powerful counter-discourses that undermine the legitimacy of creating state-like institutions on the regional level.

Integral federalism

If state-centred federalism was about a political project, integral federalism developed the opposite view of integration as a societal process. Integral federalists thought that the problem with state-centred federalism was exactly that it did not transform the state system, which after all they considered the main purpose of integration. Such a transformation could only be achieved through continuous societal transformation. This perspective is "integral" in the sense that transforming politics and society are conceptualised as inherently intertwined. While integral federalists also thought of political institutions, their visions, articulated in particular in post-Second World War Europe, were often rather vague. Their idea of a federal state was a limited one, and their focus was on far-reaching decentralisation and overlapping societal, economic and political units with smaller regions as the base, in order to provide the context in which their idea of a continuous societal transformation could take place.

This notion of integration is not only focused on the process and on society, it is also radically anti-sovereigntist in nature. It is therefore no surprise that integral federalists such as de Rougemont (de Rougemont 1987) and Marc (Lépine 2012) made explicit reference to philosophers as diverse as Althusius and Proudhon, who provided a critique of the modern state (Hueglin 1999). Integration thus problematises territorial borders while, at the same time, safeguarding the rights of smaller communities. This allows us to think beyond the clear inside/outside distinctions of modern territorial statehood. Yet, some integral federalists have been highly conservative if not racist in their political outlook (Hellman 2002), in which case their emphasis on local and regional communities has an exclusionary component that sits uneasily with the challenges to identity in a supranational and globalised context.

Integral federalists have been marginalised in integration debates not least because of their focus on process rather than project: they failed to put forward an intuitively comprehensible plan for the building of European institutions. Yet there are traces of integral federalism in European integration in ideas such as a "Europe of the Regions", institutionalised in the Committee of the Regions, or "subsidiarity", which was inserted into the EU Treaty in Maastricht, and became itself a contested concept used by some member states who were not in favour of widespread decentralisation but who wanted to safeguard the interests of member states (Jeffrey 2002).

(Neo)functionalism

Functionalism shares with integral federalism the basic conceptualisation of integration as a process. When Mitrany wrote of a "working peace system", he set this against state-centred federalism which would not work because in a state system it was unlikely that states were willing to surrender their sovereignty voluntarily to a higher level. Instead, Mitrany wanted to undermine states through functional linkages across them. Because of the technical linkages between functional areas, this would lead to increased integration in other fields as well as in what became known as a "spillover" process. Mitrany's focus is therefore on the integration process and societal actors in the various functional areas. In the neofunctionalist European integration project of Monnet, however, while there was still a focus on process, the conceptualisation of integration became more openly political in the sense that it emphasised the High Authority in the ECSC and later the Commission in the European Communities. Spillover could not be expected to come about entirely spontaneously, it had to be "cultivated" by a central actor that guarded and promoted it (Tranholm-Mikkelsen 1991).

Neofunctionalism also expects a shift of allegiances as a result of the integration process – a point that later led to intense discussion about the extent to which neofunctionalism resembles an early form of social constructivism. This neo-functionalist rearticulation of integration empowered not only experts and functional leaders within their functional communities but constructed an important role for supranational bureaucrats/politicians. It also reinstated a territorial logic into the integration process. Thus, federalists tended to see neofunctionalism as being closer to their political project than neofunctionalists would openly admit, differing more in the means than in the aims of integration (e.g. Burgess 2009).

This first meant that the new centre, despite its openly political function of cultivating spillover, was designed as a group of experts governing not through political decisions in the light of competing visions and interests, but managing on the basis of evidence and knowledge. Furthermore, there was initially at least a teleological understanding of integration that would inevitably lead to the "ever closer union". The possibility of a politicisation of integration as such, in the form of resistances and possible reversals, was only theorised from the late 1960s onwards (Schmitter 1970). If integration was the rational thing to do, managed by experts, how could one possibly object to it? Those who one saw as possibly objecting were misguided because they were against the transcendence of the nation-state. Consequently, the legitimacy of integration, which came to haunt the EU as much as other regional and global governance projects from the 1990s onwards, was not a real issue under these circumstances. Integration was seen as being carried by a "permissive consensus" (Lindberg and Scheingold 1970) where legitimacy was created by the output the system generated and which seemed to satisfy the masses, as they obviously did not protest. It was only when the legitimacy question became more urgent that neofunctionalists-turned-governance-scholars rediscovered their pluralist roots and became interested in alternative models of democracy, building on the participation of interest groups in the policy-making process.

Intergovernmentalism

While for federalists and neofunctionalists integration is valuable in its own right because it is supposed to transcend the state system, opponents see integration as limited to "low politics" areas and intensified cooperation between states in order to meet their interests. Accordingly, there is no grand project to strive for, and integration is reversible. Such a position does not necessarily deny integration as such, but its conception of integration is very limited and precarious as it is controlled by member state governments to achieve their aims. Such a conception of integration thus reifies the position of states, state/nation identities and governments as their representatives in a state system. We can witness this position not only in resistances to supranationalism in Europe, but also at the heart of the "ASEAN way" and in many de facto practices within the AU, where state leaders are cautious to turn aims ambitiously set out in treaties into reality.

Such a pluralist conception cannot be dismissed as "unethical" and pure power politics. Instead, it formulates its limited vision of integration within the nationalist imagery, reifying national communities and empowering state actors. Hoffmann (1966) foresaw many of the legitimacy problems discussed today, predicting that integration would lead to resistance from national publics. There are geopolitical, identity and sovereignty concerns that are at the centre of both cooperation and resistance to it. In the liberal intergovernmentalism of Moravcsik (1998), integration is a two-level game where interests are formulated on the domestic level and represented within the European context by governments, who in turn can use the European level to influence domestic debates. In this game, governments design institutions on the European level to enshrine the agreed rules and to ensure the credibility of a bargain for the foreseeable future (Moravcsik 1998). Nonetheless, governments remain the main actors that are empowered by the integration process. Governance, from this perspective, even seems over-legitimised because there is not only indirect legitimisation via member state governments but also direct legitimisation with the increased scope of the European Parliament to approve legislation.

Because both the state federalists and the intergovernmental reading of integration work within a statist conception of politics and focus on treaties, they ignore process in the sense of a continuous transformation, especially on the societal level. Thus, one of the core criticisms of the intergovernmental perspective is its neglect of day-to-day politics (Wincott 1995). This angle is highlighted by constructivist scholars who tend to read integration through a thicker sociological lens, which allows them to point to societal integration and processes of socialisation, although these take place on the elite level more than among the wider public (e.g. Øhrgaard 1997; Glarbo 1999; Lewis 2005).

Economic community

Finally, integration can be seen as limited to a specific functional area. In contrast to viewing integration as state cooperation, such a conceptualisation recognises the need for the building up of irreversible governance structures in specific policy fields. And in contrast to functionalist renderings of integration, there is no spillover from one sector to another, as the borders of integration and the realm where it takes place are clearly defined. In practice, such a conception of integration mostly rests on a strict distinction between economics and politics, where the field of economics is understood as the realm of a liberal market. Because such a market transcends political boundaries, existing territorial barriers to trade ought to be abolished. At the same time, a truly global market seems unfeasible because even a barrier-free market is not necessarily self-regulating but needs rules in relation to product standards or competition, which in turn need to be monitored. While such rules are seen as "objective" within a liberal economic framework, they are nonetheless contested politically, which makes their global implementation problematic.

Importantly, the presumed "objectivity" of the rules and logic of the market implies that the setting of these rules is not a political issue and ought to be left to experts. Questions pertaining to the management of the market are to be strictly separated from politics. Politics, in contrast to economics, is where choices (as opposed to expert knowledge) have to be made, and it therefore requires participation by publics that can only be conceptualised in national terms, which relies on choices to be made. Legitimacy therefore can only be achieved within the nation-state, its political identity and decision-making procedures. Integration therefore cannot spill over into other, "political" areas thus defined. This conception of integration also implies a concrete project in that the result of an integrated market is clearly outlined, even though the rules of the market will always be revised according to the latest expert knowledge, empowering those who can claim such expertise accordingly.

The conception of integration as leading to an economic community is most elaborate in the British context. While many analysts of European integration see the British position within the EU context as a pure form of safeguarding national interests and therefore of a state cooperation model, they ignore the degree to which the British government has actively promoted market integration, for instance by pushing the Single European Act in the mid-1980s. It is also telling that the EU in the UK is still referred to as the "Common Market". It is a construction of Europe that is in line with the neo-liberal restructuring of UK politics and society since Margaret Thatcher in the 1980s and shows how the concept of integration can be used to stabilise particular meanings that are essentially contested (Diez 1999, 2001).

Conclusion

As with many other core concepts in IR, integration is an opaque concept that is essentially contested. This has made it attractive for scholars and politicians alike to pursue their political goals, interests and persuasions under the mantle of integration. At the same time, this has meant that integration has been at the heart of intense political and scholarly debates. The only agreement is that integration is about cooperation and interaction across state borders.

In this chapter, I have suggested structuring the debates over the concept of integration around two dimensions: the sphere and the telos of integration. I have reviewed both political and academic conceptualisations of integration, and we have seen how they are closely related to each other. Their respective integration concepts come with strong political implications about the scope and legitimacy of governance, the type of actors empowered and the future path of societal identities. I have also tried to show how such articulations of integration try to fix a set of meanings to construct and stabilise a particular model of societal organisation. Most "project"-focused concepts of integration operate within statist parameters and thus tend to reify a territorial logic of politics, empowering state representatives and spatial communities. "Process"-oriented articulations, in contrast, emphasise the fluidity of social organisation and thus legitimise a broader spectrum of societal actors as agents of governance.

Historically, the majority of integration discourse was linked to a liberal conception of society and politics. This has given credence to the importance of economic actors, but also, in the case of (neo)functionalism, of experts and bureaucrats. This liberal underbelly of integration has in turn provoked serious contestation regarding the legitimacy of the underpinning economic model, based on a separation from the political sphere, as well as the decision-making procedures disjointed from a clearly identifiable electoral base. Articulations of integration, as I suggested in the introduction to this chapter, are therefore always also attempts to fix a broader set of understandings of socio-political order. Whether they come in the form of political schemes or academic analyses, they are part of integration discourses that empower and marginalise actors, and legitimate and de-legitimate social, economic and political actions. The use of the concept of integration is therefore deeply political. This chapter could only draw out some of the main lines of this political contestation. More detailed case studies within different national and functional contexts are necessary to enhance our understanding of how the articulation of integration is also an articulation of politics.

Suggested Readings

Diez, Thomas (2001) 'Europe as a Discursive Battleground: European Integration Studies and Discourse Analysis', *Cooperation and Conflict* 36(1), 5–38.

Makes an argument about the role of discourse in the study of European integration, and introduces the idea of contested concepts of integration and how they are tied to broader understandings of politics and society.

Hansen, Lene; Williams, Michael C. (1999) 'The Myths of Europe: Legitimacy, Community and the "Crisis" of the EU', *Journal of Common Market Studies* 37(2), 233–49.

Hansen and Williams disentangle the notion of "myth" related to the EU and see the technical governance of functionalism as a myth that underpins this form of integration.

Hettne, Björn; Söderbaum, Fredrik (1998) 'The New Regionalism Approach', *Politeia* 17(3), 6–21.

An influential article discussing the rise of a new kind of regionalism in the post-Cold War world.

Risse, Thomas; Engelmann-Martin, Daniela; Knopf, Hans-Joachim; Roscher, Klaus (1999) 'To Euro or not to Euro? EMU and Identity Politics in the European Union', *European Journal of International Relations* 5(2), 147–87.

The authors were part of one of a number of project teams in the late 1990s trying to identify different conceptions of integration in Britain, France and Germany.

Ruggie, John Gerard (1993) 'Territoriality and Beyond: Problematizing Modernity in International Relations', *International Organization* 47(1), 139–74.

A sophisticated analysis of the changing structures of international governance in a wider historical setting, of which European integration is one example.

Bibliography

Bickerton Christopher J. (2012) *European Integration: From Nation States to Member States*, Oxford: Oxford University Press.

Boomgaarden, Hajo G.; Schuck, Andreas R.T.; Elenbaas, Matthijs; de Vreese, Claes H. (2011) 'Mapping EU Attitudes: Conceptual and Empirical Dimensions of Euroscepticism and EU Support', *European Union Politics* 12(2), 241–66.

Borg, Stefan (2013) 'European Integration and the Problem of the State: Universality, Particularity and Exemplarity in the Crafting of the European Union', *Journal of International Relations and Development* 17(3), 339–66.

Burgess, Michael (2009) 'Federalism', in: Wiener, Antje; Diez, Thomas (eds) *European Integration Theory*, 2nd edn, Oxford: Oxford University Press, 25–44.

Caporaso, James A.; Marks, Gary; Moravcsik, Andrew; Pollack, Mark A. (1997) 'Does the European Union Represent an N of 1?', *ECSA Review* 10(3), 1–5.

Cini, Michelle; Borragan, N.P.-S. (eds) (2013) *European Union Politics*, 4th rev. edn, Oxford: Oxford University Press.

Deutsch, Karl (1954) *Political Community at the International Level: Problems of Definition and Measurement*, Garden City (New York): Doubleday.

Deutsch, Karl Wolfgang; Burrell, Sidney A.; Kann, Robert A.; Lee Jr, Maurice (1957) *Political Community and the North Atlantic Area: International Organization in the Light of Historical Experience*, Princeton, NJ: Princeton University Press.

de Rougemont, Denis (1987) *Die Zukunft ist unsere Sache*, Stuttgart: Klett-Cotta.

de Witte, Bruno (1999) 'Direct Effect, Supremacy and the Nature of the Legal Order', in: Craig, P.; de Burca, G. (eds) *The Evolution of EU Law*, Oxford: Oxford University Press, 177–213.

Diez, Thomas (1999) 'Constructing Threat, Constructing Political Order: On the Legitimisation of an Economic Community in Western Europe', *Journal of International Relations and Development* 2(1), 29–49.

Diez, Thomas (2001) 'Europe as a Discursive Battleground: European Integration Studies and Discourse Analysis', *Cooperation and Conflict* 36(1), 5–38.

Doornbos, M. (2001) '"Good Governance": The Rise and Decline of a Policy Metaphor?', *Journal of Development Studies* 37(6), 93–108.

Ethier, Wilfried J. (1998) 'The New Regionalism', *The Economic Journal* 108(449), 1149–61.

Farrell, Mary (2009) 'EU Policy towards other Regions: Policy Learning in the External Promotion of Regional Integration', *Journal of European Public Policy* 16(8), 1165–84.

Fioramonti, Lorenzo (2013) 'The Bumper Sticker: Why Africa isn't Following the European Model of Regional Integration', International Studies Association (ISA) Convention, San Francisco, 3–6 April.

Follesdal, Andreas (2006) 'The Legitimacy Deficits of the European Union', *The Journal of Political Philosophy* 14(4), 441–68.

Glarbo, Kenneth (1999) 'Wide-awake Diplomacy: Reconstructing the Common Foreign and Security Policy of the European Union', *Journal of European Public Policy* 6(2), 634–51.

Haas, Ernst B. (1958) *The Uniting of Europe: Political, Social and Economic Forces 1950–57*, Stanford, CA: Stanford University Press.

Hansen, Lene; Williams, Michael C. (1999) 'The Myths of Europe: Legitimacy, Community and the "Crisis" of the EU', *Journal of Common Market Studies* 37(2), 233–49.

Hellman, John (2002) *The Communitarian Third Way: Alexandre Marc and Ordre Nouveau 1930–2000*, Montreal: McGill-Queen's University Press.

Hettne, Björn; Inotai, Andras; Sunkel, Osvaldo (eds) (1999) *Globalism and the New Regionalism*, Basingstoke: Macmillan.

Hettne, Björn; Söderbaum, Fredrik (1998) 'The new Regionalism Approach', *Politeia* 17(3), 6–21.

Hoffmann, Stanley (1966) 'Obstinate or Obsolete? The Fate of the Nation-State and the Case of Western Europe', *Daedalus* 95, 862–915.

Hueglin, Thomas O. (1999) *Early Modern Concepts for a late Modern World: Althusius on Community and Federalism*, Waterloo, Ontario: Wilfried Laurier University Press.

Jachtenfuchs, Markus; Diez, Thomas; Jung, Sabine (1998) 'Which Europe? Conflicting Models of a Legitimate European Order', *European Journal of International Relations* 4(4), 409–45.

Jeffrey, Charlie (2002) 'The Europe of the Regions from Maastricht to Nice', *Queen's Papers on Europeanisation* 7, 1–9.

Jørgensen, Knud Erik; Pollack, Mark A.; Rosamond, Ben (2006) *Handbook of European Union Politics*, London: Sage.

Kleingeld, Pauline (2004) 'Approaching Perpetual Peace: Kant's Defence of a League of States and his Ideal of a World Federation', *European Journal of Philosophy* 12(3), 304–25.

Laclau, Ernesto; Mouffe, Chantal (1985) *Hegemony and Socialist Strategy: Towards a Radical Democratic Politics*. London: Verso.

Lee, Moosung; Diez, Thomas (2016) 'Introduction: The EU, East Asian Conflicts and the Norm of Integration', *Asia-Europe Journal* 14, forthcoming.

Lépine, Frédéric (2012) 'A Journey through the History of Federalism: Is Multilevel Governance a Form of Federalism?', *L'Europe En Formation* 363, 21–62.

Lewis, John (2005) 'The Janus Face of Brussels: Socialization and Everyday Decision Making in the European Union', *International Organization* 59(4), 937–71.
Lindberg, Leon; Scheingold, Stuart (1970) *Europe's Would-be Polity: Patterns of Change in the European Community*, Englewood Cliffs, NJ: Prentice-Hall.
Linklater, Andrew (1996) 'Citizenship and Sovereignty in the Post-Westphalian State', *European Journal of International Relations* 2(1), 77–103.
MacMillan, John (2006) 'Immanuel Kant and the Democratic Peace', in Beate Jahn (ed.) *Classical Theory in International Relations*, Cambridge: Cambridge University Press, 52–73.
Marcussen, Martin; Risse, Thomas; Engel-Martin, Daniele; Kopf, Hans Joachim; Roscher, Klaus (1999) 'Constructing Europe? The Evolution of French, British and German Nation State Identities', *Journal of European Public Policy* 6(4), 614–33.
Matthews, Alan (2003) 'Regional Integration and Food Security in Developing Countries', *Training Materials for Agricultural Planning*, Rome: Food and Agricultural Organisation.
Mitrany, David (1966) *A Working Peace System*, Chicago: Quadrangle Books.
Mols, Manfred (1996) *Integration und Kooperation in zwei Kontinenten: das Streben nach Einheit in Lateinamerika und in Südostasien*, Stuttgart: Steiner.
Moravcsik, Andrew (1998) *The Choice for Europe: Social Purpose and State Power from Messina to Maastricht*, London: Routledge.
Moravcsik, Andrew (2002) 'Reassessing Legitimacy in the European Union', *Journal of Common Market Studies* 40(4): 603–24.
Øhrgaard, Jakob C. (1997) '"Less than Supranational, more than Intergovernmental": European Political Cooperation and the Dynamics of Intergovernmental Integration', *Millennium: Journal of International Studies* 26(1): 1–29.
Petras, James; Veltmeyer, Henry (2011) *Beyond Neoliberalism: A World to Win*, Farnham: Ashgate.
Phelps, Nicholas A. (1997) *Multinationals and European Integration: Trade, Investment and Regional Development*, London: Jessica Kingsley Publishers.
Polat, Necati (2011) 'European Integration as a Colonial Discourse', *Review of International Studies* 37(3), 1255–72.
Risse, Thomas (2010) *A Community of Europeans? Transnational Identities and Public Spheres*, Ithaca, NY: Cornell University Press.
Ross, George (1995) 'Assessing the Delors Era and Social Policy', in: Leibfried, Stephan; Pierson, Paul (eds) *European Social Policy: Between Fragmentation and Integration*, Washington, DC: Brookings, 357–88.
Ruggie, John Gerard (1993) 'Territoriality and Beyond: Problematizing Modernity in International Relations', *International Organization* 47(1), 139–74.
Schimmelfennig, Frank; Sedelmeier, Ulrich (2002) 'Theorizing EU Enlargement: Research Focus, Hypotheses, and the State of Research', *Journal of European Public Policy* 9(4), 500–28.
Schmitter, Philippe C. (1970) 'A Revised Theory of Regional Integration', *International Organization* 24(4), 836–68.
Stubb, Alexander C.-G. (1996) 'A Categorization of Differentiated Integration', *Journal of Common Market Studies* 34(2), 283–95.
Tranholm-Mikkelsen, Jeppe (1991) 'Neo-functionalism: Obstinate or Obsolete? A Reappraisal in the Light of the New Dynamism of the EC', *Millennium: Journal of International Studies* 20(1), 1–22.
Weiss, Thomas G. (2000) 'Governance, Good Governance and Global Governance: Conceptual and Actual Challenges', *Third World Quarterly* 21(5), 795–814.
Wincott, Daniel (1995) 'Institutional Interaction and European Integration: Towards an Everyday Critique of Liberal Intergovernmentalism', *Journal of Common Market Studies* 33(4), 597–609.

18

Globalization

Stephan Stetter

It was in the 1980s that the term "globalization" – originally invented in the 1960s – turned into a buzz-word. Widely used by policy-makers, academics, business elites, journalists and ordinary citizens, it was (and still is) used not only to describe the world we live in, but also to prescribe how to live in it. "Globalization", thus, never was a neutral concept to make sense of political, cultural, and economic developments of our time. In addition to serving as a semantic anchor of communication that describes complex social processes in modernity (even those before the actual term "globalization" came into existence), "globalization" is a concept that helps in mobilizing diverse social forces, engendering various types of agency and legitimizing a wide set of practices in different social realms.

Roughly put, we can identify three main protagonists in the discursive struggle over the meaning and legitimacy, or desirability, of "globalization". First, a large bulk of socio-political projects of our times, such as financial deregulation, democracy promotion, state-building, or improving the GDP, educational standards and one's own CV are often framed as being necessitated by "globalization". Globalization is then seen as an opportunity as well as a challenge that societies and individuals have to meet. Second, precisely because of its inherently political nature, others treat "globalization", or at least its neo-liberal component, as a threat to social cohesion, ecological sustainability (e.g. globalization critics) and cultural cohesion (e.g. traditionalists, nationalists). Yet, third, there are also those who think that the fuss about globalization is exaggerated. They argue that the age of globalization is not yet there or might never be fully reached due to the political, theoretical, and normative prevalence of the nation-state and the staying power of territorial and cultural as well as particularistic identities.

The fact that globalization is widely referred to in contemporary societal debates in different parts of the world in an affirmative, rejectionist, or relativist manner only underlines the pervasiveness of "globalization" as a key concept in socio-political and academic discourses. It is a concept that, naturally, is contested but that can hardly be ignored, and if only by denying its importance. As theories of globalization in the social sciences consequently argue, globalization is not only a "basically contested process" amongst many, but also an encompassing "global condition" (Robertson 1990, 1992) that shapes social structures around the world, not only in the contemporary era but, as students of Global History are aware, for centuries. It is true that "globalization" is often perceived as a process that originates in the West and that serves mainly Western interests and values, thereby triggering or enforcing homogenization. Yet, a plethora of studies on the African, Far Eastern, and Middle Eastern origins of globalization, as well as studies on the actual diversity of historical and contemporary forms of globalization(s) – for example, multitudes of global–local interplays, defined as glocalizations by Robertson – show the limits and pitfalls of such a bifurcated equation between globalization and Westernization/homogenization (see below).

This chapter addresses some of the manifold ways in which the concept of globalization figures in socio-political and academic discourses. It also discusses the political and academic practices triggered on that basis, i.e. how the concept of globalization engenders specific ideologies and practices in socio-political life and specific forms of theorizing in the social sciences. In the following section, I draw on the framework developed by Felix Berenskoetter in Chapter 1 and discuss four key contexts of use in the history and evolution of the concept of globalization (temporal, material, socio-political, theoretical). In the subsequent section, I will then address three main approaches of globalization (historical, scientific and political), focusing in particular on how "globalization" has triggered novel ways of theorizing in the social sciences, thereby also challenging IR's traditional and still dominant focus on the "inter-national" instead of the global.

History and Evolution of the Concept and its Contexts

While the term "globalization" only emerged in the 1960s, actual social processes associated with the concept date way back in time. This globalization *avant-la-lettre* (Wimmer 2001) has two main dimensions. First, it comprises a material "compression of the world" (Robertson 1992) based on a decreasing significance of worldwide space/time differences since at least the late 15th century, a process which engenders a material form of global interconnectedness. More specifically, global space/time compression became a physical reality due to the outreach and conquest, since the 15th century, of mainly European powers, intellectuals and adventurers, as a result of which people across the globe gradually became integrated into a very hierarchical and Western-dominated global system, in, amongst other realms, politics, economy, science, and lifestyle. Second, in addition to such material processes, globalization also entails a more subtle, cognitive dimension, referred to in the literature as the "intensification of consciousness of the world as a whole" (Robertson 1992: 8). Globalization thus can also be understood as a reflexive process, as encompassing a set of ideas that frame the way we think about the world we live and act in. This cognitive process also has historical depth and is tied to technological developments, starting with the invention of the printing press in the 15th century, which supported the creation and spread of knowledge about this interconnected world to an ever-growing range of people. Mass circulation of reports about – and encounters with – "exotic" people, maps of distant territories, all the way to images of the globe as a whole contributed to the construction of knowledge about interconnectedness and a shared space for a growing audience, gradually forging a deepened societal consciousness about the global condition.

This interplay between material and cognitive dynamics culminates not only in the emergence of the term "globalization" in the 1960s, but also shaped earlier semantic innovations, such as semantics centring on notions of the "world". Scholars have observed a decisive "deepening and specification of the consciousness of globality" (Bach 2013: 59) in the 19th century in different parts of the world, through which decision-makers, intellectuals and ordinary people tried to make sense of these material and cognitive features of globalization shaping their everyday life. Induced by technological, cultural, and political dynamics that further accelerated space–time compression, such as the invention of the steamship, the railway or the telegraph, as well as the invention of universal ideas of self-determination and human rights, and many others, the global condition underwent a transformation into a distinctively *modern* global condition. Indeed, modernity and modernization became key concepts associated with the radical transformation of social structures throughout the globe, ranging from industrialization and urbanization to colonialism and the formation of mass parties and ideologies, which are intrinsically connected to our conception of globalization. Broadly speaking, global modernity was characterized by a fundamental change in both the "spaces of experience" and "horizons of expectation" (Koselleck 1988), which, for Jens Bartelson (2000: 192), rendered globalization "a metapolitical concept insofar as it fuses the conditions of meaningful experience with the conditions of expectation".

In doing so, globalization transcends mere interdependence, which is usually highlighted by regime theories and governance approaches in IR. Globalization is a much richer and, indeed, more radical concept because it points to a variety of processes and discourses and because of its ability to shape our thinking about the world and our place in it. Globalization relates, for example, to the spread of ideas and the isomorphism of social structures, such as the idea of nationalism and self-determination, as well as the diffusion of the organizing principle of the nation-state. So, rather than saying that the nation-state is threatened by globalization, we can say that globalization is a condition of its emergence in different parts of the world. Globalization also relates to the aforementioned consciousness about being embedded in a world that constitutes a social whole. This reflexive process became visible in the 19th century, through, for instance, the invention of so-called "world exhibitions", the first being held in London in 1851, which contributed to and constructed a growing awareness of the "world as a single place" (Clark 2002) shared beyond the West, as the visit of Ottoman Sultan Abdülaziz to the world fair in 1867 in Paris attests (Bilgin 2014). This consciousness was also expressed in semantic innovations surrounding the concept of the "world" (Tyrell 2005: 35). For example, since 1800, the German language has experienced a spread of "globalized" compound words such as *Weltliteratur* (world literature), *Welthandel* (world trade), *Weltbürger* (world citizen), *Weltreligionen* (world religions), and *Weltherrschaft* (world domination). In the context of the Enlightenment, and in particular through socio-political theories like socialism/Marxism and liberalism which gained a foothold throughout Europe in the 19th century, the notion of a modern global consciousness and a shared fate of humanity as a whole consolidated, also seeing the birth of the idea of global human rights (Bach 2013: 57).

It took several decades until these structural dynamics were reflected in everyday language through explicit semantic recourse to the term "globalization" (for an excellent study of the genealogy of globalization, see James/Steger 2014). An increasing reference to the adjective "global" instead of "world" can be observed in English language dictionaries from the end of the First World War onwards. Starting in the 1920s, the Oxford English Dictionary referred to an increasing number of new semantic connotations of the global condition such as, unsurprisingly, "global warfare", but also "global attitude", "global bombers", "global challenge", "global telecommunication systems", and many more (Bach 2013: 87–88). As Bach (2013: 86) notes, the first-ever entry for "globalization" in an English-language dictionary dates from 1961 and can be found in the American edition of Webster, roughly at the same time that McLuhan invented the term "global village". When the term became widely used during the 1980s (Fiss/Hirsch 2005: 38; Robertson/Khondker 1998), it also became more one-dimensional, referring primarily to economic processes that constitute the world as a single market and humans as consumers. As Fiss and Hirsch (2005: 38) observe, globalization was from the mid-1980s onwards largely equated with "a political-economic construct promoted mainly by financial actors and institutions, with the idea of the free market at its center". This was reflected in Theodore Levitt's 'The Globalization of Markets' (1983) and, with an equally neo-liberal ideological outlook, Ohmae's (1999) notion of the world as a borderless place, which dominated not only public and political debates, but academic discourse as well.

The late 1980s witnessed political and academic opposition to such a narrow neo-liberal conceptualization of globalization. On the one hand, it gave rise to the anti-globalization movement, which adopted the concept but opposed what it stood for. On the other hand, scholars, often from postcolonial and critical perspectives, argued that the concept of "globalization" is a powerful ideological term that invisibilizes the West's structural power. As one critic notes, the widespread reference to "globalization" bears testimony to the "poverty of contemporary social science" in adequately analyzing "processes that are large-scale, but not universal" and that are characterized by "crucial linkages that cut across state borders and lines of cultural difference but which nevertheless are based on specific mechanisms within certain boundaries" (Cooper 2005: 191–192).

These debates highlight the contested socio-political character of globalization (Held/McGrew 2003). On the discursive level, the contestation is characterized more by a juxtaposition of "globalization" vs. "anti-globalization" rather than a battle for hegemony between different ideas of globalization or "alter-globalizations" (Lenco 2013). As a *material and cognitive process* associated with worldwide modern dynamics such as industrialization, urbanization, individualization, and secularism, globalization remains heavily contested and is characterized by fault lines that underpin major societal confrontations and conflicts. Take only the tension between "tradition" and "modernity" that underpins many local and global conflicts during the last two centuries, both in the West and in other parts of the world. Or take those open and latent conflicts linked to the "uneven and combined development" (Rosenberg 2007) of human society that result from the huge socio-economic and political discrepancies between the Global North and the Global South. And, finally, consider the new cleavages, forms of social mobilization and societal struggle that unfold in the context of the emergence of modern and global political ideas such as state sovereignty, nationalism and human rights.

As Abu-Lughod (2000) notes, the increasingly "global system" need not only be studied empirically, but also requires comprehensive theorizing. And, of course, the socio-political context both informs and is informed by the theoretical contexts in which the concept of globalization is embedded. Political programs, such as economic neo-liberalism, democracy promotion, and also the geopolitical aspirations of various modern political ideologies (racism, fascism, democracy, anti-colonialism, communism, cosmopolitanism, etc.), have influenced academic thinking of the global (Hobson 2012). At the same time, it is possible to witness a decoupling of the popular and the academic treatment of the concept. While in the popular discourse globalization tends still to be equated with economic processes and homogenization, the academic debate increasingly highlights the concept's complexity, which allows an accounting for the *simultaneity* of homogeneity and heterogeneity. For many scholars, seeing the world through the concept of globalization shines light on both integration and conflict throughout the world and in relation to dynamics of contemporary conflict or integration within and across manifold social spheres such as religion, culture, politics, education, economics and sports (Meyer 2000; Robertson 1992; Werron 2012).

It is important to keep in mind that most comprehensive conceptions of globalization that exist today have their roots in sociological classics in the late 19th century, which also established the conceptual entanglement of "globalization" and notions of global modernity. Drawing from the social theories of Marx, Durkheim, Weber and Simmel, there is agreement among scholars today that the global condition is in fact a *modern* global condition. Although "globalization" did not figure as an explicit analytical term in classical social theories, it fully developed the "idea of a single modern society that encompasses the whole of humanity" (Chernilo 2006: 17) on which much of contemporary academic theorizing about globalization rests. As Chernilo (2006: 21; my emphasis) explains:

> from Kant's writings onwards, it became increasingly clear that the rise of modernity could only be meaningfully understood if attached to an image of a *global* modernity ... Classical societal theory tries to answer the key question of to what extent a geographically particular set of historically circumscribed processes have led to the rise of a number of evolutionary tendencies that were having a universalistic impact all over the world. The simple but by no means trivial normative corollary of this claim is that despite all differences, humankind is effectively one and could justly be *theorized* only as such.

Since the 1970s, classical social theories have seen a comeback in the emergence of various "world theories", such as world systems theory, world polity theory and world society theory in sociology and other disciplines. Scholars took recourse to classical social theories not only in order to think about globalization in a manner that allowed transcending modernization theory, but also because they wished to overcome the methodological nationalism that dominated in the social sciences after the Second World War. And, while the public debate remained centered on a narrow and neo-liberal theorization of globalization, the academic debate, in particular in sociology and global history, became much more nuanced and conceptually ambitious in trying to make sense of the "world as a single place" while not reducing globalization to mere physical interconnectedness, Western domination, or market-driven economic exchange (Cohen/Kennedy 2013; Robertson/Khondker 1998). Thus, following Bartelson (2000), the "global" has over time turned into a defining object of thought and theorizing, which addresses not only technologically induced interconnectedness and exchanges of economic goods, but also how the idea and practice of globalization engenders cultural and political transformations and conflicts in all regions of the world.

This is not to suggest that there is a consensus on how to theorize globalization. There are fierce controversies over the origin of "globalization", the social mechanisms that drive it, and the question of whether, or to what extent, it has changed in character in the age of "post-modernity" (Bartelson 2000; Beck 2000; Chase-Dunn 1999; Chernilo 2006; Lipschutz/Rowe 2005; Luhmann 2012). But at least the more encompassing theories of globalization agree that globalization not only triggers integration but also underpins fragmentation and (increasing) heterogeneity. Scholars have suggested that globalization "involves the promotion or 'invention' of difference and variety" (Robertson/Khondker 1998: 28) and that "global modernization appears as an uneven and fragmented social transformation" (Jung 2001: 464). Luhmann notes that difference and not unity is the hallmark of globalization theory (see also Sparke 2013). Even if homogenizing effects can be discerned, for instance with a view to consumption patterns or the global spread of modern subjectivities, when globalizing trends fuse with local practices they inevitably engender diversity. As Robertson (1990; see also Sassen 2004) elegantly puts it, globalization is characterized by a universalization of particularisms *and* a particularization of universalisms. Scholars from different theoretical schools emphasize this ambivalence, or hybridity, of globalization (Bartelson 2000; Nederveen Pieterse 2009; Stichweh 2000; Thomas et al. 2008). And there is a broad consensus that the manifold "contradictions of globalization" (Jung 2001: 464) cannot be properly analyzed on the basis of modernist, linear conceptualizations of globalization or by taking recourse to *sui generis* explanations but require an understanding of modernity/-ies as inherently contradictory and ambivalent, yet global (Eisenstadt 2002). So, instead of synthesizing such contradictions (e.g. universal/particular, global/local, traditional/modern, integration/fragmentation) and merging them into a unitary concept of globalization, we must recognize the persistent ambivalence of the concept and the phenomena it captures.

To say that "globalization" has become a central concept that informs a wide range of social science theories in some parts of academia is not to deny that, more broadly, the social sciences still need to pay greater attention to the concept. The discipline of international relations (IR) certainly still struggles with theorizing globalization in an encompassing way, given its traditional focus on the international instead of the global (Walker 2010). To be sure, there is no shortage of attempts to rebrand IR in a way that overcomes the discipline's procrastinated focus on the "international" (Bigo/Walker 2007) by referring to "world politics" (Jackson 2002), "global politics" (Barnett/Finnemore 2004) or a "world polity" (Boli/Thomas 1997). Yet, the difficulty IR has with accommodating encompassing theories of globalization beyond such noteworthy exceptions is reflected in one of the most popular textbooks of the discipline, entitled, after all, *Globalization of World Politics* (Baylis et al. 2011). To begin with, the title is a tautological statement that raises the question of how something that is global by definition, i.e. world politics, can be globalized when it already is. Tellingly, then, globalization is presented in this textbook as a conceptual add-on. The seven major IR theories (realism, liberalism, neo-neo approaches, Marxist theories, social constructivism, alternative approaches and international ethics) are discussed without engaging the concept of globalization; it is only in the concluding section devoted to each theory that a brief discussion of how it relates to "globalization" is offered. While globalization as a process that somehow affects international politics thus gets attention, it hardly figures as a concept in its own right or, more precisely, as a concept integrated in and underpinning all theorizing (in different ways). Such a conservative view that leaves traditional ways of theorizing in IR untouched is even more stunning given the current debate in IR about the discipline's "impoverished view of the global" (Buzan/Little 2001: 28) and suggestions of the "end" (Dunne et al. 2013) of traditional IR theorizing. To stimulate a more substantial engagement with the concept rather than treating it as an add-on, the remainder of this chapter will outline how "globalization" can be explored from a historical, scientific and political angle.

Historical Approaches: Globalization as Historical Sociology and Global History

Historical approaches locate globalization in global time. Without necessarily attributing teleological or linear attributes to this temporal dimension, historical approaches nevertheless view globalization as something that originates and progresses on a temporal scale. Such approaches draw mainly from historical sociology and global history and they also figure strongly in the scientific approaches referred to in the subsequent section, in particular world systems analysis which perceives modern capitalism in terms of a *longue durée* somewhat reminiscent of Fernand Braudel's famous study on the Mediterranean, world polity research with its focus on the 19th century and world society studies, as well as Foucauldian governmentality studies with their strong focus on empirical sources from the 16th, 17th and 18th centuries. While these conceptual approaches will be studied further below, it is important to keep in mind that, in particular with a view to the wealth of empirical data on which they rely, they are inherently linked to more "classical" approaches in global history and historical sociology. Central in that regard is the work of Charles Tilly and Michael Mann who have both highlighted the linkages between globalization, power, and violence, both historically and in the 20th century (Mann 2012a, 2012b; Tilly 1992).

Christopher Bayly and Jürgen Osterhammel have, in that context, identified the 19th century as the historical epoch in which the world was transformed, through globalization dynamics (Bayly 2003; Osterhammel 2014), into a distinctively modern global order. This happened both violently (e.g. via colonialism) and through subtle global social dynamics, such as *inter alia* global comparisons. Historical sociology, more generally speaking, looks at global history with a specific interest in providing a "historically sensitive, yet generally applicable, account of the emergence of capitalism, industrialization, rationalism, bureaucratization, urbanization and other core features of the modern world" and at how these features shape *contemporary* global politics at global, regional, national, and local levels (Lawson 2007: 344). These core features of the modern world – many of which indeed point to the 19th century – are understood in historical sociology as "the underlying reality that provides the environment for everyday actions, events and processes" and provide an "account of order" in world politics (Lawson 2007: 357–358). In other words, rather than falling into the trap of "temporalo-centrism" (Wimmer 2001), i.e. explaining a given research question by focusing mainly on the immediate temporal context that surrounds it, the social sciences and IR specifically are, in the view of protagonists of historical approaches, well advised to focus on the *longue durée* of globalization, in particular how the global transformation of the 19th century shaped the contours of society and politics in the present era.

Apart from the English School, which championed a wealth of historically saturated accounts of international society from the 17th century until today, history does not usually figure prominently in IR. Empirically, it is mainly a discipline of the post-World-War-II world, while, theoretically speaking, key IR theories operate with more or less sophisticated models (e.g. international system; agency–structure) that are, however, usually discussed in abstract rather than historical terms. That is why Hobden (2002: 53–57; see also Halliday 1987: 216) rightly notes that much of IR has turned into "ahistorical international relations". The discipline, by and large, prefers to focus on "puzzles", being mainly thrilled with epistemological or theoretical concerns, rather than putting its analyses into broader historical contexts – in particular, those that require knowledge of non-Western languages. Historical sociology and global history challenge this understanding. Drawing from concepts of globalization developed in these two research traditions allows for a study of the "international system" not as a universe of its own but as a system that is embedded in and emerges from larger historical processes, such as *inter alia* modernization, industrialization, colonialism, and individualization. As Buzan and Little (2001: 38) emphasize, "only when IR integrates with world history, and recaptures a vision of the international systems as grand theory, will it be able to truly take off the Westphalian straitjacket". Over the last few years, some parts of IR have resorted back to historical analysis in the tradition of historical sociology and global history. Unsurprisingly, in that scholarship the 19th century is regularly identified as a key object of study for IR since this was the period in which key features of (political) global modernity emerged that fundamentally shaped the way global politics has developed since then. To take but two examples, Buzan and Lawson (2013) study in that context the transformation of organized violence in global modernity, while Pella (2014) focuses on the abolition of the transatlantic slave trade which was one of the building blocks of the global human rights revolution.

Scientific Approaches: Globalization as Social Theory

As already alluded to, a number of approaches that tried to grasp the "thick reality" of globalization in general models gained momentum in the 1970s. Rooted in classical social theory, these scientific approaches did not carry the label "globalization" but referred to the "world" as their conceptual core: Wallerstein's world system analysis, Meyer's world polity and Luhmann's (and Peter Heintz's) world society. Wallerstein developed his concept of the world system by drawing in particular from the social theory of Karl Marx. His understanding of globalization is one that hinges on the global expansion, in the modern era, of capitalism and how this process underpinned the radical transformation of societal and political structures throughout the world, in particular the stratification of "world social structure" (Wallerstein 1979) in Western core and non-Western peripheral states. According to Wallerstein, particularistic entities such as nations, classes, and so on need to be analyzed against the backdrop of their structural embedding within the "global formation" (Chase-Dunn 1999) of an economically driven and highly stratified, uneven world system. In IR, it has been Justin Rosenberg (2007) who has offered a conceptually rich discussion of key tenets from Wallerstein's – and Karl Marx's – theory of the global modern. According to Rosenberg, economic development is the central driving force of globalization, yet not in a unifying manner. Thus, the "anterior sociological attribute of development itself [is] its intrinsic unevenness" (Rosenberg 2007: 453). The process of globalization, in fact, deepens "the existing unevenness of worldwide social development, while simultaneously drawing its parts into a single system. With this conjunction, unevenness itself was increasingly transformed from a latent descriptive fact about human diversity into an active causal structure of determinations and pressures" (2007: 456). Drawing from Trotzky, Rosenberg argues that the concept of "uneven and combined development" could indeed become "a theory of modern world history" (Rosenberg 2007: 457). The global (in Rosenberg's terminology the "international") thus constitutes the "fundamental dimension of social existence" (Rosenberg 2007: 450).

The world polity approach, initially developed by John W. Meyer, is then inspired by Max Weber's social theory. While world polity theory has many facets, its conceptual core assumption is that at least since the late 19th century the world constitutes a single polity, namely the world polity. As John Boli and George Thomas (1999: 14) elaborate, "by this we mean that the world has been conceptualized as a unitary social system, increasingly integrated by networks of exchange, competition, and cooperation, such that actors have found it 'natural' to view the whole world as their arena of action and discourse". This world polity is, however, not merely a space of global interconnectedness. "Like all polities, the world polity is constituted by a distinct culture" (1999: 14), a world culture shaped by a modern belief in rationalization and organization. It is this belief that then underpins the process of isomorphism through which distinct forms of rationally organizing society – the nation-state, business models, universities, airports, educational ideas, conceptions of the environment, etc. – spread globally (with a view to environmental rationalities, see Stetter et al. 2011). This includes the "rules for the world" that emerge due to the bureaucratization of world politics, in general, and the agency of International Organizations (IOs) as (rationalized) bureaucracies, in particular, and through which world polity theory was popularized in IR (Barnett and Finnemore 2004).

However, it is pivotal here to note that world polity theory considers this process of isomorphic diffusion as both pervasive and evasive. Beyond the surface of isomorphic mimicry lie difference and ambivalence. Actual practice always differs, often fundamentally, from the "pure" model and it is, in fact, a key feature of organizations to camouflage this de-coupling of "pure" globalized model and actual practice. Modern organizations (and modern individuals too) become experts in the "organization of hypocrisy" (Brunsson 1993), characterized by a de-coupling of talk, decision and action. In IR, Stephen Krasner (1999) used this notion of organized hypocrisy and argued that the international system as a whole is a prime example of organized hypocrisy since its guiding principle of state sovereignty allows states to regularly violate key norms of that system in practice without challenging the legitimacy of these norms.

Niklas Luhmann's theory of world society has probably more implicit roots in classical social theory when compared with world-systems analysis and world polity theory (see also Chapter 9, this volume). Yet, the relevance of Georg Simmel's and Emile Durkheim's work on *Vergesellschaftung* (societation) and societal differentiation for Luhmann's theory of a functionally differentiated world society cannot be overlooked (Luhmann 2012; Stichweh 2000). Luhmann argues that society is constituted by communication (Albert et al. 2008) and highlights that, at least since the global discoveries and conquests by Europeans since the 15th century, society thus necessarily is global in outreach. In the modern era, communications have, not least due to technological innovations such as the invention of the printing press and the parallel process of an increasing primacy of functional differentiation, acquired increasingly reflexive connotations. (Written) knowledge was produced and consumed on an unprecedented scale and was available in other spatial and temporal contexts. Luhmann observes, in a similar way as Meyer, that this process unleashes organizational specialization (e.g. a tremendous boost in professions since the end of the Middle Ages), as well as highly specialized and rationalized functional forms of organizing society within distinct social spheres or systems (i.e. functional differentiation). While Luhmann attributes a primacy in the global modern era to functional forms of differentiation – the interplay between self-generating systems such as politics, economics, science, art, etc. that all reproduce themselves on the basis of specific codes – he emphasizes that other forms of differentiation matter too, in particular the differentiation between centre and periphery that world systems theory talks about.

Mathias Albert and Barry Buzan (2010: 262) argue that differentiation theory "holds out to IR a major possibility for theoretical development" not only because it allows the study of the integration of world politics in a larger social whole, but also because it provides a sociologically and historically grounded narrative of "structural change and world history" (Albert/Buzan 2010: 262; Albert et al. 2013). One of the central structural changes in global modernity – and one that stands in a co-constitutive relation with functional differentiation – is "that modern society reproduces itself in distinction to the individual" (Jung et al. 2014: 18). Modern society is no longer a place in which the social status of a person is fixed. Inclusion/exclusion becomes the constant challenge "disembedded modern subjects" have to face (2014). While functional differentiation thus triggers the emergence of modern subjectivities, including the idea of individual and human rights, it simultaneously renders social exclusion a constant risk that modern subjects have to encounter. Modern disembedded subjects thus need to engage "in continuing reflexive projects of establishing a coherent and explicit narrative of self-identity in light of social exclusion" (2014: 18). Such modern and globalized configurations of *individual* inclusion/exclusion, for example, underpin the antagonization of collective identities in key conflict areas in world society, such as the Middle

East (Stetter 2008), as also Reus-Smit (2011) has argued when pointing to the centrality of the human rights discourse to collective ideas about national self-determination in colonialized, non-Western parts of the world since the 19th century.

Political Approaches: Globalization as Critical and Cosmopolitan Studies

Political approaches to globalization have become highly popular since the late 1980s, primarily in (political) sociology and cultural studies, and with the objective of "mapping the global condition" (Robertson 1990) in a manner that transcends the simplistic caricature of globalization as a mere justification for neo-liberal homogenization and Western dominance (thereby building on earlier theories such as dependence theory). Similar to the "world theories" mentioned above, such political approaches of globalization highlight the historical dimension of globalization, its origins in different world regions (Turner/Khondker 2010) and the structural embedding of national society in a "concrete structuration of the world as a whole" (Robertson 1992: 54).

In addition, political approaches focus strongly on how globalization and culture interrelate. Thus, a key research focus has been how local practices merge with the global condition, and, arguably an extension of the notion of world culture in world polity theory, globalization is therefore primarily considered as a process of cultural hybridization and multiple globalizations (Nederveen Pieterse 2009). Thus, on a structural level, modern notions of rational organization, bureaucratic politics, individualization and market economy matter, but do not diffuse in a homogenous manner. In fact, these modern forms of organizing society evoke "local" responses that range from "mimicry to counter-hegemony" (2009). This also includes what Alexander (2013) calls the dark side of modernity, i.e. that totalitarian and genocidal practices on an unprecedented scale are one of the defining features of the global modern rather than a "barbaric" deviation. On a cultural level, a similar oscillation between mimicry and counter-hegemony can be studied. On the one hand, we observe cultural politics throughout the world in which people try to reconcile the modern myth of individuality with their local (imagined and often newly invented) traditions. While this merging of the universal and the particularistic often gives rise to a tasty global *mélange* (Nederveen Pieterse 2009), for instance when celebrating human diversity, it also shapes the antagonization of exclusive (national, ethnic, religious, civilizational, political) identities that underpins many of modernity's violent conflicts. Thus, on the other hand, culture – understood as the social realm in which, following Ernst Bloch, the *contemporaneity of the non-contemporaneous* in global modernity is particularly visible – becomes the "ideological battleground of modernity" (Wallerstein 1990). It is against the backdrop of such notions of globalization as cultural hybridization and cultural antagonization that Kate Nash notes that cultural politics and the politics of diversity become more rather than less important in the globalized modern order. Even more than that, the notion of cultural politics encompasses the very "practices constituting social reality itself ... What was previously a separate sphere of society ... has now entered every aspect of social life" (Nash 1999: 31).

Being concerned with the underlying ambivalence, paradoxes, and tensions of globalization, it is not surprising that political approaches are particularly sensitive to the role of power in the global condition. Seen from the angle of (political) sociology and cultural studies, "globalization clearly provides opportunities to reconsider the key issues of power and politics" (Nash 1999: 44). Rather than drawing from materialist and agent-centred theories of power, it has become popular in the context of political approaches to resort to poststructuralist, often Foucauldian, notions of power. Scholars are interested in how power is embedded in and engenders global social relations, thereby addressing globalization's coercive *and* productive characteristics. In the modern, globalized condition, power is becoming not less but probably more significant – the "power of power" (Sartori 1969) increases. As Sartori observes (1969: 214), globalization

> does not merely mean that political participation and/or political mobilization are becoming world-wide phenomena. This means above all that the power of power is growing at a tremendous pace – almost with the pace of technology – both with reference to the manipulative and coercive capacity of state power and, at the other extreme, with reference to the explosive potentialities of state power vacuums.

This metaphor of a growing *power of power* in modernity underlies, arguably, both Foucault's notion of governmental power as well as Luhmann's focus on politics as a self-referential system based on the code of power/powerlessness (see Stetter 2008). Thus, power is simultaneously dispersed (i.e. not located in specific actors but embedded in social relations) and pervasive (i.e. shaping social structure in modernity, e.g. as modern governmentality or in the context of a functionally differentiated political system). And this is not primarily because we witness an increase in "relevant" actors that engage in world politics, as is often argued in mainstream IR, but because the globalization of power coincides with a globalization of the idea of (modern) governmentality. *Global governmentality* (Larner/Walters 2004) then refers to the "technologies, rationalities and instruments of governing international spaces" by optimizing the global political economy, the conduct of populations and the apparatuses of security that underpin global order. At the same time, global governmentality entails "technologies of the Self" (Foucault 2010), i.e. the contribution of individuals – as disembedded modern subjects – in the maintenance of this order, including in non-Western parts of the world (Busse/Stetter 2014). A political sociology of globalization is thus not merely a study "of today's 'globalism'", but accounts for the "political rationalities and technologies of imperialism, internationalism, cosmopolitanism and much else beside" (Larner and Walters 2004: 2) that pervade the modern condition.

A second major strand of political approaches links globalization with normative political theory. It has two main facets. First, scholars study the transformative potential of globalization in shaping new political communities, such as humanity as a whole. They discuss in particular the possibilities and limits of global democracy and a democratization of global governance. Second, and in addition to these questions, normative social theories address the question of which reconfigurations of power characterize human history, in general, and the modern era, in particular. In this latter context, the work of Andrew Linklater is especially relevant. Linklater draws from Norbert Elias' notion of a global civilizing process. Elias views civilization as a mechanism in the transformation of social behavior. More specifically speaking, increasing societal differentiation leads to various practices of self-restraint. On that basis, Linklater (2010: 155) argues that "global civilizing processes", triggered by an increase in social power and a consciousness about global interconnectedness, are underway, that "harness ... solidarities to restrain the human capacity to cause violent and non-violent harm to distant people". Linklater does not argue that this process is all-encompassing. Yet, he maintains that it gained momentum in the modern era, not least due to the notion of a "sacrality of the person" (Joas 2011) that underpins the idea of the modern subject. Yet, as the history of political violence, human rights violations, colonialism, war, terrorism, and genocide in the 19th and 20th centuries amply illustrates, global civilizing processes are anything but linear, rather they are – as globalization as such – ambivalent and marked by contradictions. In fact, Linklater (2009: 493) argues that "modern societies live in what may be an early stage of human interconnectedness, or in 'humanity's pre-history'". Yet, the civilizing dynamics that can be observed are still "reason enough for wishing to place international relations at the heart of a grand narrative that tries to understand the history of human ingenuity in multiplying the ways of causing harm, and to comprehend the slower evolution of measures to eradicate violent and non-violent harm from relations between social groups" (2009: 493).

Civilizing processes are always linked to the imagination of political communities within which self-restraint is exercised (Elias 2000). A global civilizing process thus evokes questions about the status of global civil society and a global political community. And this is precisely how concepts of globalization underpin the debate in IR on the reach and limits of global democracy (Archibugi/Held 1995; Held 1996) and the possibilities for democratizing global governance. Thus, although Rosenau (2006: 121) once famously stated that global governance comprises "systems of rule at all levels of human activity – from the family to the international organization – in which the pursuit of goals through the exercise of control has transnational repercussions", it seems safe to argue that the political practice and the academic focus on global governance is mainly concerned with how formal actors with epistemic expertise (IOs, national governments, technical experts, and NGOs) provide rules and regulations for the world. Democratizing global governance, for instance by enabling broader participation for civil society and more transparency, has been one of the constant calls of scholars criticizing such a "depoliticization of global governance" (Jaeger 2007; Scholte 2014).

Conclusion

This chapter has given an overview of the various contextual uses and approaches to the concept of globalization. It has also been argued that in mainstream IR theory discourse, the concept of globalization is an outsider. This is not only because many scholars have become frustrated with and turned away from what they see as an over-hyped, vague and politicized concept. More significantly, the concept is largely absent because a substantial engagement with it poses significant challenges to mainstream IR theorizing. IR scholars cannot simply press the "replace all" button with a view to exchanging the concept of "international" with the concept of "global(ization)", and then everything will be fine. As Bigo and Walker (2007: 731) rightly alert us, "the problem is less to find a new definition of the international or to dissolve it into some other label such as a global politics or a world politics, than to examine very carefully the way we think about it in relation to boundaries that are so easily framed as simply present or absent". The usefulness of concepts – and it might indeed be more useful to speak of it in plural terms – of globalization for IR depends on the discipline's ability to sketch a picture of the global (modern) condition, that points to its inherent fragmentation, ambivalence and paradoxes and that draws a more nuanced picture of politics in a multi-faceted world than mainstream IR theories usually do. In line with Rosenberg (2007: 450–451), more careful thinking about globalization – as, for instance, in the historical, scientific, and political approaches outlined above – should be seen as a pathway leading out of IR's conceptual disciplinary isolation and internal fragmentation. "Globalization" may not be *the* master concept for IR, but it can provide a platform that shows "that there exists a level of reflection at which the particular theories of international relations (IR) can be resolved into a more general, 'supradisciplinary' idiom, providing not just a point of integration with, but also a distinctive contribution to the wider field of social theory" (2007: 450–451). Embracing the concept of globalization both more forcefully and more critically would almost certainly make us better analysts of world politics.

Suggested Readings

Bartelson, Jens (2000) 'Three Concepts of Globalization', *International Sociology* 15 (2), 180–196.
A very good and useful text for first encounters with globalization studies.

Bayly, Christopher A. (2003) *The Birth of the Modern World, 1780–1914*. Malden, MA: Wiley-Blackwell.
This book is a must read for understanding globalization from a historical perspective.

Meyer, John W. (2000) 'Globalization Sources and Effects on National States and Societies', *International Sociology* 15 (2), 233–248.
Presents a sociological account of how the nation-state is embedded in processes of globalization from the perspective of the Stanford School of neo-institutionalism, or world polity theory.

Nederveen Pieterse, Jan (2009) *Globalization and Culture: Global Mélange*. Lanham, MD: Rowman & Littlefield.
A valuable book discussing the diversity and complexity associated with globalization and its encounters of cultures and traditions, including invoking and inventing traditions.

Robertson, Roland (1990) 'Mapping the Global Condition: Globalization as the Central Concept', *Theory, Culture & Society* 7 (2), 15–30.
This text was essential in launching a sophisticated scientific debate on globalization in the early 1990s in contrast to thin approaches that focused on economic globalization only.

Bibliography

Abu-Lughod, Janet L. (2000) *Sociology for the Twenty-First Century*. Chicago: University of Chicago Press.

Albert, Mathias and Buzan, Barry (2010) 'Differentiation: A Sociological Approach to International Relations Theory', *European Journal of International Relations* 16 (3), 315–337.

Albert, Mathias, Buzan, Barry and Zürn, Michael (eds) (2013) *Bringing Sociology to International Relations*. Cambridge: Cambridge University Press.
Albert, Mathias, Kessler, Oliver and Stetter, Stephan (2008) 'On Order and Conflict: International Relations and the "Communicative Turn"', *Review of International Studies* 34 (Supplement S1), 43–67.
Alexander, Jeffrey C. (2013) *The Dark Side of Modernity*. Cambridge; Malden, MA: John Wiley & Sons.
Archibugi, Daniele and Held, David (eds) (1995) *Cosmopolitan Democracy*. Oxford; Cambridge, MA: Polity.
Bach, Olaf (2013) *Die Erfindung der Globalisierung*. Frankfurt: Campus Verlag.
Barnett, Michael and Finnemore, Martha (2004) *Rules for the World*. Ithaca, NY: Cornell University Press.
Bartelson, Jens (2000) 'Three Concepts of Globalization', *International Sociology* 15 (2), 180–196.
Baylis, John, Smith, Steve and Owens, Patricia (2011) *The Globalization of World Politics*. New York: Oxford University Press.
Bayly, Christopher A. (2003) *The Birth of the Modern World, 1780–1914*. Malden, MA: Wiley-Blackwell.
Beck, Ulrich (2000) 'The Cosmopolitan Perspective: Sociology of the Second Age of Modernity', *The British Journal of Sociology* 51 (1), 79–105.
Bigo, Didier and Walker, R. B. J. (2007) 'Political Sociology and the Problem of the International', *Millennium: Journal of International Studies* 35 (3), 725–739.
Bilgin, Pinar (2014) 'The International in Security', http://kclrcir.org/2014/10/27/the-international-in-security/ (accessed 4 November 2014).
Boli, John and Thomas, George M. (1997) 'World Culture in the World Polity: A Century of International Non-Governmental Organization', *American Sociological Review* 62 (2), 171–190.
Boli, John and Thomas, George M. (1999) *Constructing World Culture*. Stanford, CA: Stanford University Press.
Brunsson, Nils (1993) 'The Necessary Hypocrisy', *The International Executive* 35 (1), 1–9.
Busse, Jan and Stetter, Stephan (2014) 'Gouvernementalität im Nahen Osten: Machtpraktiken in Israel und Palästina aus weltgesellschaftstheoretischer Perspektive', in: Andreas Vasilache (ed.), *Gouvernementalität, Staat und Weltgesellschaft*. Wiesbaden: Springer, 197–224.
Buzan, Barry and Albert, Mathias (2010) 'Differentiation: A Sociological Approach to International Relations Theory', *European Journal of International Relations* 16 (3), 315–337.
Buzan, Barry and Lawson, George (2013) 'The Global Transformation: The Nineteenth Century and the Making of Modern International Relations', *International Studies Quarterly* 57 (3), 620–634.
Buzan, Barry and Little, Richard (2001) 'Why International Relations has Failed as an Intellectual Project and What to do About it', *Millennium: Journal of International Studies* 30 (1), 19–39.
Chase-Dunn, Christopher (1999) 'Globalizations: a World-Systems Perspective', *Journal of World- Systems Research* 5 (2), 187–215.
Chernilo, Daniel (2006) 'Social Theory's Methodological Nationalism: Myth and Reality', *European Journal of Social Theory* 9 (1), 5–22.
Clark, Robert P. (2002) *Global Awareness*. Lanham, MD: Rowman & Littlefield.
Cohen, Robin and Kennedy, Paul (2013) *Global Sociology*. New York: NYU Press.
Cooper, Frederick (2005) *Colonialism in Question*. Berkeley, CA: University of California Press.
Dunne, Tim, Hansen, Lene and Wight, Colin (2013) 'The End of International Relations Theory?', *European Journal of International Relations* 19 (3), 405–425.
Eisenstadt, Shmuel N. (ed.) (2002) *Multiple Modernities*. New Brunswick, NJ: Transaction.

Elias, Norbert (2000) *The Civilizing Process*. Oxford; Malden, MA: Blackwell.
Fiss, Peer C. and Hirsch, Paul M. (2005) 'The Discourse of Globalization: Framing and Sensemaking of an Emerging Concept', *American Sociological Review* 70 (1), 29–52.
Foucault, Michel (2010) *The Birth of Biopolitics*. New York: Picador.
Halliday, Fred (1987) 'State and Society in International Relations: A Second Agenda', *Millennium: Journal of International Studies* 16 (2), 215–230.
Held, David (1996) *Democracy and the Global Order*. Stanford, CA: Stanford University Press.
Held, David and McGrew, Anthony (2003) *The Global Transformations Reader*. Cambridge; Malden, MA: Blackwell.
Hobden, Stephen (2002) 'Historical Sociology: Back to the Future of International Relations', in: *Historical Sociology of International Relations*. Cambridge: Cambridge University Press, 42–62.
Hobson, John M. (2012) *The Eurocentric Conception of World Politics*. Cambridge: Cambridge University Press.
Jackson, Patrick Thaddeus (2002) 'Rethinking Weber: Towards a Non-individualist Sociology of World Politics', *International Review of Sociology* 12 (3), 439–468.
Jaeger, Hans-Martin (2007) '"Global Civil Society" and the Political Depoliticization of Global Governance', *International Political Sociology* 1 (3), 257–277.
James, Paul and Steger, Manfred B. (2014) 'A Genealogy of "Globalization": The Career of a Concept', *Globalizations* 11 (4), 417–434.
Joas, Hans (2011) *Die Sakralität der Person*. Berlin: Suhrkamp.
Jung, Dietrich (2001) 'The Political Sociology of World Society', *European Journal of International Relations* 7 (4), 443–474.
Jung, Dietrich, Petersen, Marie Juul and Sparre, Sara Lei (2014) *Politics of Modern Muslim Subjectivities*. New York: Palgrave Macmillan.
Koselleck, Reinhart (1988) *Vergangene Zukunft*. Frankfurt: Suhrkamp.
Krasner, Stephen D. (1999) *Sovereignty*. Princeton, NJ: Princeton University Press.
Larner, Wendy and Walters, William (2004) *Global Governmentality*. London: Routledge.
Lawson, George (2007) 'Historical Sociology in International Relations: Open Society, Research Programme and Vocation', *International Politics* 44 (4), 343–368.
Lenco, Peter (2013) *Deleuze and World Politics*. London: Routledge.
Levitt, Theodore (1983) 'The Globalization of Markets', *Harvard Business Review*, May–June.
Linklater, Andrew (2009) 'Human Interconnectedness', *International Relations* 23 (3), 481–497.
Linklater, Andrew (2010) 'Global Civilizing Processes and the Ambiguities of Human Interconnectedness', *European Journal of International Relations* 16 (2), 155–178.
Lipschutz, Ronnie and Rowe, James K. (2005) *Globalization, Governmentality and Global Politics*. Abingdon; New York: Routledge.
Luhmann, Niklas (2012) *Theory of Society, Vol. 1*. Stanford, CA: Stanford University Press.
Mann, Michael (2012a) *The Sources of Social Power, Vol. 1: A History of Power from the Beginning to AD 1760*. New York: Cambridge University Press.
Mann, Michael (2012b) *The Sources of Social Power, Vol. 4: Globalizations, 1945–2011*. New York: Cambridge University Press.
Meyer, John W. (2000) 'Globalization Sources and Effects on National States and Societies', *International Sociology* 15 (2), 233–248.
Nash, Kate (1999) *Contemporary Political Sociology*. Malden, MA: Wiley-Blackwell.
Nederveen Pieterse, Jan (2009) *Globalization and Culture*. Lanham, MD: Rowman & Littlefield.
Ohmae, Kenichi (1999) *The Borderless World: Power and Strategy in the Interlinked Economy*. New York: HarperBusiness.
Osterhammel, Jürgen (2014) *The Transformation of the World*. Princeton, NJ: Princeton University Press.

Pella, John Anthony (2014) 'Expanding the Expansion of International Society: A New Approach with Empirical Illustrations from West African and European Interaction, 1400–1883', *Journal of International Relations and Development* 17 (1), 89–111.

Reus-Smit, Christian (2011) 'Struggles for Individual Rights and the Expansion of the International System', *International Organization* 65 (2), 207–242.

Robertson, Roland (1990) 'Mapping the Global Condition: Globalization as the Central Concept', *Theory, Culture & Society* 7 (2), 15–30.

Robertson, Roland (1992) *Globalization*. London: Sage.

Robertson, Roland and Khondker, Habib H. (1998) 'Discourses of Globalization: Preliminary Considerations', *International Sociology* 13 (1), 25–40.

Rosenau, James N. (2006) *The Study of World Politics, Vol. 2: Globalization and Governance*. London; New York: Routledge.

Rosenberg, Justin (2007) 'International Relations: The "Higher Bullshit" – A Reply to the Globalization Theory Debate', *International Politics* 44 (4), 450–482.

Sartori, Giovanni (1969) 'From the Sociology of Politics to Political Sociology', *Government and Opposition* 4 (2), 195–214.

Sassen, Saskia (2004) 'Local Actors in Global Politics', *Current Sociology* 52 (4), 649–670.

Scholte, Jan A. (2014) 'Reinventing Global Democracy', *European Journal of International Relations* 20 (1), 3–28.

Sparke, Matthew (2013) *Introducing Globalization*. Chichester; Malden, MA: Wiley-Blackwell.

Stetter, Stephan (2008) *World Society and the Middle East*. Basingstoke; New York: Palgrave.

Stetter, Stephan, Herschinger, Eva, Teichler, Thomas and Albert, Mathias (2011) 'Conflicts about Water: Securitizations in a Global Context', *Cooperation and Conflict* 46 (4), 441–459.

Stichweh, Rudolf (2000) *Die Weltgesellschaft: Soziologische Analysen*. Frankfurt: Suhrkamp.

Thomas, George M., Chhetri, Nalini and Hussaini, Khaleel (2008) 'Legitimacy and the Rise of NGOs: the Global and Local in South Asia', *Journal of Civil Society* 4 (1), 31–42.

Tilly, Charles (1992) *Coercion, Capital and European States: AD 990–1992*. Cambridge, MA: Wiley-Blackwell.

Turner, Bryan S. and Khondker, Habib H. (2010) *Globalization East and West*. Thousand Oaks, CA: Sage.

Tyrell, Hartmann (2005) 'Singular oder Plural: Einleitende Bemerkungen zu Globalisierung und Weltgesellschaft', in: Bettina Heintz, Richard Münch and Hartmann Tyrell (eds), *Weltgesellschaft*. Stuttgart: Lucius & Lucius, 1–50.

Walker, Rob B. J. (2010) *After the Globe, before the World*. London: Routledge.

Wallerstein, Immanuel (1979) *The Capitalist World-Economy*. Cambridge: Cambridge University Press.

Wallerstein, Immanuel (1990) 'Culture as the Ideological Battleground of the Modern World-System', in: M. Featherstone (ed.), *Global Culture*. London: Sage, 31–56.

Werron, Tobias (2012) 'Worum konkurrieren Nationalstaaten? Zu Begriff und Geschichte der Konkurrenz um "weiche" globale Güter', *Zeitschrift für Soziologie* 41 (5), 338–355.

Wimmer, Andreas (2001) 'Globalizations Avant la Lettre: A Comparative View of Isomorphization and Heteromorphization in an Inter-Connecting World', *Comparative Studies in Society and History* 43 (3), 435–466.

Index